D1273349

Reed-Solomon Codes and Their Applications

Irving S. Reed and Gustave Solomon

Reed-Solomon Codes and Their Applications

Edited by

Stephen B. Wicker
Georgia Institute of Technology

Vijay K. Bhargava
University of Victoria

IEEE Communications Society and IEEE Information Theory Society, *Co-sponsors*

The Institute of Electrical and Electronics Engineers, Inc., New York

This book may be purchased at a discount from the publisher when ordered in bulk quantities. For more information contact:

IEEE PRESS Marketing
Attn: Special Sales
P.O. Box 1331
445 Hoes Lane
Piscataway, NJ 08855-1331
Fax: (908) 981-8062

Printed in the United States of America

10   9   8   7   6   5   4   3   2

ISBN 0-7803-1025-X

IEEE Order Number: PC3749

Library of Congress Cataloging-in-Publication Data

Reed-Solomon codes and their applications / edited by Stephen B.
Wicker, Vijay Bhargava.
    p.   cm.
    "IEEE Communications Society and IEEE Information Theory Society,
co-sponsors."
    Includes bibliographical references and index.
    ISBN 0-7803-1025-X
    1. Data transmission systems—Design and construction—
Mathematics.   2. Reed-Solomon codes.   I. Wicker, Stephen B.
II. Bhargava, Vijay K.   III. IEEE Communications Society.
IV. Information Theory Society.
TK5103.7.R44   1994   94-3160
621.382'2–dc20   CIP

Dedication

With applications ranging from digital audio disc players to the *Voyager* spacecraft, Reed-Solomon codes are the most frequently used error control codes in this corner of the galaxy. It is thus entirely possible that there are users of these codes that know nothing of the two men after whom these codes are named. And that is indeed a pity. Aside from being brilliant coding theorists, Irving Reed and Gus Solomon are great engineers, teachers, mentors, and, above all, world-class gentlemen. This book is dedicated to Irving and Gus by those who are proud to know them as colleagues and as friends.

Stephen B. Wicker
Vijay K. Bhargava

Contents

Preface

In June, 1992 we decided to collect a series of papers in honor of Irving Reed and Gustave Solomon. This effort was motivated by Gus's retirement from Hughes Aircraft, where he had worked with distinction for many years. We compiled a list of some of the top researchers that have worked with Reed-Solomon codes, and asked them to submit a chapter. The response was overwhelming, and the results lie in the pages that follow.

The chapters in this book can be loosely grouped into three categories: historical, tutorial, and advanced research. The book begins with a simple overview of the theory of Reed-Solomon codes. The historical elements then begin with a joint paper by Irving Reed and Gustave Solomon that describes the early years of error control coding, leading up to their discovery of Reed-Solomon codes. The book continues with a discussion of the use of Reed-Solomon codes in two extremely important applications: deep space telecommunications and the compact disc. These initial chapters will provide the reader who has a basic background in engineering, math, and/or science with a feel for how Reed-Solomon codes work and the impact that they have had on telecommunications in the past 35 years.

The next few chapters provide more details on how Reed-Solomon codes are implemented. Two chapters treat the general problem of designing and building Reed-Solomon decoders. The first of these chapters emphasizes the issues that surround VLSI implementations of Reed-Solomon decoders. The second of these chapters brings the reader up to the state-of-the-art on the subject of soft decision decoding for Reed-Solomon codes, a problem that remains unsolved. The book then continues with an examination of how Reed-Solomon codes can be used in systems that have two-way communication channels. These "intermediate-level" chapters are intended for the reader who wants to explore the rich area of error control coding in more depth. They provide an excellent background for the material that follows, and a good supplement for a senior/entry-level graduate course in block error control coding.

The remaining chapters describe results from research programs that define the state-of-the-art in error control coding in general and Reed-Solomon codes in particular. The practicing engineer can use these chapters as a reference for the development of advanced communication systems, while the student will find any one of these chapters an excellent starting point for a research program.

We would like to thank all of our authors for their contributions. It is a tribute to Irving Reed and Gus Solomon that researchers of such eminence were willing to take the time to write chapters of such quality.

We also thank Dr. David Forney and Professors Carl Baum, Shih-Chun Chang, and Wayne Stark for their valuable contributions as technical reviewers. They have made this a better book. We gratefully acknowledge the support of the IEEE Communications Society and the IEEE Information Theory Society, and thank their respective liasons to the IEEE Press, Professors Tom Robertazzi and John Anderson. And finally, we thank Valerie Zaborski and Dudley Kay of the IEEE Press for their extensive efforts in bringing this project to completion. It was a pleasure to work with them.

Professor Wicker would like to acknowledge and thank the British Columbia Advanced Systems Institute for naming him a Visiting Fellow in 1992. It was during a two-week visit to Victoria associated with this fellowship that this book was conceived. He would also like to thank his co-editor, Professor Bhargava, for an enjoyable, productive collaboration.

Professor Bhargava would like to thank Mr. Micha Avni for encouraging him to undertake the software and hardware implementation of Reed-Solomon codes. He would also like to thank his co-editor, Professor Wicker, for an enjoyable, productive collaboration, and for making it easy for Professor Bhargava to carry out his duties as a Director of the IEEE during the editing of this book.

The editors and authors extend their thanks to Richard Austin of NASA's Jet Propulsion Laboratory for providing the photograph of Irving Reed and Gus Solomon.

Stephen B. Wicker
Vijay K. Bhargava

An Introduction to Reed-Solomon Codes

Stephen B. Wicker
School of Electrical and Computer Engineering
Georgia Institute of Technology
Atlanta, Georgia 30332

Vijay K. Bhargava
Department of Electrical and Computer Engineering
University of Victoria
Victoria, British Columbia, Canada V8W 2Y2

1 POLYNOMIAL CODES OVER CERTAIN FINITE FIELDS

On January 21, 1959, Irving Reed and Gus Solomon submitted a paper to the *Journal of the Society for Industrial and Applied Mathematics.* In June of 1960 the paper was published: five pages under the rather unpretentious title "Polynomial Codes over Certain Finite Fields" [17]. This paper described a new class of error-correcting codes that are now called Reed-Solomon codes. In the decades since their discovery, Reed-Solomon codes have enjoyed countless applications, from compact disc™ players in living rooms all over the planet to spacecraft that are now well beyond the orbit of Pluto. Reed-Solomon codes have been an integral part of the telecommunications revolution in the last half of the twentieth century. This book has been written in an attempt to capture the power and utility of these codes, as well as the history of their use. Each chapter has been written by specialists in digital communications who have used Reed-Solomon codes in their engineering designs or have made the analysis and implementation of Reed-Solomon codes a focus of their research. The chapters can be loosely grouped into four classes: history, code construction, applications, and decoding techniques. The chapter immediately following this introduction is a joint effort by Irving Reed and Gus Solomon. In this chapter they describe the events that led up to the discovery of Reed-Solomon codes and their experiences afterwards. It is basically historical in nature and provides some excellent insights into a great event in the history of digital communications technology. The remaining chapters deal with Reed-Solomon codes in a more detailed, technical manner. It is thus appropriate that the reader be prepared with a bit of introductory material. The remainder of this chapter presents the three basic techniques for constructing Reed-Solomon codes and briefly discusses some typical applications and the decoding problem. In the process, the remaining chapters in this book are introduced.

2 THE ORIGINAL APPROACH TO REED-SOLOMON CODES

Reed-Solomon codes are constructed and decoded through the use of finite field arithmetic. Finite fields were the discovery of the French mathematician Evariste Galois and are thus sometimes referred to as Galois fields. A finite field of q elements is usually denoted as GF(q). The number of elements in a finite field must be of the form p^m, where p is a prime integer and m is a positive integer [12, 21]. For any given q of this form, the field GF(q) is unique up to isomorphisms (in other words, one can rename the elements in the field, but it is still the same field). We can thus completely describe a finite field by giving its size.

The *order* of an element α in GF(q) is the smallest positive integer m such that $\alpha^m = 1$. GF(q) always contains at least one element, called a primitive element, that has order $(q - 1)$. Let α be primitive in GF(q). Since $(q - 1)$ consecutive powers of α, $\{1, \alpha, \alpha^2, \ldots, \alpha^{q-2}\}$, must be distinct, they are the $(q - 1)$ nonzero elements of GF(q). The "exponential representation" of the nonzero elements in the field provides an obvious means for describing the multiplication operation: $\alpha^x \cdot \alpha^y = \alpha^{(x+y)}$.

Addition in GF(q) is almost as easy. A primitive element is a root of a *primitive polynomial* $p(x)$. The exponential representations for the nonzero elements of GF(q) are reduced *modulo* the primitive polynomial to obtain a "polynomial representation," which is used in the addition operation.

EXAMPLE: GF(8) $p(x) = x^3 + x + 1$ is a primitive binary polynomial. Let α be a root of $p(x)$. This implies that $\alpha^3 + \alpha + 1 = 0$, or equivalently, $\alpha^3 = \alpha + 1$ (addition and subtraction are the same in binary arithmetic).

Exponential Representation		Polynomial Representation
1	=	1
α^1	=	α
α^2	=	α^2
α^3	=	$\alpha + 1$
α^4	=	$\alpha^2 + \alpha$
α^5	=	$\alpha^3 + \alpha^2 = \alpha^2 + \alpha + 1$
α^6	=	$\alpha^3 + \alpha^2 + \alpha = \alpha^2 + 1$
0	=	0

Addition is performed using the polynomial representation. To compute $\alpha^2 + \alpha^5$ in GF(8), one begins by substituting the polynomial representations for the exponential representations α^2 and α^5. The polynomials are then summed to obtain a third polynomial representation, which may then be reexpressed as a power of α.

$$\alpha^2 + \alpha^5 = (\alpha^2) + (\alpha^2 + \alpha + 1) = (\alpha + 1) = \alpha^3$$

The original approach to constructing Reed-Solomon codes is extremely simple (brilliant ideas usually are). Suppose that we have a packet of k information symbols, $\{m_0, m_1, \ldots, m_{k-2}, m_{k-1}\}$, taken from the finite field GF(q). These symbols can be used to construct a polynomial $P(x) = m_0 + m_1 x + \cdots + m_{k-2} x^{k-2} + m_{k-1} x^{k-1}$. A Reed-Solomon code word $\mathbf{c}$ is formed by evaluating $P(x)$ at each of the q elements in the finite field GF(q).

$$\mathbf{c} = (c_0, c_1, c_2, \ldots, c_{q-1}) = \left[P(0), P(\alpha), P(\alpha^2), \ldots, P(\alpha^{q-1}) \right] \quad (1)$$

A complete set of code words is constructed by allowing the k information symbols to take on all possible values. Since the information symbols are selected from GF(q), they can each take on q different values. There are thus q^k code words in this Reed-Solomon code. A code is said to be linear if the sum of any two code words is also a code word. It follows from Equation (1) that Reed-Solomon codes are linear, for the sum of two polynomials of degree $(k - 1)$ is simply another polynomial of degree less than or equal to $(k - 1)$.

The number of information symbols k is frequently called the *dimension* of the code. This term is derived from the fact that the Reed-Solomon code words form a vector space of dimension k over GF(q). Since each code word has q coordinates [see equation (1)], it is usually said that the code has *length* $n = q$. When Reed-Solomon codes (and any other linear codes) are discussed, they are usually denoted by their length n and dimension k as (n, k) codes.

Each Reed-Solomon code word can be related by equation (1) to a system of q linear equations in k variables, as shown below.

$$
\begin{aligned}
P(0) &= m_0 \\
P(\alpha) &= m_0 + m_1\alpha + m_2\alpha^2 + \cdots + m_{k-1}\alpha^{k-1} \\
P(\alpha^2) &= m_0 + m_1\alpha^2 + m_2\alpha^4 + \cdots + m_{k-1}\alpha^{2(k-1)} \\
&\vdots \\
P(\alpha^{q-1}) &= m_0 + m_1\alpha^{q-1} + m_2\alpha^{2(q-1)} + \cdots + m_{k-1}\alpha^{(k-1)(q-1)}
\end{aligned}
\quad (2)
$$

Any k of these expressions can be used to construct a system of k equations in k variables. For example, the first k of the above expressions form the following system.

$$
\begin{bmatrix}
1 & 0 & 0 & \cdots & 0 \\
1 & \alpha & \alpha^2 & \cdots & \alpha^{(k-1)} \\
1 & \alpha^2 & \alpha^4 & \cdots & \alpha^{2(k-1)} \\
\vdots & \vdots & \vdots & \ddots & \vdots \\
1 & \alpha^{k-1} & \alpha^{2(k-1)} & \cdots & \alpha^{(k-1)(k-1)}
\end{bmatrix}
\cdot
\begin{bmatrix}
m_0 \\
m_1 \\
m_2 \\
\vdots \\
m_{k-1}
\end{bmatrix}
=
\begin{bmatrix}
P(0) \\
P(\alpha) \\
P(\alpha^2) \\
\vdots \\
P(\alpha^{k-1})
\end{bmatrix}
\tag{3}
$$

This system can be shown to have a unique solution for the k information symbols $\{m_0, m_1, \ldots, m_{k-2}, m_{k-1}\}$ by computing the determinant of the following coefficient matrix.

$$
\begin{bmatrix}
1 & 0 & 0 & \cdots & 0 \\
1 & \alpha & \alpha^2 & \cdots & \alpha^{(k-1)} \\
1 & \alpha^2 & \alpha^4 & \cdots & \alpha^{2(k-1)} \\
\vdots & \vdots & \vdots & \ddots & \vdots \\
1 & \alpha^{k-1} & \alpha^{2(k-1)} & \cdots & \alpha^{(k-1)(k-1)}
\end{bmatrix}
\tag{4}
$$

Using cofactor expansion across the top row, the determinant of this matrix reduces to that of a *Vandermonde* matrix, and it can be shown that all Vandermonde matrices are nonsingular [21]. The coefficient matrix for any system formed by a combination of k expressions from equation (2) can be reduced to Vandermonde form, so it follows that any k of the expressions in equation (2) can be used to determine the values of the information coordinates.

We are now in a position to evaluate the ability of the Reed-Solomon code to correct errors. Suppose that t of the code word coordinates are corrupted by noise during transmission and received incorrectly. The corresponding expressions in equation (2) are thus incorrect and would lead to an incorrect solution if one or more of them were used in the system of equations in (3). Assuming that we do not know where the errors are, we might construct all possible distinct systems of k expressions from the set of expressions in equation (2). There are $\binom{q}{k}$ such systems, $\binom{t+k-1}{k}$ of which will give incorrect information symbols [17]. If we take the majority opinion among the solutions to all possible linear systems, we will get the correct information bits so long as $\binom{t+k-1}{k} < \binom{q-t}{k}$. This condition holds if and only if $t + k - 1 < q - t$, which in turn holds if and only if $2t < q - k + 1$. A Reed-Solomon code of length q and dimension k can thus correct up to t errors, where t is as follows. Note that $\lfloor x \rfloor$ is the largest integer less than or equal to x.

$$
t = \left\lfloor \frac{q - k + 1}{2} \right\rfloor
\tag{5}
$$

In 1964 Singleton showed that this was the best possible error correction capability for any code of the same length and dimension [18]. Codes that achieve this "optimal" error correction capability are called *maximum distance separable* (MDS). Reed-Solomon codes are by far the dominant members, both in number and utility, of the class of MDS codes. MDS codes have a number of interesting properties that lead to many practical consequences. This is discussed in some detail in Chapter 7.

We have shown that erroneous expressions in equation (2) can be corrected up to some maximum number of errors. But what if some of the expressions in equation (2) are missing altogether? In many digital communication systems, the demodulator can make a rough estimate as to whether a given symbol at the output of the detector is reliable. For example, a binary detector might consist of a simple hard limiter: analog received signals below a certain threshold are made into zeros, those above the threshold become ones. If we know that a particular signal is very close to the threshold, we may want to declare that signal as being "erased" instead of assigning a binary value that has a significant probability of being incorrect. When we erase a Reed-Solomon code word coordinate, we are deleting the corresponding expression in equation (2) from consideration. Since we need only k correct expressions to recover the information bits, we can erase up to $q - k$ of the code word coordinates. Combining this result with the above result for error correction, it can be shown that a Reed-Solomon code can correct t errors and v erasures so long as

$$2t + v < q - k + 1. \tag{6}$$

Reed and Solomon's original approach to constructing their codes fell out of favor following the discovery of the "generator polynomial approach" (the subject of the next section). At the time it was felt that the latter approach led to better decoding algorithms. It was not until 1982 that Tsfasman, Vladut, and Zink, using a technique developed by Goppa, extended Reed and Solomon's construction to develop a class of codes whose performance exceeded the Gilbert-Varshamov bound [20]. The Gilbert-Varshamov bound is a lower bound on the performance of error-correcting codes that many were beginning to believe was also an upper bound. Tsfasman, Vladut, and Zink's work uses several powerful tools from algebraic geometry to break open an entirely new field of research that continues to attract a great deal of interest from coding theorists. Yaghoobian and Blake explore this field in detail in Chapter 13. They begin by considering Reed and Solomon's construction from an algebra-geometric perspective. The Galois field elements $\{0, \alpha, \alpha^2, \ldots, \alpha^{q-1} = 1\}$ are treated as points on a rational curve; along with the point at infinity, they form the one-dimensional *projective line*. The operation in equation (1) translates these points onto points on a curve in a higher-dimensional projective space. Yaghoobian and Blake show that by changing the "base" curve from the projective line to a curve with more structure (i.e., one with higher genus), codes defined by the transformation in equation (1) can yield new codes that are extremely powerful.

3 THE GENERATOR POLYNOMIAL APPROACH

The generator polynomial construction for Reed-Solomon codes is the approach most commonly used today in the error control literature. This approach initially evolved independently from Reed-Solomon codes as a means for describing *cyclic codes*. A code is said to be cyclic if, for any code word $\mathbf{c} = (c_0, c_1, c_2, \ldots, c_{n-2}, c_{n-1})$, the cyclically shifted word $\mathbf{c}' = (c_1, c_2, c_3, \ldots, c_{n-1}, c_0)$ is also a code word. Cyclic codes were first discussed in a series of technical notes and reports written between 1957 and 1959 by Prange at the Air Force Cambridge Research Labs [14–16]. This led directly to the work published in March and September of 1960 by Bose and Ray-Chaudhuri on what are now called BCH codes [4, 5]. (The "H" in BCH is for Hocquenghem, whose 1959 paper presented independent work that included a description of BCH codes as a "generalization of Hamming's work" [9].) Gorenstein and Zierler then generalized Bose and Ray-Chaudhuri's work to arbitrary Galois fields of size p^m, discovering along the way that they had developed a new means for describing Reed and Solomon's "polynomial codes" [8].

If an (n, k) code is cyclic, it can be shown that the code can always be defined using a generator polynomial $g(x) = g_0 + g_1 x + g_2 x^2 + \cdots + g_{n-k} x^{n-k}$. In this definition each code word is interpreted as a *code polynomial*.

$$(c_0, c_1, c_2, \cdots, c_{n-1}) \Rightarrow c_0 + c_1 x + c_2 x^2 + \cdots + c_{n-1} x^{n-1} \qquad (7)$$

A vector $\mathbf{c}$ is a code word in the code defined by $g(x)$ if and only if its corresponding code polynomial $c(x)$ is a multiple of $g(x)$. This provides a very convenient means for mapping information symbols onto code words. Let $\mathbf{m} = (m_0, m_1, \ldots, m_{k-1})$ be a block of k information symbols. These symbols can be associated with an information polynomial $m(x) = m_0 + m_1 x + \cdots + m_{k-1} x^{k-1}$, which is encoded through multiplication by $g(x)$.

$$c(x) = m(x)g(x) \qquad (8)$$

Cyclic Reed-Solomon codes with code word symbols from GF(q) have length $q - 1$, one coordinate less than that obtained through the original construction. A cyclic Reed-Solomon code can be extended to have length q, or even length $q + 1$, but in both cases the resulting code is usually no longer cyclic [21]. As the generator polynomial approach to constructing

Reed-Solomon codes is currently the most popular, the reader may note that Reed-Solomon codes with symbols in the field GF(q) usually have length $q - 1$. For example, the field GF(256) is used in many applications because each of the 256 field elements can be represented as an 8-bit sequence, or byte. Reed-Solomon codes of length 255 are thus very popular error control codes (see the deep space coding standard in Chapters 3 and 11).

The cyclic Reed-Solomon code construction process proceeds as follows. Suppose that we want to build a t-error-correcting Reed-Solomon code of length $q - 1$ with symbols in GF(q). Recall that the nonzero elements in the Galois field GF(q) can be represented as ($q - 1$) powers of some primitive element α. The Reed-Solomon design criterion is as follows: *The generator polynomial for a t-error-correcting code must have as roots 2t consecutive powers of α.*

$$g(x) = \prod_{j=1}^{2t} \left(x - \alpha^j \right) \tag{9}$$

Valid code polynomials can thus have degrees from $2t$ up to $q - 2$ [a degree-($q - 2$) code polynomial corresponds to a code word with ($q - 1$) coordinates]. It follows that the dimension of a code with a degree-$2t$ generator polynomial is $k = q - 2t - 1$. Once again we see the MDS relation

$$\text{Error correction capability} = \frac{\text{length} - \text{dimension}}{2}. \tag{10}$$

Any valid code polynomial must be a multiple of the generator polynomial. It follows that any valid code polynomial must have as roots the same $2t$ consecutive powers of α that form the roots of $g(x)$. This provides us with a very convenient means for determining whether a received word is a valid code word. We simply make sure that the corresponding polynomial has the necessary roots. This approach leads to a powerful and efficient set of decoding algorithms that are introduced later in this chapter and discussed in detail in Chapters 5 and 10.

4 THE GALOIS FIELD FOURIER TRANSFORM APPROACH

The third approach to Reed-Solomon codes uses the various techniques of Fourier transforms to achieve some interesting interpretations of the encoding and decoding process. Once again, let α be a primitive element in the Galois field GF(q). The Galois field Fourier transform (GFFT) of an n-bit vector $\mathbf{c} = (c_0, c_1, \ldots, c_{n-1})$ is defined as follows.

$$\mathcal{F}\{(c_0, c_1, \ldots, c_{n-1})\} = (C_0, C_1, \ldots, C_{n-1}),$$
$$\text{where } C_j = \sum_{i=0}^{n-1} c_i \alpha^{ij}, \, j = 0, 1, \ldots, n - 1 \tag{11}$$

This is clearly a revisitation of Reed and Solomon's original approach, but using the vocabulary and power of Fourier transforms.

Unlike the conventional analysis of signals in a communication system, it is not entirely clear what is meant by the terms "time domain" and "frequency domain" when we are working with coordinate values from finite fields. Despite this bit of fogginess, we can press on to some very interesting and useful results. Suppose that our n-bit word in the time domain is a code word c from a cyclic, t-error-correcting Reed-Solomon code. c thus corresponds to a code polynomial that has as roots some $2t$ consecutive powers of α. When we take the GFFT of this n-bit word, we find that the frequency domain word, or *spectrum*, has $2t$ consecutive zero coordinates! It can be shown that the two conditions are equivalent: a word polynomial has $2t$ consecutive powers of α as roots if and only if the spectrum of the corresponding word has $2t$ consecutive zero coordinates. The GFFT approach is thus a dual to the generator polynomial approach. The transform relationship leads to a series of efficient encoders and decoders. The interested reader is referred to the pioneering work in [3].

5 APPLICATIONS OF REED-SOLOMON CODES

5.1 The Digital Audio Disc

It can safely be claimed that Reed-Solomon codes are the most frequently used digital error control codes in the world. This claim rests firmly on the fact that the digital audio disc, or compact disc uses Reed-Solomon codes for error correction and error concealment. In Chapter 4, Immink describes how digital audio systems make use of Reed-Solomon codes and how the special properties of Reed-Solomon codes make the sound quality of the compact disc as impressive as it is (the signal-to-noise ratio at the output exceeds 90 dB).

The compact disc system uses a pair of *cross-interleaved* Reed-Solomon codes. The details are left for presentation in Chapter 4, but three items of particular interest will be noted here. Since Reed-Solomon codes are nonbinary, each code word symbol becomes a string of bits when transmitted across a binary channel. If a noise burst corrupts several consecutive bits on the channel, the resulting bit errors are "trapped" within a small number of nonbinary symbols. For each burst of noise, the Reed-Solomon decoder needs only to correct a few symbol errors, as opposed to a longer string of bit errors.

Reed-Solomon codes can also correct erasures in an efficient manner. The compact disc error control system uses the first of the cross-interleaved

Reed-Solomon codes to declare erasures, and the second code to correct them. This brilliant piece of engineering allows for accurate reproduction of sound despite material imperfections and damage to the surface of the disc.

Finally, Reed-Solomon codes, as with any block code used in a systematic context, can be "shortened" to an arbitrary extent. Most error control codes have a natural length. For example, Reed-Solomon codes defined over the field GF(256) can be said to have a natural length of 256 (the original approach) or 255 (the generator polynomial approach). The compact disc system is able to use Reed-Solomon codes of length 32 and 28 symbols, while still retaining the 8-bit symbol structure of a length-255 code. The shorter code word length keeps the implementation of the interleaver simple, while the 8-bit symbols provide protection against error bursts and provide a good match for the 16-bit samples taken from the analog music source.

5.2 Deep Space Telecommunication Systems

It has been said that deep space telecommunications and coding are a "match made in heaven" [11]. For Reed-Solomon codes this has certainly been the case. In Chapter 3 McEliece and Swanson examine the use of Reed-Solomon codes in several of NASA and ESA's planetary exploration missions. They begin by noting that Reed-Solomon codes were not an obvious choice for deep space telecommunication systems because the deep space channel does not usually induce burst errors in transmitted data. It was soon found, however, that when convolutional and Reed-Solomon codes are used in concatenated systems, enormous coding gains are achievable. A convolutional code is used as an "inner code," while a Reed-Solomon code is used to correct errors at the output of the convolutional (Viterbi) decoder. The Viterbi decoder output happens to be bursty, providing a perfect match for a Reed-Solomon code. The most famous application of the concatenated convolutional/Reed-Solomon system was in the *Voyager* expeditions to Uranus and to Neptune. Reed-Solomon codes were used in the transmission of photographs from these outer planets, providing close-up images of worlds that, to the residents of this planet, were once tiny smudges made visible only through the use of powerful telescopes. Chapter 3 contains the first photograph of Uranus taken by *Voyager*, a photograph that is also the first Reed-Solomon-encoded image ever transmitted from deep space.

Chapter 3 also discusses the problems encountered by the *Galileo* mission to Jupiter. The high-gain antenna on board the spacecraft has refused to deploy properly and is thus useless. All data collected by the probe must now be sent to the earth by way of a low-gain antenna, resulting in a drastic lowering of the rate at which the spacecraft can reliably transmit data. Engineers all over the world have been frantically working to find ways to increase the coding gain provided by the concatenated codes used by *Galileo*. In Chapter 11, Hagenauer, Offer, and Papke discuss several powerful means for attacking this problem. These include the use of iterative decoding and the soft-output Viterbi algorithm (SOVA). The SOVA provides for the declaration of erasures at the input to the Reed-Solomon decoder, thus improving performance considerably. One key result that emerges from this work is the demonstration that a concatenated convolutional/Reed-Solomon system can provide for reliable data transmission beyond the *cutoff rate*. The cutoff rate is an information-theoretic concept that many believe denotes the best possible performance for an error control system. The results in Chapter 11 show that, for a concatenated error control system, this supposed barrier can be surpassed. Hagenauer, Offer, and Papke have brought the performance of a Reed-Solomon error control system within a few decibels of the ultimate barrier: channel capacity. A series of photos of the lunar surface are used to display the impact of these results.

5.3 Error Control for Systems with Feedback

In Chapter 7, Wicker and Bartz examine various means for using Reed-Solomon codes in applications that allow the transmission of information from the receiver back to the transmitter. Such applications include mobile data transmission systems and high-reliability military communication systems. Along with their powerful error correction capabilities, Reed-Solomon codes can also provide a substantial amount of *simultaneous* error detection. The key lies in the distinction between a *decoder error* and a *decoder failure*. Consider the decoding of a t-error-correcting Reed-Solomon code. If a received word differs from an incorrect code word in t or fewer coordinates, then that code word will be selected by the decoder, resulting in a decoder error. This is an undetectable condition that causes errors in the decoded data. On the other hand, if a noise-corrupted word differs from *all* code words in $(t + 1)$ or more coordinates, then the decoder declares a *decoder failure*. Decoder failures are detectable, so the receiver is able to request a retransmission of the problematic word. In Chapter 7 it is shown that decoder errors are actually quite rare and that retransmission requests can be used to develop Reed-Solomon error control systems with extremely high levels of reliability. Two such systems are discussed. The first is a simple extension of the standard forward-error-correcting Reed-Solomon error control system. The second system uses the special properties of Reed-Solomon codes to a create a *code-combining system*. Multiple received words are combined to create code words from increasingly powerful Reed-Solomon codes. No matter how noisy the channel may be, this system ensures that reliable data will eventually be provided to the end user.

5.4 Spread-Spectrum Systems

Spread-spectrum systems can be grouped into two basic types: frequency-hopping spread spectrum (FH/SS) and direct-sequence spread spectrum (DS/SS). An FH/SS system modulates information onto a carrier that is systematically moved from frequency to frequency. Frequency hopping has been used in military communications systems as a powerful means for defeating partial-band jamming. In general a frequency-hopped system provides protection against any partial-band disturbance. In a peaceful environment, such disturbances may arise from FH multiple-access interference or from narrow-band noise sources. They may also be caused by frequency selective fading on a mobile communication channel. For these reasons and others, frequency hopping is receiving serious consideration for use in personal communication systems in the United States. GSM, the European cellular telephone system, has already provided for a limited amount of frequency hopping.

A DS/SS system creates a wideband signal by phase-shift-keying its RF carrier with the sum of the data sequence and a spreading sequence whose pulse rate is much larger than that of the data sequence. When the received signal is "despread," narrowband interfering signals are spread out so that only a small fraction of their power falls within the bandwidth of the recovered data sequence. As with FH/SS systems, DS/SS systems perform well against partial-band disturbances. DS/SS systems have the added benefit of a low-probability-of-intercept (LPI) spectrum. Since the transmitted signal energy is spread across a wide spectrum, only a small amount of signal energy is found in any given narrowband slot in which an enemy may be searching for activity. DS/SS systems are also being considered for use in mobile radio applications.

In Chapter 9, Sarwate begins by describing the design and performance of several FH/SS systems. He then proceeds to discuss how Reed-Solomon codes can be used in the design of the hopping sequences. If these sequences are carefully selected, the interference caused by other users in a multiple-access environment can be greatly reduced. Sarwate shows that some of the hopping sequences that have been described using other terminology can also be viewed as low-rate Reed-Solomon code words. He then proceeds to a description of several DS/SS systems and shows that the familiar Gold and Kasami sequences can also be interpreted using the language of Reed-Solomon codes.

In Chapter 8, Pursley explores in greater detail the application of Reed-Solomon codes for error correction in FH/SS systems. He focuses on various means by which side information may be obtained from a frequency-hopped system and used to declare erasures at the input to the Reed-Solomon decoder. He begins by considering the use of test symbols and threshold tests, which require very little modification to an existing FH/SS system but provide a significant improvement in performance. He then considers more powerful techniques, including the use of binary parity checks on individual code word symbols and the derivation of side information from the inner decoder in a concatenated system. Pursley concludes by examining the use of side information in routing algorithms in packet radio networks.

5.5 Computer Memory

In Chapter 12, Saitoh and Imai describe the error control problems caused by faults in the integrated circuits used to control data flow in computers. The resulting error patterns in these systems are generally unidirectional; in other words, the erroneous bits have the same value. Saitoh and Imai show that this unidirectional tendency can be exploited to develop codes based on Reed-Solomon codes that outperform standard Reed-Solomon codes. Such advanced error control systems play an integral role in the development of extremely high-speed super computers.

6 DECODING REED-SOLOMON CODES

After the discovery of Reed-Solomon codes, a search began for an efficient decoding algorithm. None of the standard decoding techniques used at the time were very helpful. For example, some simple codes can be decoded through the use of a syndrome look-up table. The syndrome for a received word is computed, and the corresponding minimum-weight error pattern found in a table. This error pattern is subtracted from the received word, producing a code word. Unfortunately this approach is out of the question for all but the most trivial Reed-Solomon codes. For example, the (63,53) five-error-correcting Reed-Solomon code has approximately 10^{20} syndromes. The construction of a syndrome look-up table for this particular Reed-Solomon code is thus somewhat problematic.

In their 1960 paper, Reed and Solomon proposed a decoding algorithm based on the solution of sets of simultaneous equations (see Section 2). Though much more efficient than a look-up table, Reed and Solomon's algorithm is still useful only for the smallest Reed-Solomon codes. In the early 1960s, progress in the search for an efficient decoding algorithm was slow but steady. In 1960 Peterson provided the first explicit description of a decoding algorithm for binary BCH codes [13]. His "direct solution" algorithm is quite useful for correcting small numbers of errors but becomes computationally intractable as the number of errors increases. Peterson's algorithm was improved and extended to nonbinary codes by Gorenstein and Zierler (1961) [8], Chien (1964) [6], and Forney (1965) [7]. These efforts were productive, but Reed-Solomon codes capable of correcting more than six or seven errors still could not be used in an efficient manner. Detractors of coding research in the early 1960s had used the lack of an efficient decoding algorithm to claim that Reed-Solomon codes were nothing more than a mathematical curiosity. Fortunately the detractors' assessment proved to be completely wrong.

The breakthrough came in 1967 when Berlekamp demonstrated his efficient decoding algorithm for both nonbinary BCH and Reed-Solomon codes [1, 2]. Berlekamp's algorithm allows for the efficient decoding of dozens of errors at a time using very powerful Reed-Solomon codes. In 1968 Massey showed that the BCH decoding problem is equivalent to the problem of synthesizing the shortest linear feedback shift register capable of generating a given sequence [10]. Massey then demonstrated a fast shift register-based decoding algorithm for BCH and Reed-Solomon codes that is equivalent to Berlekamp's algorithm. This shift register-based approach is now commonly referred to as the *Berlekamp-Massey algorithm*.

In 1975 Sugiyama, Kasahara, Hirasawa, and Namekawa showed that Euclid's algorithm can also be used to efficiently decode BCH and Reed-Solomon codes [19]. Euclid's algorithm, named after its discoverer, the father of geometry, is a means for finding the greatest common divisor of a pair of integers. It can also be extended to more complex collections of objects, including certain sets of polynomials with coefficients from finite fields.

A detailed discussion of the various decoding algorithms for Reed-Solomon codes can be found in Chapter 5. Hasan, Bhargava, and Le-Ngoc begin this chapter by showing how various finite field operations can be implemented in software or hardware. They then proceed to the various decoding algorithms and describe the architectures through which these algorithms can be implemented. Hasan, Bhargava, and Le-Ngoc emphasize the techniques that allow for fast, efficient Reed-Solomon decoders, the very techniques that have made Reed-Solomon codes popular in so many different applications.

In Chapter 10 Berlekamp, Seroussi, and Tong describe a state-of-the-art Reed-Solomon decoder that is based on a hypersystolic architecture. This architecture is well-suited for very high-speed applications with sustained data rates that approach one gigabit per second. The hypersystolic architecture is described in detail, and it is shown how the algebraic algorithms in traditional RS decoding are adapted to it. The complexity of the cells in the hypersystolic array is limited to one Galois field multiplier, a few Galois field registers, and some simple control logic. Signal paths between cells are limited to two symbol-wide data lines and a few 1-bit control lines. Every signal, including control signals and the clock, has a fan-out and fan-in of only one line. The decoder supports codes of any length $n \leq 2^m - 1$, and redundancy $r < n/3$ over $GF(2^m)$. A prototype of this decoder was built and demonstrated in 1987. This prototype decoder corrected all patterns of up to five errors per block in the (63,53) code mentioned earlier while running at a sustained data rate of 820 Mbits/s.

The "Holy Grail" of Reed-Solomon decoding research, to quote Cooper in Chapter 6, is the maximum-likelihood soft-decision decoder. A soft-decision decoder accepts analog values directly from the channel; the demodulator is not forced to decide which of the q possible symbols a given signal is supposed to represent. The decoder is thus able to make decisions based on the quality of a received signal. For example, the decoder is more willing to assume that a noisy value is indicating an incorrect symbol than that a clean, noise-free signal is doing so. All of the information on the "noisiness" of a particular received signal is lost when the demodulator assigns a symbol to the signal prior to decoding. It has been estimated that this results in a 2- to 3-dB loss in performance. Cooper examines the various means by which researchers are currently recovering some of this lost performance. He shows that the gap is closing but that there is still a great deal of work to be done before the Grail is found and the knights can go home.

7 THE FUTURE OF REED-SOLOMON CODES

The CD player is just the first of the many commercial, mass applications that Reed-Solomon codes can expect to enjoy in the coming years. The commercial world is becoming increasingly mobile, while simultaneously demanding reliable, rapid access to sales, marketing, and accounting information. Unfortunately the mobile channel is a nasty environment in which to communicate, with deep fades an ever-present phenomenon. Reed-Solomon codes are the single best solution; there is no other error control system that can match their reliability performance in the mobile environment. The optical channel provides another set of problems altogether. Shot noise and a dispersive, noisy medium plague line-of-sight optical systems, creating noise bursts that are best handled by Reed-Solomon codes. As optical fibers see increased use in high-speed multiprocessors, we can expect to see Reed-Solomon codes used there as well. In more specialized, single-use applications such as the occasional deep space probe, Reed-Solomon codes will continue to be used to force communication system performance ever closer to the line drawn by

Shannon. These are but a few of the applications showing that Irving Reed and Gus Solomon's codes have brought us a long way and that we can expect them to be with us for a very long time to come.

REFERENCES

[1] E. R. Berlekamp, "Nonbinary BCH Decoding," paper presented at the 1967 International Symposium on Information Theory, San Remo, Italy.

[2] E. R. Berlekamp, *Algebraic Coding Theory*, New York: McGraw-Hill, 1968. (Revised edition, Laguna Hills: Aegean Park Press, 1984.)

[3] R. E. Blahut, "Transform Techniques for Error Control Codes," *IBM Journal of Research and Development*, Volume 23, pp. 299–315, 1979.

[4] R. C. Bose and D. K. Ray-Chaudhuri, "On a Class of Error Correcting Binary Group Codes," *Information and Control*, Volume 3, pp. 68–79, March 1960.

[5] R. C. Bose and D. K. Ray-Chaudhuri, "Further Results on Error Correcting Binary Group Codes," *Information and Control*, Volume 3, pp. 279–290, September 1960.

[6] R. T. Chien, "Cyclic Decoding Procedure for the Bose-Chaudhuri-Hocquenghem Codes," *IEEE Transactions on Information Theory*, Volume IT-10, pp. 357–363, October 1964.

[7] G. D. Forney, "On Decoding BCH Codes," *IEEE Transactions on Information Theory*, Volume IT-11, pp. 549–557, October 1965.

[8] D. Gorenstein and N. Zierler, "A Class of Error Correcting Codes in p^m Symbols," *Journal of the Society of Industrial and Applied Mathematics*, Volume 9, pp. 207–214, June 1961.

[9] A. Hocquenghem, "Codes correcteurs d'erreurs," *Chiffres*, Volume 2, pp. 147–156, 1959.

[10] J. L. Massey, "Shift Register Synthesis and BCH Decoding," *IEEE Transactions on Information Theory*, Volume IT-15, Number 1, pp. 122–127, January 1969.

[11] J. L. Massey, "Deep Space Communications and Coding: A Match Made in Heaven," in *Advanced Methods for Satellite and Deep Space Communications*, J. Hagenauer (ed.), Lecture Notes in Control and Information Sciences, Volume 182, Berlin: Springer-Verlag, 1992.

[12] R. J. McEliece, *Finite Fields for Computer Scientists and Engineers*, Boston: Kluwer Academic, 1987.

[13] W. W. Peterson, "Encoding and Error-Correction Procedures for the Bose-Chaudhuri Codes," *IRE Transactions on Information Theory*, Volume IT-6, pp. 459–470, September 1960.

[14] E. Prange, "Cyclic Error-Correcting Codes in Two Symbols," Air Force Cambridge Research Center-TN-57-103, Cambridge, Mass., September 1957.

[15] E. Prange, "Some Cyclic Error-Correcting Codes with Simple Decoding Algorithms," Air Force Cambridge Research Center-TN-58-156, Cambridge, Mass., April 1958.

[16] E. Prange, "The Use of Coset Equivalence in the Analysis and Decoding of Group Codes," Air Force Cambridge Research Center-TR-59-164, Cambridge, Mass., 1959.

[17] I. S. Reed and G. Solomon, "Polynomial Codes over Certain Finite Fields," *SIAM Journal of Applied Mathematics*, Volume 8, pp. 300–304, 1960.

[18] R. C. Singleton, "Maximum Distance Q-nary Codes," *IEEE Transactions on Information Theory*, Volume IT-10, pp. 116–118, 1964.

[19] Y. Sugiyama, Y. Kasahara, S. Hirasawa, and T. Namekawa, "A Method for Solving Key Equation for Goppa Codes," *Information and Control*, Volume 27, pp. 87–99, 1975.

[20] M. A. Tsfasman, S. G. Vladut, and T. Zink, "Modular Curves, Shimura Curves and Goppa Codes Which Are Better Than the Varshamov-Gilbert Bound," *Mathematische Nachrichten*, Number 109, pp. 21–28, 1982.

[21] S. B. Wicker, *Error Control Systems for Digital Communication and Storage*, Englewood Cliffs, N.J.: Prentice-Hall, 1994.

Chapter 2

Reed-Solomon Codes: A Historical Overview

Irving S. Reed
Communication Sciences Institute
Electrical Engineering Systems
University of Southern California
Los Angeles, California 90089

Gustave Solomon
Jet Propulsion Laboratory
Pasadena, California 91109

1 INTRODUCTION

It is difficult to recapture the drama and excitement that infused the early workers in information theory and coding in the 1950s. Claude Shannon in 1948 had proven the existence of error-correcting codes that, under suitable conditions and at rates less than channel capacity, would transmit error-free information for all practical applications. The hunt for optimal, mechanizable error-correcting codes was on!

The evolution of algebraic coding theory in the 1950s and 1960s was driven by the development of simplified encoders and less complex decoders by a host of researchers. While perusing the literature years later, after everything has been organized and recognized as subsets of this theory or belonging to that framework, it is difficult to see where the difficulty lay. But one must recall that it took some time before the positive integers found their full and proper setting in the complex field of characteristic zero. Human discoveries, inventions, reinventions, and rediscoveries often seem terribly, sometimes painfully, slow to those who are personally involved.

In this chapter the authors hope to share some of the excitement of the early years of error control coding for digital communication systems. We begin by considering Hamming's work in the early 1950s and lead up to the development of what are now called Reed-Solomon codes. We will then discuss our discovery of these codes and provide a brief definition. Finally we follow the progress of the authors and their codes up until the present date.

2 PRECODE

The theory of Reed-Solomon codes is inextricably entwined with the history of block and more particularly algebraic coding theory. With the introduction of increasingly complex mathematical structures, broader classes of machine-encodable block codes emerged along with the algebraic means of decoding.

It is the early 1950s, Richard Hamming had already produced the first practical binary codes using the techniques of linear algebra. In fact, he had both introduced and completed the theory of optimal single-error-correcting binary codes. At almost the same time, Marcel Golay gave us the perfect triple-error-correcting code of length 23 and dimension 12. Golay's results opened up a Pandora's box for mathematical theorists searching for perfect optimal binary codes. David Muller, trained as a theoretical physicist, had invented a class of codes in a language of his own called "Boolean net functions." Shortly thereafter, a Caltech Ph.D. in mathematics with a minor in physics, Irving Reed, recognized an inherent algebraic structure in Muller's codes. They were multinomials over the Galois field of two elements [i.e., GF(2)].

Using the notion of multinomials over the primitive field GF(2) and constraining the maximum product degree, Reed constructed an error-correcting code that was equivalent to Muller's codes. The algebraic structure Reed imposed led to a decoding algorithm, the Reed algorithm, the first example of what is now called majority logic decoding. Reed and Muller's codes were demonstrated to be group codes, or vector spaces over GF(2). Now called Reed-Muller codes, the codes were introduced in September 1954 at the first International Symposium on Information Theory in Cambridge, Massachusetts. The Grassmann algebra people later recognized this structure as belonging to them and extended Reed-Muller codes to algebraic number fields and other structures. With the work of Neal Zierler, Solomon Golomb, and Eugene Prange, these codes were soon generated by linear shift registers (with parity added) and thus became endowed with a cyclic structure. The introduction of deeper abstract algebraic structures as a tool for generating new codes was on the horizon, and Reed and others were leading the way.

In the mid-1950s, Reed spent much of his time developing automatic digital processors for use in radar applications. This work culminated in 1957–1958 in the design of the first all-solid-state (transistor) computer, then called CG-24. This led to many firsts: the first machine to be designed and developed using the RTL language, the first machine to be emulated on another computer, and the first all-purpose machine to have a rudimentary interrupt structure. At this time, Reed became enamored of Galois theory and thought of using nonbinary finite field symbols in byte-level operations as opposed to the traditional focus on bit-oriented algorithms. This thought process ultimately led to Reed-Solomon codes.

In the late 1950s, Gustave Solomon, a young MIT Ph.D. mathematician specializing in algebra, was brought into the field by Reed. Reed introduced him to the world of coding theory and applied algebra through his ideas and conjectures. (Many scientists, mathematicians, and engineers started this way in the new burgeoning interdisciplinary fields, whether in computer science, artificial intelligence, information theory, or related fields.)

In December 1958, an internal memorandum was distributed (MIT Lincoln Laboratory Group Report 47.23) and an article was submitted to the *Journal of the Society of Industrial and Applied Mathematics* (*JSIAM*). The memorandum and article described a new class of codes and provided an intuitive, direct decoding algorithm. On March 6, 1959, Reed and Solomon followed up their initial work with a report that included an algebraic setting that introduced symmetric sums as syndromes for a decoding algorithm (MIT Lincoln Laboratory Group Report 47.24).

3 THE CODES

Reed-Solomon codes first appeared to the outside world in June 1960, in a five-page paper entitled "Polynomial Codes over Certain Finite Fields" in *JSIAM*. The codes were given their present name by W. Wesley Peterson in his *Error Correcting Codes* published by John Wiley and Sons (1961). Peterson also redefined them in a cyclic context to complement his own work in algebraic decoding. (More coders and their codes owe their name and fame to Peterson than anyone of whom we know. We owe him for the naming, the recognition, and the occasional lunches this honor has brought us.)

What are Reed-Solomon codes? They are simply sets of algebraic curves defined by polynomials with a limited range of degrees. These curves when graphed are a set of discrete points—the abscissas and ordinates are values in a Galois field. The degree limitation allows recovery of the complete curve even when the graph is assumed to be smudged and erased at many points. The relation of this idea to error control on noise-corrupted digital communication channels is immediate.

To be specific, an (n, k) Reed-Solomon code of length n and dimension k over a Galois field GF(q), $q = p^m$, where p is a prime, is a cyclic group code of minimum distance d, where $d = n - k + 1$ and $n = q - 1$. The code words are the values taken by the set of all possible polynomials $x^j P(x)$ with coefficients in GF(q), where $P(x)$ is of degree $k - 1$. The values are taken over the n elements of the multiplicative group of GF(q) or, in its extended form, over all of the elements in the field GF(q). These n elements may be represented and ordered as ascending powers of a primitive nth root of unity. For $p = 2$, the field elements may be identified algebraically with binary m-tuples that have a field structure. Consequently, for GF(2^8) addition and multiplication operations can be performed upon binary 8-tuples, or bytes.

The paper as written has a combinatoric-algebraic orientation. A combinatoric decoding algorithm was used in the presentation of the code's properties. This decoding algorithm provided maximum likelihood hard-decision decoding but was unfortunately not very efficient. The particular encoding algorithm presented was nonsystematic and did not invoke the cyclic structure inherent in the definition. It was Golomb who suggested that we include an explicit algebraic representation for the m-tuples for clarity, and we followed his suggestions.

4 APRES CODE

With the introduction of these codes, applied algebra and Galois fields became a major subject of investigation for discrete mathematicians and engineers. The search for an efficient decoding algorithm had begun, and the electronic mechanization of the operations of finite fields became the primary challenge. Simplification and complexity emerged simultaneously as key issues for hardware implementation. In the digital communication field, the work was greeted with indifferent admiration. Electronics was slow, the work was abstract, the algebra was new (only 100 years old), and the demand was limited to a few Air Force colonels who had taken information theory and had heard the word "Shannon."

However, in the world of pure research in electrical engineering and applied mathematics, applied algebra and Galois fields was a smash hit. (Recall, kind older reader, that in the 1960s after *Sputnik*, the United States was in the golden age of research and development.) The task of simplifying encoding and decoding operations became an international craze; old mathematics was invigorated, and new mathematics was invented. For example, the Chinese remainder theorem was revitalized and reintroduced to a waiting world as an efficient decoding procedure. The general framework of cyclic codes was established, and a relation with the later Bose-Chaudhuri-Hocquenheim (BCH) codes was described by Peterson in his text on coding. It was Peterson who introduced an algebraic decoding algorithm relying on the transformation of power sum symmetric functions (the syndromes) into elementary symmetric functions. This leads to a matrix equation relating the syndromes to the coefficients of an "error location polynomial" whose roots specify the locations of erroneous coordinates in a received word.

More significantly, it was the individual work of G. David Forney, Jr., and Elwyn Berlekamp in the mid- to late 1960s that effectively brought Reed-Solomon codes into the mainstream of both the practical and theoretical sides of the field of communications. Forney, in his thesis and later book *Concatenated Codes* (MIT Press), produced the constructive algorithms that achieve Shannon's bound for the additive white Gaussian noise and other noisy channels. He introduced a concatenated scheme of inner and outer codes: the inner code is decoded using soft-decision channel information, while the outer Reed-Solomon code uses errors and erasures decoding to correct inner decoder errors as m-bit symbols. The effort to achieve the Shannon bound for noisy channels became a search for concatenated codes that would do the job. The new proviso was of course real-time decodability without the consumption of a good fraction of the gross national product.

Berlekamp's work in decoding cyclic codes, including Reed-Solomon and BCH codes, was the brilliant tour de force of the decade. The Peterson technique of using matrix inversion to find the coefficients of the error location polynomials was far too complicated for the decoding of large numbers of errors. Berlekamp developed a brilliant, easily mechanizable algorithm that replaced this procedure. The decoding of large numbers of errors using RS codes of long lengths became immediately practical and was in many applications already a necessity. For example, the NASA standard (255,223) 16-error-correcting code (see Chapters 3 and 11 of this book) has since used the Berlekamp algorithm on many planetary exploration spacecraft. Berlekamp's attack on the decoding problem was so inventive and original that it took 10 years and a team of four Japanese mathematicians (Sugiyama, Kasahara, Hirasawa, and Namekawa, 1975) before it was recognized as an improvisation on, reframing of, and improvement of Euclid's algorithm. Mathematically speaking, Berlekamp's algorithm was shown by James Massey to be a new method for finding the least-degree recursion polynomial for a set of given initial conditions. Berlekamp has also contributed a simplification of the Reed-Solomon encoding computations through his work on bit-serial encoding. A single VLSI RS decoder chip using Berlekamp's bit-serial multiplier, was realized in 1984 by Reed, his students at USC, and T. K. Truong of the Jet Propulsion Laboratory (JPL).

Coding theory as now practiced, used, and taught is the evolutionary product of many workers in the field. For every coder who was fortunate enough to have a code or an algorithm named after him or her, there are several whose contributions and insights, known or anonymous, planted conscious or subliminal seeds that others, including these authors, harvested. Our acknowledgment and appreciation goes out to them.

5 LIFE AFTER THE CODES

5.1 Irving Reed

As for the authors, I. S. Reed went off to California to eventually become a professor in the Electrical Engineering Department of the University of Southern California. His first position after returning to the West Coast was with the RAND Corporation in Santa Monica (1960–1963). There he studied the structural aspects of both air and missile defense systems, focusing on the computer, communication, and radar components. The reliability problems of the processors of the early 1960s led Reed to write the RAND report *On Increasing the Lifetimes of Unattended Machines* with D. E. Brimley in 1962. The automatic error detection and unit replacement techniques of these reports influenced JPL in the design of the computer systems in their planetary exploration probes, including the Mars lander and the *Voyager* spacecraft. Reed has also, in collaboration with W. B. Kendall, then at RAND, contributed to the development of comma-free codes, a subject originally pioneered by Golomb at JPL.

The revised edition of Peterson's coding book describes a systematic algorithm for computing arithmetic binary distances. This was contained in "Arithmetic Norms and Bounds on AN Codes" by former student A. C. L. Chiang and I. S. Reed in *IEEE Transactions on Information Theory* (1970). Reed also studied radar detection theory and its associated stochastic processes for many years, beginning with his stay at MIT's Lincoln Laboratory. This work led ultimately to a collaboration with L. E. Brennan and the application of adaptive signal detection to radar, resulting in such papers as "Theory of Adaptive Radar" and "Rapid Convergence Rate in Adaptive Arrays" in the 1972–1974 era. This work in adaptivity led Reed most recently to consider the related subject of neural nets and its possible application to the decoding of error correction codes. Very recently (1993), in collaboration with former student K. A. Al-Mashouq, he wrote the paper "The Use of Neural Nets to Decode Adaptively in a Variety of Channels," which appeared in *Digital Signal Processing*.

The sudden advent of silicon-chip processors, semiconductor memories, and several important breakthroughs in computer software led to small, reliable, and inexpensive microprocessor systems. This resulted in an enormous increase during the 1970s and 1980s in research into and development of encoder and decoder algorithms based on these new small chip processors. Reed's 1977 paper, "The Fast Decoding of Reed-Solomon Codes Using Fermat Theoretic Transforms and Continued Fractions," written in collaboration with R. A. Scholtz, L. R. Welch, and former student T. K. Truong, was one of the many early contributions in this period. This paper was an effort to combine the very efficient FFT-like algorithms (called number-theoretic transforms) known for Fermat primes with a transform decoder that utilized a predecessor of the Euclidean algorithm, namely, the continued fraction algorithm, to find the error location polynomial. This paper was based on previous research Reed and Truong had done on number-theoretic transforms that perform fast convolutions and on transform decoders for BCH and Reed-Solomon codes.

More recently Reed has focused his attention on the decoding of quadratic residue codes and the possible use of ideals in polynomial rings for this purpose. The 1992 paper "The Algebraic Decoding of the (41,21) Quadratic Residue Code" with T. K. Truong and his graduate student X. Chen is his most recent effort in this direction. His collaboration with the same authors in "A Performance Comparison of the Binary QR codes with the 1/2 rate Convolutional Codes" demonstrated that for every rate-1/2 convolutional code there exists a corresponding rate-1/2 extended QR code with equal or better performance. This means, of course, that the concatenated code performance found originally by Forney can be accomplished equally well with a QR code that has two nice properties: QR codes are block codes, and they are algebraically decodable in a polynomial number of operations.

5.2 Gus Solomon

Gus Solomon stayed at Lincoln Laboratory until 1961, when he was recruited by Golomb at the Jet Propulsion Laboratory. From 1967 to 1989, Solomon worked on developing new communication systems in the aerospace industry, punctuated by occasional visiting professorships at UCLA and Caltech. He also developed an interest in medical electronics, an area in which he holds a patent.

From 1960 on, Solomon undertook many fruitful collaborations with other mathematicians and communication theorists. His collaborative work with H. F. Mattson (1961), "A New Treatment of Bose-Chaudhuri Codes," appears in two collected works of classical coding papers. His association with R. J. McEliece (1966) led to "Weights of Cyclic Codes," yielding new usable formulas. The collaboration with H. van Tilborg (1977), "A Connection Between Block and Convolutional Codes," introduced trellis decoding to algebraic codes. An eightieth birthday dedication to Marcel Golay by

Solomon and M. M. Sweet (1980), "A Golay Puzzle," presented an entirely new decoding algorithm and led Solomon to a whole new area of box codes and pseudoquadratic residue codes. These are currently under investigation and extension at Caltech and the Jet Propulsion Laboratory. Finally, he is most proud of his contribution "Algebraic Coding Theory" to *Communication Theory*, McGraw-Hill (1966), edited by A. V. Balakrishnan, who was also a contributor. The text is self-contained due to a key section that is prefaced by a set of mathematical problems. This provides the learning process that gives the reader all the mathematical tools needed. On a personal note of satisfaction and forbidden pleasure, he traces the word "punctured" as now used in convolutional coding to "Punctured Cyclic Codes," a paper cowritten with J. J. Stiffler.

Solomon still consults extensively in the area of digital communications and is occasionally honored to serve as thesis reader and coadvisor for the brilliant students in the Electrical Engineering Department at Caltech. His current main interest is in the learning process, both in the technical area and in the performance area of voice/speech production and physical movement. He teaches both privately.

As Solomon has not pursued a career in academia, this book's dedication, along with the invitation to write this chapter, has been a signal and unexpected honor.

Reed-Solomon Codes
and the Exploration
of the Solar System[1]

Robert J. McEliece
Department of Electrical Engineering
and
Jet Propulsion Laboratory
California Institute of Technology
4800 Oak Grove Drive
Pasadena, California 91109

Laif Swanson
Jet Propulsion Laboratory
California Institute of Technology
4800 Oak Grove Drive
Pasadena, California 91109

1 INTRODUCTION

The exploration of the solar system by unmanned spacecraft is one of the triumphs of the twentieth century. The dramatic photographs of Mercury, Venus, Mars, Jupiter, Saturn, Uranus, and Neptune transmitted by spacecraft with romantic names like *Mariner*, *Voyager*, *Viking*, etc., over distances of hundreds of millions, even billions, of miles, have made these planets, which were previously known to us only as fuzzy telescopic images in textbooks, as real to us in the 1990s as, say, the Himalayas, the Sahara Desert, or Antarctica.

In a book devoted to Reed-Solomon (RS) codes, it is surely appropriate to include a chapter on deep space applications since error control coding in general, and Reed-Solomon coding in particular, have been part of the communications technology of planetary exploration almost from the beginning. So in this article, we will trace the use of RS codes in space applications from "prehistoric" times (about 1970) to the present—and into the future!

---

[1]This chapter was written at the California Institute of Technology's Jet Propulsion Laboratory, under contract with the National Aeronautics and Space Administration.

First, some general remarks. In deep space communication, the channel is, to a very close approximation, a power-limited, wideband, additive Gaussian channel. (See [36 (Chap. 2)] or [30 (Chap. 4)] for good descriptions of this model.) RS codes are not effective *directly* on such a channel for two main reasons. First, RS codes are best at combatting bursts of errors, but the Gaussian channel is memoryless. Second, there is no known practical way to "soft-decode" RS codes, and the 2-dB loss resulting from hard quantization prior to decoding is intolerable in all but a few applications.

Nevertheless, RS codes can be effectively used *indirectly* on the space channel, as "outer" codes in concatenated systems. The general idea of concatenation, which was introduced by Forney in 1967 [15], is shown in Figure 3-1. The idea is to use an "inner" encoder/decoder pair directly adjacent to the unreliable channel over which reliable communication must be achieved. No matter how well it is designed, the inner decoder will occasionally make errors, which will normally be bursty and hard-quantized. It is the job of the outer code to correct these errors. As Forney was the first to observe, Reed-Solomon codes are ideal choices for the outer code since they are naturally able to correct complex, bursty error patterns. They turn out to be *so* ideal, in fact, that other codes are rarely used as outer codes in concatenated systems.

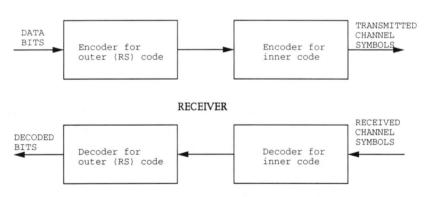

Figure 3-1. A general concatenated coding system.

Shortly after the appearance of Forney's work, Odenwalder, under the direction of Viterbi [22], realized that concatenation could be used to great advantage on the space channel if the inner code is a convolutional code decoded with Viterbi's algorithm and the outer code is RS (possibly with the addition of an interleaver), as shown in Figure 3-2. In Figure 3-3, we see typical performance curves for the space channel that illustrate the advantages of using RS codes. Without the outer RS code (the "unconcatenated" curve in Figure 3-3), the tradeoff between bit signal-to-noise ratio and decoder error probability is relatively shallow, whereas when the outer RS code is added to the system, the resulting curve is comparatively steep, so that if a decoded bit error probability of 10^{-5} or less is required, the concatenated system is markedly superior to the unconcatenated one. Note, however, that if the desired bit error probability is 10^{-3} or greater, concatenation offers no significant advantage. As we will see below, this fact, together with the fact that *uncompressed images*, which until recently comprised the bulk of the data returned by planetary probes, are usually acceptable if the bit error probability is 10^{-2} or less, explains why RS codes made a relatively late appearance in space communication systems.

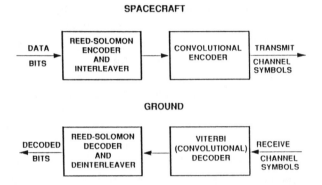

Figure 3-2. An Odenwalder-Viterbi concatenated coding system for the space channel.

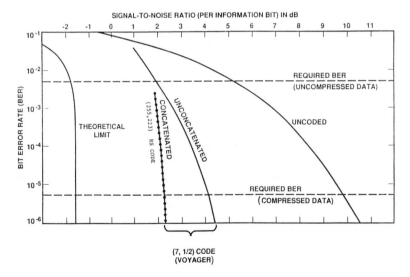

Figure 3-3. Typical performance curves for concatenated and unconcatenated coding systems for the space channel.

2 PREHISTORY—THE 1971 *MARINER* MARS MISSION

If we stretch our definitions a little, we can argue that the first space application of RS codes was on NASA's 1971 *Mariner* Mars orbiter mission, which was launched on May 30, 1971. On that mission, the main downlink code was the (32, 6) biorthogonal code, which was decoded using a fast Hadamard transform or "green machine" decoder [29]. The bulk of the data returned by *Mariner 71* was in the form of digital images of the surface of Mars, for which a decoded error probability of 5×10^{-3} was acceptable. However, the spacecraft also returned data from another experiment, the infrared interferometer spectrometer (IRIS), which required a bit error probability almost two orders of magnitude smaller. Since the IRIS data comprised only a small fraction of the total data delivered by *Mariner*, it obviously would have been wasteful to transmit the entire data stream at a bit SNR large enough to produce a decoded error probability of 5×10^{-5}. A solution to this dilemma, devised by Dorsch and Miller [14], was to use concatenation *only* on the IRIS data. Their idea was to use a concatenation system of the general type depicted in Figure 3-1, with the inner code being the (32, 6) biorthogonal code and the outer code being a (6, 4) RS code over $GF(2^6)$. Dorsch and Miller rightly called the outer code a "generalized Hamming code," since with redundancy 2 it could correct only one error, but they also observed that "the described code is a specific case of a Reed-Solomon code," which is of course also true. Thus in a sense, this concatenated system was the first space-borne use of Reed-Solomon codes. However, the first "full-blown" use of RS concatenated coding on a space mission was on the *Voyager* mission, which we describe in the next section.

3 THE *VOYAGER* MISSION

3.1 History

Multierror-correcting Reed-Solomon codes were used for the first time in deep space exploration in the spectacularly successful *Voyager* mission that began in the summer of 1977 with the launch of twin spacecraft (*Voyager 1* and *Voyager 2*) from Cape Kennedy, towards the outer planets Jupiter and Saturn. (See Murray [21] for an insider's reminiscences about this historic mission.) Earlier deep space missions like *Pioneer*, *Mariner*, *Viking*, and indeed *Voyager* itself to Jupiter and Saturn, used sophisticated error correction but had no need for Reed-Solomon codes because their digital images were not *compressed* prior to transmission. At Uranus and Neptune, however, *Voyager* transmitted some (though not all) of its images in compressed format, which made RS coding essential. Let us see why this was so.

A *Voyager* full-color image is digitized by the spacecraft's imaging hardware into three 800×800 arrays of 8-bit pixels, or $3 \times 800 \times 800 \times 8 = 15,360,000$ bits. In an *uncompressed* spacecraft telecommunication system, these bits are transmitted, one by one, to earth, where the image is reconstructed. Of course, if some of the received bits are in error, the quality and scientific usefulness of the image is degraded, and early studies by planetary scientists established 5×10^{-3} as the maximum bit error probability acceptable for images from NASA planetary missions.[2] Thus when telecommunications engineers designed the error control coding for these missions, they invariably sought to maximize the "coding gain" at a decoded bit error probability of 5×10^{-3}. For example, in the baseline *Voyager* telecommunication system, which uses a $K = 7$, rate 1/2 convolutional code (originally suggested by Odenwalder [22,23]), the coding gain at $P_b = 5 \times 10^{-3}$ is about 3.5 dB (see Figure 3-3).

Odenwalder [22,23] also showed that by concatenating the $K = 7$, rate-1/2 code with an outer RS code, as shown in Figure 3-2, the coding gain for low bit error rates can be improved considerably. For example, in Figure 3-3, we see the comparative performance of the baseline $(7, 1/2)$ convolutional code and the same code concatenated with a $(255, 223)$ RS code (assuming an interleaving depth large enough that the RS symbol errors can be assumed independent). We see that while the concatenated system is only slightly superior to the baseline system at $P_b = 5 \times 10^{-3}$ (about 0.2 dB), at smaller values of P_b the concatenated system is markedly superior. For example, at $P_b = 10^{-6}$, the concatenated system is about 2.5 dB superior, which implies that at $P_b = 10^{-6}$, the concatenated system can transmit at a 78% higher data rate than the baseline system. However, as we have seen, planetary missions required only $P_b = 5 \times 10^{-3}$, and so these potential gains at lower values of P_b were apparently of no practical value. Shortly after Odenwalder's work appeared, however, an important breakthrough in data compression occurred that changed this situation dramatically.

It had been realized since the early 1960s that planetary images are extremely redundant, and that far fewer than 15 million bits should suffice to represent one of them. However, the known techniques for reducing this redundancy were too complex to be implemented onboard a spacecraft. But this situation changed in the early 1970s when Robert Rice at Caltech's Jet Propulsion Laboratory devised a data compression algorithm that typically compressed a planetary image by a factor of 2.5, with no loss of fidelity,

---

[2]Unaccountably, in 1977 Murray and Burgess [20], recalling the 1973 *Mariner 10* mission to Mercury, wrote that "Three errors in 100 bits had been established by the imaging team years earlier as an acceptable level." Presumably it should read "three errors in 1000 bits."

and which was simple enough to be implemented in *Voyager*'s software (see [31]–[34]. (In modern data compression parlance, Rice's algorithm could be called "line-by-line adaptive entropy coding of the pixel differences.") A factor of 2.5 achieved by data compression translates to 4 dB in system gain, a figure that would be difficult to obtain in any other way. Still, conservative spacecraft engineers judged the Rice algorithm too risky for the all-important basic mission to Jupiter and Saturn, although they were willing to include it as part of a backup system in case the primary communication link failed and as a way of enhancing the hoped-for "extended mission" to distant Uranus and Neptune. Even so, there was a stumbling block.

The stumbling block was that Rice's *decompression* algorithm, like most decompression algorithms, is quite sensitive to bit errors. If a compressed line contains even one bit error, Rice's algorithm will, as a rule, garble the line beyond recognition. Thus it was determined that the venerable value of $P_b = 5 \times 10^{-3}$ was no longer acceptable; a much lower value was required, a value that could be achieved efficiently only by using concatenation with RS codes, as prescribed by Odenwalder! After considerable study, which took into account the fact that decoder errors, when they occur, tend to occur in bursts, it was determined that $P_b = 10^{-6}$ was necessary for Rice-compressed planetary images. A glance at Figure 3-3 shows that the RS concatenated system requires an E_b/N_0 of 2.8 dB to achieve a $P_b = 10^{-6}$, whereas the baseline $K = 7$, rate-1/2 system requires 2.6 dB for $P_b = 5 \times 10^{-3}$. Thus the net energy cost of going from $P_b = 5 \times 10^{-3}$ to $P_b = 10^{-6}$ is 0.2 dB, which means that using the Rice compression algorithm together with the concatenated RS/convolutional system results in a net gain of about 3.8 dB over the baseline system. Indeed, this system was implemented on *Voyager*, and in Figure 3-4 we see the first deep space photograph ever sent using Reed-Solomon technology.

In the next section, we outline the operational details of *Voyager*'s RS-enhanced coding system.

3.2 Operational Details

The *Voyager* RS code is a $(255, 223)$ code over the field GF(2^8). The field is represented by the primitive polynomial $m(x) = x^8 + x^4 + x^3 + x^2 + 1$, which is the first degree-8 polynomial listed in the famous tables of Peterson-Weldon [27]. The generator polynomial for the code is

$$g(x) = (x - \alpha)(x - \alpha^2) \cdots (x - a^{32}),$$

where α is a zero of $m(x)$. The code is interleaved to a depth of 4, which means that the overall performance will not be quite as good as that shown in Figure 3-3, which is for infinite interleaving. A careful study, however,

Figure 3-4. Uranus as seen through the eyes of Reed and Solomon, April 5, 1985, from a distance of over 200 million miles.

shows that for this system the loss due to finite interleaving is only 0.02 dB at a decoded error probability of 10^{-6} [6].

The *Voyager* onboard RS encoder is a special-purpose hardware device built from several dozen SSI space-qualified CMOS parts [11]. In essence, it is a hardware implementation of the usual systematic shift register encoder as depicted, say, in [10 (Sec. 4.3)] requiring 32 hard-wired Galois field multipliers, corresponding to the coefficients of $1, x, \ldots, x^{31}$ in $g(x)$.

The *Voyager* ground-based decoder was built by Charles Lahmeyer of the Jet Propulsion Laboratory [17]. It implements the RS decoding algorithm outlined in [18 (Table 8.6)]. In particular, it uses the Euclidean algorithm to solve the key equation, then a Chien search to locate the errors, and finally the usual $w(x)/\sigma'(x)$ formula to evaluate the errors. The actual physical device is a special-purpose circuit built from discrete-component TTL logic, primarily 74S Schottky logic. The decoder uses no microprocessors. Instead, processing is done by dedicated "nanosequencers," which are specially developed microprogrammable controllers. During the Uranus encounter and Neptune encounters, the *Voyager* data rate was a maximum of 44.8 kbps, but the decoder was capable of running at speeds up to 1 Mbit/s [17].

4 THE *GALILEO* MISSION

4.1 History

Galileo is a 2 1/2-ton NASA spacecraft that was launched towards Jupiter in October 1989. It will arrive in late 1995 and will then begin a 2-year study of the Jovian atmosphere, satellites, and surrounding magnetosphere. In the summer of 1995, a probe will detach itself from the main body of the spacecraft, and in December 1995 this probe will plunge into Jupiter's stormy atmosphere, from which it will bravely return data until its inevitable destruction a few hours later. Much, though not all, of *Galileo*'s data will be protected by Reed-Solomon codes.

Unfortunately, the *Galileo* mission has suffered two major operational misfortunes, both of which have caused engineers to make significant alterations in the communications technology. The first of these was the *Challenger* disaster (January 28, 1986), which delayed the launch of *Galileo* by more than 3 years. The coding system on the pre-*Challenger Galileo* mission was virtually identical to that of *Voyager*, viz. a $K = 7$, rate-1/2 convolutional code concatenated with a $(255, 223)$ RS code over GF(256). The only significant difference was that for unavoidable engineering reasons, the interleaving depth on *Galileo* was only 2, vs. 4 for *Voyager*.

The launch delay and propulsion restrictions caused by the *Challenger* accident resulted in both a longer travel time to Jupiter and a less favorable planetary geometry. Because of this, there was the potential for a significant loss of data return. This potential loss was, however, partially compensated for by a last-minute decision by spacecraft engineers to include an enhanced error correction system on the *Galileo* spacecraft. Instead of the *Voyager*-like, NASA standard $K = 7$, rate-1/2, convolutional code, a $K = 15$, rate-1/4 code was proposed and adopted and a corresponding encoder was built into the spacecraft prior to launch [12,35]. But no changes were made to the RS part of the coding system, and so we will not discuss this interesting system further.

However, a further calamity was to befall *Galileo*, and RS codes were heavily involved in this story, which we shall tell in the next section.

4.2 The *S*-Band Mission

In April 1991, the high-gain, or "*X*-band" spacecraft antenna, which had been "furled" like an umbrella for launch, failed to unfurl properly when commanded to do so. Repeated attempts to open the antenna failed, and mission managers declared the *X*-band antenna dead.

Because of the failure of *Galileo*'s high-gain antenna, it became necessary to use the low-gain, or *S*-band, antenna whose gain was 40 dB less than that of the high-gain antenna. This reduced the useful data rate from *Galileo* from 100,000 bits/s to only 10 bits/s! It fell to JPL engineers, including coding specialists, to increase this data rate by making postlaunch enhancements to the *Galileo* communications system. The major system-level enhancement was the addition of 15:1 image data compression [5,7]. As with the *Voyager* system, the presence of data compression means that the required decoded bit error probability is very small, this time on the order of 10^{-7}, and a RS convolutional concatenated coding system is indicated. However, the importance of every tenth of a decibel to the success of the mission, and the fact that the received data rate is so small, motivated JPL coding engineers to propose a very elaborate, high-performance system which we will describe briefly. The key idea of these coding enhancements is *redecoding*, which means making several decoding passes through the data. This idea seems to have originated independently in [8], [9], and [24].

The *Galileo* *S*-band coding system is of the same general form as the original *Galileo* system, but both the inner codes and outer codes are somewhat modified. The original *Galileo* $K = 15$, rate-1/4 code could not be used because it was inextricably linked to the crippled *X*-band antenna. Furthermore, the only transmission path through the *S*-band antenna passes through a hard-wired NASA standard $K = 7$, rate-1/2 code. In order to obtain the coding gains achievable from a long-constraint-length convolutional code, coding engineers were forced to program *Galileo*'s onboard computers to encode a $K = 11$, rate-1/2 convolutional code, which, when then cascaded with the hardware $K = 7$ code, formed a $K = 14$, rate-1/4 convolutional code [5,28].

The outer code for the *Galileo* *S*-band mission is Reed-Solomon, over the field $GF(2^8)$, interleaved to depth 8. However, the 8 code words in each interleaved block don't all have the same redundancy (see Figure 3-5).

The redundancies chosen for the eight RS code words in each interleaved block are, as shown, 100, 10, 32, 10, 60, 10, 32, 10, which works out to an average redundancy of 33 symbols per code word. The code words with higher

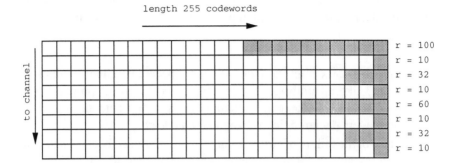

Figure 3-5. The *Galileo* S-band interleaved RS block.

redundancy are called *strong* code words, and those with lower redundancy are called *weak* code words. (In fact, there is a 256th byte in each RS block that is a synch marker so that each S-band *Galileo* data frame is actually a 256×8 array of bytes, consisting of 8 bytes of synch marker, 1776 information bytes, and 264 bytes of RS parity.)

The idea is that in the presence of a long burst (or several long bursts) of errors from the inner Viterbi decoder, the strongest RS code word will be very likely to decode, even though some or all of the weaker code words may not. Once the RS decoding is complete, the Viterbi decoder then makes a second pass, aided this time by the sure knowledge of those bits decoded by the RS decoder. This knowledge is used to force the Viterbi decoder to consider only paths that are consistent with the known bits; i.e., the paths are "pinned down" at certain locations. (In fact, since a state of the inner code is specified by 13 bits, and since typically no two consecutive 8-bit RS symbols will be known, the full Viterbi decoder state will typically not be known. Still, the partial state information provided by the RS decoder allows the Viterbi decoder to discard many formerly attractive paths.) Because any long Viterbi decoder bursts have been broken up by the states that are pinned, or partially pinned, by the knowledge provided by the RS decoder, the Viterbi decoder can do a better job of decoding on the second pass.

After the second pass of the Viterbi decoder, RS decoding is repeated. This time, the hope is that the second strongest RS word will decode, so that even more knowledge of the correct bits can be used by the Viterbi on a *third* pass. Finally, after four passes through both decoders, the process stops.

Another *Galileo* decoding enhancement, involving only the RS decoder, is *error forecasting*. If one word in an interleaved RS block decodes, but others do not, the corrections made by the decoded word can be used to predict, or *forecast*, locations of some of the errors in the adjacent undecodable RS words. If sufficiently many of the erroneous symbols in the uncorrectable RS words are successfully forecasted (erased), then some or all of these words may decode on a second try, since any RS code can correct twice as many erasures as errors. However, in the *Galileo* scheme, the pinning of states shortens the Viterbi bursts enough so that error forecasting is of relatively little value. The entire variable-redundancy, quadruple-pass scheme adopted for use on the *Galileo* S-band mission gains 0.53 dB over the "plain vanilla," constant-redundancy, one-pass, RS concatenated scheme, at a decoder error probability of 2×10^{-7}.

Although at the time this article was being written (summer 1993), no documentation for the *Galileo* decoder, as eventually implemented, yet existed, in an earlier article [13], a similar but simpler system was analyzed in detail. In that system, the redundancies chosen for the 8 RS code words in each interleaved block were 64, 20, 20, 20, 64, 20, 20, 20, an average of 31 symbols per code word, and only two decoding passes were used. The performance of this scheme and three simpler schemes, taken from [13], is summarized in Table 1.

TABLE 1 Performance of Four RS-Viterbi Concatenated Systems with Decoded 8-Bit Symbol Error Probability of 2×10^{-7}

Decoding passes	1	1	2	2
Error forecasting	No	Yes	No	Yes
Redundancy profile	(32)	(44,28,28,28)	(66,20,22,20)	(64,20,20,20)
E_b/N_0 required (dB)	1.17	0.98	0.78	0.76

In Table 1, we see comparisons of four possible schemes of the type described above. In each case, the inner code is the $K = 14$, rate-1/4 "cascaded" convolutional code described above, and the RS code words are length 255 and interleaved to depth 8. The four options listed in Table 1 correspond roughly to the four combinations of yes-no answers to the two questions (1) Is error forecasting used when decoding a RS block? and (2) Is Viterbi redecoding done? The first column corresponds to a plain vanilla system with constant RS redundancy 32, no error forecasting, and only one decoding pass. On the bottom line, we see that the value of E_b/N_0 required for this system to achieve a decoded (8-bit) symbol error probability of 2×10^{-7} is 1.17 dB. In the second column, variable-redundancy RS codes (44, 28, 28, 28, 44, 28, 28, 28) plus error forecasting, but only one pass, yields an improvement of 0.19 dB. In the third column, we see the performance of a system with variable-redundancy (66, 20, 22, 20, 66, 20, 22, 20) but no error forecasting, but with two passes through the decoders. This yields a further improvement of 0.20 dB. Finally, in column 4, we see the performance of a two-pass, error-forecasting system with redundancy profile $(64, 20, 20, 20, 64, 20, 20, 20)$. The improvement over column 3 is only 0.02 dB but is nevertheless positive and was judged to be worth the slight increase in complexity over system 3. The overall improvement over the plain vanilla system is thus seen to be $1.17 - 0.76 = 0.41$ dB, compared to the 0.53-dB improvement for the full-blown *Galileo* system described above.

Encoding, both for the $K = 11$, $r = 1/2$ convolutional code, which cascades with the hardware $K = 7$, $r = 1/2$ code to form the inner $K = 14$, $r = 1/4$ convolutional code, and for the various interleaved RS codes, will be done in software by *Galileo*'s command data subsystem that consists primarily of eight space-qualified RCA 1802 microprocessors. These same processors will in addition perform the onboard data compression. (All this is in addition to the tasks they were programmed to do before the high-gain antenna failed!)

On the ground, decoding and redecoding for both the RS and convolutional codes will be done in software, by a Sun SC 1000 workstation. The RS decoding program was written by Todd Chauvin using the time domain RS errors-and-erasures decoding algorithm described on p. 155 of [19]. The Euclidean algorithm is used to solve the key equation.

In summary, the star-crossed *Galileo* mission has provided a once-in-a-lifetime opportunity for coding engineers to pull out all the stops and design what is arguably the highest performance, highest-complexity error control coding system ever built, and Reed-Solomon codes form a central part of this system.

5 THE CCSDS STANDARD

By now the use of Reed-Solomon codes on spacecraft telemetry systems has become relatively routine, and so it is not surprising that a committee has written standards. Indeed, in May 1984, the Consultative Committee for Space Data Systems, representing the space agencies for most of the world (including NASA and ESA, the European Space Agency), issued an official recommendation for a telemetry channel coding standard [2–4], which has since been adopted for use by numerous planetary missions, including NASA's ill-fated Mars *Observer* (to Mars: was launched in September 1992, arrived in August 1993), *Cassini* (to Saturn: will be launched in 1997, arrive 2004), the joint NASA/ESA *Ulysses* mission (to the sun's polar regions: was launched October 1990, will arrive June 1994), and ESA missions *Giotto*[3] (1985–1986

---

[3]In fact, *Giotto* was launched on July 2, 1985, and arrived at Halley's comet in the spring of 1986, and so it was transmitting RS-encoded data from deep space almost as soon as *Voyager* was. (See Figure 3-4.)

mission to to Halley's comet), *Huigens* (the Titan probe that will fly aboard *Cassini*), and *Cluster* and *Soho* (both spacecraft in the International Solar and Terrestrial Physics Program).

The CCSDD recommended coding standard is twofold: a convolutional coding system without concatenation and a convolutional coding system with concatenation. The unconcatenated system contains no surprises: the recommendation is for the venerable $K = 7$, rate-1/2 code that has been used so many times before. The *concatenated* system, however, does contain some surprises. The recommended RS code is a (255, 223) code over $GF(2^8)$, with recommended interleaving depths of 1, 2, 3, 4, and 5. However, (cf. Section 3.2), the field $GF(2^8)$ is to be represented by the polynomial $m(x) = x^8 + x^7 + x^2 + x + 1$ rather than the expected $x^8 + x^4 + x^3 + x^2 + 1$, and the generator polynomial for the CCSDS's (255, 223) code is

$$g(x) = \prod_{j=112}^{143} (x - \alpha^{11j}),$$

where α is a primitive root in the field $GF(2^8)$, i.e, a root of the equation $m(x) = 0$. This choice of parameters is the result of work done by Belekamp and Perleman [1,25,26] in the early stages of the *Galileo* project. In particular, Berlekamp discovered a way to simplify the encoding of RS codes using bit-serial arithmetic, using the so-called *dual basis* for $GF(2^8)$ relative to the "standard" basis $\{1, \alpha, \ldots, \alpha^7\}$. The particular choice of field representation and generator polynomial given above, recommended by the CCSDS, was motivated by a desired to minimize the encoder hardware for a bit-serial, dual-basis, encoder.

In 1990, Paaske [24] discussed the possibility of using a "two-pass" decoding strategy on the CCSDS standard system. This work had a substantial influence on the final design of the *Galileo* S-band coding system even though that system does not conform to the CCSDS standard.

6 SUMMARY AND CONCLUSIONS

Coding has been an essential part of space communications systems for 30 years. Reed-Solomon coding for this application is a relative newcomer, but for the past decade it too has been an integral part of space exploration. Space applications represent some of the earliest and most important uses of these powerful codes. We have seen that in deep space applications, RS codes are always used as outer codes in concatenated systems of the type originally proposed by Forney and Odenwalder, when the required decoded bit or symbol probability is of the order 10^{-5} or less, as is usually dictated by the presence of data compression. Despite the fact that the theory of RS codes is quite mature, we have seen that the needs of space communication have driven research in RS codes into directions that would probably not have occurred otherwise, e.g., bit-serial encoders, variable-redundancy interleaving, and so on.

As planetary missions become increasingly sophisticated and cost-constrained, and in particular, as data compression becomes standard practice, we may be sure that Reed-Solomon codes, by now old friends to the communication system designers, will find their way into the farthest reaches of the solar system—and beyond!

REFERENCES

[1] E. R. Berlekamp, "Bit Serial Reed-Solomon Encoders," *IEEE Transactions on Information Theory*, Volume IT–28, pp. 869–874, 1982.

[2] Recommendation for Space Data System Standards: Telemetry Channel Coding, Issue 1, Washington, D.C., May 1984.

[3] Consultative Committee for Space Data Systems, Blue Book CCSDS 101.0-B-2, Washington, D.C.: NASA, 1987.

[4] Consultative Committee for Space Data Systems, Blue Book CCSDS 101.0-B-3, Washington, D.C.: NASA, 1992.

[5] K. -M. Cheung, D. Divsalar, S. Dolinar, I. Onyszchuk, F. Pollara, and L. Swanson, "Changing the Coding System on a Spacecraft in Flight," *Abstracts 1993 International Symposium on Information Theory*, p. 381.

[6] K. -M. Cheung and S. J. Dolinar, Jr., "Performance of *Galileo*'s Concatenated Codes with Nonideal Interleaving," JPL TDA Progress Reports, Volume 42-95, pp. 148–152, November 1988.

[7] K. -M. Cheung and K. Tong, "Proposed Data Compression Schemes for the *Galileo S*-Band Contigency Mission," *Proceedings of the 1993 Space and Earth Science Data Compression Workshop, Snowbird, Utah, April 1993*, NASA Conference Publication 3191, pp. 99–109.

[8] O. Collins, *Coding Beyond the Computational Cutoff Rate*, Ph.D. Thesis, California Insititute of Technology, Pasadena, May 1989.

[9] O. Collins and M. Hinzla, "Determinate-State Convolutional Codes," JPL TDA Progress Reports, Volume 42-107, pp. 36–56, November 1991.

[10] S. Lin and D. J. Costello, *Error Control Coding*, Englewood Cliffs, N.J.: Prentice-Hall, 1983.

[11] J. P. deVries, *Voyager: Functional Requirement Voyager Dual Processor Data System*, NASA Jet Propulsion Laboratory Document D-238, Pasadena, Calif., October 1982.

[12] S. Dolinar, "A New Code for *Galileo*," JPL TDA Progress Reports, Volume 42-93, pp. 83–96, May 1988.

[13] S. Dolinar and M. Belongie, "Enhanced Decoding for the *Galileo* S-Band Mission," JPL TDA Progress Report, Volume 42-114, August 1993.

[14] B. Dorsch and W. H. Miller, "Error Control Using a Concatenated Code," Washington, D.C.: NASA Technical Note D–5775, June 1970.

[15] G. D. Forney, *Concatenated Codes*, Cambridge, Mass.: MIT Press, 1967.

[16] E. Hilbert, J. Lee, E. Popard, and R. F. Rice, "Reed-Solomon Coding for *Galileo* Project," Jet Propulsion Laboratory Document GLL-625-303, Pasadena, Calif., April 1979.

[17] C. R. Lahmeyer, *Reed-Solomon Decoder Manual*, NASA Jet Propulsion Laboratory Document D-1665, Pasadena, Calif., April 1985.

[18] R. J. McEliece, *The Theory of Information and Coding*, Reading, Mass.: Addison Wesley, 1977.

[19] R. J. McEliece, "The Decoding of Reed-Solomon Codes," JPL TDA Progress Reports, Volume 42-95, pp. 153–167, November 1988.

[20] B. C. Murray and E. Burgess, *Flight to Mercury*, New York: Columbia University Press, 1977.

[21] B. C. Murray, *Journey into Space*, New York: Norton, 1989.

[22] J. P. Odenwalder, *Optimal Decoding of Convolutional Codes*, Ph.D. Thesis, Systems Science Department, University of California, Los Angeles, 1970.

[23] J. P. Odenwalder et al., *Hybrid Coding Systems Study Final Report*, NASA Document NASA-CR-114486, San Diego, Calif.: Linkabit, 1972.

[24] E. Paaske, "Improved Decoding for a Concatenated Coding System Recommended by CCSDS," *IEEE Transactions on Communications*, Volume 38, pp. 1138–1144, August 1990.

[25] M. Perlman, *Space Flight Operations Center Reed-Solomon Subsystem (RSS) Mappings Between Codewords of Two Distinct (N, K) Reed-Solomon Codes over* GF(2^J), NASA Jet Propulsion Laboratory Document D-8351 Change 1, Pasadena, Calif., September 1991.

[26] M. Perlman and J. -J. Lee. *Reed-Solomon Encoders—Conventional vs. Berlekamp's Architecture*, NASA Jet Propulsion Laboratory Publication 82-71, November 1982.

[27] W. W. Peterson and E. J. Weldon, Jr., *Error-Correcting Codes* (2nd ed.), Cambridge, Mass.: MIT Press, 1972.

[28] F. Pollara and D. Divsalar, "Cascaded Convolutional Codes," JPL TDA Progress Reports, Volume 42-110, pp. 202–207, August 1992.

[29] E. C. Posner, "Combinatorial Structures in Planetary Reconnaissance," in *Error Correcting Codes*, H. B. Mann (ed.), New York: John Wiley, 1968.

[30] J. G. Proakis, *Digital Communications* (2nd ed.), New York: McGraw-Hill, 1989.

[31] R. F. Rice, *Channel Coding and Data Compression System Considerations for Efficient Communication of Planetary Imaging Data*, NASA Jet Propulsion Laboratory Technical Memo 33-695, Pasadena, Calif., September 1974.

[32] R. F. Rice, "An Advanced Imaging Communication System for Planetary Exploration," *SPIE Seminar Proceedings*, Volume 66, pp. 70–89, August 1975.

[33] R. F. Rice, *Potential End-to-End Imaging Information Rate Advantages of Various Alternative Communication Systems*, NASA Jet Propulsion Laboratory Publication, 78-52, Pasadena, Calif., June 1978.

[34] R. F. Rice, E. Hilbert, J. -J. Lee, and A. Schlutsmeyer, "Block Adaptive Rate Controlled Image Data Compression," *Proceedings ITC*, pp. 53.5.1–53.5.6, 1979.

[35] L. Swanson, "A New Code for Galileo," *Abstracts 1988 International Symposium on Information Theory*, p. 94.

[36] A. J. Viterbi and J. K. Omura, *Principles of Digital Communication and Coding*, New York: McGraw-Hill, 1979.

Reed-Solomon Codes
and the Compact Disc

Kees A. Schouhamer Immink
Philips Research Laboratories
5600 JA Eindhoven, The Netherlands

1 INTRODUCTION

The compact disc digital audio system, compact disc for short, can be considered as a transmission system that brings sound from the studio into the living room. The sound encoded into data bits and modulated into channel bits is sent along the "transmission channel" consisting of write laser, master disc, user disc, and optical pickup. Imperfections of the disc will produce errors in the recovered data. The nature of the errors leads, in a natural fashion, to the adoption of Reed-Solomon codes. The compact disc system was the first example of the introduction of Reed-Solomon codes in a consumer product. In this chapter, we shall provide a description of the various factors that play a role in the design of the compact disc error control code.

The advantages of digital audio and video recording have been appreciated for a long time and, of course, computers have long been operated in the digital domain. The advent of ever cheaper and faster digital circuitry has made feasible the creation of new devices such as the compact disc and Digital Compact Cassette (DCC) recorder, an impracticable possibility using previous generations of conventional analog hardware. The principal advantage that digital implementation confers over analog systems is that in a well-engineered digital recording system the sole significant degradation takes place at the initial digitization and the fidelity lasts until the point of ultimate failure. In an analog system, sound fidelity is diminished at each stage of signal processing and clearly the number of recording generations is limited. The provision of error-correcting codes, which by necessity work in the digital domain, has made it possible to almost perfectly reconstitute the recorded signal, even in the presence of imperfections in the recording medium and the replay mechanism. It is not an exaggeration to say that, without error-correcting codes, digital audio would not be technically feasible. There are two kinds of errors: those that are distributed randomly among the individual bits, called *random errors*, and those that occur in groups that cover hundreds or even thousands of bits, called *burst errors*. Burst errors, caused by dropouts, are usually the result of surface contamination from fingerprints and scratches on the disc. The above characterization of the recording channel is by necessity qualitative. Any statement beyond truisms such as "some error bursts are longer than others" is speculative and must be handled with great care.

Coding techniques are used in communication systems to improve the reliability and efficiency of the communication channel. The *reliability* is commonly expressed in statistical terms such as the probability of receiving the wrong information, that is, information that differs from what was originally transmitted. Error control is concerned with techniques of delivering information from a source (the sender) to a destination (the receiver) with a minimum of errors. In a digital audio recorder system, the sound signal is digitized in the form of (binary) symbols. The digital data stream so obtained is not directly recorded on tape. In order to make it possible to reliably record the digital data, the data are, prior to recording, translated in two successive steps: (a) error correction code and (b) recording code.[1] The output generated by the recording code is stored on the storage medium in the form of binary physical quantities, for example, pits and lands or positive and negative magnetizations. During readout, the data are obtained via the decoders for the recording code and the error correction code. Schematically the elements of the coding steps in a digital recorder are similar to those of a "point-to-point" communication link. The physical quantities written on the medium are generally very small, and this means that dropouts caused by fingerprints or defects on the medium as well as the methods to cope with them are of the greatest importance. Error correction control is realized by adding extra symbols to the conveyed message. These extra symbols make it possible for the receiver to detect and/or correct some of the errors that may occur in the

---

[1] In some audio recorders, we may find a third coding step called *source coding*. Source coding is, roughly speaking, a technique to reduce the source symbol rate by removing the redundancy in the source signal. State-of-the-art audio source coders can reduce the symbol rate by a factor of 4 or 5 without sacrificing too much sound fidelity. Source coding is not a part of the compact disc system and therefore is not discussed here.

retrieved message. The main challenge is to achieve the required protection against the inevitable transmission errors without paying too high a price in adding extra symbols (the addition of the extra symbols will lower the effective capacity, say, playing time, of the storage medium). There are many different families of error-correcting codes. Of major importance for recording applications is the family of *Reed-Solomon* (*RS*) *codes*. The reason for their preeminence in recording systems is that they can combat combinations of random as well as burst errors. The success story of RS codes started with its first practical application in digital audio recorders. Pioneering research in this field was conducted by Tanaka et al. in 1978 [13]. Tanaka's design team opted for an RS code constituted by 3-bit symbols, i.e., elements of $GF(2^3)$, and code words of length 8 (symbols). The compact disc, as standardized by Sony and Philips in 1980, was the first example of the widespread introduction of Reed-Solomon codes in the consumer market. Thereafter, Reed-Solomon codes have held undivided sway in digital audio and video storage products such as the DAT recorder [9], the Digital Compact Cassette (DCC) [8], and D1-D2 video recorders [15].

   This chapter starts with a brief outline of the system aspects of the compact disc followed by a description of the coding techniques employed. Details of the physical context of optical recording systems are not discussed; the reader is referred to the literature [2].

2 DESCRIPTION OF THE COMPACT DISC SYSTEM

In this section, we shall deal in some detail with the various factors that had to be weighed one against the other in the design of the coding techniques employed in the compact disc system. With its high information density and a playing time of 73 min, the outside diameter of the disc is only 120 mm. Because the disc is so compact, the dimensions of the player can also be small. The way in which the digital information is derived from the analog sound signal gives a frequency characteristic that is flat from 20 to 20,000 Hz. With this digital system the well-known "wow and flutter" of conventional players are a thing of the past.

   In the compact disc system, the analog audio signal is sampled at a rate of 44.1 kHz, which is, according to Nyquist's sampling theorem, sufficient for the reproduction of the maximum audio frequency of 20 kHz. The signal is quantized by the method of uniform quantization: the sampled amplitude is divided into equal parts. The number of bits per sample is 32, that is, 16 for the left and 16 for the right audio channel. This corresponds to a signal-to-noise ratio (where the noise is caused by quantization error) of more than 90 dB. The net bit rate is thus $44,100 \times 32 = 1.41$ Mbits/s. The audio bits are grouped into blocks of information, called *frames,* each containing six of the original stereo samples. Figure 4-1 represents the complete compact disc system as a "transmission link" that brings the sound from the studio into the living room. The orchestral sound is converted at the recording end into a bit stream B_i, which is recorded on the master disc. The master disc is used as the "pattern" for replicating the discs for the user. The player in the living room derives the bit stream B_0 from the user disc, which in the ideal case should be a facsimile of B_i, and reconverts it to the orchestral sound. The system between COD and DECOD is the actual transmission channel. Figure 4-2 shows the encoding system in more detail. The audio signal is first converted into a stream B_1 of audio bits by means of pulse-code modulation (PCM). The parity bits for error correction and a number of bits for "control and display" are then added to the bit stream [3]. This results in the data bit stream B_2. The modulator converts this stream into channel bits (B_3). The bit stream B_i is obtained by adding a synchronization signal. The bit stream B_i in Figure 4-1 is converted into a signal at P that switches the light beam from the write laser on and off. The channel should be of high enough quality to allow the bit stream B_i to be reconstituted from the read signal at Q. To achieve this quality, all the stages in the transmission path must meet exacting requirements, from the recording on the master disc, through the disc manufacture, to the actual playing of the disc. The quality of the channel is determined by the player and the disc: these are mass-produced, and the tolerances cannot be made unacceptably small. A general picture can be obtained from Table 1, which gives the manufacturing tolerances of a number of relevant parameters, both for the player and for

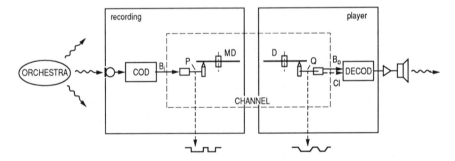

Figure 4-1. Compact disc system considered as a transmission system that brings sound from the studio into the living room. The transmission channel between the encoding system (COD) at the recording side and the decoding system (DECOD) in the player "transmits" the bit stream B_i to DECOD via the write laser, the master disc (MD), the disc manufacture, the disc (D) in the player, and the optical pickup; in the ideal case B_0 is the same as B_i. The bits of B_0, as well as the clock signal (Cl) for further digital operations, have to be detected from the output signal of the pickup unit at Q. Taken from [6].

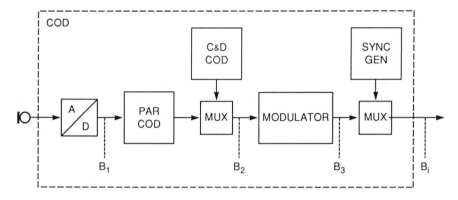

Figure 4-2. Encoding system (COD in Figure 4-1). The system is highly simplified here. In practice there are two channels for stereo which together supply the bit stream B_1. The bit steam B_1 is supplemented by parity and control display bits (B_2) translated by the encoder (B_3) and provided with synchronization signals (B_i). MUX: multiplexers. Taken from [6].

TABLE 1   Manufacturing Tolerances

Player	Objective-lens tilt $\pm 0.2°$
	Tracking $\pm 0.1\ \mu$m
	Focusing $\pm 0.5\ \mu$m
Disc	Thickness 1.2 ± 0.1 mm
	Flatness $\pm 0.6°$
	Pit-edge positioning ± 50 nm
	Pit depth 120 ± 10 nm

the disc. With properly manufactured players and discs, the channel quality can still be impaired by dirt and scratches forming on the discs during use. By its nature, the optical system is fairly insensitive to these damages [3,6], and any errors they may introduce can nearly always be corrected or masked. In the following, we shall see that the recording code also helps to reduce the sensitivity of imperfections.

Successive blocks of audio bits have blocks of parity symbols added to them in accordance with a coding technique called cross-interleaved Reed-Solomon code (CIRC) [11,14] which will be detailed in Section 4. The ratio of the number of bits before and after this operation, the *rate* of the CIRC code, is 3:4. The parity symbols can be used here to correct errors. Due to the nature of optical recording, it is impossible to fully correct all possible error patterns. A well-engineered system must be able to offer a graceful degradation during errors. Error concealment is required if error correction is found to be impossible. Errors may stem from defects in the manufacturing process, for example, undesired particles or air bubbles in the plastic substrate, or damage during use, or fingermarks or dust on the disc. Since the information with the CIRC code is "interleaved" in time, errors that occur at the input of the error correction system are spread over a large number of frames during decoding. The built-in error correction system can correct a burst of up to 4000 data bits, largely because the errors are spread out by interleaving. If more errors than the permitted maximum occur, they can only be detected; the errors detected can be masked.

Each frame then has subcode control and display (C & D) bits added to it. The function of the C & D bits is providing the "information for the listener." In some versions of the player, the information for the listener can be represented on a display and the different sections of the music can be played in the order selected by the user. After the previous operation the bits are called *data bits*. Next the bit stream is encoded into a sequence of binary symbols, called *channel bits*, which are suitable for storage on the disc. The eight-to-fourteen modulation (EFM) code is used for this. Under EFM coding rules, data blocks of 8 bits are translated into blocks of 14 channel bits that have special properties. The blocks of 14 bits are linked by three *merging bits*. The ratio of the number of data bits entering the EFM encoding stage and the number of channel bits leaving it is 8:17.

For synchronization of the bit stream an identical synchronization pattern consisting of 27 channel bits is added to each frame. The total bit rate after all these manipulations is approximately 4.32×10^6 channel bits/s. Table 2 gives a survey of the successive operations with the associated bit rates and their names.

TABLE 2 Successive Signals, Associated Bit Rates, and Operations During Processing of an Audio Signal

Name	Bit rate (Mbits/s)	Operations
Audio signal		PCM (44.1 kHz)
Audio bit stream	1.41	CIRC
Data bit stream	1.94	EFM (+ sync. bits + C & D)
Channel bit stream	4.32	

As the track velocity is constant, the playing time of a disc is equal to the track length divided by the track velocity. The track length is simply the useful disc area divided by the track pitch. For the given disc diameter, 120 mm, and track pitch, 1.6 μm, it follows that the track length is about 5.3 km. The playing time increases if we decrease the track velocity in the system (the track velocity of both the master disc and of the user disc). If we decrease the track velocity, however, the physical length of a channel bit becomes smaller and, therefore, the readout becomes more sensitive to perturbations such as additive noise. The anticipated level of noise and perturbation sets a lower limit to the minimum distinguishable channel bit length, which in turn sets a lower limit to the minimum the track velocity. After ample experiments, it was concluded that the minimum length of a channel bit on the disc is 0.3 μm, from which we conclude a minimum velocity of 1.2 m/s and a maximum playing time of 73 min. As said, the track velocity is constant, which means that the rotational frequency, or angular velocity, of the disc is inversely proportional to the scanning radius. At the inner radius, the rotational frequency is approximately 10 Hz, while at the outer radius it is approximately 3 Hz. During readout, the rotational frequency is automatically adjusted by the player's electronics.

3 EFM RECORDING CODE

The EFM code is a member of the family of *run-length-limited codes*. In this context, the number of consecutive zeros or ones in a (binary) sequence is known as *run length*. A run-length-limited sequence is a sequence of binary symbols characterized by two parameters, $d + 1$ and $k + 1$, which stipulate the minimum and maximum run length, respectively, that may occur in the sequence. The parameter d controls the highest transition frequency and thus has a bearing on intersymbol interference when the sequence is transmitted over a bandwidth-limited channel. In the transmission of binary data it is generally desirable that the received signal is self-synchronizing or self-clocking. Timing is commonly recovered with a phase-locked loop that adjusts the phase of the detection instant according to observed transitions of the received waveform. The maximum run-length parameter k ensures adequate frequency of transitions for synchronization of the read clock. The grounds on which d and k values are chosen, in turn, depend on various factors such as the channel response, the desired data rate (or information density), and the jitter and noise characteristics. The design considerations underlying a certain choice are outside the scope of this chapter. The interested reader is referred to [7], which also provides more details of the EFM code and other run-length-limited codes.

Figure 4-3 gives a schematic general picture of the bit streams in the encoding system. The information is divided into frames. One frame contains 6 sampling periods, each of 32 audio bits (16 bits for each of the two audio channels). These 32 audio bits are divided into 4 words of 8 bits. The bit stream B_1 thus contains 24 words per frame. In B_2, 8 parity words and 1 C & D word have been added to each frame, resulting in 33 data words. The modulator translates each byte (8 bits) into a new word of 14 bits. Added to these are 3 merging bits, for reasons that will appear shortly. After the addition of a synchronization pattern of 27 bits to the frame, the bit stream B_i is obtained. B_i therefore contains $33 \times 17 + 27 = 588$ channel bits per frame. Finally, B_i is converted into a control signal for the write laser. It should be noted that in B_i a 1 or a 0 does not mean "pit" or "land," but a 1 indicates a pit edge. The information is thus completely recorded by the position of the pit edges; it therefore makes no difference to the decoding system if pit and land are interchanged on the disc.

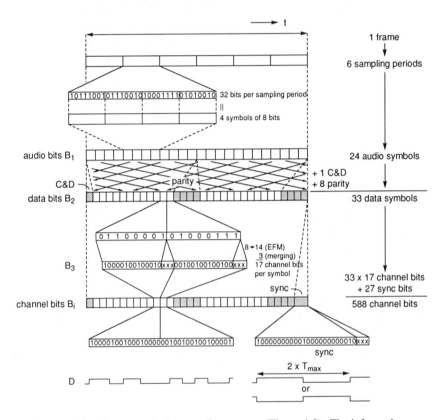

Figure 4-3. Bit streams in the encoding process (Figure 4-2). The information is divided into frames; the figure shows one frame of the successive bit streams. Six audio sampling periods constitute one frame, each sampling period giving 32 bits (16 for each of the two audio channels). The EFM code translates 8 data bits B_2 into 14 channel bits, to which 3 merging bits are added. At B_3 the frames are marked with a synchronization pattern of the form illustrated (bottom right); the final result is the channel bit stream B_i used for writing on the master disc in such a way that each 1 indicates a pit edge (D). Taken from [6].

Opting for the translation of series of 8 bits following the division into words in the parity coding has the effect of avoiding error propagation. One channel bit error will spoil an entire word, but because of the correspondence between channel words and data words, never more than one word. If a different recording code is used, in which the data bits are not translated in groups of 8 but in groups of 6 or 10, say, then the bit stream B_2 is in fact first divided up into 6- or 10-bit channel words. Although one channel-bit error then spoils only one channel word, it usually spoils two of the original 8-bit words. A quantitative description of the above error propagation phenomenon has been given by Blaum [1]. Under EFM rules, the data bits are translated 8 at a time into 14 channel bits, with a minimum run-length parameter d of 2 and a maximum run-length parameter k of 10 channel bits (this means at least 2 and at the most 10 successive zeros in B_i). The grounds for chosing these specific values of d and k are not easily explained. This choice came about more or less as follows. The minimum run-length parameter $d = 2$, with about 16 channel bits on 8 data bits, is about the optimum for the compact disc system. A simple calculation shows that at least 14 channel bits are necessary for the reproduction of all the 256 possible words of 8 data bits under the conditions $d = 2$, $k = 10$. The choice of the maximum run-length parameter k was dictated by the fact that a larger choice does not make things very much easier, whereas a smaller choice does create far more difficulties. With 14 channel bits it is possible to make up 267 words that satisfy the minimum run-length condition $d = 2$. Since we require only 256, we omitted 10 to make it possible to limit the maximum run length to $k = 10$. One other code word was deleted more or less at random. In order to reduce the complexity of the decoder logic, the relationship between (output) data patterns and (input) code patterns has to be optimized. The codebook was compiled with the aid of computer optimization in such a way that the translation in the player can be carried out with the simplest possible circuit, i.e., a circuit that contains the minimum of logic gates. In the compact disc player, the EFM conversion can be performed with a logic array of approximately 50 logic functions. Part of the EFM coding table is presented in Table 3, which shows the decimal representation of the 8-bit source word (left column) and its 14-bit channel representation (right column). The merging bits are primarily intended to ensure that the run-length conditions continue to be satisfied when the code words are merged. If the run length is in danger of becoming too short, we choose zeros for the merging bits; if it is too long, we choose a one for one of them.

TABLE 3   Part of the EFM Coding Table

Data	Code	Data	Code
100	01000100100010	114	10010010000010
101	00000000100010	115	00100000100010
102	01000000100010	116	01000010000010
103	00100100100010	117	00000010000010
104	01001001000010	118	00010001000010
105	10000001000010	119	00100001000010
106	10010001000010	120	01001000000010
107	10001001000010	121	00001001001000
108	01000001000010	122	10010000000010
109	00000001000010	123	10001000000010
110	00010001000010	124	01000000000010
111	00100001000010	125	00001000000010
112	10000000100010	126	00010000100010
113	10000010000010	127	00100000000010

4 THE CIRC CODE

CIRC code (cross-interleaved Reed-Solomon code) is the name of the error control code used in the CD system. The system requirements are

- High random error correctability
- Long burst error correctability
- In case burst correction capability is exceeded, we still have good concealment possibility
- Simple decoder strategy possibility with reasonable sized external random access memory
- Low redundancy
- Possibility for future introduction of four audio channels without major changes in the format.

The errors found in the CD system are a combination of a random and bursty character, and in order to alleviate the load on the error control code some form of interleaving is required. The interleaving scheme is tailored to the specific requirements of the compact disc system. In particular, the adopted cross-interleaving technique will make it possible to effectively mask errors if correction is found to be impossible. Depending on the magnitude of the error to be concealed, this can be done by interpolating or by muting the audio signal. If a large error has occurred and a single audio sample cannot be reconstituted by the error control circuitry, it is possible to obtain an approximation to it by interpolating the neighboring audio samples. The concealment will make errors almost inaudible, and as a result, it offers a graceful degradation of the sound quality. Specifically, most of the sharp, temporary degradations of the audio signal, "clicks," are avoided. The judicious positioning of the left and right stereo channels as well as the audio samples on even- or odd-number instants within the interleaving scheme are key parameters to the success of the concealment strategy. There are a number of interleaved structures used in the CD, each of which makes it possible to correct and detect errors with a minimum of redundancy. The CIRC interleaving scheme will be discussed in the next section.

5 THE ART OF INTERLEAVING

There are a number of different ways in which interleaving can be performed. The simplest interleaving method is termed *block interleaving*. In block interleaving, data are written into a memory that is organized as an $n_1 \times n_2$ matrix. The data are written column-wise and read row-wise. The code words have a length of n_2 symbols. It can easily be verified that if the code is single-error-correcting, bursts of a length at most n_1 symbols can be corrected. Note that the required memory capacity of the interleaver is $n_1 \times n_2$ symbols. The compact disc uses a more effective type of interleaver called a *cross-interleave*. This type of interleave structure, due to Ramsey [12], is also known as a periodic or convolutional interleaver [5]. The essence of the convolutional interleave can be understood from Figure 4-4. Here, code words are constituted by four symbols $\{w_i \ldots w_{i+3}\}$. Before transmission, the symbols of the code words are multiplexed over four delay lines with differing delays. The outputs of the delay lines are combined (demultiplexed) and forwarded to the channel. At the receiver end, the data are subjected to the inverse operation. The CIRC code employs a similar approach of interleaving. A schematic description of the CIRC encoder is displayed in Figure 4-5. The error control code used in the CD system employs not one but two Reed-Solomon codes (C_1, C_2), which are interleaved cross-wise. In particular, the synergy of the two RS codes gives excellent results. For code C_1 we have $n_1 = 32, k_1 = 28$, and for C_2 we have $n_2 = 28, k_2 = 24$. The code symbols are 8 bits long, i.e., elements of $GF(2^8)$. Clearly, the rate of the CIRC code is $(k_1/n_1)(k_2/n_2) = 3/4$. For both of the codes the minimum distance is 5, which makes it possible to directly correct a maximum of two errors in one code or to make a maximum correction of four erasures. The various steps of interleaving can be observed in Figure 4-5. Each frame of information accommodates 12 right and left channel audio samples, denoted by R and L. Each 16-bit sample is divided into 2 bytes indicated by W. The even- and odd-number audio samples are separated by subjecting them to a delay of two

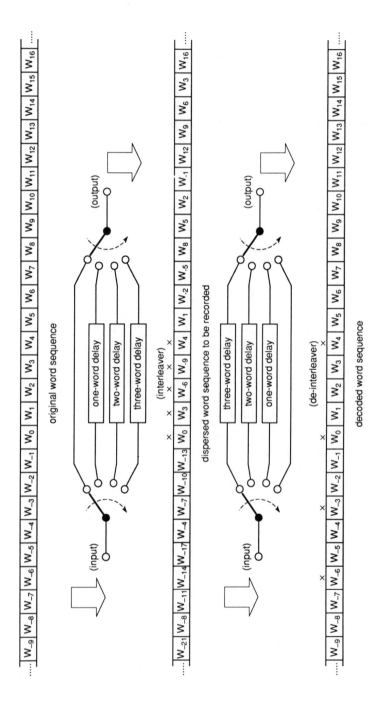

Figure 4-4. Simple interleave and deinterleave scheme using delay lines of differing lengths. As an example, we assume that a burst will damage w_0, w_{-3}, w_{-6}, and w_{-9}. Errors made during transmission are denoted by *. The example shows that correction of four consecutive errors is possible even with a one-error correcting code.

52

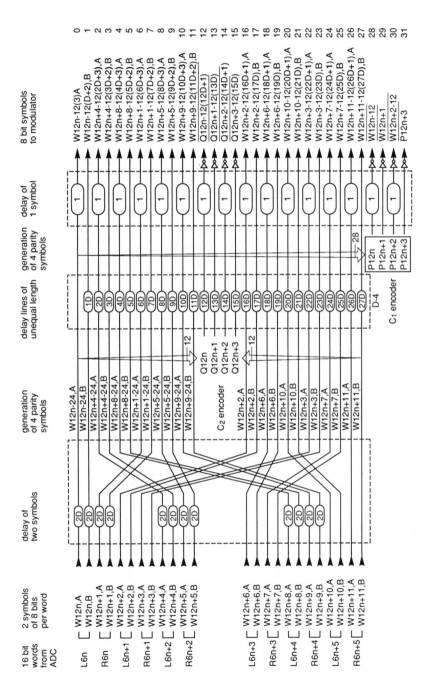

Figure 4-5. Block diagram of CIRC encoder.

53

symbols. This makes it much easier to conceal uncorrectable errors. The 24 symbols in a frame are regrouped so as to give a separation of the even- and odd-number samples, and the odd- and even-number samples are further separated by the four parity symbols Q. The four check symbols Q_{12n}, Q_{12n+1}, Q_{12n+2}, and Q_{12n+3} are formed in accordance with the RS code C_2. The 28 output symbols are multiplexed and subjected to 28 differing delays in accordance with the principle of operation of the convolutional interleaver of Figure 4-4. Note that D denotes the unit delay operator. In CIRC $D = 4$. As a result of the convolutional interleave, one C_2 code word is stored in 28 different blocks spread over a distance of 109 blocks. The memory space required for the CIRC interleave is easily computed: $4 \times 27 \times 28/2 = 1502$ bytes. Encoder C_2 forms the check symbols P_{12n}, P_{12n+1}, P_{12n+2}, and P_{12n+3}. A delay of one symbol is inserted into every other line. This is done to separate two adjacent symbol errors which are the result of relatively small bursts. A nice trick of the trade is that the eight check symbols are inverted in order to prevent producing the all-zero code word. This is important, as it makes it possible to detect bit insertions or deletions caused by clocking difficulties (bit slip).

The error correction circuitry consists of two decoders termed DEC_1 and DEC_2. They are schematically represented in Figure 4-6. The CIRC decoder strategy has not been standardized, and in fact each manufacturer can choose his or her own "optimum" or "super" strategy. Various strategies with accompanying performance analyses have been published in the literature, e.g., [4]. In most decoder strategies, decoder DEC_1 corrects one error. If more than one error may occur, DEC_1 will attach to the 28 outgoing symbols an erasure flag (represented as dashed lines in Figure 4-6). Owing to the different lengths of the delay lines, erasures will be spread over a number of code words at the input of DEC_2. Decoder DEC_2 can correct at maximum four erasures. If more than four erasures may occur, DEC_2 will attach to the 24 outgoing symbols an erasure flag. These flags are an indication for the concealment circuitry that the corresponding sound samples are unreliable. The ability of the error control system to correct and conceal both error bursts and random errors is of great importance. The maximum fully correctable burst length and the maximum interpolation length are determined by the CIRC format. It is easily seen that the correctability is $d = 4$ blocks, since the code C_2 is quadruple-erasure-correcting, that is, the maximum fully correctable burst length is about 4000 data bits, which corresponds to a track length on the disc of 2.5 mm (the effective length on track of a data bit is about 0.6 μm.)[2]

---

[2]Note that only channel bits (the bits leaving the EFM encoder) have physical dimensions as they can be observed on a CD disc. Data bits, on the other hand (the bits entering the CIRC and EFM encoders) are not physical units, but one may say that they have an effective length, that is, the channel bit length divided by the code rate.

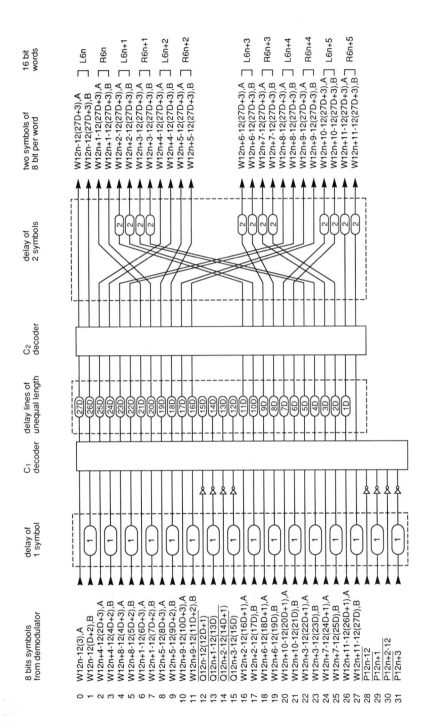

Figure 4-6. Block diagram of CIRC decoder.

55

The length of errors that can be concealed by interpolation is about 12,000 bits (50 blocks), which amounts to nearly 7.5 mm of track length. The main features of the CIRC code are summarized in Table 4. Given the standardized format of the compact disc, a designer of a decoding VLSI can opt for a certain decoding strategy. The choice may depend upon many considerations such as price, power consumption, and performance. Below we will describe two decoding strategies of increasing complexity taken from [4]. For each strategy the C_1 and C_2 decoders are specified separately. We assume that there is no erasure information entering the C_1 decoder. In the description of the C_2 decoder strategy, the integer f denotes the number of erasures at its input. We start with Strategy 1, the simplest of the two strategies described.

Strategy 1

C_1 decoder

if single- or zero-error syndrome

then modify at most one symbol accordingly

else assign erasure flags to all symbols of the received words.

C_2 decoder

if single- or zero-error syndrome

then modify at most one symbol accordingly

else if $f > 2$

then copy C_2 erasure flags from C_1 erasure flags

else begin if $f = 2$

then try 2-erasure decoding;

if $f < 2$ **or if** 2-erasure decoding fails

then assign erasure flags to all symbols of the received word;

end.

For decoder Strategy 2, we need some extra terminology. Assume a t-error-correcting decoder for a code C with minimum distance d, where $2t \leq d - 1$. Assume the decoder finds an estimate of the error pattern of weight $l \leq t$, initially ignoring erasure information presented at its input. For this decoding situation we define a parameter $v \leq l$, denoting the number of nonzero symbols in the estimated error pattern that occur in erasure positions.

Strategy 2

C_1 decoder

if single- or zero-error syndrome

then modify at most one symbol accordingly

else begin if double-error syndrome

then modify two symbols accordingly;

assign erasure flags to all symbols of the received word.

end

C_2 decoder

if single- or zero-error syndrome

then modify at most one symbol accordingly

else if $f \leq 4$

then if double-error syndrome "and" $[(v = 1$ "and" $f \leq 3)$ "or" $(v = 0$ "and" $f \leq 2)]$ or $(f \leq 2$ "and" "not" double-error syndrome)

then assign erasure flags to all symbols of the received word

else copy C_2 erasure flags from C_1 erasure flags

else copy C_2 from C_1 erasure flags.

TABLE 4   Specifications of CIRC

Aspect	Specifications
Maximum *completely* correctable burst length	$\approx$ 4000 data bits, i.e., $\approx$ 2.5-mm track length
Maximum interpolatable burst length in the *worst* case	$\approx$ 12,300 data bits, i.e., $\approx$ 7.7-mm track length
Sample interpolation rate	One sample every 10 h at BER = 10^{-4}; 1000 samples per minute at BER = 10^{-3}
Undetected error samples (click)	Less than one every 750 h at BER = 10^{-3}; negligible at BER $\leq 10^{-4}$
Code rate	3/4
Structure of decoder	One special LSI chip plus one random-access memory of 2048 bytes

Performance calculations, which are based on the assumption that errors occur at random, have been conducted by Driessen and Vries [4] and are shown in Figure 4-7. The figure displays P_{click} (the probability that errors slip through the net) and $P_{\text{interpolate}}$ (the probability that CIRC cannot cope with the errors) as a function of the channel error probability under the assumption that the input errors are random (no burst errors are assumed).

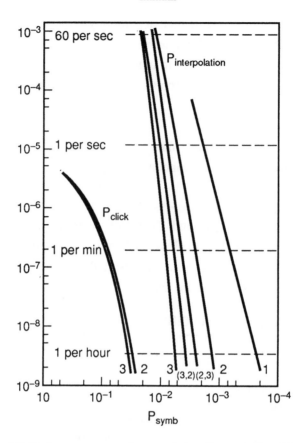

Figure 4-7. Performance curves for several decoding strategies. The quantity P_{click} is the probability that errors pass without being detected, and $P_{interpolate}$ is the probability that errors detected but cannot be corrected as they are beyond the capacity of the CIRC error control system.

REFERENCES

[1] M. Blaum, "Combining ECC with Modulation: Performance Comparisons," *IEEE Transactions on Information Theory*, Volume IT-37, Number 3, pp. 945–949, May 1991.

[2] G. Bouwhuis, J. Braat, A. Huijser, J. Pasman, G. van Rosmalen, and K. A. S. Immink, *Principles of Optical Disc Systems*, Bristol, U.K.: Adam Hilger, 1985.

[3] M. G. Carasso, J. B. H. Peek, and J .P. Sinjou, "The Compact Disc Digital Audio System," *Philips Technical Review*, Volume 40, Number 6, pp. 151–156, 1982.

[4] L. M. H. E. Driessen and L. B. Vries, "Performance Calculation of the COMPACT DISC Error Correcting Code on the Memoryless Channel," *Proceedings of the Fourth International Conference on Video and Data Recording, Southampton, U.K.*, pp. 385–395, April 1982.

[5] G. D. Forney, Jr., "Burst-Correcting Codes for the Classic Bursty Channel," *IEEE Transactions on Commununications*, Volume COM-19, pp. 772–781, October 1971.

[6] J. P. J. Heemskerk and K. A. S. Immink, "Compact Disc: System Aspects and Modulation," *Philips Technical Review*, Volume 40, Number 6, pp. 157–164, 1982.

[7] K. A. S. Immink, *Coding Techniques for Digital Recorders*, Englewood Cliffs, N.J.: Prentice-Hall International, 1991.

[8] G. C. P. Lokhoff, "DCC, Digital Compact Cassette," *IEEE Transactions on Consumer Electronics*, Volume CE-37, pp. 702–706, August 1991.

[9] H. Nakajima and M. Kosaka, "The DAT Conference: Its Activities and Results," *IEEE Transactions on Consumer Electronics*, Volume CE-32, pp. 404–415, August 1986.

[10] K. Odaka, T. Furuya, and A. Taki, "LSIs for Digital Signal Processing to Be Used in Compact Disc Players," *71th AES Convention, New York*, Preprint 1860, May 1982.

[11] J. B. H. Peek, "Communications Aspects of the Compact Disc Digital Audio System," *IEEE Communications Magazine*, Volume 23, pp. 7–15, February 1985.

[12] J. L. Ramsey, "Realization of Optimum Interleavers," *IEEE Transactions on Information Theory*, Volume IT-15, pp. 338–345, May 1970.

[13] K. Tanaka, T. Furukawa, K. Ohnishi, T. Inoue, S. Kunii, and T. Sat, "Two-Channel PCM Tape Recorder for Professional Use," *61th AES Convention, New York*, Preprint 1408 (F-3), November 1978.

[14] L. B. Vries and K. Odaka, "CIRC—The Error-Correcting Code for the Compact Disc Digital Audio System," *Collected Papers AES Premiere Conference, Rye, New York*, pp. 178–188, New York: Audio Engineering Society, 1982.

[15] J. Watkinson, *The D-2 Digital Video Recorder*, London: Focal Press, 1990.

Algorithms and Architectures for the Design of a VLSI Reed-Solomon Codec

M. Anwarul Hasan
University of Waterloo
Waterloo, Ontario, Canada

Vijay K. Bhargava
University of Victoria
Victoria, British Columbia, Canada

Tho Le-Ngoc
Concordia University
Montreal, Quebec, Canada

1 INTRODUCTION

Reed-Solomon (RS) codes are among the most versatile and powerful error control codes. The RS code has the capability of correcting both random and burst errors [1,2]. This feature has been one of the key factors in adopting RS codes in many practical applications such as deep space communications, magnetic recording systems, etc.

The basic concept of the RS code is well understood, but the problem of designing a low-complexity, high-bit-rate RS encoder and decoder still remains an active area of research. In the recent past, quite a few decoding algorithms have been proposed, and side-by-side corresponding architectures have been developed, e.g., [3]–[5]. In addition to proposing improved decoding algorithms, efforts have been made to perform finite field arithmetic operations in efficient ways, e.g., [6]–[8]. These efforts have been made because finite field arithmetic is the underlying operation in decoding algorithms. Its efficient implementation plays an important role in the development of the codec with acceptable levels of circuit complexity and data speed to suit a particular application.

The codec design complexity increases considerably as the code length and the error-correcting capability of the code increase. However, recent advances in VLSI technologies and the development of efficient decoding algorithms have made it possible to implement an RS decoder in a single chip. The implementation of the complete decoder in a single-chip results in higher throughput and provides other advantages inherent to a single-chip device, including, for example, high reliability, low weight, and low cost.

The VLSI design is, in general, a time-consuming and costly process. Using encoding/decoding algorithms which will result in modular/cellular structures, one can reduce the codec design time and cost. Implementing universal-type codec which can be used in different applications, one can reduce the cost further. However, a modular or/and universal design may not yield an area-efficient codec, and there are some applications where the silicon area and, consequently, the weight are of prime concern. As a result, the decision of choosing an algorithm and architecture for the hardware implementation of a codec is very much influenced by the particular application. In this chapter, several important codec algorithms and architectures are presented.

The organization of this chapter is as follows. In Section 2, the RS code is briefly described. In Section 3, finite field arithmetic operations required for the realization of RS encoders and decoders are discussed. Section 4 deals with RS encoding. Decoding algorithms and architectures are presented in Section 5. ASIC implementations of an RS encoder and decoder are presented in Section 6. Finally, concluding remarks are made in Section 7.

2 REED-SOLOMON CODES

Reed-Solomon (RS) codes are a special subclass of generalized BCH codes [1,2]. An (n, k) primitive RS code defined in the Galois field GF(2^m) has code words of length $n = 2^m - 1$, where m is a positive integer. The ratio k/n is called the rate of the RS code. This code has a minimum distance of $n - k + 1$, and the number of parity-check symbols is $n - k$. The error-correcting capability of the code is $t = \lfloor (n-k)/2 \rfloor$. The generator polynomial $g(x)$ of the code is

$$g(x) = \prod_{i=0}^{n-k-1} (x + \alpha^{h+i}), \tag{1}$$

where α is a primitive element in GF(2^m) and h is an integer constant. Different generating polynomials are formed with different values for h; by carefully choosing the constant h, the circuit complexity of the encoder and decoder can be reduced [6]. In the rest of our discussion, however, we consider only $h = 1$. In this case the generator polynomial $g(x)$ is

$$g(x) = \prod_{i=0}^{n-k+1} (x + \alpha^{1+i})$$

$$\stackrel{\Delta}{=} g_0 + g_1 x + \cdots + g_{n-k} x^{n-k}$$

$$(2)$$

RS codes can use 1 bit of soft-decision per symbol. This information, called an *erasure indicator*, is an indication that the received symbol is incorrect. In fact, an erasure is an error with known location. An RS (n, k) code is capable of correcting up to $(n - k)$ erased symbols. Any pattern of v symbol errors and ρ symbol erasures can be corrected provided that $2v + \rho \leq n - k$. To correct an error, the decoder must find both its location and its value, whereas to correct an erasure, only the value of the correct symbol must be found.

3 ARITHMETIC OPERATIONS IN GF(2^m)

Arithmetic operations in finite fields GF(2^m) are quite distinct from their counterparts in the binary number system. The elements of GF(2^m) can be represented with respect to a basis. With basis representation, addition and subtraction operations are simple, but multiplication and division operations are not. However, since multiplication and division are used in decoding algorithms the realization of these operations has received considerable attention and several approaches have been presented [6–8].

3.1 Representation of Field Elements

GF(2^m) is an extension field of GF(2), where m is a positive integer [9]. The extension field has 2^m elements. Any element a of GF(2^m) can be represented as a sum of m linearly independent elements of the field, i.e.,

$$a = a_0 \gamma_0 + a_1 \gamma_1 + \cdots + a_{m-1} \gamma_{m-1}, \tag{3}$$

where, for $0 \leq i \leq m - 1$, $a_i \in$ GF(2) and $\gamma_i \in$ GF(2^m). The set of m elements $\{\gamma_0, \gamma_1, \ldots, \gamma_{m-1}\}$ is called a *basis* of GF(2^m) over GF(2), and a_i, $i = 0, 1, \ldots, m - 1$, are the coordinates of a with respect to this basis. Let

$$f(x) = \sum_{i=0}^{m} f_i x^i$$

be a *primitive monic* polynomial over GF(2) of degree m. (For simplicity we consider only primitive polynomials. An extension to a more general discussion involving irreducible polynomials is straightforward.) Let $\alpha \in$ GF(2^m) satisfy $f(\alpha) = 0$. Then it can be shown that $\{1, \alpha, \alpha^2, \ldots, \alpha^{m-1}\}$

forms a basis called a *canonical basis*. Moreover, α, $\alpha^{2^1}, \ldots, \alpha^{2^{m-1}}$ are linearly independent and form another basis called a *normal basis*. Canonical and normal bases are widely used to represent field elements.

Let $\{\tau_0, \tau_1, \ldots, \tau_{m-1}\}$ be any basis of $GF(2^m)$ over $GF(2)$. Then the basis is dual to the primal basis $\{\gamma_0, \gamma_1, \ldots, \gamma_{m-1}\}$ if

$$\text{Tr}(\tau_i \gamma_j) = \delta_{i,j} \tag{4}$$

where the trace function $\text{Tr}(x) = \sum_{l=0}^{m-1} x^{2^l}$ and $\delta_{i,j}$ is the Kronecker delta function which is equal to 1 if $i = j$ and 0 otherwise.

If the canonical basis $\{1, \alpha, \ldots, \alpha^{m-1}\}$ is chosen as the primal basis, the dual basis coordinates of a field element can be easily obtained—in fact, they can be obtained using a simple linear feedback shift register. However, the reverse transformation is not always simple [10]. The combination of the canonical basis and its corresponding dual basis plays an important role in an efficient realization of finite field multiplication operation [6]. However, there does not seem to be an efficient realization using the combination of normal basis and its dual basis. What follows is a discussion of a triangular basis [11,12].

For $j = 0, 1, \ldots, m - 1$, let $\beta_j = \sum_{i=0}^{m-1-j} f_{i+j+1} \alpha^i$, where f_i's, $0 \leq i \leq m - 1$, are the coefficients of the primitive polynomial defining the field $GF(2^m)$. Then $\{\beta_0, \beta_1, \ldots, \beta_{m-1}\}$ is the triangular basis (TB) corresponding to the canonical basis (CB) $\{1, \alpha, \ldots, \alpha^{m-1}\}$, and forms a basis of $GF(2^m)$ over $GF(2)$. This can be seen by arranging the basis elements in the following matrix form and then noting that the $m \times m$ transformation matrix is nonsingular.

$$\begin{bmatrix} \beta_0 \\ \beta_1 \\ \vdots \\ \beta_{m-1} \end{bmatrix} = \begin{bmatrix} f_1 & f_2 & \cdots & f_{m-1} & 1 \\ f_2 & f_3 & \cdots & 1 & 0 \\ \vdots & \vdots & \ddots & \vdots & \vdots \\ 1 & 0 & \cdots & 0 & 0 \end{bmatrix} \begin{bmatrix} 1 \\ \alpha \\ \vdots \\ \alpha^{m-1} \end{bmatrix}. \tag{5}$$

Representing the element a with respect to the triangular basis we obtain

$$a = \sum_{i=0}^{m-1} \tilde{a}_i \beta_i, \tag{6}$$

where $\tilde{a}_i \in GF(2)$, for $0 \leq i \leq m - 1$, are the TB coordinates of a.

A basis other than the canonical basis can be chosen as the primal basis, and a corresponding triangular basis can be found. As a simple illustration consider the following example.

Example 1. Let $f(x)$ be $1 + x^3 + x^4$ which is a primitive polynomial of degree 4 over GF(2). Then the CB is $\{1, \alpha, \alpha^2, \alpha^3\}$, and using (5) the corresponding TB is obtained as $\{\alpha^{14}, \alpha^{13}, \alpha^{12}, 1\}$.

Any element represented with respect to either the CB or TB can be uniquely represented with respect to the other basis. In this connection, from (3) and (6) one obtains

$$\sum_{i=0}^{m-1} a_i \alpha^i = \sum_{j=0}^{m-1} \tilde{a}_j \sum_{l=0}^{m-1-j} f_{l+j+1} \alpha^l. \tag{7}$$

Equating the coefficients of α^i, for $0 \le i \le m - 1$, on both sides of (7) we have

$$\tilde{a}_i = a_{m-1-i} + (1 - \delta_{i,0}) \sum_{l=1}^{i} \tilde{a}_{i-l} f_{m-l} \pmod{2} \quad 0 \le i \le m - 1, \tag{8}$$

and

$$a_{m-1-i} = \sum_{l=0}^{i} \tilde{a}_{i-l} f_{m-l} \pmod{2}\ 0 \le i \le m - 1. \tag{9}$$

Equations (8) and (9) correspond to transformations of coordinates from the CB to the TB and vice versa; they can be realized by well-known shift register configurations.

3.2 Multiplication

Bartee and Schneider suggest a direct implementation of the multiplication by combinational logic [13]. They use a canonical basis to represent the elements of the field. Depending on the polynomial $f(x)$, this implementation requires as many as $(m^3 - m)$ two-input adders over GF(2) [1]. Because of the high circuit complexity and lack of regularity, it is often advantageous to use other techniques for hardware implementation of multiplication.

In the last decade, two important contributions to multiplication in GF(2^m) were made: one is the dual basis multiplication algorithm by Berlekamp [6], and the other is the normal basis multiplication algorithm by Massey and Omura [14]. The representation of field elements with respect to a normal basis is unconventional, but it results in a very simple squaring operation. This is advantageous for the design of inversion and exponentiation circuitry. Multiplication using the Massey-Omura algorithm requires the same logic circuitry for all product coordinates. In the following discussion we briefly present the two multipliers.

Massey-Omura Multiplier.   Let $a \in GF(2^m)$ be represented with respect to the normal basis $\left\{\alpha, \alpha^2, \ldots, \alpha^{2^{m-1}}\right\}$, i.e.,

$$a = \breve{a}_0\alpha + \breve{a}_1\alpha^2 + \cdots + \breve{a}_{m-1}\alpha^{2^{m-1}}$$

$$= \begin{bmatrix} \breve{a}_0, & \breve{a}_1, & \cdots, \breve{a}_{m-1} \end{bmatrix} \begin{bmatrix} \alpha \\ \alpha^{2^1} \\ \vdots \\ \alpha^{2^{m-1}} \end{bmatrix}, \tag{10}$$

where $\breve{a}_i \in GF(2)$, $0 \le i \le m - 1$, is the ith coordinate of a with respect to the normal basis.

Let u be the product of any two elements a and b of $GF(2^m)$, i.e.,

$$u = \begin{bmatrix} \breve{a}_0, & \breve{a}_1, & \cdots, \breve{a}_{m-1} \end{bmatrix} \begin{bmatrix} \alpha \\ \alpha^{2^1} \\ \vdots \\ \alpha^{2^{m-1}} \end{bmatrix}$$

$$\cdot \begin{bmatrix} \alpha, & \alpha^{2^1}, & \cdots, \alpha^{2^{m-1}} \end{bmatrix} \begin{bmatrix} \breve{b}_0 \\ \breve{b}_1 \\ \vdots \\ \breve{b}_{m-1} \end{bmatrix} = \mathbf{a}\,\mathbf{M}\mathbf{b}^T, \tag{11}$$

where T denotes transposition, $\mathbf{a} = [\breve{a}_0, \breve{a}_1, \ldots, \breve{a}_{m-1}]$, $\mathbf{b} = [\breve{b}_0, \breve{b}_1, \ldots, \breve{b}_{m-1}]$, and the *multiplication* matrix $\mathbf{M}$ is defined as

$$\mathbf{M} = \begin{bmatrix} \alpha^{2^0+2^0} & \alpha^{2^0+2^1} & \cdots & \alpha^{2^0+2^{m-1}} \\ \alpha^{2^1+2^0} & \alpha^{2^1+2^1} & \cdots & \alpha^{2^1+2^{m-1}} \\ \vdots & \vdots & \ddots & \vdots \\ \alpha^{2^{m-1}+2^0} & \alpha^{2^{m-1}+2^1} & \cdots & \alpha^{2^{m-1}+2^{m-1}} \end{bmatrix}. \tag{12}$$

Following [15],

$$\mathbf{M} = \mathbf{M}_0\alpha + \mathbf{M}_1\alpha^2 + \cdots + \mathbf{M}_{m-1}\alpha^{2^{m-1}} \tag{13}$$

where the entries of the $m \times m$ Boolean matrix $\mathbf{M}_l$ ($0 \le l \le m - 1$) belong to $GF(2)$. In $\mathbf{M}_l$, each row and column is numbered as $0, 1, \ldots, m - 1$.

Then, row i and column j of $\mathbf{M}_l$ contain the coefficient of α^{2^l} when $\alpha^{2^i+2^j}$ is expressed in terms of the normal basis using (10) with $l = 0, 1, \ldots, m-1$.

From (11) and (13), one obtains the coordinates of the product as

$$\begin{aligned}
\breve{u}_{m-1-l} &= \mathbf{a}\mathbf{M}_{m-1-l}\mathbf{b}^T \quad l = 0, 1, \ldots, m-1 \\
&= \mathbf{a}^{(l)}\mathbf{M}_{m-1}\mathbf{b}^{(l)T}
\end{aligned} \tag{14}$$

where $\mathbf{a}^{(l)}$ is the l-fold right cyclic shift of $\mathbf{a}$ [15].

A bit-serial multiplier based on equation (14) is shown in Figure 5-1, and it is known as a serial-type Massey-Omura multiplier. Shift registers A and B are initially loaded with the normal basis coordinates of a and b, respectively. The contents of the registers can be rotated l times to generate the vectors $\mathbf{a}^{(l)}$ and $\mathbf{b}^{(l)}$. The contents of the registers are input to an AND-XOR plane which generates the coordinates of the product using equation (14). The complexity of the plane and consequently that of the multiplier depend on the polynomial $f(x)$ defining the field. On average, the circuit complexity of the serial-type Massey-Omura multiplier is $O(m^2)$ gates; however, there are certain low-complexity normal bases that require only $O(m)$ gates [15,16].

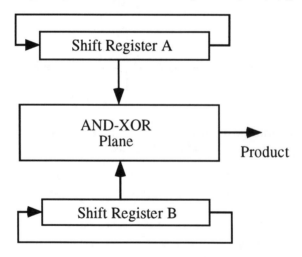

Figure 5-1. Massey-Omura bit-serial multiplier.

Berlekamp's Dual Basis Multiplier.   Let $\{\tau_0, \tau_1, \ldots, \tau_{m-1}\}$ be the dual to the canonical basis $\{1, \alpha, \ldots, \alpha^{m-1}\}$. Let $a'_i, i = 0, 1, \ldots, m-1$, be the coordinates of a with respect to the dual basis, i.e.,

$$a = \sum_{i=0}^{m-1} a_i\alpha^i = \sum_{i=0}^{m-1} a'_i\tau_i. \tag{15}$$

If u is the product of any two elements a and b, then for $l = 0, 1, \ldots, m - 1$ we have

$$u'_l = \text{Tr}(\alpha^l u) = \text{Tr}(\alpha^l ab)$$

$$= \text{Tr}\left(\alpha^l a \sum_{j=0}^{m-1} b_j \alpha^j\right)$$

$$= \sum_{j}^{m-1} b_j \text{Tr}(\alpha^{l+j} a) \tag{16}$$

$$= \sum_{j=0}^{m-1} b_j \text{Tr}[\alpha^j (\alpha^l a)] = \sum_{j=0}^{m-1} b_j (\alpha^l a)'_j.$$

Equation (16) requires calculation of an inner product over GF(2) involving the canonical basis coordinates of b and the dual basis coordinates $(\alpha^l a)$. The latter can be recursively obtained as follows:

$$(\alpha^l a)'_j = \text{Tr}\left(\alpha^j \alpha^l a\right)$$

$$= \begin{cases} \text{Tr}\left(\alpha^{j+1} \alpha^{l-1} a\right) & j = 0, 1, \ldots, m - 2 \\ \text{Tr}\left(\alpha^m \alpha^{l-1} a\right) & j = m - 1, \end{cases}$$

$$= \begin{cases} (\alpha^{l-1} a)'_{j+1} & j = 0, 1, \ldots, m - 2 \\ \sum_{i=0}^{m-1} f_i (\alpha^{l-1} a)'_i & j = m - 1. \end{cases} \tag{17}$$

The realization of the Berlekamp's dual basis multiplier in bit-serial form is shown in Figure 5-2. The circuit requires $O(m)$ gates. The registers are initially loaded with the dual basis coordinates of a, and the inner product output is u'_0. After the first shift, the register contains the dual basis coordinates of αa, and the output is u'_1. After the second shift, the register contains the dual basis coordinates of $\alpha^2 a$, and the output is u'_2, and so on.

The advantage of Berlekamp's bit-serial multiplier is that it requires minimum circuitry when the multiplier b is a constant. However, note that one factor (the multiplier b) is represented with respect to the canonical basis and the other factor (the multiplicand a) is represented with respect to the corresponding dual basis. The product is obtained with respect to the dual basis.

The involvement of two bases in Berlekamp's multiplication algorithm is a drawback, especially when the multiplier is to be used as part of a larger circuit. In general, the canonical basis representation of both the multiplicand

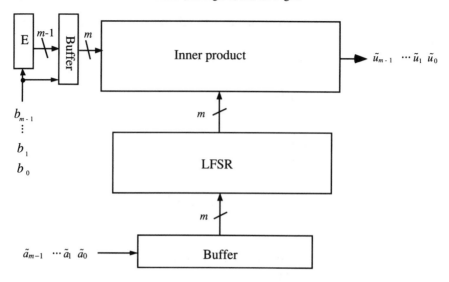

Figure 5-2. Berlekamp's dual basis bit-serial multiplier.

and multiplier are available, and the product is also expected to be represented relative to this basis. As a result, circuitry is required at the input to transform one of the factors (the multiplicand) from the canonical basis to the dual basis, and at the output to transform the product from the dual basis back to the canonical basis. Recent work by Morii, Kasahara, and Whiting [17] shows that bit-serial multiplication can be made efficient if the polynomial $f(x)$ is a trinomial. However, irreducible trinomials do not exist for all degrees. Wang and Blake [18] present a bit-serial multiplier featuring regular basis transformation circuitry at the input and output which works for all irreducible polynomials. The multiplier of [19] is equivalent to that of [18] in the sense that all the input and output elements are expressed with respect to a canonical basis. However, the multiplier of [19] has lower circuit complexity than that of [18]. In the following subsection, we present a triangular basis multiplier [11].

Triangular Basis Multiplication.   A multiplication algorithm can be obtained by formulating the problem as a discrete-time Wiener-Hopf equation (DTWHE). For $ab = u$, we have [19]

$$
\begin{bmatrix}
\tilde{a}_0 & \tilde{a}_1 & \cdots & \tilde{a}_{m-1} \\
\tilde{a}_1 & \tilde{a}_2 & \cdots & \tilde{a}_m \\
\vdots & \vdots & \ddots & \vdots \\
\tilde{a}_{m-1} & \tilde{a}_m & \cdots & \tilde{a}_{2m-2}
\end{bmatrix}
\begin{bmatrix}
b_0 \\
b_1 \\
\vdots \\
b_{m-1}
\end{bmatrix}
=
\begin{bmatrix}
\tilde{u}_0 \\
\tilde{u}_1 \\
\vdots \\
\tilde{u}_{m-1}
\end{bmatrix},
\qquad (18)
$$

where

$$\tilde{a}_i = \sum_{l=0}^{m-1} \tilde{a}_{i-1-l} f_{m-1-l} \pmod{2} \quad m \le i \le 2m - 2, \tag{19}$$

and $\tilde{a}_i$ and $\tilde{u}_i$, $0 \le i \le m - 1$, are the TB coordinates of a and u, respectively. Then we have the following multiplication algorithm [12].

Step 1: For $0 \le i \le m - 1$, transform CB coordinates a_i to TB coordinates $\tilde{a}_i$ using (8).

Step 2: Generate the rows of the Hankel matrix in (18).

Step 3: Perform the matrix-vector multiplication described in (18) to obtain $\tilde{u}_i$ for $0 \le i \le m - 1$.

Step 4: For $0 \le i \le m - 1$, transform TB coordinates $\tilde{u}_i$ to CB coordinates u_i using (9).

A pipeline bit-serial multiplier that uses the above multiplication algorithm is shown in Figure 5-3. The CB coordinates of a and b serially enter the LFSR_1 and the $(m - 1)$-stage register E, respectively. As the CB coordinates of a enter the LFSR_1 they are transformed to the TB coordinates $\tilde{a}_0, \tilde{a}_1, \ldots, \tilde{a}_{m-1}$. At the mth clock cycle, the vector $[\tilde{a}_0, \tilde{a}_1, \ldots, \tilde{a}_{m-1}]$, which is the 0th row of the Hankel matrix, is loaded into the LFSR_2. The CB coordinates of b are also loaded into the m-stage buffer F and the registers of both the LFSR_1 and the FFSR (feed forward shift register) are cleared to zero. During the clock cycles from m to $2m - 1$, all rows of the Hankel matrix are obtained as the outputs of the LFSR_2, and an inner product over GF(2) is formed in each clock cycle, yielding the TB coordinates of the product u. During these clock cycles, the CB coordinates of u are also obtained from the output of the FFSR, and the coordinates of a and b of the next problem enter the LFSR_1 and buffer E to give a pipeline operation.

Note that without the LFSR_1 and FFSR in Figure 5-3, the triangular basis multiplier is the same as Berlekamp's dual basis multiplier. The advantages of the structure shown in Figure 5-3 are that its input and output are represented with respect to a canonical basis and it provides pipeline operation.

3.3 Inversion

Computing inversion is one of the most complicated operations in $GF(2^m)$. With the exception of the encoder discussed in [20], encoders do not require finite field inversion. However, most decoders do.

A straightforward approach for computation of the inverse of a nonzero element in $GF(2^m)$ is to use a ROM in which inverses of the field elements

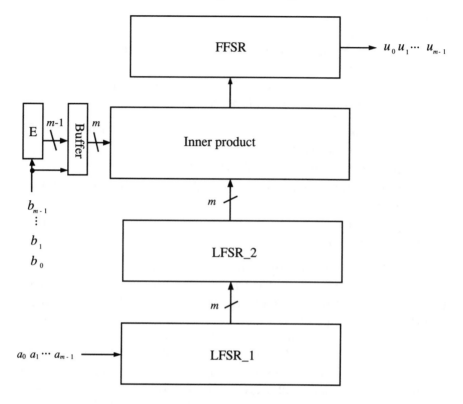

Figure 5-3. A triangular basis pipeline bit-serial multiplier.

are stored. For GF(2^m), the size of the ROM is on the order of $m2^m$ bits. The coordinates of an element are used as the address of the location in the ROM where the corresponding inverse has been stored. For most of the practically used RS codes, the size of the ROM is not very large. As a result, many RS decoders that rely on this ROM-based approach to compute inverses can be found. However, the use of ROM is not advantageous for designing a universal RS decoder where codes are defined over GF(2^m) for different values of m [21].

Two alternate methods for computing an inverse have received considerable attention in the literature. They are based on Euclid's algorithm and Fermat's theorem. Let the field elements be represented with respect to the canonical basis $\{1, \alpha, \ldots, \alpha^{m-1}\}$. The representation of an element a with respect to this basis can be considered as a polynomial in α over GF(2) whose degree is less than m; i.e., $a(\alpha) = \sum_{i=0}^{m-1} a_i \alpha^i$. Since $f(x)$ is a primitive polynomial of degree m over GF(2), $f(x)$ is relatively prime to $a(x)$, and using Euclid's algorithm we can find polynomials $b(x)$ and $d(x)$ such that

$$a(x)b(x) + f(x)d(x) = 1 \qquad (20)$$

where $\deg[b(x)] < \deg[f(x)]$. Therefore, $a(\alpha)b(\alpha) = 1$, and $b(\alpha)$ is the canonical basis representation of the inverse of the element a.

Inversion circuits based on Euclid's algorithm require polynomial divisions and multiplications. An inverter with a modular structure based on Euclid's algorithm is presented in [22].

Since $a \in GF(2^m)$, following Fermat's theorem,

$$a^{2^m-1} = 1,$$
$$a^{-1} = a^{2^m-2} = a^{2^1}a^{2^2}\cdots a^{2^{m-1}}.$$

Thus, inverters based on Fermat's theorem require recursive squaring and multiplication operations over finite fields. Accordingly, they are suitable when a normal basis is used for the representation of the elements of GF(2^m) [7]. The attractive feature of a normal basis representation is that the squaring can be performed by a simple cyclic shift of a field element's binary digits. A recursive pipeline inverter that uses a Massey-Omura parallel-type multiplier and requires $(m - 2)$ multiplications and $(m - 1)$ cyclic shifts is discussed in [7].

It has been shown that inverting an element of GF(2^m) can be achieved by solving $(2m - 1)$ simultaneous linear equations in $(2m - 1)$ unknowns over GF(2) [23]. However, more efficient inversion methods based on the solution of linear equations over GF(2) have also been developed [17,19]. The division algorithm developed in [19] requires a solution of m linear equations over GF(2). A discussion of this algorithm follows.

The product u of a and b is simply the polynomial multiplication of $\sum_{i=0}^{m-1} a_i\alpha^i$ and $\sum_{i=0}^{m-1} b_i\alpha^i$ modulo $f(\alpha)$. Direct polynomial multiplication of a and b results in a polynomial in α, say, $\hat{u}(\alpha)$, with degree less than or equal to $2m - 2$. The elements α^i, $i = 0, 1, \ldots, 2m - 2$, are known as the supporting elements [19]. If the coordinates of these supporting elements are known, substitution of these coordinates into $\hat{u}(\alpha)$ will result in a polynomial of degree less than m. The coefficients of this polynomial are the coordinates of the product u.

Now, if b is the inverse of a, then $ab = u = 1$. Thus, computation of the inverse of a reduces to finding the coordinates of b in terms of the coordinates of a and the supporting elements. Let α^l, $0 \le l \le 2m - 2$, be a supporting element that can be represented with respect to the canonical basis as follows:

$$\alpha^l = \sum_{i=0}^{m-1} s_i^{(l)} \alpha^i, \tag{21}$$

where $s_i^{(l)}$, $0 \le l \le 2m - 2$, $0 \le i \le m - 1$, is the ith coordinate of the supporting element α^l. Let $a \ne 0$ and let b be the inverse of a. Following [19] we have the following matrix equation:

$$
\begin{bmatrix}
\sum_{l=0}^{m-1} a_l s_{m-1}^{(l)} & \sum_{l=0}^{m-1} a_l s_{m-1}^{(l+1)} & \cdots & \sum_{l=0}^{m-1} a_l s_{m-1}^{(l+m-1)} \\[2ex]
\sum_{l=0}^{m-1} a_l s_{m-2}^{(l)} & \sum_{l=0}^{m-1} a_l s_{m-2}^{(l+1)} & \cdots & \sum_{l=0}^{m-1} a_l s_{m-2}^{(l+m-1)} \\[2ex]
\vdots & \vdots & \ddots & \vdots \\[2ex]
\sum_{l=0}^{m-1} a_l s_0^{(l)} & \sum_{l=0}^{m-1} a_l s_0^{(l+1)} & \cdots & \sum_{l=0}^{m-1} a_l s_0^{(l+m-1)}
\end{bmatrix}
\begin{bmatrix}
b_0 \\ b_1 \\ \vdots \\ b_{m-1}
\end{bmatrix}
=
\begin{bmatrix}
0 \\ 0 \\ \vdots \\ 1
\end{bmatrix},
\tag{22}
$$

Boolean expressions for the coordinates of b in terms of the coordinates of a can be obtained by symbolically solving equation (22). These expressions lead to combinational logic circuits which perform an inversion operation in one time step. Such an inverter is suitable for fast computation and can be used for applications where high throughput is a prime concern. The main disadvantage of this inversion procedure is that any change in the value of m or polynomial $f(x)$ will result in a completely new circuit. A flexible design that can be used for different values of m and $f(x)$ would increase the overall circuit complexity significantly.

Systolic inversion circuitry based on equation (22) is presented in [8]. This circuitry does not depend on the coefficients of the polynomial $f(x)$ of degree m. As shown in Figure 5-4, it has two main parts: a one-dimensional systolic array for the formation of the coefficient matrix of equation (22) (SAFCM) and a two-dimensional systolic array for solving the linear equations (SASLE). Although the inverter cannot complete the computation in one clock cycle, it supports pipeline and bit-serial operations that are suited to bit-serial decoders.

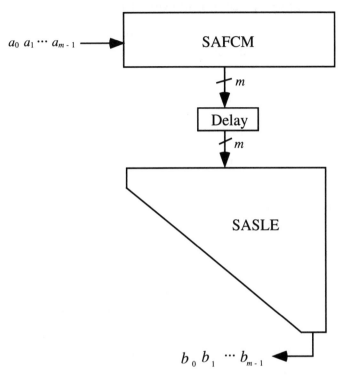

Figure 5-4. Block diagram for a systolic finite field inverter.

4 ENCODING

In the previous section, we discussed several approaches to implementing arithmetic operations of $GF(2^m)$, especially multiplication and inversion. These two operations are used in the encoding and decoding of RS codes. In this section, we discuss different encoding methods.

Let the sequence of k data symbols in $GF(2^m)$ be $d = [d_0, d_1, \ldots, d_{k-1}]$. The data vector can be represented by a polynomial as follows:

$$d(x) = d_0 + d_1 x + \cdots + d_{k-1} x^{k-1}.$$

Code word polynomials could be formed as $d(x)g(x)$, but this code would be nonsystematic because the k data symbols would not be explicitly present in the code word. Hence, one extra step is needed in the decoding process to extract the information from the corrected code word.

4.1 Encoding by Polynomial Division

A code word can be obtained in systematic form by adding $n - k$ ($= 2t$) parity-check symbols to the data symbols. Let us denote the corresponding parity-check vector by $p = [p_0, p_1, \ldots, p_{2t-1}]$. Then the code word vector

$$C = [c_0, c_1, \ldots, c_{n-1}] = [p_0, p_1, \ldots, p_{2t-1}, d_0, d_1, \ldots, d_{k-1}].$$

Using polynomial notation, we can write

$$c(x) = p(x) + x^{n-k}d(x), \tag{23}$$

where $p(x) = \sum_{i=0}^{2t-1} p_i x^i$ is a polynomial over GF(2^m) of degree $2t - 1$ or less. The parity symbols p_i are chosen such that $c(x)$ is divisible by the generator polynomial $g(x)$, i.e.,

$$p(x) = R_{g(x)}\left[x^{n-k}d(x)\right], \tag{24}$$

where $R_{g(x)}[\cdot]$ denotes the remainder after division by $g(x)$.

Thus the encoding of an RS code can be performed using the following algorithm:

Step 1: Premultiply the data polynomial $d(x)$ by x^{n-k}.

Step 2: Obtain $p(x)$ as defined in (24).

Step 3: Combine $p(x)$ and $x^{n-k}d(x)$ to obtain code word $c(x)$ as indicated in (23).

Although not explicitly shown in the above algorithm, $k(n - k)$ multiplications in GF(2^m) are required in Step 2. If the input information symbols are received in a bit-serial fashion, a bit-serial multiplication scheme can be used to give low encoder complexity at the expense of throughput.

4.2 Encoding in the Frequency Domain

An RS code can also be generated in the so-called frequency domain [2]. To encode the information symbols in the frequency domain, the first $(n - k)$ symbols, i.e., $C_i, i = 0, 1, \ldots, n - k - 1$, are set to zero. The remaining k symbols are assigned the information symbols. An inverse finite field Fourier transform, defined by the relationship

$$c_i = \sum_{j=0}^{n-1} C_j \alpha^{-ij}, \quad i = 0, 1, \ldots, n - 1, \tag{25}$$

is performed to obtain time domain RS codes.

It can be seen from equation (25) that the number of multiplications required for encoding using the Fourier transform is the same as the number required using polynomial division. However, when the number of information symbols is variable, it may be advantageous to use the Fourier transform encoding technique since it can accommodate different k simply by setting the appropriate number of C_i to zero without any change in the hardware.

4.3 Encoding Using the Cauchy Matrix

Consider a systematic generator matrix for the RS (n, k) code. This matrix has the form

$$G = [I \; A], \tag{26}$$

where I is the identity matrix of order k and A is a $k \times (n - k)$ matrix [20]. The matrix A is known as a *Cauchy matrix* and has entries

$$A_{i,j} = \frac{u_i v_j}{x_i + y_j}, \quad 0 \le i \le k - 1, \; 0 \le j \le n - k - 1. \tag{27}$$

where u_i, v_j, x_i, and y_j are elements of $GF(2^m)$ and are defined as:

$$x_i = \alpha^{n-1-i}, \quad 0 \le i \le k - 1, \tag{28}$$

$$y_j = \alpha^{n-1-k-j}, \quad 0 \le j \le n - k - 1, \tag{29}$$

$$u_i = \frac{1}{\displaystyle\prod_{\substack{0 \le l \le k-1 \\ l \ne i}} \left(\alpha^{n-1-i} - \alpha^{n-1-l}\right)}, \quad 0 \le i \le k - 1, \tag{30}$$

$$v_j = \prod_{0 \le l \le k-1} \left(\alpha^{n-1-k-j} - \alpha^{n-1-l}\right), \quad 0 \le j \le n - k - 1. \tag{31}$$

For systematic RS codes, the parity-check vector $p = [p_0, p_1, \ldots, p_{n-k-1}]$ is

$$p = dA,$$

$$p_j = \sum_{i=0}^{k-1} d_i A_{i,j} \tag{32}$$

$$= v_j \sum_{i=0}^{k-1} \frac{d_i u_i}{x_i + y_j}, \quad 0 \le j \le n - k - 1.$$

Due to the inversion operations in (32), it is clear that encoding using a Cauchy matrix requires more finite field computation than the other two methods. In the following subsection, we discuss encoder structures based on the three algorithms.

4.4 Encoder Architectures

The conventional encoder depends on the structure for polynomial division. Since polynomial division requires multiplications in $GF(2^m)$, the complexity of the structure depends on the multiplier used. For the parallel-type multiplier, the circuit complexity could be as high as $O(m^2t)$. However, using Berlekamp's bit-serial dual basis multiplier, the complexity can be reduced to $O(mt)$ [6]. An encoder with a similar complexity can also be obtained using the triangular basis multiplier shown in Figure 5-5 [12]. This last structure is divided into three main units whose functions are briefly described below.

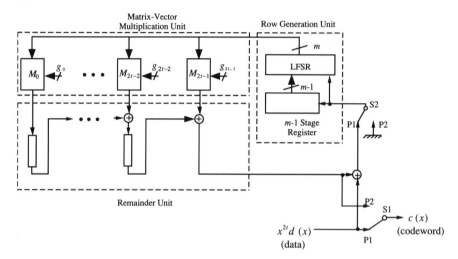

Figure 5-5. A fixed-rate pipeline bit-serial encoder.

1. Row generation unit: The incoming bit stream is first buffered into the $(m - 1)$-stage shift register before a block of m bits is loaded into the linear feedback shift register (LFSR). Each m-bit data block is considered to be the TB coordinates of an element of $GF(2^m)$. As a result, the loading operation corresponds to the formation of the 0th row of the Hankel matrix as discussed in the previous section. The other rows are generated by the LFSR in subsequent clock cycles.

2. Matrix-vector multiplication unit: This unit consists of $2t$ identical modules $M_0, M_1, \ldots, M_{2t-1}$. Each module evaluates the inner product of two input vectors. The common input to all modules is a row of the Hankel matrix. The other input to module M_i is the vector consisting of the CB coordinates of g_i. For a fixed-rate encoder, g_i can be hardwired to M_i.

3. Remainder unit: This unit stores the coefficients of the remainder polynomial whose coefficients are elements of $GF(2^m)$ and are represented with respect to the TB. Modulo-2 additions are performed serially with respect to the TB.

To obtain a structure using frequency domain encoding, note that equation (25) can be written as

$$c_i = (\cdots (C_{n-1}\alpha^{-i} + C_{n-2})\alpha^{-i} + \cdots + C_1)\alpha^{-i} + C_0. \qquad (33)$$

As a result, code word c_i can be generated recursively using one α^{-i} multiplier and one adder. This structure is shown in Figure 5-6 where triangular basis multiplication has been used. At the 0th clock cycle, the LFSR is initialized to 1. In the next nm cycles the coordinates of C_i, for $i = n - 1, n - 2, \ldots, 0$, enter the cells in a bit-serial fashion. After nm clock cycles, the cell shift registers contain code word symbols that are then downloaded onto an associated shift register outside the cells. During the next nm clock cycles the code word is transmitted in a bit-serial fashion, and C_i, for $i = n - 1, n - 2, \ldots, 0$, can enter the structure yielding a pipeline operation. Note that the structure is independent of the value of t and can be used to generate RS codes of different code rates. It has a circuit complexity of $O(mn)$ gates. Although the structure has a higher circuit complexity than the structure based on polynomial division, it is more suitable for a programmable code rate encoder since it does not depend on t.

Using (32), an encoder structure that is systolic and does not have any feedback connections has been proposed [20]. Since interleaving is not required, this structure also results in a reduction in the latency delay, which makes it suitable for applications in which a high throughput is required. The block diagram of the basic encoder structure is shown in Figure 5-7. The leftmost cell C_{pre} computes $d_i u_i$, for $0 \le i \le k - 1$. In addition to cell C_{pre}, the structure has $(n - k)$ identical cells $(CC_j, j = 0, 1, \ldots, n - k - 1)$. Cell CC_j computes the component p_j of the parity-check vector during time steps $n - k - j$ to $n - 1 - j$. During these time steps, the switch is at position A and it allows data symbols to propagate. At the $(n - j)$th time step, the switch is placed at position B and p_j is tapped out. In the next k time steps the switch is at position C so that the parity symbols from the left side cells can propagate rightward. Implementation of each cell requires one divider, two fixed multipliers,[1] and two adders, all of which perform operations over $GF(2^m)$ and are of a parallel type. The computational delay in each cell is mainly determined by the divider. Because of the involvement of the divider

---

[1] Only one multiplier is required if time multiplexing is used.

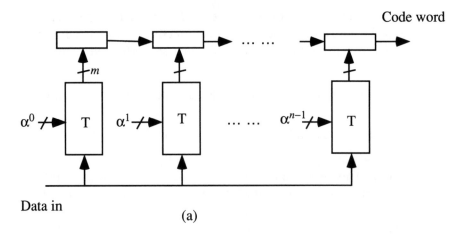

(a)

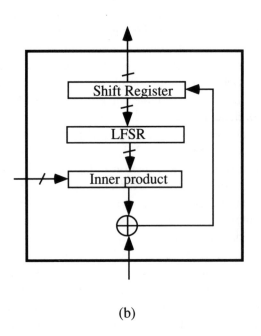

(b)

Figure 5-6. (a) Structure for a bit-serial transform encoding. (b) Cell T.

and multiplier, the complexity of the encoder can be as high as $O(m^3 t)$ gates. Bit-serial dividers and multipliers can be used to reduce the complexity at the expense of reduction in throughput.

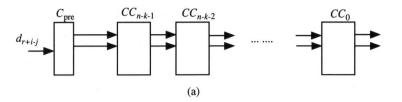

(a)

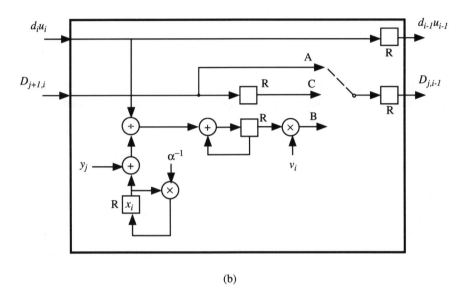

(b)

Figure 5-7. (a) A systolic encoder structure. (b) Cauchy cell CC_j. $D_j \overset{\Delta}{=}$ $\left[D_{j,i} \right]_{i=0}^{n-1} = \left[d_0, d_1, \ldots, d_{k-1}, p_j, p_{j+1}, \ldots, p_{r-1}, 0, \ldots, 0 \right]$, $0 \le j \le r-1$, and $r = n - k$.

5 DECODING

In this section we discuss different decoding algorithms and compare them from a structural point of view. We then present different decoder architectures.

5.1 Syndrome-Based Decoding

Let the error vector be $e = [e_0, e_1, \ldots, e_{n-1}]$ with polynomial representation

$$e(x) = e_0 + e_1 x + \cdots + e_{n-1} x^{n-1}. \tag{34}$$

The received polynomial at the input of the decoder is then

$$v(x) = c(x) + e(x) = v_0 + v_1 x + \cdots + v_{n-1} x^{n-1}, \tag{35}$$

where the polynomial coefficients are components of the received vector v. We can evaluate this polynomial at the roots of the generator polynomial $g(x)$, which are $\alpha, \alpha^2, \ldots, \alpha^{2t}$. Since the code word polynomial $c(x)$ is divisible by $g(x)$, and $g(\alpha^i) = 0$ for $i = 1, 2, \ldots, 2t$, we have

$$
\begin{aligned}
v(\alpha^j) &= c(\alpha^j) + e(\alpha^j) \\
&= e(\alpha^j) = \sum_{i=0}^{n-1} e_i \alpha^{ij}, \quad j = 1, 2, \ldots, 2t.
\end{aligned}
\tag{36}
$$

This final set of $2t$ equations involves only components of the error pattern, not those of the code word. They can be used to compute syndromes S_j, $j = 1, 2, \ldots, 2t$, where

$$S_j \triangleq v(\alpha^j) = \sum_{i=0}^{n-1} v_i \alpha^{ij}, \quad j = 1, 2, \ldots, 2t. \tag{37}$$

Following evaluation of the syndromes, the error pattern e_i, $i = 0, 1, \ldots,$ $n - 1$, can be determined. Suppose that v errors, $0 \le v \le t$, occur in unknown locations $i_1, i_2, \ldots, i_v$. Then the error polynomial can be written as

$$e(x) = e_{i_1} x^{i_1} + e_{i_2} x^{i_2} + \cdots + e_{i_v} x^{i_v}, \tag{38}$$

where e_{i_l} is the value of the lth error. We do not know $i_1, i_2, \ldots, i_v$, nor do we know $e_{i_1}, e_{i_2}, \ldots, e_{i_v}$. In fact, we do not even know the value of v. All these values must be computed in order to correct the errors.

The first step in decoding is the evaluation of syndromes given by equation (37). Let us evaluate the received polynomial at α to obtain the syndrome S_1:

$$
\begin{aligned}
S_1 &= v(\alpha) \\
&= e(\alpha) = e_{i_1} \alpha^{i_1} + e_{i_2} \alpha^{i_2} + \cdots + e_{i_v} \alpha^{i_v}.
\end{aligned}
$$

Changing the notation [2], we define the error values $Y_l = e_{i_l}$, for $l = 1, 2, \ldots, v$, and the error location number $X_l = \alpha^{i_l}$, for $l = 1, 2, \ldots, v$, where i_l is the actual location of the lth error and X_l is the field element associated with this location. Using this notation, the first syndrome is given by

$$S_1 = Y_1 X_1 + Y_2 X_2 + \cdots + Y_v X_v. \tag{39}$$

Similarly, we can evaluate the received polynomial at each of the powers of α which are roots of $g(x)$. We then have the following set of $2t$ equations in ν unknown error location numbers $X_1, X_2, \ldots, X_\nu$ and ν unknown error values $Y_1, Y_2, \ldots, Y_\nu$:

$$S_j = Y_1 X_1^j + Y_2 X_2^j + \cdots + Y_\nu X_\nu^j, \quad j = 1, 2, \ldots, 2t. \tag{40}$$

This set of equations must have at least one solution because of the way in which the syndromes are defined. It can be shown that the solution is unique for $0 \le \nu \le t$ [2].

We summarize the decoding process in the following two steps:

1. Syndrome evaluation using equation (37).
2. Solving the system of $2t$ nonlinear equations given by equation (40) to find the error locations and error values.

The first step, syndrome evaluation, can be regarded as evaluation of a Fourier transform of the received vector v where $2t$ frequency domain components are calculated according to equation (37) [2]. In the second step, the direct solution of a system of nonlinear equations is difficult except for small values of t. A better approach requires intermediate steps. For this purpose, the error locator polynomial $\Lambda(x)$ is introduced as follows:

$$\Lambda(x) = 1 + \Lambda_1 x + \cdots + \Lambda_\nu x^\nu. \tag{41}$$

This polynomial is defined to have as roots the inverse error location numbers X_l^{-1}, for $l = 1, 2, \ldots, \nu$. That is,

$$\Lambda(x) = \prod_{l=1}^{\nu} (1 - x X_l), \quad X_l = \alpha^{i_l}. \tag{42}$$

Methods for finding the error locator polynomial from the syndromes are explained later in this section. Once the coefficients of the error locator polynomial are determined, the error locations and error values can be found as shown in the following subsections.

Algebraic Decoding.   In algebraic decoding, syndromes are evaluated using equation (37). Then, based on the syndromes, the error locator polynomial $\Lambda(x)$ is found. Once the error locator polynomial is found, its roots are evaluated in order to find the locations of the errors. The Chien search method can be used to evaluate the roots. This method simply consists of the computation of $\Lambda(\alpha^j)$ for $j = 0, 1, \ldots, n - 1$ and checking for a result equal to zero. Use of this trial-and-error method is feasible, since the number of elements in a Galois field is finite [24].

After evaluation of the roots of $\Lambda(x)$, the error location number $X_l = \alpha^{i_l}$ is substituted in equation (40). Now this system of $2t$ equations becomes linear and can be solved for the error values Y_j, $j = 1, 2, \ldots, v$ [25]. Straightforward solution involves one matrix inversion for each error value. This method is not efficient because of the extensive computation required for the matrix inversion.

A more efficient method to find the error values is called Forney's algorithm [26]. Once again, this algorithm follows evaluation of $\Lambda(x)$. Define the syndrome polynomial

$$S(x) = \sum_{i=1}^{2t} S_i x^i \tag{43}$$

and define the error evaluator polynomial $\Omega(x)$ in terms of these known polynomials by the key equation,

$$\Omega(x) = [1 + S(x)]\,\Lambda(x) \mod x^{2t+1}. \tag{44}$$

The error evaluator polynomial is related to the error locations and error values as [26]

$$\Omega(X_l^{-1}) = Y_l \prod_{i \neq l}(1 - X_i X_l^{-1}), \tag{45}$$

and the error values are given by [2]

$$Y_l = -X_l \frac{\Omega(X_l^{-1})}{\dot{\Lambda}(X_l^{-1})}, \quad l = 1, 2, \cdots, v, \tag{46}$$

where $\dot{\Lambda}(x)$ is the formal derivative of $\Lambda(x)$. The above equation defines the Forney algorithm which is a considerable improvement over matrix inversion but requires division in $GF(2^m)$. After evaluation of the error values, the received vector can be corrected by subtracting the error values from the received vector.

In the algebraic decoding algorithm, we note that first the received vector is transformed to the frequency domain by evaluating the syndromes, and then, based on the syndromes, the error locations and error values are found in the time domain. Because of the mixture of frequency and time domain techniques, this algorithm is sometimes called the *hybrid decoding algorithm* [2].

Transform Decoding.   In transform decoding [2], the code word c is assumed to have been transformed into the frequency domain. The syndromes of the noisy code word $v = c + e$ are defined by the set of $2t$ equations in equation (37). Clearly, from the definition of a finite field Fourier transform, the syndromes are computed as $2t$ components of a Fourier transform. The received noisy code word has a Fourier transform given by $V_j = C_j + E_j$, for $j = 0, 1, \ldots, n - 1$, and the syndromes are the $2t$ components of this spectrum from 1 to $2t$. According to the construction of a Reed-Solomon code in the frequency domain,

$$C_j = 0, \quad j = 1, 2, \ldots, 2t \tag{47}$$

which yields

$$S_j = V_j = E_j, \quad j = 1, 2, \ldots, 2t. \tag{48}$$

The above equation implies that out of n components of the error pattern, $2t$ can be directly obtained from the syndromes. Given the $2t$ frequency domain components and the additional information that at most t components of the time domain error pattern are nonzero, the decoder must find the entire transform of the error pattern. After evaluation of the frequency domain vector E, decoding can be completed by evaluating the inverse Fourier transform to find the time domain error vector e and subtracting e from v [2].

Let Λ be the vector whose components are coefficients of the polynomial $\Lambda(x)$. The vector Λ has an inverse transform $\lambda = [\lambda_0, \lambda_1, \ldots, \lambda_{n-1}]$, where

$$\lambda_i = \sum_{j=0}^{n-1} \Lambda_j \alpha^{-ij} = \Lambda(\alpha^{-i}). \tag{49}$$

Now, using equation (42), we find

$$\lambda_i = \prod_{l=1}^{v} (1 - \alpha^{-i} \alpha^{i_l}). \tag{50}$$

Clearly, $\lambda_i = 0$ if $i = i_l$ for $l = 1, 2, \ldots, v$; λ_i is nonzero otherwise. Consequently, $\lambda_i = 0$ if and only if $e_i \neq 0$. That is, in the time domain, $\lambda_i e_i = 0$ for $i = 0, 1, \ldots, n - 1$. Therefore, the convolution in the frequency domain is zero, i.e.,

$$\Lambda * E = \sum_{j=0}^{n-1} \Lambda_j E_{i-j} = 0, \quad i = 0, 1, \ldots, n - 1. \tag{51}$$

Assuming that the coefficients of the error locator polynomial $\Lambda(x)$ are known, the convolution can be considered as a set of n equations in k unknown components of E. The known frequency components of E are given by equation (48); the remaining components of E can be obtained by recursive extension [2]. Since $\Lambda_0 = 1$, equation (51) can be written in the following form:

$$E_i = - \sum_{j=1}^{n-1} \Lambda_j E_{i-j}, \quad i = 0, 1, \ldots, n - 1. \tag{52}$$

In this way all the components of E can be computed.

Thus, with transform decoding, the received vector is first transformed to the frequency domain by computing syndromes. Then, the frequency domain error vector is recursively obtained, and finally an inverse Fourier transform is performed to find the time domain error vector. Therefore, all computations involved in finding the error values are performed in the frequency domain.

5.2 Evaluation of Error Locator Polynomial

We now discuss the procedure for evaluating the coefficients of the error locator polynomial $\Lambda(x)$ given by equation (41). This polynomial has ν roots at X_l^{-1} for $l = 1, 2, \ldots, \nu$. The error location numbers X_l indicate errors at locations i_l for $l = 1, 2, \ldots, \nu$.

Multiplying both sides of equation (41) by $Y_l X_l^{j+\nu}$ and setting $x = X_l^{-1}$ yields [2]

$$Y_l(X_l^{j+\nu} + \Lambda_1 X_l^{j+\nu-1} + \cdots + \Lambda_\nu X_l^{j}) = 0. \tag{53}$$

Such an equation holds for each l and j. Summing these equations for $l = 1, 2, \ldots, \nu$ gives

$$\sum_{l=1}^{\nu} Y_l X_l^{j+\nu} + \Lambda_1 \sum_{l=1}^{\nu} Y_l X^{j+\nu-1} + \cdots + \Lambda_\nu \sum_{l=1}^{\nu} Y_l X_l^{j} = 0. \tag{54}$$

Combining equations (54) and (40) yields

$$\Lambda_1 S_{j+\nu-1} + \Lambda_2 S_{j+\nu-2} + \cdots + \Lambda_\nu S_j = -S_{j+\nu}, \quad j = 1, 2, \ldots, \nu, \tag{55}$$

which can be written in the following matrix form

$$\begin{bmatrix} S_1 & S_2 & \cdots & S_\nu \\ S_2 & S_3 & \cdots & S_{\nu+1} \\ \vdots & \vdots & \ddots & \cdots \\ S_\nu & S_{\nu+1} & \cdots & S_{2\nu-1} \end{bmatrix} \begin{bmatrix} \Lambda_\nu \\ \Lambda_{\nu-1} \\ \vdots \\ \Lambda_1 \end{bmatrix} = \begin{bmatrix} -S_{\nu+1} \\ -S_{\nu+2} \\ \vdots \\ -S_{2\nu} \end{bmatrix}. \tag{56}$$

One straightforward way to solve the system of equations would be to find the inverse of the matrix. However, the value of the number of errors ν is not known yet. It can be found as follows. As a trial value, set ν to the error-correcting capability of the code t and compute the determinant of the matrix in equation (56). It can be shown that if the determinant is nonzero, this is the correct value of ν [2]. If the determinant is zero, reduce the trial value of ν by 1 and repeat. Continue this process until a nonzero determinant is obtained; the actual number of errors can be determined from the size of the matrix. The coefficients of $\Lambda(x)$ can then be evaluated using the value of ν and equation (56). However, this method is quite inefficient, especially for codes with high error-correcting capability. There are several alternate techniques for solving this problem. We discuss two in the following.

Berlekamp-Massey Algorithm.   The matrix in equation (56) is not arbitrary in its form but is highly structured. This structure can be used to advantage to obtain the polynomial $\Lambda(x)$ by a method that is conceptually more complicated but computationally much simpler than the method discussed above.

Equation (56) can be written in the following form:

$$S_j = -\sum_{i=1}^{\nu} \Lambda_i S_{j-i} \quad j = \nu+1, \nu+2, \ldots, 2\nu. \tag{57}$$

For a fixed $\Lambda(x)$, this is the equation of an autoregressive filter. It may be implemented as a linear feedback shift register with taps given by the coefficients of $\Lambda(x)$.

Linear feedback shift registers can be designed to generate the known sequence of syndromes. Many such registers exist; however, we wish to find the smallest of such shift registers so that $\Lambda(x)$ will be of the smallest degree. The polynomial of the smallest degree will have degree ν, and it is unique since the $\nu \times \nu$ matrix of the original problem is invertible.

The Berlekamp-Massey algorithm is best explained using the following set of recursive equations which computes $\lambda^{(2t)}(x)$ [2]:

$$\Delta_i = \sum_{j=0}^{i-1} \Lambda_j^{(i-1)} S_{i-j}, \tag{58}$$

$$L_i = \delta(i - L_{i-1}) + (1 - \delta)L_{i-1}, \tag{59}$$

$$\begin{bmatrix} \Lambda^{(i)}(x) \\ B^{(i)}(x) \end{bmatrix} = \begin{bmatrix} 1 & -\Delta_i x \\ \Delta_i^{-1}\delta & (1-\delta)x \end{bmatrix} \begin{bmatrix} \Lambda^{(i-1)}(x) \\ B^{(i-1)}(x) \end{bmatrix}, \tag{60}$$

for $i = 1, 2, \ldots, 2t$. The initial conditions are $\Lambda_i^{(0)}(x) = 1$, $B^{(0)}(x) = 1$, $L_0 = 0$, and $\delta = 1$ if both $\Delta_i \neq 0$ and $2L_{i-1} \leq i - 1$, otherwise $\delta = 0$. Then $\Lambda^{(2t)}(x)$ is the smallest-degree polynomial with the properties that $\Lambda_0^{(2t)} = 1$ and

$$S_i + \sum_{j=1}^{i-1} \Lambda_j^{(2t)} S_{i-j} = 0, \quad i = L_{2t+1}, \ldots, 2t. \tag{61}$$

It is also possible to find the error evaluator polynomial $\Omega(x)$ of equation (44). To find $\Omega(x)$ we combine equation (44) with the above recursion relationship to get

$$
\begin{bmatrix} \Omega^{(i)}(x) \\ A^{(i)}(x) \end{bmatrix} = \begin{bmatrix} 1 & -\Delta_i x \\ \Delta_i^{-1}\delta & (1-\delta)x \end{bmatrix} \begin{bmatrix} \Omega^{(i-1)}(x) \\ A^{(i-1)}(x) \end{bmatrix}. \tag{62}
$$

Initially, the temporary polynomial $A(x)$ is set to zero, and $\Omega^{(0)}(x)$ is set to 1. After $2t$ iterations, $\Omega^{(2t)}(x)$ is the error evaluator polynomial.

Euclidean Algorithm.   The error locator as well as the error evaluator polynomials can also be obtained using the Euclidean algorithm, a method for finding the greatest common divisor (gcd) of two polynomials [27].

The Euclidean algorithm can be explained using the following set of recursive equations:

$$
Q^{(i)}(x) = \left\lfloor \frac{R^{(i)}(x)}{T^{(i)}(x)} \right\rfloor, \tag{63}
$$

$$
A^{(i+1)}(x) = \begin{bmatrix} 0 & 1 \\ 1 & Q^{(i)}(x) \end{bmatrix} A^{(i)}(x),
$$

$$
\begin{bmatrix} R^{(i+1)}(x) \\ T^{(i+1)}(x) \end{bmatrix} = \begin{bmatrix} 0 & 1 \\ 1 & Q^{(i)}(x) \end{bmatrix} \begin{bmatrix} R^{(i)}(x) \\ T^{(i)}(x) \end{bmatrix}. \tag{64}
$$

The initial conditions are $R^{(0)}(x) = x^{2t}$, $T^{(0)}(x) = \sum_{j=1}^{2t} S_j x^{j-1}$, and $A^{(0)}(x) = \begin{bmatrix} 1 & 0 \\ 0 & 1 \end{bmatrix}$. The algorithm terminates when the degree of $T^{(i)}(x)$ is less than t. Suppose this occurs when $i = i'$. Then

$$
\Omega(x) = \Delta^{-1} T^{(i')}(x) \tag{65}
$$

$$
\Lambda(x) = \Delta^{-1} A_{22}^{(i')}(x), \tag{66}
$$

where $\Delta = A_{22}^{(i')}(0)$ and A_{22} is the element of the matrix A in the second column and the second row. Solutions of equations (65) and (66) uniquely satisfy equation (44) when degrees of $\Lambda(x)$ and $\Omega(x)$ are less than $t+1$ and t, respectively, and $\Lambda_0 = 1$ [2].

Comparison.   Using shift registers, the realization of the Berlekamp-Massey algorithm is straightforward [2] and it does not involve polynomial multiplication and division. Note that the coefficients of the polynomial that determine the tap weights of the feedback shift register are elements of $GF(2^m)$.

Hardware implementation of the Euclidean algorithm includes both shift registers polynomial multiplication and division circuitry. A modified Euclidean algorithm [4] that is very similar to the Berlekamp-Massey algorithm can be used to reduce hardware complexity.

5.3 Remainder-Based Decoding

The decoding algorithms discussed so far use syndrome calculation. Welch and Berlekamp developed an algorithm that does not require evaluation of these syndromes [3]. Their algorithm instead relies on the remainder polynomial $r(x)$ obtained from the division of the received polynomial $v(x)$ by the generator polynomial $g(x)$, i.e.,

$$r(x) \triangleq r_0 + r_1 x + \cdots + r_{n-k-1} x^{n-k-1}$$
$$= v(x) \mod g(x).$$

Let the errors be only in the information symbols. Let the locations of the errors be $X_1, X_2, \ldots, X_v$ and the corresponding error locator polynomial be

$$W(x) = (x - X_1)(x - X_2) \cdots (x - X_v). \tag{67}$$

Since α is a root of the generator polynomial $g(x)$, $x - \alpha$ divides $g(x)$. Let $\hat{g}(x)$ be the polynomial obtained after dividing $g(x)$ by $x - \alpha$, i.e.,

$$\hat{g}(x) = \frac{g(x)}{x - \alpha}$$
$$\triangleq \hat{g}_0 + \hat{g}_1 x + \cdots + \hat{g}_{n-k-1} x^{n-k-1} \tag{68}$$

The Welch-Berlekamp algorithm can then be described as follows:

Step 1:

$$\begin{bmatrix} a_l \\ b_l \end{bmatrix} = \begin{bmatrix} N^{(l)}(\alpha^l) & -W^{(l)}(\alpha^l) \\ M^{(l)}(\alpha^l) & -V^{(l)}(\alpha^l) \end{bmatrix} \begin{bmatrix} \alpha^l \hat{g}_l \\ r_l \end{bmatrix}. \tag{69}$$

If $a_l = 0$, then $b_l = 1$.

Step 2: If $\deg[a_l M^{(l)}(x)] < \deg[b_l W^{(l)}(x)]$, then

$$\begin{bmatrix} N^{(l+1)}(x) \\ W^{(l+1)}(x) \end{bmatrix} = \begin{bmatrix} N^{(l)}(x) & -M^{(l)}(x) \\ W^{(l)}(x) & -V^{(l)}(x) \end{bmatrix} \begin{bmatrix} b_l \\ a_l \end{bmatrix},$$

$$\begin{bmatrix} M^{(l+1)}(x) \\ V^{(l+1)}(x) \end{bmatrix} = (x - \alpha^l) \begin{bmatrix} M^{(l)}(x) \\ V^{(l)}(x) \end{bmatrix}.$$

Else

$$\begin{bmatrix} M^{(l+1)}(x) \\ V^{(l+1)}(x) \end{bmatrix} = \begin{bmatrix} N^{(l)}(x) & -M^{(l)}(x) \\ W^{(l)}(x) & -V^{(l)}(x) \end{bmatrix} \begin{bmatrix} b_l \\ a_l \end{bmatrix}$$

$$\begin{bmatrix} N^{(l+1)}(x) \\ W^{(l+1)}(x) \end{bmatrix} = (x - \alpha^l) \begin{bmatrix} N^{(l)}(x) \\ W^{(l)}(x) \end{bmatrix}.$$

Steps 1 and 2 are performed for $l = 0, 1, \ldots, n-k-1$. The initial conditions are $N^{(0)}(x) = V^{(0)}(x) = 0$ and $M^{(0)}(x) = W^{(0)}(x) = 1$. Following completion of the iterations we have $W(x) = W^{(n-k-1)}(x)$ and $N(x) = N^{(n-k-1)}(x)$.

Once $W(x)$ is found, the Chien search can be performed to find the roots of $W(x)$. These roots give the error locations. If $W(\alpha^l) = 0$, then the corresponding error value Y_l is [3]:

$$Y_l = Z(\alpha^l) \frac{N(\alpha^l)}{\dot{W}(\alpha^l)}, \tag{70}$$

where $\dot{W}(x)$ is the formal derivative of $W(x)$ and

$$Z(X) = X^{-1} \sum_{i=0}^{n-k-1} \frac{\hat{g}_i \alpha^{2i}}{\alpha^i - X}. \tag{71}$$

Coefficients of the remainder polynomial can be obtained using the encoder structure given in Figure 5-5. Conversely, circuitry designed for calculation of the reminder polynomial can be used to generate the RS code. Determination of $Z(X)$ is difficult, but for a particular code it is fixed and can be stored in ROM. The use of ROM, however, may not be advantageous if the decoder is to operate with variable code rates. Note that there is no circuitry required for syndrome computations. However, additional registers, multipliers, and adders are required since there are four polynomials involved in this algorithm compared to only two polynomials in other decoding algorithms. Also note that this algorithm does not directly correct errors that occur in the parity-check locations. Errors in these locations can be found, after correcting errors located in the information symbols, by reencoding and comparing the received and regenerated parity-check symbols. More on remainder-based decoding can be found in [3], [28], and [29].

5.4 Decoding in the Time Domain

We have seen that transform decoding starts with a Fourier transform and ends with an inverse Fourier transform. We have also seen that there is a Fourier transform at the beginning of the algebraic decoding algorithm. However, it is also possible to find a decoding algorithm in which the received word is not transformed into the frequency domain. Fourier transforms are not required in these time domain algorithms.

As discussed above, the Berlekamp-Massey algorithm has a simple structure. A time domain version of this algorithm is discussed in this section. Transforming this algorithm to the time domain is particularly easy, and the resulting structure is very simple because it does not involve polynomial division.

Time Domain Algorithm Based on Transform Decoding.   In addition to the Fourier transform at the beginning and the inverse transform at the end of the algorithm, transform decoding uses the Berlekamp-Massey algorithm to find the error locator polynomial $\Lambda(x)$ and recursive extension to evaluate components of the frequency domain error pattern [2].

To find a time domain equivalent of the Berlekamp-Massey algorithm, let λ and b denote the inverse Fourier transform of the vectors Λ and B, respectively. To transform the Berlekamp-Massey equations into the time domain, simply replace the frequency domain variables Λ_j and B_j with the time domain variables λ_i and b_i, replace the delay operator x with α^{-i}, and replace product terms with convolution terms. The Berlekamp-Massey algorithm is then transformed into a recursive procedure in the time domain, as described below [2].

Let v be the received noisy RS code word. The following set of recursive equations can be used to compute $\lambda_l^{(2t)}$ for $l = 0, 1, \ldots, n-1$:

$$\Delta_i = \sum_{l=0}^{n-1} \alpha^{il} \left[\lambda_l^{(i-1)} v_l \right], \tag{72}$$

$$L_i = \delta(i - L_{i-1}) + (1 - \delta)L_{i-1}, \tag{73}$$

$$\begin{bmatrix} \lambda_l^{(i)} \\ b_l^{(i)} \end{bmatrix} = \begin{bmatrix} 1 & -\Delta_i \alpha^{-l} \\ \Delta_i^{-1}\delta & (1-\delta)\alpha^{-l} \end{bmatrix} \begin{bmatrix} \lambda_l^{(i-1)} \\ b_l^{(i-1)} \end{bmatrix}, \tag{74}$$

for $i = 1, 2, \ldots, 2t$. The initial conditions are $\lambda_l^{(0)} = 1, b_l^{(0)} = 1$ for all l, and $\delta = 1$ if both $\Delta_i \neq 0$ and $2L_{i-1} \leq i - 1$, otherwise $\delta = 0$. Then $\lambda_l^{(2t)} = 0$ if and only if $e_l \neq 0$.

We can use the result to compute error values. First note that in the frequency domain, the error values can be computed using the following recursion [2,5]:

$$E_j = - \sum_{i=1}^{n-1} \Lambda_i E_{j-i} \quad j = 0, 2t + 1, 2t + 2, \ldots, n - 1. \tag{75}$$

Once the error locator polynomial is known, this relationship can be used to extend the $2t$ known components of E to all components of E through $(n - 2t)$ iterations. To obtain the time domain equivalent of equation (75), consider the received noisy RS code word $v = c + e$. Given the time domain error location indicator λ_l, it can be shown [2] that the following set of recursive equations:

$$\Delta_i = \sum_{l=0}^{n-1} \alpha^{il} v_l^{(i-1)} \lambda_l, \tag{76}$$

$$v_l^{(i)} = v_l^{(i-1)} - \Delta_i \alpha^{-il}, \tag{77}$$

evaluated for $i = 2t + 1, \ldots, n$, results in

$$v_l^{(n)} = e_l, \quad l = 0, 1, \ldots, n - 1. \tag{78}$$

The decoding algorithm then has only two steps. In the first $2t$ iterations the error locator vector λ is found. In the next $(n - 2t)$ iterations, the error vector $e = v^{(n)}$ is calculated. Error correction can then be performed.

5.5 Decoding Errors and Erasures in the Frequency Domain

An RS (n, k) code is capable of correcting up to $(n - k)$ erased symbols. Any pattern of v symbol errors and ρ symbol errors can be corrected provided that $2v + \rho \leq n - k$ [2]. To correct an error, the decoder must find both its location and its value; to correct an erasure, only the value must be found.

Syndrome-Based Decoding.   To modify syndrome-based algorithms to correct both errors and erasures, the following erasure locator polynomial is formed [2]:

$$\Gamma(x) = \prod_{i=1}^{\rho}(1 - x\alpha^{j_i}) \tag{79}$$

where j_i, $i = 1, 2, \ldots, \rho$ are locations of ρ erasure. This polynomial can be combined with the error locator polynomial $\Lambda(x)$ to form the errata locator polynomial $\hat{\Lambda}(x)$,

$$\hat{\Lambda}(x) = \Gamma(x)\Lambda(x). \tag{80}$$

Roots of the polynomial $\hat{\Lambda}(x)$ indicate the locations of errors and erasures. To form the errata locator polynomial, first the erasure locator polynomial is formed based on equation (79), and then the Berlekamp algorithm is performed for only $(n - k - \rho)$ iterations. Here, the polynomials $\Lambda(x)$ and $B(x)$ are initialized with the erasure locator polynomial instead of with value equal to 1, and the errata locator polynomial is obtained [2]. We will now drop the notation $\hat{\Lambda}(x)$ and replace it with $\Lambda(x)$, which we call the errata locator polynomial.

Based on the above discussion, the complete algebraic decoding algorithm for errors and erasures is summarized in the following steps:

Step 1: Calculate the syndromes using equation (37).

Step 2: Evaluate the erasure locator polynomial $\Gamma(x)$ using equation (79), where $i_l, l = 1, 2, \ldots, \rho$, are locations of ρ erasures.

Step 3: Perform the Berlekamp-Massey algorithm to obtain the errata locator polynomial $\Lambda(x)$. This algorithm, when modified to decode erasures as well as errors, uses the recursive relation

$$L_i = \delta(i - L_{i-1} - \rho) + (1 - \delta)L_{i-1}. \tag{81}$$

along with equations (58) and (60) to compute $\Lambda^{(n-k)}(x)$, for $i = \rho + 1, \ldots, n - k$. The initial conditions are $\Lambda^{(\rho)}(x) = B^{(\rho)}(x) = \Gamma(x)$, $L_0 = 0$, and $\delta = 1$ if both $\Delta_i \neq 0$ and $2L_{i-1} \leq i - 1 + \rho$, otherwise $\delta = 0$.

Step 4: Perform the Chien search to find the roots of $\Lambda(x)$. The roots of this polynomial indicate the error locations in the received word. If $X_j^{-1} = \alpha^{-i}$ is one of the roots, the received symbol v_i is in error. The Chien search is performed by calculating $\Lambda(\alpha^{-i})$, $i = 0, 1, \ldots, n - 1$, and comparing the result with zero.

Step 5: Find the errata value polynomial using equation (44) and the errata values from equation (46).

Step 6: Correct the received vector $v = [v_0, v_1, \ldots, v_{n-1}]$. This vector can be corrected from knowledge of the errata locations and the errata values. The corrected code word c is found by subtracting the errata values from the received vector.

The transform decoding algorithm can also be modified to correct both errors and erasures [2]. This algorithm has six steps:

Steps 1, 2, 3: Compute syndromes, the erasure locator polynomial, and the errata locator polynomial using the first three steps of the algebraic decoding algorithm.

Step 4: Calculate the remaining components of $E = (E_0, E_1, \ldots, E_{n-1})$ by recursive extension using equation (52).

Step 5: Compute the inverse transform of E_j, $j = 0, 1, \ldots, n-1$, over $GF(2^m)$, to obtain the error vector e.

Step 6: Estimate the original code vector by subtracting the error vector e from the received vector v.

5.6 Decoding Errors and Erasures in the Time Domain

To correct errors and erasures in the time domain, the erasure locator vector $\gamma = [\gamma_0, \gamma_1, \ldots, \gamma_{n-1}]$ can be introduced. This vector is equivalent to the time domain erasure locator polynomial [2].

$$\gamma_l = \prod_{i=1}^{\rho} (1 - \alpha^{j_i} \alpha^{-l}), \quad l = 0, 1, \ldots, n-1, \tag{82}$$

where the received noisy vector v has erasures at locations j_i, $i = 1, 2, \ldots, \rho$.

Time domain decoding that corrects both errors and erasures is summarized below.

Step 1: Evaluate the erasure locator vector γ according to

$$\gamma_l^{(i)} = \gamma_l^{(i-1)} (1 - \alpha^{j_i} \alpha^{-l}), \tag{83}$$

for $i = 1, 2, \ldots, \rho$ and $l = 0, 1, \ldots, n-1$. The initial conditions are $\gamma_l^{(0)} = \alpha^0 = 1$; the result is $\gamma_l = \gamma_l^{(\rho)}$.

Step 2: Calculate the time domain errata locator vector $\lambda = [\lambda_0, \lambda_1, \ldots, \lambda_{n-1}]$ using the time domain Berlekamp-Massey algorithm. This algorithm computes $\lambda_l^{(n-k)}$, for $l = 0, 1, \ldots, n-1$ and $i = \rho + 1, \rho + 2, \ldots, n-k$, using equations (72), (74), and (81). The initial conditions are $\lambda_l^{(\rho)} = b_l^{(\rho)} = \gamma_l$ for all l, $L_\rho = 0$, and $\delta = 1$ if both $\Delta_i \neq 0$ and $2L_{i-1} - \rho \neq i - 1$, otherwise $\delta = 0$. Then $\lambda_l^{(n-k)} = 0$ if and only if the lth symbol of the received vector v is in error, and hence the components of the errata locator vector are $\lambda_l = \lambda_l^{(n-k)}$ for all l.

Step 3: Find the errata values $e_l = v_l^{(n)}$, for $l = 0, 1, \ldots, n - 1$, using recursive equations (76) and (77) with $i = n - k + 1, \ldots, n$. The last iteration results in the errata value vector when λ_l is initialized as $\lambda_l^{(n-k)}$, $l = 0, 1, \ldots, n - 1$.

Step 4: Estimate the errata vector e as

$$
\begin{aligned}
e_l &= v_l^{(n)} \qquad \text{if } \lambda_l = 0 \\
e_l &= 0 \qquad \text{if } \lambda_l \neq 0,
\end{aligned}
\tag{84}
$$

and subtract it from the received vector v to form the corrected vector c.

5.7 Decoder Architectures

The decoding algorithms presented in the previous subsection can be divided into three main classes: syndrome-based decoding, remainder-based decoding, and time domain decoding. The algebraic and transform decoding methods fall into the class of syndrome-based decoding. The algebraic decoding is quite similar to the remainder-based decoding in the sense that both of them solve equations[2] to find the error locator polynomial, use the Chien search to find error locations, and evaluate functions at error locations to calculate error values.

An Architecture Based on Algebraic Decoding. A decoder architecture based on the algebraic decoding is shown in Figure 5-8. It mainly consists of three processing blocks. Each block requires computation in $GF(2^m)$ which can be performed in either a bit-serial or bit-parallel fashion. While bit-parallel operations provide increased throughput, a significant reduction in circuit complexity, in terms of number of gates as well as connectivity, is obtained using bit-serial operations.

The first step of the algebraic decoding is to compute the syndromes. For $i = 1, 2, \ldots, 2t$, equation (37) can be written as

$$
S_i = [\cdots (v_{n-1}\alpha^i + v_{n-2})\alpha^i + \cdots + v_1]\alpha^i + v_0.
\tag{85}
$$

Equation (85) has the same form as that of (33), and the syndrome computation block in Figure 5-8 can be built with $2t$ cells used in the transform encoder shown earlier in Figure 5-6. As the constant input to cell i, however, we need to use α^i instead of α^{-i}.

---

[2]The equations are not, however, the same.

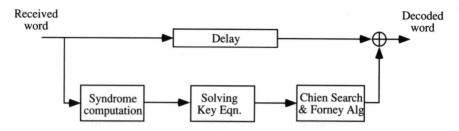

Figure 5-8. An overall block diagram for the algebraic decoding.

The second step of the algebraic decoding is to find the error locator polynomial. For this purpose, the Berlekamp-Massey algorithm can be used. A shift register configuration for the Berlekamp-Massey algorithm is shown in Figure 5-9 [2]. It is assumed that the control unit generates δ and all other necessary control signals. Registers S, Λ, and B are for polynomials $S(x)$, $\Lambda(x)$, and $B(x)$, respectively. Each register is large enough to hold the largest possible degree of its respective polynomial. Short-degree polynomials are stored with the register filled out with zeros. During one iteration, register Λ is shifted twice, first to compute Δ_r, then to be updated. Switches S1, $\cdots$, S4 are to pass data in the appropriate direction so that equations (58)-(60) can be realized. When B is being updated, if $\delta = 0$ (reps. 1) S1 is at position P1 (resp. P2). When Λ is begin updated, S2 remains closed. Switches S3 and S4 remain closed during the formation of Δ. Once $\Lambda(x)$ has been formed, the error evaluator polynomial $\Omega(x)$ can be calculated from $S(x)$ and $\Lambda(x)$, and the coefficients of $\Omega(x)$ can be shifted into the Ω register.

The next step of the algebraic decoding is to find the roots of the error locator polynomial. For this purpose, the Chien search method can be used. This method provides a simple and general algorithm for finding zeros of a polynomial over a finite field. In the Chien search method we compute

$$\Lambda(1), \ \Lambda(\alpha), \ \ldots, \ \Lambda(\alpha^{2^m-2}).$$

Each zero in the sequence corresponds to an error, the value of which can be computed using the Forney algorithm. Since $\Lambda(x) = \sum_{j=0}^{2t} \Lambda_j x$, for $i = 0, 1, \ldots, n-1$, we have

$$\Lambda(\alpha^i) = \sum_{j=0}^{2t} \Lambda_j \alpha^{ij}, \qquad (86)$$

which is similar to the syndrome computation. However, this summation extends to $j = 2t$ only.

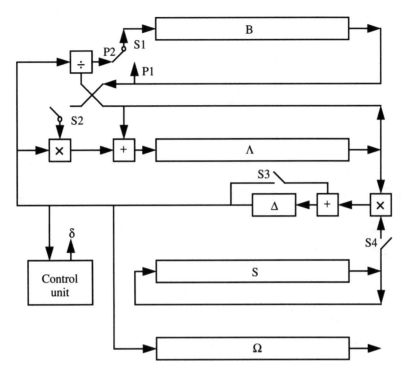

Figure 5-9. A structure for realization of the Berlekamp-Massey algorithm.

The previous equation can be written in the following form:

$$\Lambda(\alpha^i) = \sum_{j=0}^{2t} \Lambda_j \alpha^{ij} = \sum_{j=0}^{2t} \Lambda_j \alpha^{(i-1)j} \alpha^j, \tag{87}$$

that is, for $j = 0, 1, \ldots, 2t$, the multiplication of α^j with the jth term of $\Lambda(\alpha^{i-1})$ yields the corresponding term of $\Lambda(\alpha^i)$. Thus, for the calculation of each term, we simply need a constant multiplier and a register. Figure 5-10 shows a structure for the Chien search method. In the figure, the odd- and even-numbered terms are summed separately to facilitate implementation of the Forney algorithm as discussed below.

Once the error locations are known, the error values can be found using Forney's algorithm. This requires evaluation of the polynomial $\Omega(x)$ at α^l if $\Lambda(\alpha^l) = 0$. The error values are

$$e_l = \begin{cases} 0 & \Lambda(\alpha^{-l}) \neq 0 \\ \dfrac{\Omega(\alpha^{-l})}{\Lambda(\alpha^{-l})} & \Lambda(\alpha^{-l}) = 0, \end{cases} \tag{88}$$

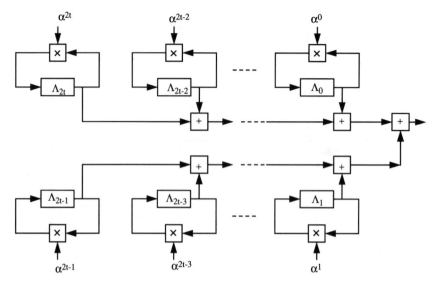

Figure 5-10. A structure for the Chien search.

where $\dot{\Lambda}(x)$ is the derivative of $\Lambda(x)$. Since

$$\dot{\Lambda}(x) = \sum_{\text{odd}} \Lambda_j x^{j-1}, \tag{89}$$

$\dot{\Lambda}(\alpha^{-l})$ can be can obtained from the summation of the odd-numbered terms of $\Lambda(\alpha^{-l})$ as given in the Chien search circuitry. Note also that for $\Lambda(\alpha^l) = 0$, these two summations are equal. Let Δ_0 be the summation of odd coefficients. It then follows that [3]

$$\Delta_0 = \sum_{\text{odd}} \Lambda_j \alpha^{lj} = \alpha^l \sum_{\text{odd}} \Lambda_j \alpha^{l(j-1)} \tag{90}$$

$$= \alpha^l \dot{\Lambda}(\alpha^l). \tag{91}$$

Thus, when $\Lambda(\alpha^l) = 0$, the corresponding error value is

$$e_l = \alpha^l \Omega(\alpha^{-l}) \Delta_0^{-1}. \tag{92}$$

Figure 5-11 shows a realization of Forney's algorithm for computing the error values. The delay element is introduced to compensate for the delay through the divider.

5.8 Transform Decoder

The overall block diagram of a transform RS decoder is shown in Figure 5-12. In addition to two delay elements, it has four processing blocks.

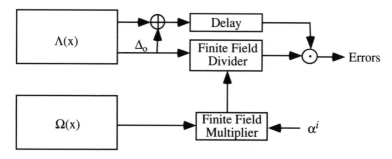

Figure 5-11. Realization of the Forney algorithm.

The functions of Blocks 1 and 2 are to compute syndromes and perform the Berlekamp-Massey algorithm, respectively. Details of these two blocks are discussed in the previous section. The syndromes are the first $2t$ components of E. The remaining components of E are recursively computed in Block 3. This block is essentially an LFSR that uses the error locator polynomial, forwarded from Block 2, as its feedback polynomial. The storage devices, multipliers, and adders of the LFSR are for elements of $GF(2^m)$ so that equation (52) can be realized. Block 4 in Figure 5-12 computes the inverse transform of E and results in the error vector e. Since

$$e_i = \sum_{j=0}^{n-1} E_j \alpha^{-ij}, \quad i = 0, 1, \ldots, n - 1, \tag{93}$$

Block 4 can be realized by the structure shown in Figure 5-6.

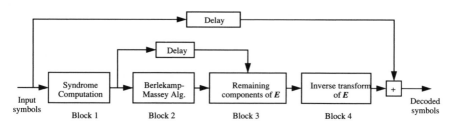

Figure 5-12. An overall block diagram for the transform RS decoder.

Time Domain Decoder.   Using the time domain decoding algorithm (see Section 5.6), an architecture for the hardware realization of the RS decoder can be obtained [2,31]. The decoder in [30] can correct both errors and erasures and is versatile in the sense that it can decode any RS code defined in a particular field $GF(2^m)$. To obtain the erasure locator vector, instead of (83), the following set of equations is used:

$$\Delta = \alpha^{ji},$$

$$\delta = 0,$$

$$\begin{bmatrix} \lambda_l \\ b_l \end{bmatrix} \leftarrow \begin{bmatrix} 1 & \Delta\alpha^{-l} \\ \Delta^{-1}\delta & (1-\delta)\alpha^{-l} \end{bmatrix} \begin{bmatrix} \lambda_l \\ b_l \end{bmatrix},$$

$$b_l \leftarrow \lambda_l,$$

where $\gamma = \lambda$ at the end of ρ iterations. The above equations make it possible to use the same hardware that also realizes equations (72), (74), and (81) for determining the error locator vector.

Figure 5-13 shows an overall block diagram for the time domain RS decoder. It consists of an I/O unit, a control unit, and a decoding unit. Before being forwarded to the decoding unit, input code words $v_0, v_1, \ldots, v_{n-1}$ are buffered into the I/O unit. If v_l is an erased symbol, the I/O unit generates $\alpha^l, l = 0, 1, \ldots, n - 1$. The I/O unit also counts the number of erasures and passes this number ρ to the control unit. The control unit generates δ and counts the number of iterations i. Using the values of k and ρ, this unit also generates necessary signals for the switches that control the direction of data flow in the decoding unit.

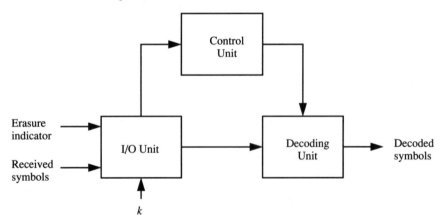

Figure 5-13. An overall block diagram for the time domain RS decoder.

Figure 5-14 shows details of the decoding unit. There are three sets of n-stage shift registers for storing s_l, λ_l, and b_l, $l = 0, 1, \ldots, n - 1$. The shifting operation is performed until the end of the decoding process. In iteration $i = 0$, received symbols $v_l, l = 0, 1, \ldots, n - 1$, are multiplied by α^l and the products are loaded into the shift register s. At the same time, the products are accumulated in register Δ_l to form Δ for iteration $i = 1$. In this iteration, shift registers λ and b are loaded with the initial value of $\alpha^0 = 1$. In iterations

1 to ρ, the decoding unit iteratively generates the erasure locator vector. At the end of iteration ρ, this vector is available in both λ and b registers. In the next $(n-k-\rho)$ iterations, the decoding unit generates the error locator vector. In the next k iterations, the following equations derived from (76) and (77),

$$\Delta = \sum_{l=0}^{n-1} \lambda_l s_l,$$

$$s_l \leftarrow s_l - \Delta,$$

are used to obtain the errata value vector. In the last, i.e., the nth iteration, s_l is added to the previous value of Δ to be used for correcting v_l. For proper correction, the value of $\lambda_l s_l$ is compared with zero, and if $\lambda_l s_l = 0$, then the corresponding component of v is corrected.

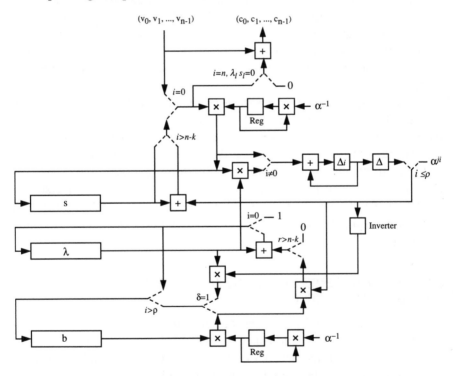

Figure 5-14. Decoding unit of the time domain RS decoder.

The register part of the decoding unit can be designed in a fairly straightforward way. The rest of the decoding unit mainly consists of one inverter and seven multipliers of GF(2^m). However, this part is quite small compared to the register part, and one needs to design only one multiplier and duplicate it as required.

The decoding time of the decoder is determined by the longest delay path. This path has a delay τ equivalent to the delay of 19 gates [30]. In each iterations, the registers are shifted n times and there are $(n + 1)$ iterations, resulting in a total delay of $n(n + 1)\tau$. Thus, when implemented in hardware, the time domain decoder requires a high computation time but less silicon area.

5.9 Other Time Domain Decoder Architectures

A time domain cellular RS decoder has been presented in [30]. The decoder can correct both errors and erasures and can be used for any RS codes defined in the field $GF(2^m)$. This cellular decoder can be viewed as a spatial expansion of the versatile decoder presented above. Unlike the versatile decoder, which has only one decoding unit, the cellular decoder has n decoding *cells*. Each cell performs one of n iterations of the time domain algorithm. Clearly, the circuit complexity of the cellular decoder is significantly higher (about n times) than that of the versatile decoder. However, a proportionate increase in throughput is obtained only at the expense of additional circuit complexity [30].

A universal RS decoder has been presented in [21]. The decoder can be used for any RS codes defined over $GF(2^m)$ for $3 \leq m \leq 8$. It uses the time domain decoding algorithm and can be viewed as a generalization of the versatile decoder. Since the decoder supports different values of m, its arithmetic units are capable of performing operations in the corresponding fields. It has been estimated that the design of a universal decoder capable of correcting errors will require less than 100,000 gates, and hence using 1.0 μm technology the decoder can be fabricated on a single chip [21].

6 HARDWARE IMPLEMENTATION: AN EXAMPLE DESIGN OF AN RS (31, k) CODEC

In this section we briefly describe the implementation of an RS encoder and decoder using application-specific integrated circuit (ASIC) technologies. These encoder and decoder circuits were designed for advanced train control systems and other mobile radio systems [31].

The two major categories of ASIC technologies are *array-based* and *cell-based*. Array-based ASICs configure a customer design at metal layers, whereas cell-based ASICs are uniquely fabricated at all layers of silicon processing including the diffusion layers. The array-based design was chosen for the RS encoder and decoder mainly because of its fast turnaround and fewer number of programmable masks, resulting in lower initial cost.

6.1 Encoder RS31KE

The encoder called RS31KE operates in a 5-bit Galois field $GF(2^5)$, and it accepts a block of k information symbols. This information block length is user-programmable up to the code word length of 31. The code is based on the nonsystematic method of transform encoding; i.e., if the k information symbols are $(D_{k-1}, D_{k-2}, \ldots, D_0)$, then the output of the encoder is the code word $(C_{30}, C_{29}, \ldots, C_0)$, where

$$C_l = \sum_{i=0}^{k-1} D_i \alpha^{il} \quad l = 0, 1, \ldots, 30 \tag{94}$$

and α is a primitive element of $GF(2^5)$.

The RS31KE has been implemented using low-power, 1.5-μm, two-layer metal HCMOS technology. It requires approximately 6200 gates divided among three main logic blocks, namely, INPUT, OUTPUT, and TEST [31]. A simplified block diagram of the RS31KE is shown in Figure 5-15. The INPUT block requiring about 1500 gates generates signals to initiate the encoding of the information block. This block also contains a 5-bit serial shift in/155-bit parallel shift out register used to hold the incoming symbols for the information block to be encoded. The OUTPUT block requiring about 4200 gates contains a temporary code word latch, a working code word register, the transform-processing element, the α^i generator, and an output symbol register. The TEST block requires 400 gates and contains necessary circuitry to provide built-in self-testing.

6.2 Decoder RS31KD

The decoder called RS31KD is also user-programmable and can be used with the encoder described above. It can decode standard and shortened systematic and transform codes. Like the encoder, the decoder operates in $GF(2^5)$. It receives a code word of L symbols and erasures flags, if available, and produces a block of k decoded symbols.

The decoder is based on the time domain decoding algorithm. For a received code word, it first looks for erasures (indicated by the erasure flags). Second, it performs the time domain Berlekamp-Massey algorithm. Then it finds the errata vector and performs error and erasure correction. If the received code word is in transformed form, the decoder also performs an inverse transformation to complete the decoding process.

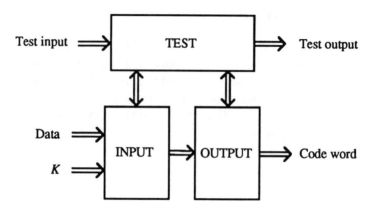

Figure 5-15. Simplified block diagram of the RS31KE.

The decoder can correct v symbols errors and ρ symbol erasures provided that $2v + \rho \le 31 - k$. In the absence of erasure flags, it can correct one burst of length $b_1 = 5(t - 1) + 1$ bits or two bursts of length $b_2 = 5(t - 3) + 1$, etc., where $t = (31 - k)/2$. It can be used for RS (n, k) shortened transform codes to correct v symbol errors and ρ symbol erasures as long as $2v + \rho \le (n - k)$.

The RS31KD has also been implemented using low-power, 1.5-μm, two-layer metal HCMOS technology. It requires about 20,500 gates divided among seven top-level logic blocks, namely, BREG31, LREG31, ERASURE, CTRL_DELTA and IN_OUT, IN_ROUTE and OUT_ROUTE [31]. The IN_ROUTE and OUT_ROUTE blocks are used for the purpose of testing the decoder chip. A simplified block diagram of the RS31KD without these testing blocks is shown in Figure 5-16. The BREG31 and LREG31 blocks contain the logic circuitry required for computing and storing temporary results. The ERASURE block contains the erasure register, a counter to keep track of the currently updated number of erasures, and two 31-symbol registers to store the roots of the erasures locator vector. The CTRL_DELTA block contains logic for computation of a set of recursive equations needed in the time domain Berlekamp-Massey algorithm and for the generation of necessary control signals needed for routing all sorts of data. The IN_OUT block is used for input and output storage.

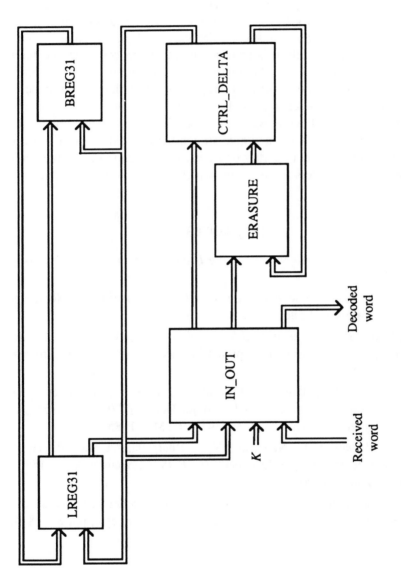

Figure 5-16. Simplified block diagram of the RS31KD.

7 CONCLUDING REMARKS

In this chapter, algorithms and architectures for Reed-Solomon (RS) encoders and decoders have been considered. Encoding and decoding of RS codes require arithmetic operations in $GF(2^m)$; the operations of finite field multiplication and inversion have been discussed. Different encoding and decoding algorithms have been outlined and compared with regard to circuit complexity. Different architectures for RS codecs have also been discussed. Finally, one hardware implementation of an RS encoder and decoder has been presented.

Although conceptually it is possible to extend RS codec architectures to different finite fields to yield a universal encoder and decoder [32], their realization in VLSI appears difficult. Recently, efforts have been made to realize a universal decoder in a single chip [5,21]. However, the proposed solutions are not quite flexible, and the corresponding implementation for RS codes of larger length is not a simple straightforward extension in silicon. Thus it is still of practical importance to develop algorithms and architectures for universal RS encoders and decoders which can be easily implemented in VLSI.

REFERENCES

[1] E. R. Berlekamp, *Algebraic Coding Theory*, McGraw-Hill: New York, 1968.

[2] R. E. Blahut, *Theory and Practice of Error Control Codes*, Reading, Mass.: Addison Wesley, 1984.

[3] D. L. Whiting, *Bit-Serial Reed-Solomon Decoder in VLSI*, Ph.D. Thesis, School of Engineering and Applied Science, University of California, Los Angeles, 1985.

[4] H. M. Shao, T. K. Truong, L. J. Deutsch, J. H. Yuen, and I. S. Reed, "A VLSI Design of a Pipeline Reed-Solomon Decoder," *IEEE Transactions on Computers*, Volume C-34, pp. 393–403, May 1985.

[5] Y. R. Shayan, T. Le-Ngoc, and V. K. Bhargava, "A Versatile Time-Domain Reed-Solomon Decoder," *IEEE JSAC*, Volume 8, pp. 1535–1542, October 1990.

[6] E. R. Berlekamp, "Bit-Serial Reed-Solomon Encoder," *IEEE Transactions on Information Theory*, Volume IT-28, Number 6, pp. 869–874, November 1982.

[7] C. C. Wang, T. K. Truong, H. M. Shao, L. J. Deutsch, J. K. Omura, and I. S. Reed, "VLSI Architecture for Computing Multiplications and Inverses in GF(2^m)," *IEEE Transactions on Computers*, Volume C-34, pp. 709–717, August 1985.

[8] M. A. Hasan and V. K. Bhargava, "Bit-Serial Systolic Divider and Multiplier for GF(2^m)," *IEEE Transactions on Computers*, Volume 41, pp. 972–980, August 1992.

[9] R. Lidl and H. Niederreiter, *Introduction to Finite Fields and Their Applications*," Cambridge: Cambridge University Press, 1986.

[10] D. R. Stinson, "On Bit-Serial Multiplication and Dual Bases in GF(2^m)," *IEEE Transactions on Information Theory*, Volume IT-37, Number 6, pp. 1733–1736, November 1991.

[11] M. A. Hasan, *Efficient Computations in Galois Fields*, Ph.D. Thesis, Department of Electrical and Computer Engineering, University of Victoria, British Columbia, 1992.

[12] M. A. Hasan and V. K. Bhargava, "A VLSI Architecture for a Low Complexity Rate-Adaptive Reed-Solomon Encoder," *Proceedings of the 16th Biennial Symposium on Communications*, Kingston, Ontario, pp. 331–334, May 1992.

[13] T. C. Bartee and D. I. Schneider, "Computation with Finite Fields," *Information and Computers*, Volume 6, pp. 79–98, March 1963.

[14] J. L. Massey and J. K. Omura, "Apparatus for Finite Field Computation," U.S. Patent Application, pp. 21–40, 1984.

[15] P. K. S. Wah and M. Z. Wang, "Realization and Application of the Massey-Omura Lock," *International Zurich Seminar*, 1984.

[16] D. W. Ash, I. F. Blake, and S. A. Vanstone, "Low Complexity Normal Bases," *Discrete Applied Mathematics*, Volume 25, pp. 191–210, 1989.

[17] M. Morii, M. Kasahara, and D. L. Whiting, "Efficient Bit-Serial Multiplication and the Discrete-Time Wiener-Hopf Equations over Finite Fields," *IEEE Transactions on Information Theory*, Volume IT-35, Number 6, pp. 1177–1183, November 1989.

[18] M. Z. Wang and I. F. Blake, "Bit Serial Multiplication in Finite Fields," *SIAM Journal of Discrete Mathematics*, Volume 3 pp. 140–148, February 1990.

[19] M. A. Hasan and V. K. Bhargava, "Division and Bit-Serial Multiplication over GF(q^m)," *IEE Proceedings: Part E*, Volume 139, pp. 230–236, May 1992.

[20] G. Seroussi, "A Systolic Reed-Solomon Encoder, *IEEE Transactions on Information Theory*, Volume IT-37, pp. 1217–1220, July 1991.

[21] B. Green and G. Drolet, "A Universal Reed-Solomon Decoder Chip," *Proceedings of the 16th Biennial Symposium on Communications, Kingston, Ontario*, pp. 327–330, May 1992.

[22] K. Araki, I. Fujita, and M. Morisue, "Fast Inverter over Finite Field Based on Euclid's Algorithm," *Transactions of the IEICE*, Volume E 72, Number 11, pp. 1230–1234, November 1989.

[23] G. I. Davida, "Inverse of Elements of a Galois Field," *Electronic Letters*, Volume 8, Number 21, pp. 518–520, October 1972.

[24] R. T. Chien, "Cyclic Decoding Procedures for BCH Codes," *IEEE Transactions on Information Theory*, Volume IT-27, pp. 254–256, October 1981.

[25] D. Gorenstein and N. Zierler, "A Class of Cyclic Linear Error-Correcting Codes in p^m Symbols," *Journal of the Society for Industrial and Applied Mathematics*, Volume 9, June 1961.

[26] G. D. Forney, "On Decoding BCH Codes," *IEEE Transactions on Information Theory*, Volume IT-11, pp. 393–403, October 1965.

[27] Y. M. Sugiyama, S. H. Kasahara, and T. Namekawa, "A Method for Solving the Key Equation for Decoding of Goppa Codes," *Information and Control*, Volume 27, pp. 87–89, January 1975.

[28] Tomic Yaghoobian, "*On Reed-Solomon and Algebraic Geometry Codes*," Ph.D. Thesis, Department of Electrical and Computer Engineering, University of Waterloo, Ontario, 1993.

[29] M. Morii and M. Kasahara, "Generalized Key-Equation of Remainder Decoding Algorithm for Reed-Solomon Codes," *IEEE Transactions on Information Theory*, Volume IT-38, Number 6, pp. 1801–1807, November 1992.

[30] Y. R. Shayan, *Versatile Reed-Solomon Decoders*, Ph.D. Thesis, Concordia University, Montreal, 1990.

[31] V. K. Bhargava, T. Le-Ngoc, G. E. Seguin, and Y. R. Shayan, *ASIC Implementation of a* $(31, k)$ *Reed-Solomon Codec for Advanced Train Control Systems and Other Mobile Radio Systems,* Volume I, Victoria, British Columbia: Binary Communications, 1991.

[32] R. E. Blahut, "A Universal Reed-Solomon Decoder," *IBM Journal of Research and Development*, pp. 150–158, March 1984.

ACKNOWLEDGEMENT

This work was supported in part, by the University of Waterloo under a start-up grant and, in part, by the Canadian Insitute for Telecommunications Research under the NCE program of the Government of Canada.

Soft-Decision Decoding
of Reed-Solomon Codes

A. Brinton Cooper III
U.S. Army Research Laboratory
Aberdeen Proving Ground, Maryland 21005-5067

1 INTRODUCTION

Early in the development of coding theory, it was found convenient to represent communication channels as conveyors of symbols drawn from finite sets. The effects of channel noise were represented by the occasional (random) reception of a symbol other than the one that was transmitted. This abstraction of reality permitted the application of powerful algebraic and combinatoric tools to the code design and decoding problems. RS codes themselves were developed through this abstraction.

In reality, however, channel noise is almost always a continuous phenomenon. What is transmitted may be selected from a discrete set, but what is received comes from a continuum of values. This viewpoint leads to the *soft-decision decoder* (SDD), which accepts a vector of real samples of the noisy channel output and estimates the vector of channel input symbols that was transmitted. By contrast the *hard-decision decoder* (HDD) requires that its input be from the same alphabet as the channel input. It is now well known that soft-decision decoding techniques can provide approximately 2 dB more *coding gain* for the white Gaussian channel.

For many years the primary focus of SDD research was on convolutional codes. Convolutional codes (and their trellis-coded progeny) allow for a very natural use of channel state information. Unfortunately the application of channel state information in the decoding of Reed-Solomon (RS) codes is not as obvious, and many have contended that it is equally unnecessary. RS codes are maximum distance separable (MDS) and thus have the largest possible minimum distance (and thus random error-correcting capability) for any algebraic code of the same length and dimension. In extremely hostile communication environments (e.g., fading and jamming), however, SDD can strengthen RS code performance. In fact, it is suggested in [20] that RS codes cannot be used effectively at all with certain m-ary modulation schemes such as QAM unless SDD techniques are used.

A SDD for a binary code generally presents an estimate or "guess" of the binary value of each transmitted symbol and a real number expressing the "goodness" or reliability of the binary estimate. The design of a binary SDD includes the means by which it produces the hard-decision estimate, computes the reliability, and combines the two into a symbol or word estimate. SDDs for RS (or other nonbinary) codes fall into one of two classes. One class considers expansion of the symbol field over its ground field, e.g., $GF(2^m)$ over $GF(2)$, and applies soft-decision decoding to the ground field symbols [17]. The other class makes estimates of value and reliability in the actual transmitted symbol field [11].

In this chapter, we present first those SDDs operating on the binary symbols of RS codes over symbol fields of characteristic 2. Then we review several symbol-oriented SDDs, including some attempts at maximum-likelihood decoding (MLD), the "Holy Grail" of this subject. Some symbol-oriented decoders are not specific to RS codes but are presented nonetheless because of their power and potential or because they are used as bases for other decoders.

The reader will not find a comprehensive discussion of so-called coding gains for the various decoders. We assume that the reader is aware of the theoretical 2-dB gain provided by soft-decision decoding of binary codes on the additive white Gaussian channel. Beyond that, computations of coding gain reported in the literature assume a variety of reference channels and schemes and are quite disparate. It makes no sense, for example, to compare the performance of codes used on the Gaussian channel with those designed for the deep fading channel. Since this is a treatise on decoders, we leave applications—and their coding gains—to the needs and interests of the reader.

2 SOFT DECISION AT THE BIT LEVEL

"The major drawback with RS codes (for satellite use) is that the present generation of decoders do not make full use of bit-based soft-decision information ..." [4]. Since Berlekamp et al. gave us that 1987 observation, significant progress has been made in refuting its thesis.

This section begins with an elegant method [21] of writing an RS code in terms of the cosets of a related binary code and presents a SDD based upon that expansion. This stands in contrast to the method [20] of quantizing the binary channel output and producing the "soft weight" of a code symbol in terms of the soft weights of the constituent binary symbols.

2.1 A Coset Expansion and Decoder

In this application, the RS code alphabet is $GF(2^m)$. Symbols are expanded over the binary ground field and transmitted over a binary channel. Expanding each symbol from $GF(2^m)$ to m binary symbols requires a *basis* of $GF(2^m)$ over $GF(2)$. When the mapping to $GF(2)$ is linear, the resulting binary code is also linear.

Either a radix-m representation or the powers of a root α of a primitive polynomial of degree m over $GF(2)$ can be used as the basis.

Bit-Level Code Generation.   For every RS code over $GF(2^m)$ there is a binary BCH code of the same length and having minimum distance at least as large. This BCH code, together with a basis for $GF(2^m)$ over $GF(2)$, provides a partitioning of the RS code into cosets [21] which are used in a bit-level SDD that first (soft) decodes the associated BCH code, then searches across the cosets for the most likely code word.

Let $\{\alpha^s, \ldots, \alpha^{s+N-K-1}\}$ be the roots of $\mathcal{R}$, an (N, K) RS code over $GF(2^m)$, and let α be primitive in $GF(2^m)$. The minimum distance is $d_{\min} = N - K + 1$. The BCH code $\mathcal{B}$ having the same roots (plus their cyclotomic conjugates) has length N and $d_{\min}^b \geq N - K + 1$; it is a subfield subcode of $\mathcal{R}$ [13].

Let ϕ be a mapping from $GF(2^m)$ to $GF(2)$.[1] This mapping has the basis $\gamma_1, \gamma_2, \ldots, \gamma_m, \gamma_j \in GF(2^m)$. Define m nonbinary subcodes of $\mathcal{R}$.

$$\mathcal{B}_j = \{\gamma_j \mathbf{b} | \mathbf{b} \in \mathcal{B}\}, j = 1, \ldots, m \tag{1}$$

Applying the mapping ϕ to each element of the generator matrix of the RS code and reordering the columns of the resulting binary matrix results in the $mK \times mN$ binary generator matrix $\mathbf{G}$:

$$
\mathbf{G} = \begin{bmatrix}
\mathbf{B} & & & & \bigcirc \\
\bigcirc & \mathbf{B} & & & \cdot \\
\cdot & & \bigcirc & & \cdot \\
\cdot & & & \mathbf{B} & \\
\multicolumn{5}{c}{\text{Glue Vectors}}
\end{bmatrix} \tag{2}
$$

where the $(k \times N)$ matrix $\mathbf{B}$ is the generator of $\mathcal{B}$.[2]

---

[1]One could, of course, adopt the viewpoint that a mapping from $GF(2)$ to $GF(2^m)$ is needed, using the usual radix expansion. ϕ was defined in the present manner because it produces a useful result.

[2]The $m(K - k)$ "glue vectors" occur because $\mathcal{B}$ has more roots than does $\mathcal{R}$.

With this construction, we can write $\mathcal{R}$ as a union of cosets,

$$C_l = \{\mathbf{r}^l + c | c \in C\} \tag{3}$$

where C is the direct sum $C = \mathcal{B}_1 + \mathcal{B}_2 + \cdots + \mathcal{B}_m$ and $\mathbf{r}^l$ is a coset leader.

Encoding distributes the binary symbols of each character from GF(2^m) among the m BCH codes. This *interleaving* property permits burst error correction and plays an important part in these SDD decoders.

Decoding via the Coset Model.

First consider the memoryless channel and its probability transition matrix $f(v|j) = f_j(v), j \in$ GF(2), v real. Each transmitted binary symbol produces one real number v_i^j, $j = 0, \ldots, m$, $i = 0, \ldots, N-1$, at the channel output. The MLD decoder output is

$$\max_{c \in \mathcal{R}} \sum_{i=0}^{N-1} \sum_{j=1}^{m} \log f(v_i^j | c_i^j), \tag{4}$$

assuming equally probable transmitted code words. To achieve efficiency, the decoder searches $\mathcal{R}$ by cosets:

$$\max_{c \in \mathcal{R}} \sum_{i=0}^{N-1} \sum_{j=1}^{m} \log f(v_i^j | c_i^j) = \max_{C_l} \max_{c \in C_l} \sum_{i=0}^{N-1} \sum_{j=1}^{m} \log f(v_i^j | c_i^j). \tag{5}$$

The rightmost summation is a SDD decoder of the subfield BCH subcode and is the basis for the following algorithm [21] in which each coset C_l is characterized by a coset leader or "representative" $\mathbf{r}$.

ALGORITHM 1

1. For $j = 1, 2, \ldots m$ find the code word $\mathbf{b} = \hat{\mathbf{b}}_j$ which maximizes $M_j(\mathbf{b})$:

$$\hat{\mathbf{b}}_j = \arg \max_{\mathbf{b} \in B} M_j(\mathbf{b}) \tag{6}$$

where

$$M_j(\mathbf{b}) = \sum_{i=0}^{N-1} \log f(v_i^j | b_i + r_i^j) \tag{7}$$

2. For each estimate $\hat{\mathbf{b}}_j$, evaluate

$$M(\mathbf{c}) = \sum_{j=0}^{m} M_j(\hat{\mathbf{b}}_j)$$

$$= \sum_{j=1}^{m} \sum_{i=0}^{N-1} \log f(v_i^j | c_i^j) \tag{8}$$

where $c_i^j = \hat{b}_i^j + r_i^j$. Select the code word $c \in \mathcal{R}$ that maximizes (8). This algorithm has complexity less than $2^{m(K-k)}$ [21].

Algorithm 1 maximizes the sum of the binary symbol likelihoods on the memoryless channel and, therefore, does not exploit burst error correction possibilities afforded by RS codes. Now, assume that the channel noise, acting independently on each symbol in $GF(2^m)$, can be represented by $f(v|\xi) = f(v^1, v^2, \ldots, v^m|\xi^1, \xi^2, \ldots, \xi^m)$, where $(\xi^1, \xi^2, \ldots, \xi^m)$ is the expansion of ξ over the binary field. The next decoder invokes the m-fold interleaving represented in (2), following the maximization over cosets.

ALGORITHM 2

1. See Step 1 of Algorithm 1.
2. Evaluate the channel probability matrix over the channel symbols.

$$
\begin{aligned}
M(c) &= \sum_{i=0}^{N-1} \log f(v_i|c_i) \\
&= \sum_{i=0}^{N-1} \log f(v_i^1, v_i^2, \ldots, v_i^m|\hat{b}_i^1 + r_i^1, \ldots, \hat{b}_i^m + r_i^m)
\end{aligned}
\tag{9}
$$

The decoder selects that code word c which maximizes (9). The complexity is about the same [21], but burst error correction is achieved.

2.2 Minimum Weight Soft-Decision Decoding

For any cyclic code generated by $g(x)$, write the channel output as $r(x) = i(x)g(x) + e(x)$. Minimum weight decoding (MWD) [20] has been proposed:

1. Compute syndrome $s(x)$ as the remainder from dividing $r(x)$ by $g(x)$.
2. Compute Hamming weight $w = w_H[s(x)]$.
   - If $w \leq \lfloor (d-1)/2 \rfloor$, the error pattern has been found; STOP.
   - else, GOTO 3.
3. Perform a cyclic shift of $g(x)$.
   - If the total number of cyclic shifts is $\leq k + n$, GOTO 2;
   - else, GOTO 4.
4. Change one symbol in $r(x)$ to another element of $GF(2^m)$, reset the count of cyclic shifts, and GOTO 2.

Actually, the cyclic shifts of Step 3 provide a method for continuing to divide the remainder by $g(x)$ until either the weight falls to $w \leq \lfloor \frac{d-1}{2} \rfloor$ or the remainder continuously repeats some untrappable error pattern. The trial-and-error procedure, however, assures that any error pattern within $\lfloor \frac{d-1}{2} \rfloor$ will be found [9]. This "extended" minimum weight decoding is essentially error trapping [16] with a trial-and-error [10] component. It corrects all patterns of errors with weight no greater than $t = \lfloor \frac{d-1}{2} \rfloor$. While this is a HDD, any satisfactory *weight* can be used to search for valid code words. In particular, the following adds a SDD capability to MWD [9]:

1. Let $\mathbf{r} = (r_0, \ldots, r_{N-1})$ be the received real vector. Let the index $\alpha = 0$.

2. Find $\mathbf{x}_\alpha = (x_0, x_1, \ldots, x_{N-1})$, where

$$x_i = \arg \max_{\hat{x}_i \in GF(2^m)} P(r_i | \hat{x}_i), \ i = 0, \ldots, N - 1 \qquad (10)$$

and where $\mathbf{x}_\alpha$ has not been previously tried.

3. Apply MWD to $\mathbf{x}_\alpha$. If decoder finds error pattern of weight $\leq t$, STOP.

4. Otherwise $\alpha = \alpha + 1$. GOTO 2.

This decoder, merging a maximum likelihood search technique with MWD, is fairly complex except for certain special cases, e.g., amplitude shift keying where Euclidean distance can be used as the soft distance measure.

In addition, the complexity of this algorithm may be high because of the possibility of searching through all the n-tuples. To reduce this complexity, modify the trial-and-error part of the algorithm. Instead of replacing every symbol in $GF(2^m)$ with every other, we can replace each symbol from $GF(2^m)$ with another having a binary expansion that is only Hamming distance 1 or 2 from the original. Because this does not search all of $GF(2^m)$, its performance is slightly worse, while the complexity is much better [20].

3 SOFT DECISION AT THE SYMBOL LEVEL

While the foregoing bit-level methods are interesting and potentially powerful, it might be difficult to implement them in an integrated modulation/coding system (e.g., block-coded modulation) or in cases where the symbol field is of characteristic other than 2. Thus, we turn to the symbol-oriented methods, many of which are seen to be natural generalizations of binary SDDs.

3.1 Generalized Minimum-Distance Decoding

Generalized minimum-distance (GMD) decoding [11] is not specific to RS codes, but some form of it is used in many SDDs for RS codes.

Forney introduced GMD decoding so that channel state information could be used to improve algebraic decoding algorithms. It has been modified and extended by several authors [8,19,25], but the goal has remained the same: to bridge the (often considerable) gap between maximum likelihood decoding and minimum Hamming distance decoding. The GMD decoder preserves much of the likelihood information contained in the received channel symbols.

Let q be an integer power of a prime. Let $\mathbf{X} = (x_1, \ldots, x_n)$, a code word over GF($q$), be received as $\mathbf{Y} = (y_1, \ldots, y_n)$, a vector over the reals. The receiver computes two values for each symbol: a hard-decision estimate of each received symbol x_j and a reliability value α_j.

Let $\hat{x}_j$ be an estimate from GF(q) of the jth transmitted symbol x_j. The reliability of this estimate is given by the symbol log-likelihood ratio,

$$L(\hat{x}_j, y_j) = \ln \frac{P[y_j|\hat{x}_j]}{\sum\limits_{x \neq x_j} P[y_j|x]}. \tag{11}$$

Define a set of normalized reliability measures:

$$\alpha_j = \begin{cases} 1 & \text{if } L(\hat{x}_j, y_j) \geq T \\ L(\hat{x}_j, y_j)/T & \text{if } 0 \leq L(\hat{x}_j, y_j) \leq T \\ 0 & \text{if } L(\hat{x}_j, y_j) \leq 0. \end{cases} \tag{12}$$

T is a threshold that will be handled in the implementation.

Define

$$s(\hat{x}_j, x_j) = \begin{cases} +1, & x_j = \hat{x}_j, \\ -1, & x_j \neq \hat{x}_j. \end{cases} \tag{13}$$

For any code word $\mathbf{X}$, let

$$\alpha \cdot \mathbf{X} = \sum_{i-1}^{n} \alpha_i s(\hat{x}_i, x_i). \tag{14}$$

GMD is based upon the following theorem [11].

THEOREM 1   There is at most one code word $\mathbf{X}$ from a code of length n and minimum distance d such that $\alpha \cdot \mathbf{X} > n - d$.

Any algorithm that produces a code word meeting this criterion is a GMD decoding algorithm. One follows [12]:

GMD Decoder

1. Reorder the indices on the reliabilities so that $|\alpha_{i_1}| \leq |\alpha_{i_2}| \leq \cdots \leq |\alpha_{i_n}|$.
2. Set $v = 0$.

3. Erase the ν least reliable symbols:

$$q_\nu(\alpha_{i_j}) = \begin{cases} 0, & \text{if } 1 \le j \le \nu \\ \text{sgn}(y_{i_j}), & \text{otherwise.} \end{cases} \tag{15}$$

4. If an errors-and-erasures decoder can find a code word $\mathbf{X}$ corresponding to $\mathbf{q}_\nu$, decode as $\mathbf{X}$ and exit.
5. If not, set $\nu = \nu + 1$ and go to Step 3.

By iterating over the number ν of erased symbols, this decoder effectively iterates over threshold T. See [11] for more detail. It has been shown [12] that if a code word satisfying the conditions of (1) exists, such a decoder will find it in no more than than $\frac{d+1}{2}$ iterations.

Forney [11] presented a GMD algorithm specifically for BCH (and RS) codes. It demonstrates the power of GMD but suffers from severe complexity. To reduce this complexity and improve the efficiency of the decoding operation, many investigators have proposed extensions to GMD. Yu [26] extended GMD from unquantized to M-ary output channels, obtaining the full performance of GMD with somewhat less decoding effort [25]. Others [8, 19] have tried to reduce complexity by finding other ways to limit the search for the correct code word.

A complexity reduction approach that is specific to RS codes restricts the symbols to $GF(2^m)$, in which the symbol probabilities for the likelihood function are expanded into products of conditional probabilities of the bits given in the expansion of the symbol over $GF(2)$. In the white Gaussian noise channel, expansion of the conditional bit probabilities permits us to ignore most of the terms in these bitwise expansions when the signal-to-noise ratio is "sufficiently large." This simplifies computing the α_j with little loss in performance [7]. Also, the Welch-Berlekamp [23] decoder has been applied [1] to a modification of the key equation [3] for RS codes so that, following ordering of the received symbols by decreasing reliability, a single computation is made of each symbol in the estimate, requiring only one execution of an algebraic errors-and-erasures decoder. It is a full GMD decoder, but with reduced complexity [1].

3.2 Maximum Likelihood Decoders

MLD and Near-MLD.   Recent attempts [18] to achieve MLD have brought forth a MLD, for any linear code, a SDD for which an algebraic decoder exists and a SDD that admits an erasure algorithm.

A code word $\mathbf{X} = (x_0, x_1, \ldots, x_{n-1})$, $x_i \in GF(q)$, is transmitted over a memoryless channel. It is received as $\mathbf{Y} = (y_0, \ldots, y_{n-1})$ from which the maximum symbol likelihood estimate $\mathbf{r} = (r_0, r_1, \ldots, r_{n-1})$ is sought:

$$r_i = \arg \max_{\hat{r} \in GF(q)} \ln p(y_i | \hat{r}), i = 0, 1, \ldots, n - 1. \tag{16}$$

Beginning with $\mathbf{r}$, which may not be a code word, we attempt MLD using the log-likelihood matrix,

$$\mathbf{L} = \left[\ln p(y_i | c_j) \right], \ 0 \le i \le n - 1, \ 0 \le j \le q - 1, \tag{17}$$

to compute a code word estimate

$$\hat{\mathbf{x}}_m = \arg \ln \max \ p_n(\mathbf{y} | \mathbf{x}_m), \tag{18}$$

where the maximization is over the entire code. On the memoryless channel, this computation is equivalent to finding the code word

$$\mathbf{x}_m = \arg \max_{\mathbf{x}'_m} \Lambda(\mathbf{x}_m), \tag{19}$$

where

$$\Lambda(\mathbf{x}_m) = \sum_{i=0}^{n-1} \ln p(y_i | x_{mi}), \tag{20}$$

which is equivalent to selecting the code word $\mathbf{x}_m$ nearest to $\mathbf{r}$.

In a manner suggested by [6], this decoder orders all q-ary n-tuples according to log-likelihood ratio and chooses the first (most likely) code word. A new algorithm [18] follows.

A MLD Algorithm

1. Let $i = 1$ and $\mathbf{z}_i = \mathbf{z}_1 = \mathbf{r}$.
2. Compute $\mathbf{s} = \mathbf{z}_i \mathbf{H}^T$, $\mathbf{H}$ = check matrix of C.
   - If $\mathbf{s} = \mathbf{0}$, i.e., $\mathbf{z}_i \in C$, then output $\hat{\mathbf{c}} = \mathbf{z}_i$; STOP
   - else let $i = i + 1$; GOTO 3.
3. Find $\mathbf{z}_i$, the n-tuple having the ith smallest log-likelihood ratio with respect to $\mathbf{r}$ over all q-ary n-tuples: GOTO 2.

This is a maximum likelihood algorithm if permitted to run until it finds a code word. However, the complexity remains exponential. Although the test for $\mathbf{z}_i \in C$ is a simple syndrome computation, the challenge is to find efficient search schemata for generating the $\mathbf{z}_i$. C.-F. Su [18] detailed an algorithm for preprocessing and storing certain symbol log-likelihood differences. Su's results show that, when code words over GF(q) are transmitted, the complexity of the implementation is of order $M^2(n - 1) + n^2(q - 1)$ and the storage requirement is of order $Mn + n^2(q - 1)n$, where M is the number of test patterns required to find the ML code word and $1 \leq M \leq q^n - q^k + 1$. The actual value of M is not analytically predictable but is believed to be strongly sensitive to the channel signal-to-noise ratio [18]. Nevertheless, this MLD algorithm can be applied to RS codes under certain conditions.

A Near-MLD for Good Channels.   Sacrificing complete MLD can reduce complexity while preserving most of the performance benefits. The following algorithm generates only a subset of the test patterns of the MLD algorithm and so can fail to decode in some situations [18].

Let ϵ be a small number.

1. $\Lambda_{best} = -\epsilon$; $c_{best} = r$; $z_1 = r$; $i = 1$.
2. Compute $s = z_i H^T$.
    - If $s = 0$, then
      If $\Lambda(z_i) \geq \Lambda_{best}$, $c_{best} = z_i$;
      Otherwise, keep previous c_{best}.
    - If $s \neq 0$, GOTO 3.
3. Decode z_i using an errors-only, bounded distance decoder.
    - If a code word c_i is found, set $\Lambda_{best} = \Lambda(c_i)$ and $c_{best} = c_i$. Set $i = i + 1$.
    - otherwise CONTINUE.
4. If $i > M_0$, stop and output c_{best}. Otherwise, set z_i = test pattern with the ith smallest log-likelihood difference relative to r over the q-ary n-tuples and GOTO 2.

This near-MLD algorithm has a storage requirement of $M_1 n + Un$, where M_1 is the actual number of errors-only decodings used, $M_1 \leq M$, and $U \leq \min(M, (q - 1)n)$ [18]. The number of comparisons is of order $M_1^2(n - 1) + U(n-1)$, and the complexity of the errors-only algorithm (including syndrome computation) is roughly $M_1 n^2$. The latter was estimated for a transform-decoding errors-only algorithm [5]. Intuitively, we expect the effort to be small for quiet channels, and this has been borne out experimentally [18].

A Near-MLD Suitable for Fading Channels.   Use of errors-only decoding in the preceding algorithm is suitable for channels such as the white Gaussian noise channel. Channel fading over one code word yields widely varying likelihood values and surely leads to the need for many more test patterns. To prevent this increase in complexity, we can erase some of the received symbols with lowest likelihood values and use an errors-and-erasures decoder in lieu of the errors-only decoder. We are given M_0 as before, and $s < d_{min}$.

Let ϵ be a small number.

1. If $\mathbf{r}\mathbf{H}^T = 0$, stop. $\mathbf{c}_{\text{best}} = \mathbf{r}$.

2. Form $\mathbf{r}'$ from $\mathbf{r}$ by erasing the s positions having lowest reliability. Set $\Lambda_{\text{best}} = -\epsilon$; $\mathbf{c}_{\text{best}} = \mathbf{r}$; $i = 1$; $\mathbf{z}'_1 = \mathbf{r}'$.

3. If $\mathbf{z}'_i \mathbf{H}^T = 0$, $\chi = \Lambda(\mathbf{z}'_i)$; $\mathbf{x} = \mathbf{z}'_i$. GOTO 4.
   Otherwise, decode $\mathbf{z}'_i$ using an errors-and-erasures decoder.
   - If it finds a code word $\mathbf{c}_i$, set $\chi = \Lambda(\mathbf{c}_i)$; $\mathbf{x} = \mathbf{c}_i$.
   - If no code word is found, GOTO 5.

4. If $\chi > \Lambda_{\text{best}}$, $\Lambda_{\text{best}} = \chi$ and $\mathbf{c}_{\text{best}} = \mathbf{x}$, $i = i + 1$.

5. If $i > M_0$, stop and output $\mathbf{c}_{\text{best}}$. Otherwise, form another test pattern $\mathbf{z}_i$ such that
   - it has the same set of erased positions as $\mathbf{r}$, and
   - $\Lambda(\mathbf{z}'_i) - \Lambda(\mathbf{r}')$ is the $(i-1)$st smallest difference over all the q-ary n-tuples having the same set of erased positions. GOTO 3.

The number of q-ary additions and multiplications is estimated to be of order $M_0 n^2$ each [18]. Overall, the complexity is asymptotically proportional to M_0.

These algorithms are reminiscent of Chase's algorithms, originally published for binary codes. They have, however, been seen to outperform "Chasing" and to compare quite favorably, in simulation, with GMD itself [18].

Use of a Trellis.   The use of a trellis to express the state of a decoder for convolutional codes is well known [14]. One can, as well, write a trellis for the state of a decoder for any linear block code by using its parity-check matrix [24]. This provides another technique for MLD of a RS code.

Consider a (15,11), two-error-correcting RS code over $GF(2^4)$. MLD can be performed by correlating each code word with the received vector. This word correlation requires $(2^4)^{11}$ comparisons. The Viterbi algorithm [22], by contrast, requires the equivalent of searching q^{n-k} or 2^4 paths through the trellis. It computes a real number from the log-likelihood ratio for each node at depth $j = 1, \ldots, k$ in the trellis. However, it retains only the maximum likelihood path to each node from depth j to $j + 1$. When $j = n$, the single remaining path represents the maximum likelihood code word.

Viterbi decoding with a trellis is one of the few practical RS decoding algorithms that always achieves MLD. However, while $\min(q^k, q^{n-k})$ can be much smaller than $\max(q^k, q^{n-k})$, the number of states in a nonbinary Viterbi decoder continues to grow exponentially. Its advantage lies in its smaller complexity, for codes of modest size, than correlation decoding.

3.3 Bounded Distance Methods

Maximum Likelihood Sequence Detection.   Consider a sequence $(\mathbf{x}_0, \mathbf{x}_1, \ldots \mathbf{x}_i)$, where $\mathbf{x}_i$, is the ith most likely hard-decision estimate of transmitted code word $\mathbf{c}$; i.e., $p(\mathbf{r}|\mathbf{x}_0) \geq p(\mathbf{r}|\mathbf{x}_1) \geq \ldots$. The sequence stops at the first $\mathbf{x}_i$ belonging to the code. This *maximum likelihood sequence decoding* or MLSD technique becomes quite impractical for large codes because it may be required to search all the n-tuples in $GF(2^m)$ in order to find a code word [17]. However, a SDD helps to reduce the complexity of MLSD because the more refined SDD may find a code word sooner than the HDD. Instead of searching through the code's vector space, stopping only when it lands on a code word, this system adds a bounded distance decoder to find a code word within an acceptable radius, thereby terminating the search sooner.

Likelihood information is provided by a matrix of confidence values $w_{ix_{ij}} = -\log p(r_i|x_{ij})$, where $i = 0, 1, \ldots, N-1$ indexes the position in the word and $j = 1, 2, \ldots, 2^m - 1$ indexes the elements of $GF(2^m)$. The value $w_{ix_{ij}}$ is known as the *soft weight* of the received signal r_i with respect to field element x_{ij}. This notion is used with MWD (see Section 2.2) in the decoding/testing phase of the MSLD under discussion [17]. The required distance or weight measure on n-tuples is

$$w(\mathbf{x}_i|\mathbf{r}) = \sum_{j=0}^{n-1} w_{ix_{ij}}. \tag{21}$$

Finally, define t_s to be the maximum code word weight (with respect to the received signal) that guarantees correction to the correct code word. This is the soft analog of $t = \lfloor (d-1)/2 \rfloor$ which expresses the maximum number of guaranteed correctable errors per block using HDD. The search weight t_s is computed as follows:

$$t_s = \max_{\mathbf{c}'}\{w(\mathbf{c}'|\mathbf{r}), w(\mathbf{c}') \leq w(\mathbf{c}), \forall \mathbf{r}\}, \tag{22}$$

where $\mathbf{r}$ is decoded to the lowest-weight code word $\mathbf{c}'$ and $\mathbf{c}$ is the transmitted code word. The algorithm is

1. Compute t_s. Select the maximum number $i_{\max}$ of iterations.
2. $i = 0$.
3. Compute $\mathbf{x}_i$
4. Do MWD using search weight t_s.

- If search is successful, END;
- otherwise, $i = i + 1$. CONTINUE.

  If $i \leq i_{\max}$ GOTO 3;

  else END. Use most likely code word found in the search.

A Gathering of Many Ideas.   Most popular algebraic decoders for RS and BCH codes compute and manipulate power sum symmetric functions. Indeed, we have become so accustomed to handling them and hardware performance has grown so significantly that it is easy to neglect opportunities for decoders that do not require this level of complexity. What follows was introduced by Berlekamp [2] in his Shannon Lecture at the 1993 International Symposium on Information Theory. It outlines a decoder that

- exploits the RS code property that any k position is an information set;
- recursively determines the error locators and magnitudes without using power sum symmetric functions;
- improves its performance by choosing an information set that places the errors in the check positions, thereby doing less work;
- incorporates SDD in a manner reminiscent of GMD [11] in order to find the code word that minimizes a "reliability score" over sets of the most likely error patterns over all values of the error threshold.

This "bounded distance + 1" decoder is a soft-decision version of the Welch-Berlekamp (WB) algorithm [23]. Its significance in this survey is twofold: on one hand, it incorporates many ideas from algebraic coding theory and from GMD; on the other, it is by far the most recent SDD that could be incorporated in this work.

The first written report of WB was in their 1986 patent [23] which is not very accessible to many readers on at least two counts. Fortunately, Morii and Kasahara [15] have illuminated it as part of a treatise on generalized key equations. The contribution of WB is that, without syndrome computation, it produces a key equation relating error locations and coefficient values. Note that this key equation is quite different from that produced by the "standard" Berlekamp-Massey and Euclidean decoders although it serves quite the same purpose.

Typically, standard decoders compute syndromes

$$s_k = e(\alpha^k), \ k = b, b + 1, \ldots, b + d - 2 \tag{23}$$

by evaluating the received vector $R(x) = c(x) + e(x)$ at the roots of the RS code. Used as coefficients of polynomial $s(x)$, these syndromes are combined with the formal error locator polynomial $\sigma(x)$ to form the familiar key equation $\sigma(x) \equiv \omega(x) \mod x^{d-1}$ from which $\omega(x)$ is written as a function of the error locators $\{e_k\}$ and of the $(d-1)$ powers of α.

Observe that all the information needed to derive this key equation is contained in the remainder $r(x)$ obtained by dividing $R(x)$ by the code generator $g(x)$. The derivation in [23] begins with the single-error case, assuming that the error occurs in a message position.[3] If a single error of magnitude Y occurs at location Z, we can write

$$r(\alpha^k) = Y Z^k. \tag{24}$$

Let

$$p(x) = \frac{g(x)}{x - \alpha^b} = \sum_{k=b+1}^{b+d-2} p_i x^i. \tag{25}$$

Then it can be shown [15,23] that

$$Y = Z^{-b} r(\alpha^b) \tag{26}$$

$$= \tilde{A} Z^{-b} \sum_{i=0}^{d-2} \frac{p_i \alpha^{i(b+1)}}{(\alpha^i - Z)} \tag{27}$$

$$= \tilde{A} f(Z) \tag{28}$$

where the constant $\tilde{A}$ can be precomputed from $p(x)$ and the powers of α.

The result is generalized in the multiple-error case to produce the key equation. Let the error at location Z_i have magnitude Y_i for $i = 1, 2, \ldots, e$. The contributions of the errors to $r(x)$ sum linearly:

$$r_k = p_k \alpha^k \sum_{i=1}^{e} \frac{Y_i}{f(Z_i)(\alpha^k - Z)}. \tag{29}$$

Let $N(x)$ and $W(x)$ be the numerator and denominator, respectively, of the summation in the foregoing. The key equation is found by direct manipulation [15, 23] to be

$$p_k \alpha^k N(\alpha^k) = r_k W(\alpha^k) \tag{30}$$

where

$$p(x) = \prod_{k=b+1}^{b+d-2} (x - \alpha^k) = \sum_{i=0}^{d-2} p_i x^i. \tag{31}$$

As is customary, the decoder uses n symbols from GF(q) and n nonnegative real numbers, "reliabilities" of the finite field symbols. The SCORE of

---

[3] If the error occurs in a check position, that fact will become apparent using reencoding. See [23] and [15] for details.

the n-tuple from GF(q) is defined as the sum of the reliabilities of the nonzero elements. Define

$$ERRATA\_COUNT = 2t + e \qquad (32)$$

where t is the number of errors in the received word and e is the number of erasures. Then, whereas a MLD finds the error pattern having minimum SCORE over all possible error patterns, the "bounded distance + 1" decoder finds the error pattern having minimum SCORE over that subset of error patterns for which $ERRATA\_COUNT \le r + 1$, where $r = n - k$ is the redundancy of the code. This decoder also minimizes SCORE over all settings of the error threshold [11].

The decoding algorithm is

1. Sort the reliability scores of the received symbols.
2. Reencode the information positions.
3. Erase the least reliable r symbols and decode using "erasures only."
4. Treat the least reliable r symbols as check symbols and find candidate solutions using the WB algorithm.
5. For each candidate code word in Step 4, find the corresponding error pattern, if possible, and compute its SCORE.
6. Select the candidate with lowest SCORE and correct the received word.

Berlekamp has argued that, because the complexity of Step 4 is proportional to re, where e is the actual number of errors that occurred, it represents a significant improvement over prior algorithms. Further, it finds all candidate solutions in a single "pass" with erasures.

4 CONCLUSIONS

The earlier chapters of this book have shown that applications in communications, recording, and multimedia presentation systems (including entertainment) are exploiting the power of RS codes, and many uses would not be feasible without the added performance of soft-decision decoding (e.g., see Chapter 3). Increases in the speed of modern hardware and the reduced complexity of soft decoders are erasing the difficulties of implementation that might have been major road blocks just a few years ago.

No doubt, the explosion in algebraic geometry will lead to stronger new codes, but if history is an indication, the first decoding algorithms for these codes may be quite complex, to the extent that they differ in form and structure from RS and BCH codes. Meanwhile, the rich array of soft-decision decoders for RS codes continues to expand, providing system designers with ever more powerful error control capabilities to meet emerging demands.

REFERENCES

[1] K. Araki and M. Takada, "The Efficient GMD Decoders for BCH Codes," *1993 IEEE International Symposium on Information Theory, San Antonio*, January 1993.

[2] E. R. Berlekamp, "Bounded Distance + 1 Soft Decision Reed-Solomon Decoding," Shannon Lecture, *1993 IEEE International Symposium on Information Theory, San Antonio*, January 1993.

[3] E. R. Berlekamp, *Algebraic Coding Theory*, New York: McGraw-Hill, 1968.

[4] E. R. Berlekamp, R. E. Peile, and S. P. Pope, "The Application of Error Control to Communication," *IEEE Communications Magazine*, Volume 25, pp. 44–57, 1987.

[5] R. E. Blahut, *Theory and Practice of Error Control Codes,* Reading, Mass.: Addison-Wesley, 1983.

[6] D. Chase, "A Class of Algorithms for Decoding Block Codes with Channel Measurement Information, *IEEE Transactions on Information Theory*, Volume IT-18, pp. 170–182, January 1982.

[7] N. Doi, M. Izumita, S. Mita, and H. Imai, "Soft-Decision Decoding for Reed-Solomon Codes," *Electronics and Communications in Japan, Part 3*, Volume 72, Number 4, 1989.

[8] V. I. Dolgov and K. Khalimov, "Decoding of Block Codes with Erasure of the Least Reliable Symbols," *Telecommunications and Radio Engineering 2, Radio Engineering*, Volume 42, Number 4, 1987.

[9] P. G. Farrell, M. Rice, and F. Taleb, "Minimum Weight Decoding for Cyclic Codes," in *Cryptography and Coding*, H. J. Beher and F. C. Piper (eds.), Oxford: Clarendon Press, 1989.

[10] P. G. Farrell, "Code Structure and Decoding Complexity," in *The Impact of Processing Techniques on Communications*, Proceedings of the NATO Advanced Study Institute on the Impact of Processing Techniques on Communications, 1983, J. K. Skwirzynski (ed.), Dordrecht, The Netherlands: Nijhoff, pp. 159–192, 1985.

[11] G. D. Forney, *Concatenated Codes*, Cambridge: MIT Press, 1966.

[12] G. D. Forney, "Generalized Minimum Distance Decoding," *IEEE Transactions on Information Theory*, Volume IT-12, pp. 125–131, 1966.

[13] F. J. MacWilliams and N. J. Sloane, *The Theory of Error-Correcting Codes*, Amsterdam: North-Holland, 1977.

[14] A. M. Michelson and A. H. Levesque, *Error-Control Techniques for Digital Communication*, New York: John Wiley, 1985.

[15] M. Morii and M. Kasahara, "Generalized Key-Equation of Remainder Decoding Algorithm for Reed-Solomon Codes," *IEEE Transactions on Information Theory*, Volume 38, pp. 1801–1807, November 1992.

[16] W. W. Peterson and E. J. Weldon, *Error-Correcting Codes*, Cambridge: MIT Press, 1972.

[17] M. Rice, D. J. Tait, and P. G. Farrell, "A Soft-Decision Reed-Solomon Decoder," *1988 IEEE International Symposium on Information Theory, Kobe.*

[18] C.-F. Su, *Some Soft Decision Decoding Algorithms for Linear Block Codes*, Ph.D. Thesis, University of Virginia, Charlottesville, May 1992.

[19] D. J. Taipale and M. B. Pursley, "An Improvement to Generalized Maximum Likelihood Decoding," *IEEE Transactions on Information Theory*, Volume IT-37, 1991.

[20] F. Taleb and P. G. Farrell, "Minimum Weight Decoding of Reed-Solomon Codes," in *Cryptography and Coding II*, C. Mitchell (ed.), Oxford: Clarendon Press, 1992.

[21] A. Vardy and Y. Be'ery, "Bit Level Soft-Decision Decoding of Reed-Solomon Codes," *IEEE Transactions on Communications*, Volume 39, Number 3, March, 1991.

[22] A. J. Viterbi, "Error Bounds for Convolutional Codes and an Asymptotically Optimum Decoding Algorithm," *IEEE Transactions on Information Theory*, Volume IT-13, pp. 260–269, April 1967.

[23] L. R. Welch and E. R. Berlekamp, "Error Correction for Algebraic Block Codes," U. S. Patent Number 4,633,470, issued Dec 30, 1986.

[24] J. Wolf, "Efficient Maximum Likelihood Decoding of Linear Block Codes Using a Trellis," *IEEE Transactions on Information Theory*, Volume IT-24, pp. 76–80, January 1978.

[25] C. C. Yu and D. J. Costello, Jr., "Generalized Minimum Distance Decoding Algorithms for Q-ary Output Channels," *IEEE Transactions on Information Theory*, Volume IT-26, pp. 238–243, March 1980.

[26] C. C. Yu, *Efficient Decoding Algorithms for Linear Codes on Soft-Quantized Channels*, Ph.D. Thesis, Illinois Institute of Technology, Chicago, May 1978.

Chapter 7

Reed-Solomon Codes in Hybrid Automatic Repeat-Request Protocols[1]

Stephen B. Wicker
School of Electrical and Computer Engineering
Georgia Institute of Technology
Atlanta, Georgia 30332

Michael Bartz
Department of Electrical Engineering
Memphis State University
Memphis, Tennessee 38152

1 INTRODUCTION

Reed-Solomon codes provide excellent reliability performance when used for error detection or combined error detection and error correction [7]. They are thus natural candidates for use in hybrid-ARQ protocols [19], in which error detection and correction are combined in a receiver that detects unreliably decoded code words and requests their retransmission. It has been noted, however, that the combined error detection and correction capabilities of Reed-Solomon codes can become a liability when the communication channel is nonstationary [2]. Consider a type I hybrid-ARQ protocol that has been designed for a fixed channel noise level. In a type I protocol each transmitted code word is encoded for both error detection and error correction. The error correction capacity is used to correct frequently occurring error patterns, while the detection capacity is used to detect the less frequently occurring patterns, which cause the generation of retransmission requests. In a type I protocol the transmitter responds to retransmission requests by sending another copy of the transmitted code word. This error control scheme performs quite well on channels that are essentially stationary except for infrequent bursts of additional noise. However, if the channel noise level deviates from the design

[1] This work was supported by the National Science Foundation under Grant Number NCR-9009877.

level for a significant period of time, the performance of the protocol can be seriously degraded. As the channel noise level increases, the probability that each received word contains an uncorrectable error pattern also increases. The new error patterns are detected, and a flood of retransmission requests ensues that persists until the channel noise level returns to its original level. As the channel noise level decreases, the error correction capacity is sufficient to correct all error patterns, rapidly driving the frequency of retransmission requests to zero. The redundancy reserved for error detection thus assumes the status of useless overhead. In either case the throughput performance of the type I protocol is suboptimal. This problem is particularly acute when the type I protocol is based on codes whose error correction and detection performance curves have strongly negative slopes as a function of signal to noise ratio (e.g., Reed-Solomon codes).

Code combining offers a solution to this problem. The code-combining receiver concatenates received code words until their combined code rate is sufficient to reliably recover the transmitted information [3]. As the channel noise level varies, the receiver varies the effective code rate of the error control system, reducing the throughput degradation observed with a fixed-rate system. The simplest code-combining system is the type II hybrid-ARQ protocol, a truncated form that limits combining operations to a maximum of two received code words [9,10,18]. In a type II protocol the transmitter responds to an initial retransmission request by transmitting a code word containing parity bits for the first code word. The original message is obtained through decoding operations on the first or second code words alone or through a combined decoding operation on the composite code word created through the concatenation of the two received code words.

MDS codes (a large family of codes that includes the Reed-Solomon codes) possess a number of properties that make them well suited for use in type II protocols. Mandelbaum [13,14] has noted that Reed-Solomon codes can be punctured to provide a primary code word and one or more secondary blocks that provide incremental redundancy as needed. This scheme is optimal in the sense that the incremental redundancy increases the minimum distance of the composite received word by the greatest possible amount per additional symbol. Mandelbaum's work is modified and extended in this chapter by defining a type II hybrid-ARQ protocol based on the general class of punctured MDS codes.

Pursley and Sandberg have proposed the use of Reed-Solomon codes in an incremental redundancy system for meteor-burst channels [15,16]. Their version of the RS type II system is considered in this chapter as well as a modified version which requires fewer decoding operations. The analytical framework presented here can be used to accurately predict the performance of both systems.

In Section 2 an analysis of the reliability and throughput performance of a generic type II hybrid-ARQ protocol is provided. A general review of the relevant properties of MDS codes follows. It is then shown that the various properties of MDS codes can be used to construct a type II protocol from a series of type I protocols based on punctured MDS codes. The performance parameters of the individual type I protocols provide the necessary data for the complete characterization of the type II system using the general expressions derived in the earlier section. Several examples are provided to indicate the excellent throughput and reliability performance offered by the MDS type II hybrid-ARQ protocol.

2 PERFORMANCE MODEL FOR THE GENERAL TYPE II HYBRID-ARQ PROTOCOL

In a type II hybrid-ARQ protocol, a code word is encoded using two codes, C_1 and C_2, to create a pair of code words c_1 and c_2. These codes have corresponding decoding operations D_1 and D_2 which can recover the original code word from noise-corrupted versions of c_1 and c_2, respectively. c_1 forms the initial transmission, while c_2 is set aside. Upon receiving c_1, the receiver attempts decoding operation D_1 to recover the transmitted data. If the attempt is successful (i.e., no retransmission request is generated), the receiver sends an acknowledgment (ACK) to the transmitter; otherwise, a negative acknowledgment (NACK) is sent. The transmitter responds to the NACK by sending c_2. The receiver then attempts to decode c_2 by itself using decoding operation D_2. If successful, the receiver inverts the corrected version of c_2 to recover the desired information and sends an ACK to the receiver. If unsuccessful, the receiver combines c_1 and c_2 to create c_3, a code word in a lower-rate code C_3. If the third decoding operation D_3 is successful, the data are recovered and an ACK is sent to the receiver; otherwise, a NACK is sent and the entire process is repeated. After the first pair of transmissions, the combined decoding operation D_3 is always available after the receipt of subsequent copies of either c_1 or c_2. This decoding protocol is shown as a flowchart in Figure 7-1. Note that this protocol is a slight generalization of the type II protocol originally presented by Lin and Yu [5]. We are allowing the first and second packets to be independently decoded within type I HARQ protocols instead of restricting the coding for the first transmission to error detection only.

Reliability and throughput generating functions for this protocol are obtained using signal flow graph techniques [11]. A generic graph that describes

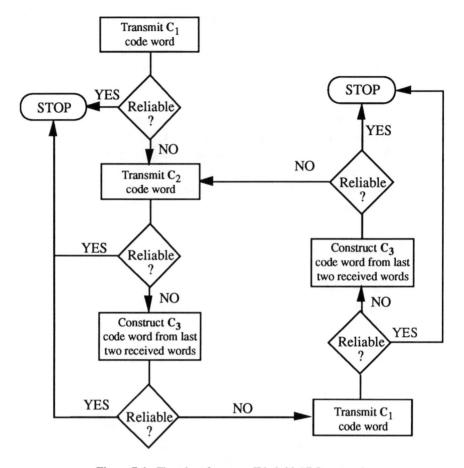

Figure 7-1. Flowchart for a type II hybrid-ARQ protocol.

this protocol is depicted in Figure 7-2. The nodes of the graph consist of the initial transmission IT, code word acceptance CA, and the decoding operations D_1, D_2, and D_3. The branches indicate the directions by which the code word transmission and decoding processes proceed. For reliability analysis the branches are labeled with the probability that the associated event occurs, whereas for throughput calculations, the branch labels help determine the number of transmitted symbols. The branch labels for determining reliability and throughput are found in Table 1. The generic graph yields the following transfer function:

$$IT = \left\{ ab + ac\,(d + ef + egh + egij)\left(\frac{1}{1 - egik}\right) \right\} CA \qquad (1)$$

Substituting the appropriate branch values, one obtains the throughput and reliability generating functions for the type II protocol.

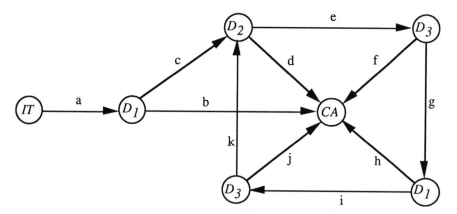

Figure 7-2. Generic graph for a type II hybrid-ARQ protocol.

TABLE 1   Graph Labels for the Derivation of Throughput and Reliability Generating Functions

Branch Label	Throughput Label	Reliability Label
a	T^{n_1}	1
b	$1 - p_R^{(1)}$	$p_E^{(1)}$
c	$p_R^{(1)} \cdot T^{n_2}$	$p_R^{(1)}$
d	$1 - p_R^{(2)}$	$p_E^{(2)}$
e	$p_R^{(2)}$	$p_R^{(1)}$
f	$1 - p_R^{(3)}$	$p_E^{(3)}$
g	$p_R^{(3)} \cdot T^{n_1}$	$p_R^{(3)}$
h	$1 - p_R^{(1)}$	$p_E^{(1)}$
i	$p_R^{(2)}$	$p_R^{(1)}$
j	$1 - p_R^{(3)}$	$p_E^{(3)}$
k	$p_R^{(3)} \cdot T^{n_2}$	$p_R^{(3)}$

For throughput calculation the branches are labeled with the probabilities of the generation of a retransmission request p_R, decoder error p_E, and code word acceptance $1 - p_R$, as appropriate. The superscripts for the various probabilities reference the probabilities to a specific decoding operation. The variable T is used to indicate the transmission of a code word, while its exponent denotes the number of code word symbols contained in the code word (n_1 or n_2 for code C_1 or C_2, respectively). For the calculation of the throughput, a selective-repeat protocol is assumed. The throughput generating function is as follows:

$$G(T) = T^{n_1} p_C^{(1)} + T^{n_1+n_2} p_R^{(1)} \left[p_C^{(2)} + T^{n_1} p_R^{(2)} p_R^{(3)} p_C^{(1)} + \right.$$

$$\left. p_C^{(3)} \left(p_R^{(2)} + T^{n_1} p_R^{(2)} p_R^{(3)} p_R^{(1)} \right) \right] \left(\frac{1}{1 - T^{n_1+n_2} p_R^{(1)} p_R^{(2)} p_R^{(3)2}} \right) \quad (2)$$

Once the throughput generating function has been obtained, the throughput η of the protocol can be computed. The throughput η is defined here as the ratio of the number of information symbols transmitted (k, the dimension of code C_1) to the average number of symbols transmitted before the code word is correctly accepted. By taking the partial derivative of equation (2) with respect to T and setting T equal to unity, the probability of each of the distinct paths through the graph in Figure 7-2 is weighted by the total number of symbols transmitted along that path. The following expression results.

$$\eta = k \left(\left. \frac{\partial}{\partial T} G(T) \right|_{T=1} \right)^{-1}$$

$$= k \left(\frac{1 - p_R^{(1)} p_R^{(2)} p_R^{(3)2}}{n_1 + n_2 p_R^{(1)} + n_1 p_R^{(1)} p_R^{(2)} p_R^{(3)} - n_1 p_R^{(1)} p_R^{(2)} p_R^{(3)2}} \right) \quad (3)$$

The reliability-generating function provides the following expression for the probability that an accepted, decoded code word contains one or more symbol errors.

$$P(E) = \left[p_E^{(1)} + p_R^{(1)} \left(p_E^{(2)} + p_R^{(2)} p_E^{(3)} + p_R^{(2)} p_R^{(3)} p_E^{(1)} + p_R^{(1)} p_R^{(2)} p_R^{(3)} p_E^{(3)} \right) \right.$$

$$\left. \cdot \left(\frac{1}{1 - p_R^{(1)} p_R^{(2)} p_R^{(3)2}} \right) \right] \quad (4)$$

3 THE PROPERTIES OF MDS CODES

The use of MDS codes in type II protocols is motivated by a series of properties that are, as a whole, unique to MDS codes. The most pertinent are listed here. The first property is frequently used as the definition for MDS codes, though it can be shown to be equivalent to a number of other definitions.

PROPERTY 1 The Singleton bound states that given a linear code **C** with length n and dimension k, the minimum distance d_{min} must satisfy $d_{min} \leq (n - k + 1)$. A code **C** is MDS if and only if it satisfies the Singleton bound with equality [17].

Property 1 shows that MDS codes are optimal in the sense that they provide "maximum distance" between code words. MDS codes were once called "optimal codes," but this proved to be confusing and was abandoned in later literature [1,12]. The Singleton bound can be used in conjunction with the BCH bound to show that Reed-Solomon codes are MDS [12].

When the "natural" length of a particular code is unsuitable for an application, the length can be changed by puncturing, extending, shortening, or lengthening the original code [1,4,12]. In this chapter the technique of interest is *puncturing*. A code is punctured through the consistent deletion of parity coordinates from each code word in the code. Puncturing j coordinates reduces an (n, k, d) code to an $(n - j, k, d')$ code. In most cases the goal is to minimize the reduction in minimum distance through the judicious selection of the deleted coordinates. In the case of MDS codes, however, the minimum distance of the resulting code is solely a function of the number of coordinates punctured. Any combination of j puncturing operations changes an $(n, k, n - k + 1)$ MDS code into an $(n - j, k, n - k - j + 1)$ MDS code.

PROPERTY 2 Punctured MDS codes are MDS.

This is easily proven by noting that the elimination of a coordinate in a code can reduce the code's minimum distance by at most 1, while the Singleton bound implies that the minimum distance of an MDS code must be reduced by at least 1 when the length is reduced by 1. The result, of course, is a consistent reduction of the minimum distance by 1 with each successive puncturing operation.

Property 1 can be shown to imply a "separability" property which proves quite useful in the development of code-combining schemes [17]. Unfortunately the term "separable" has enjoyed a variety of definitions in the literature that are not equivalent. In works focusing on MDS codes "separable" is taken to mean that a code can be partitioned (separated) into message symbols and parity symbols (i.e., a systematic representation of the code exists) [12,17]. In this sense of the word, any linear code is separable, for a generator matrix **G** for an (n, k) code must have at least one combination of k linearly independent columns. In works involving type II hybrid-ARQ protocols, however, "separable" has been used to describe any code $\{F(x)\}$ for which there is a punctured version $\{f(x)\}$ that is "capable of detecting by itself a number of errors eventually correctable by $\{F(x)\}$" [5]. In this chapter the former definition is adopted, for it is this sense of separability that leads to the construction of the desired MDS code-combining protocol. An (n, k) code shall be called *strongly separable* if *any* k code word coordinates can be used as the information symbols in a systematic representation.

PROPERTY 3   MDS codes are strongly separable [17].

A code is said to be *invertible* if the parity-check symbols of the code word can be used by themselves to uniquely determine the information symbols through an inversion process [8]. An (n, k) code shall be called *strongly invertible* if any k symbols from the code word can be used to recover the information symbols.

PROPERTY 4   MDS codes are strongly invertible.

Property 4 follows from the fact that any $(k \times k)$ submatrix of the generator matrix is nonsingular.

The final property of interest is the MDS weight enumerator, which allows for an exact determination of the probabilities of undetected error and retransmission request.

PROPERTY 5   The number of code words of weight j in an $(n, k, d_{\min})$ 2^m-ary MDS code is [1]

$$A_j = \binom{n}{j} (2^m - 1) \sum_{i=0}^{j-d_{\min}} (-1)^i \binom{j-1}{i} 2^{m(j-i-d_{\min})}. \tag{5}$$

4 PUNCTURED MDS CODES IN A TYPE II HYBRID-ARQ PROTOCOL

In the MDS type II protocol, the codes C_1, C_2, and C_3 are formed in a very natural manner. The first step is to select an (n, k) MDS code with rate less than one-half for the combined code C_3. Using decoding operation D_3, this code should provide sufficient error correction capability for the reliable transmission of information under the worst channel conditions expected. Figure 7-3 shows how code words from C_3 are punctured to form code words in C_1 and C_2. The first $n/2$ coordinates in a given C_3 code word $c_{i,3}$ form the code word $c_{i,1}$ in C_1, while the remaining $n/2$ coordinates form the code word $c_{i,2}$ in C_2. Since codes C_1 and C_2 are punctured versions of the MDS code C_3, they are themselves MDS by Property 2. Property 4 guarantees that corrected versions of code words from any of the three codes can be used to recover the information symbols. Decoding operations D_1 and D_2 are designed so as to maximize throughput while maintaining a minimum allowable level of reliability under optimum channel conditions. The design of the individual decoding operations is developed in the following section.

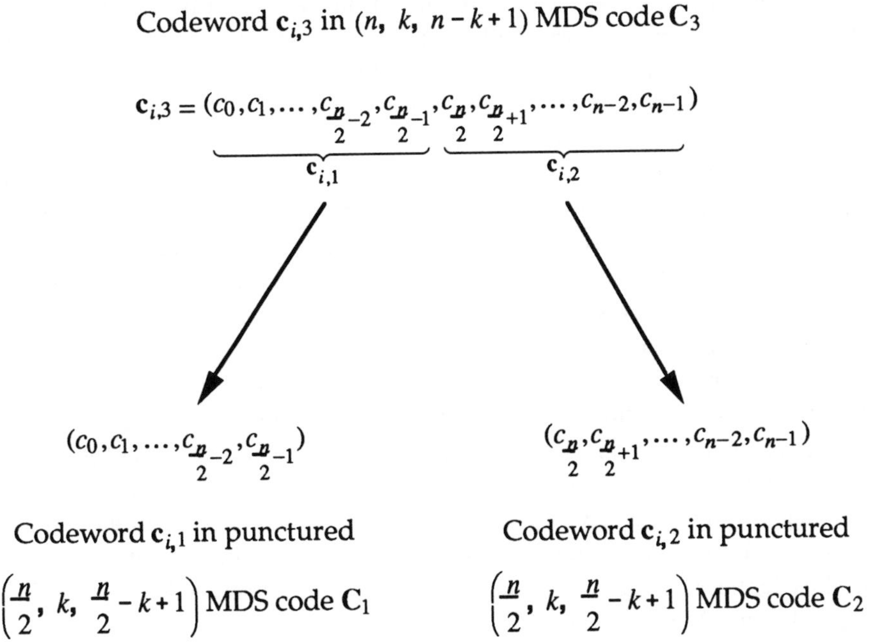

Codeword $\mathbf{c}_{i,3}$ in $(n,\ k,\ n-k+1)$ MDS code C_3

$$\mathbf{c}_{i,3} = (\underbrace{c_0, c_1, \ldots, c_{\frac{n}{2}-2}, c_{\frac{n}{2}-1}}_{\mathbf{c}_{i,1}}, \underbrace{c_{\frac{n}{2}}, c_{\frac{n}{2}+1}, \ldots, c_{n-2}, c_{n-1}}_{\mathbf{c}_{i,2}})$$

$(c_0, c_1, \ldots, c_{\frac{n}{2}-2}, c_{\frac{n}{2}-1})$

$(c_{\frac{n}{2}}, c_{\frac{n}{2}+1}, \ldots, c_{n-2}, c_{n-1})$

Codeword $\mathbf{c}_{i,1}$ in punctured

Codeword $\mathbf{c}_{i,2}$ in punctured

$\left(\frac{n}{2},\ k,\ \frac{n}{2}-k+1\right)$ MDS code C_1

$\left(\frac{n}{2},\ k,\ \frac{n}{2}-k+1\right)$ MDS code C_2

Figure 7-3. MDS code decomposition for type II HARQ protocols.

5 A RETRANSMISSION REQUEST MECHANISM FOR MDS CODES

All three of the decoding operations used in a type II protocol need a retransmission request mechanism to detect code words whose completed decoding will result in unreliable information symbols. In the MDS type II scheme, the same retransmission request mechanism is used with all three decoding operations. All three are treated as *type I* hybrid-ARQ protocols that combine to form a *type II* protocol. In this section the design and analysis of the MDS type I hybrid-ARQ protocol is discussed.

5.1 The MDS Type I Hybrid-ARQ Protocol

Wicker has demonstrated a method for modifying FEC Reed-Solomon error control systems for use in type I hybrid-ARQ protocols [19,20 (fading channels with erasure decoding)]. These systems were shown to provide excellent reliability and throughput performance on stationary channels that suffer occasional bursts of errors. The conceptual development of these systems is repeated here for the slightly more general case of bounded distance decoders for MDS codes.

Given an MDS code with minimum distance $d_{\min}$, a bounded distance decoding algorithm can correct all received words containing e symbol errors and s symbol erasures within the constraint $(2e + s) < d_{\min}$. If the received word is within e errors and s erasures of a valid code word and $(2e+s) < d_{\min}$, then the decoder will select that code word. If the selected code word is not the code word that was transmitted, then a *decoder error* has occurred. If there is no code word within e errors and s erasures, where $(2e + s) < d_{\min}$, then a *decoder failure* is declared. If decoding is completed, the values of e and s can be obtained by comparing the received and corrected words (or, in the case of the Berlekamp-Massey algorithm, by examining the degrees of the error and erasure locator polynomials, respectively).

The bounded distance MDS type I hybrid-ARQ protocol is defined as follows. Let d_e be defined as the *effective diameter* of the decoding operation. The effective diameter is the maximum value of the sum $(2e + s)$ for which decoding is allowed to be completed. The effective diameter d_e must thus be an integer in the range $[0, d_{\min} - 1]$. Whenever $(2e + s) > d_e$, or any time a decoder failure occurs, a retransmission is requested. The effective diameter d_e thus defines the balance between error correction and error detection in this type I hybrid-ARQ system.

5.2 The Performance of the MDS Type I Protocols Within the Framework of a Type II Protocol

When deriving the performance of a type II protocol, two different categories of decoding operations must be considered: those operating on newly arrived code words and those operating on code words that have caused the generation of retransmission requests. Decoding operations D_1 and D_2 fall into the former category, while D_3 falls into the latter. The rationale for this distinction lies in the fact that the average number of errors and erasures in the code word(s) to be decoded differs between the two cases. If a code word is known to have caused the generation of a retransmission request, then the expected number of errors and erasures within the code word is higher than that for a newly received code word for which decoding has not yet been attempted. An effective channel model must be developed for each of the two cases if the overall performance of the type II protocol is to be accurately determined.

For decoding operations D_1 and D_2, the probabilities of symbol error and erasure are determined using information about the modulation format and the communication channel. Figure 7-4 shows the channel model used in the following analysis. This model assumes that transmitted code symbols are independent and that incorrect symbols are equally probable. The precise values for the probabilities of symbol error p_e and symbol erasure p_s are highly application-dependent (see, for example, the case of a binary modem used over a slowly fading code symbol interleaved channel in [20]). Once p_e and p_s are known, however, the following analysis can be used in most applications.

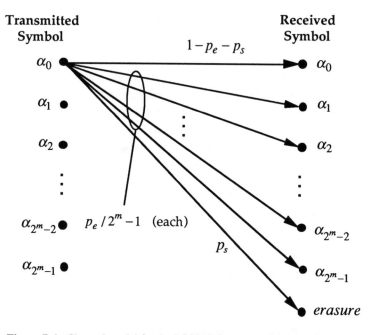

Figure 7-4. Channel model for the RS/HARQ system with erasure decoding.

Using the values for p_e and p_s the probabilities of retransmission and decoder error are determined as follows. Consider the case of an (n, k) 2^m-ary MDS code in a bounded distance type I hybrid-ARQ protocol. If only linear codes are being considered, one may assume without loss of generality that the all-zero code word has been transmitted. Let $P_{d_e}^j$ be the probability that a received word $\mathbf{r}$ is within the decoding sphere of effective diameter d_e surrounding a code word of weight j. If simple error correction is to be performed without erasure decoding, $P_{d_e}^j$ takes on the value

$$P_{d_e}^j = \sum_{v=0}^{\lfloor \frac{d_e}{2} \rfloor} \sum_{w=0}^{\lfloor \frac{d_e-2v}{2} \rfloor} \binom{n-j}{v} \binom{j}{w} (2^m - 1)^{w-j} \left(1 - \frac{p_e}{2^m - 1}\right)^w$$

$$\cdot (1 - p_e)^{n-j-v} p_e^{j+v-w}. \tag{6}$$

This expression uses a series of counting variables to enumerate all possible received words $\mathbf{r}$ of length n that fall within the decoding sphere and weights them by their probability of occurrence using the channel model in Figure 7-4.

A similar expression can be obtained for those cases in which erasure decoding is used. This expression is derived as follows. Let $\mathbf{C}$ be an (n, k) code with minimum distance $d_{\min}$ for which there exists a bounded distance erasure-decoding algorithm. We wish to determine $P_{d_e}^j$, the probability that a received word $\mathbf{r}$ falls within the decoding sphere surrounding a code word $\mathbf{c}_i$ of weight j.

Let Θ be the set containing the $(n - j)$ coordinates of $\mathbf{c}_i$ that contain zeros. Let Φ be the set containing the j coordinates of $\mathbf{c}_i$ that contain nonzero symbols. The desired probability expression can be obtained by allocating e errors and s erasures among the two sets of coordinates in all possible combinations within the constraint $(2e + s) < d_{\min}$.

There are five distinct events that must be accounted for in this derivation.

1. A Θ or Φ coordinate in $\mathbf{r}$ contains a zero symbol. This event occurs with probability $1 - p_e - p_s$.

2. A Θ or Φ coordinate in $\mathbf{r}$ contains an erasure. This event occurs with probability p_s.

3. A Θ coordinate in $\mathbf{r}$ contains a nonzero, nonerased symbol. This event occurs with probability p_e.

4. A Φ coordinate in $\mathbf{r}$ contains a nonzero, nonerased symbol that is different from the symbol at the same coordinate in $\mathbf{c}_i$. This event occurs with probability $(2^m - 2)p/(2^m - 1)$.

5. A Φ coordinate in $\mathbf{r}$ contains the same nonzero symbol as at the same coordinate in $\mathbf{c}_i$. This event occurs with probability $p/(2^m - 1)$.

The allocation of errors and erasures in the expression is controlled by five counting variables as follows:

$v =$ number of Θ coordinates for which $\mathbf{r}$ has a nonzero symbol

$w =$ number of Θ coordinates for which $\mathbf{r}$ has an erasure

$x =$ number of Φ coordinates in which $\mathbf{r}$ has a nonzero symbol other than the nonzero symbol in $\mathbf{c}_i$

$y =$ number of Φ coordinates for which $\mathbf{r}$ has an erasure

$z =$ number of Φ coordinates for which $\mathbf{r}$ has a zero.

$P_{d_e}^j$ is computed by summing over all possible error/erasure patterns for the all-zero code word such that $(2v + w + 2x + y + 2z) < d_{\min}$.

$$P_{d_e}^j = \left\{ \sum_{v=0}^{\lfloor \frac{d_e}{2} \rfloor} \binom{n-j}{v} p_e^v \sum_{w=0}^{d_e-2v} \binom{n-j-v}{w} p_s^w (1 - p_e - p_s)^{n-j-v-w} \right.$$

$$\underbrace{\qquad\qquad\qquad\qquad\qquad\qquad}_{\Theta \text{ coordinates}}$$

$$\cdot \left\{ \sum_{x=0}^{\lfloor \frac{d_e-2v-w}{2} \rfloor} \binom{j}{x} \left[\frac{(2^m-2)p_e}{(2^m-1)} \right]^x \sum_{y=0}^{d_e-2v-w-2x} \binom{j-x}{y} p_s^y \right.$$

$$\left. \cdot \sum_{z=0}^{\lfloor \frac{d_e-2v-w-2x-y}{2} \rfloor} \binom{j-x-y}{z} (1 - p_e - p_s)^z \left[\frac{p_e}{(2^m-1)} \right]^{j-x-y-z} \right\}$$

$$\underbrace{\qquad\qquad\qquad\qquad\qquad\qquad}_{\Phi \text{ coordinates}}$$

$$= \sum_{v=0}^{\lfloor \frac{d_e}{2} \rfloor} \sum_{w=0}^{d_e-2v} \sum_{x=0}^{\lfloor \frac{d_e-2v-w}{2} \rfloor} \sum_{y=0}^{d_e-2v-w-2x} \sum_{z=0}^{\lfloor \frac{d_e-2v-w-2x-y}{2} \rfloor} \tag{7}$$

$$\cdot \binom{n-j}{v} \binom{n-j-v}{w} \binom{j}{x}$$

$$\cdot \binom{j-x}{y} \binom{j-x-y}{z} (2^m - 1)^{y+z-j} (2^m - 2)^x$$

$$\cdot p_e^{j+v-y-z} p_s^{w+y} (1 - p_e - p_s)^{n+z-j-v-w}$$

Property 5 in Section 3 provides the weight distribution for MDS codes. If A_j is the number of code words of weight j, then the probability of undetected decoder error on a single code word transmission is

$$P_E = \sum_{j=d_{\min}}^{n} A_j P_{d_e}^j \tag{8}$$

A retransmission request is generated whenever the received word is not within the decoding sphere surrounding the correct or any one of the incorrect code words. For the nonerasure and erasure decoding cases the following expressions result [20].

$$P_R = \begin{cases} 1 - P_E - \sum_{v=0}^{\lfloor \frac{d_e}{2} \rfloor} \binom{n}{v} p_e^v (1 - p_e)^{n-v} & \\ & \text{nonerasure decoding} \\ 1 - P_E - \sum_{v=0}^{\lfloor \frac{d_e}{2} \rfloor} \sum_{w=0}^{d_e-2v} \binom{n}{v} \binom{n-v}{w} (1 - p_e - p_s)^{n-v-w} p_e^v p_s^w & \\ & \text{erasure decoding} \end{cases} \tag{9}$$

The value of P_E computed in equation (8) is used for both $P_E^{(1)}$ and $P_E^{(2)}$ in equations (3) and (4). The value of P_R computed in equation (9) is used for both $P_R^{(1)}$ and $P_R^{(2)}$.

If a code word is known to have failed in decoding attempts by itself or in combination with other code words, then the mean number of code symbol errors and erasures in the code word is higher than that indicated by the channel model in Figure 7-4. The increase in the channel symbol erasure and error rate must be quantified if the performance of decoding operation D_3 is to be accurately computed.

Consider the case of an (n, k) MDS code that has caused the generation of a retransmission request during a decoding attempt by a decoder with effective diameter d_e. If the probability that a code symbol transmitted over a memoryless channel has been received in error is p_e, then the expected number of errors in a received code word $\mathbf{c}$ of length n is np_e before decoding. This new p_e can be written in terms of this expected value as follows:

$$p_e = \frac{np_e}{n} = \frac{E\{\text{number of errors in } \mathbf{c}\}}{\text{length of } \mathbf{c}} \tag{10}$$

The expected value can also be computed by weighting the number of errors e by the sum of the probabilities of the error patterns of weight e and then summing over all possible values of e.

$$E\{\text{number of errors in } \mathbf{c}\} = \sum_{e=0}^{n} e\left[\binom{n}{e} p_e^e (1 - p_e)^{n-e}\right] \tag{11}$$

If it is assumed that the received code word $\mathbf{c}$ has caused the generation of a retransmission request, then $\mathbf{c}$ cannot have fallen within the decoding spheres of effective diameter d_e surrounding the correct and incorrect code words. Let Ω_0 be the summation of all terms in the above expression corresponding to error patterns that are contained within the decoding sphere surrounding the all-zero code word, i.e.,

$$\Omega_0 = \sum_{v=0}^{\lfloor \frac{d_e}{2} \rfloor} \sum_{w=0}^{d_e - 2v} v \binom{n}{v} \binom{n - v}{w} (1 - p_e - p_s)^{n-v-w} p_e^v p_s^w. \tag{12}$$

Let Ω_1 be the summation of all terms in the above expression corresponding to error patterns that are contained within the decoding spheres surrounding nonzero code words. For code words of weight j define $\Omega_1(j)$ as

$$\Omega_1(j) = \sum_{v=0}^{\lfloor \frac{d_e}{2} \rfloor} \sum_{w=0}^{d_e-2v} \sum_{x=0}^{\lfloor \frac{d_e-2v-w}{2} \rfloor} \sum_{y=0}^{d_e-2v-w-2x} \sum_{z=0}^{\lfloor \frac{d_e-2v-w-2x-y}{2} \rfloor} (j+v-y-z)\binom{n-j}{v}$$

$$\binom{n-j-v}{w}\binom{j}{x}\binom{j-x}{y}\binom{j-x-y}{z}(2^m-2)^x(2^m-1)^{y+z-j}$$

$$p_e^{j+v-y-z}p_s^{w+y}(1-p_e-p_s)^{n+z-j-v-w}.$$

(13)

The number of code words of weight j is known (Property 5), so Ω_1 can be computed as follows:

$$\Omega_1 = \sum_{j=d_{\min}}^{n} A_j \Omega_1(j) \tag{14}$$

By removing the terms in Ω_0 and Ω_1 from the right hand side of equation (11) and dividing the result by the probability of retransmission, the probability of symbol error within **c** given that **c** has caused the generation of a retransmission request can be obtained as

$$P(\text{code symbol error} \mid \text{request}) = p'_e = \frac{1}{nP_R}(np_e - \Omega_0 - \Omega_1) \tag{15}$$

The value of P_R in the above expression is the probability of retransmission for the code word for its initial decoding attempt.

A similar result is obtained for the probability of symbol erasure given that a retransmission request has been generated. The above expressions are slightly modified to yield the following:

$$\Psi_0 = \sum_{v=0}^{\lfloor \frac{d_e}{2} \rfloor} \sum_{w=0}^{d_e-2v} w\binom{n}{v}\binom{n-v}{w}(1-p_e-p_s)^{n-v-w}p_e^v p_s^w \tag{16}$$

$$\Psi_1(j) = \sum_{v=0}^{\lfloor \frac{d_e}{2} \rfloor} \sum_{w=0}^{d_e-2v} \sum_{x=0}^{\lfloor \frac{d_e-2v-w}{2} \rfloor} \sum_{y=0}^{d_e-2v-w-2x} \sum_{z=0}^{\lfloor \frac{d_e-2v-w-2x-y}{2} \rfloor}$$

$$(w+y)\binom{n-j}{v}\binom{n-j-v}{w}$$

(17)

$$\binom{j}{x}\binom{j-x}{y}\binom{j-x-y}{z}(2^m-2)^x(2^m-1)^{y+z-j}$$

$$p_e^{j+v-y-z}p_s^{w+y}(1-p_e-p_s)^{n+z-j-v-w}$$

$$\Psi_1 = \sum_{j=d_{min}}^{n} A_j \Psi_1(j) \tag{18}$$

$$P(\text{code symbol erasure} \mid \text{request}) = p'_s = \frac{1}{n P_R} (n p_s - \Psi_0 - \Psi_1). \tag{19}$$

Figure 7-5 indicates the necessity of the preceding analysis. It is assumed that a (32,12) Reed-Solomon code has been decomposed into a pair of (16,12) punctured Reed-Solomon codes. The initial decoding operation (D_1 or D_2) has an effective diameter of $d_e = 4$, and the combined operation uses $d_e = 20$. The 32-ary symbols are transmitted in bit-serial form using a coherent BPSK modem over a Rayleigh fading channel with background AWGN. Erasures are generated using channel side information with an erasure threshold of $\lambda_s = 0.1$ (assuming unity energy signaling) [6,20]. Figure 7-5 clearly shows that the probability of symbol error in code words that are known to have caused the generation of a retransmission request (p'_e) is substantially higher than that for newly arrived code words (p_e).

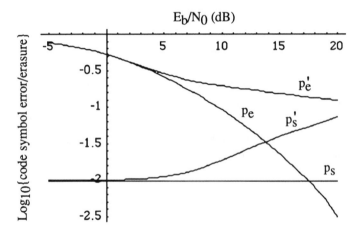

Figure 7-5. Probability of symbol error and erasure in code words that have caused the generation of retransmission requests.

This preceding analysis can be carried through one additional step to account for code words that have caused the generation of retransmission requests in decoding operation D_3 as well. The additional increase in the probability of error is small compared to the initial increase indicated by the retransmission request generated during the first decoding attempt. Therefore, the reliability and throughput calculations are tight upper and lower bounds, respectively. As will be shown in Section 6, the additional computational complexity is thus not warranted in most cases.

All of the necessary probabilities are now available for the characterization of the performance of the MDS type II hybrid-ARQ protocol. The probabilities of symbol error and erasure from Figure 7-4 (first attempt to decode) and equations (15) and (19) (second and subsequent attempts to decode) are used in equations (8) and (9) to determine the performance of the individual type I hybrid-ARQ protocols. These performance parameters are then used in equations (3) and (4) to determine the overall performance of the composite type II protocol.

6 EXAMPLES

In this section several examples of the proposed protocol are examined. Additionally, the qualitative effects of the decoding sphere sizes are considered. This section concludes with consideration of a modification of the proposed protocol that reduces the complexity of the decoder. In the following examples code symbols are transmitted in bit-serial form using a coherent BPSK modem over a code symbol interleaved Rayleigh fading channel with background AWGN. Erasures are generated using channel amplitude side information [6,20].

In the first set of performance curves (Figures 7-6 and 7-7), a (16,4) MDS code (code C_3) is decomposed into a pair of (8,4) punctured MDS codes (codes C_1 and C_2). The original (16,4) code and the punctured codes form a type II HARQ protocol using the methods discussed in previous sections of this chapter. Decoding operations D_1 and D_2 both have an effective diameter of $d_e = 2$, while D_3 has an effective diameter of $d_e = 12$. The performance of a type I protocol ($d_e = 2$) based solely on one of the punctured (8,4) codes has been included for reference. Figure 7-6 clearly shows that the type II protocol offers substantially better throughput performance at lower signal-to-noise ratios. On a nonstationary channel, the type II protocol thus offers more graceful throughput degradation as the channel deteriorates. Figure 7-7 shows an improvement in reliability performance at low signal-to-noise ratios. This is a direct result of the reduction in the number of transmission attempts per code word in the type II protocol [see the denominator in equation (4)].

In the next example a (64,24) MDS code (code C_3) is decomposed into a pair of (32,24) punctured codes (codes C_1 and C_2). Decoding operation D_3 has an effective diameter of $d_e = 38$, while operations D_1 and D_2 have effective diameters $d_e = 6$. The throughput data in Figure 7-8 indicate that the type II protocol is still substantially better than the performance provided by the comparable type I protocol. Also, as shown in Figure 7-9, the reliability of the type II system is substantially better at low SNR's.

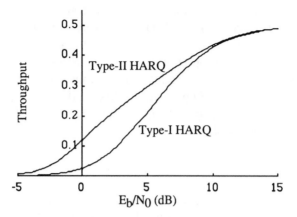

Figure 7-6. Throughput performance for (8,4)/(8,4) MDS type II HARQ protocol compared to (8,4) MDS type I HARQ protocol.

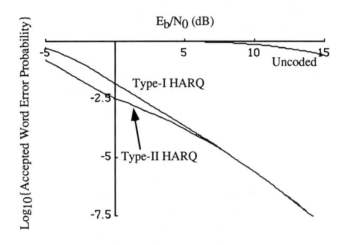

Figure 7-7. Reliability performance for (8,4)/(8,4) MDS type II HARQ protocol compared to (8,4) MDS type I HARQ protocol.

The effective diameter of the combined and single code affect both the reliability and throughput of the type II system. A lower d_e reduces the size of the decoding spheres for the punctured codes. For a type I system this reduction increases the reliability and decreases throughput. The effective diameter for decoding operation D_3, d_{e3}, shows the same tendency. The optimal setting for d_e and d_{e3} is obviously a tradeoff between reliability and throughput. For maximum throughput, the decoding diameters should be as large as possible. Consider the throughput and reliability of the (8,4) system

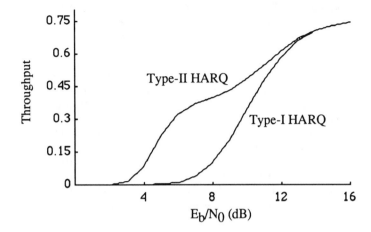

Figure 7-8. Throughput performance for (32,24)/(32,24) MDS type II HARQ protocol compared to (32,24) type I HARQ protocol.

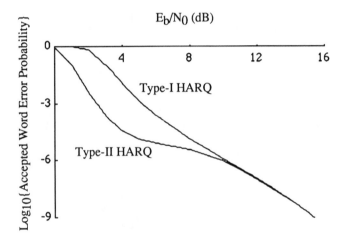

Figure 7-9. Reliability performance for (32,24)/(32,24) MDS type II HARQ protocol compared to (32,24) type I HARQ protocol.

in figures 7-6 and 7-7. The reliability and throughput at SNR of 0 dB are summarized in Table 2. The first number in each entry is the throughput, while the second is the log of the accepted word error rate. The tradeoff between reliability and throughput is very clear.

Finally, the implications of a slight modification to the proposed protocol is considered. After a retransmission, let the newly received code word be combined directly with the previously determined unreliable code word. This step reduces the overall processing time of the decoder. The direct-

TABLE 2 Performance Comparison of the (8,4) MDS Code for Various Decoding Sphere Sizes

	$d_e = 0$	$d_e = 2$	$d_e = 4$
$d_{e3} = 4$	0.0053/−3.35	0.028/−1.83	0.126/−0.62
$d_{e3} = 5$	0.0057/−3.39	0.028/−1.83	0.126/−0.62
$d_{e3} = 6$	0.0126/−3.73	0.033/−1.89	0.127/−0.63
$d_{e3} = 7$	0.0142/−3.78	0.034/−1.91	0.128/−0.63
$d_{e3} = 8$	0.032/−4.14	0.047/−2.05	0.132/−0.65
$d_{e3} = 9$	0.036/−4.18	0.05/−2.08	0.134/−0.65
$d_{e3} = 10$	0.0697/−4.38	0.077/−2.27	0.145/−0.69
$d_{e3} = 11$	0.076/−4.25	0.082/−2.3	0.148/−0.69
$d_{e3} = 12$	0.119/−3.69	0.12/−2.44	0.168/−0.75

combination system is described by the generic graph and branch label table shown in Figure 7-10 and Table 3, respectively. The generic transfer function is as follows:

$$IT = \left\{ ac + ab \left(d + \frac{eg}{1 - ef} \right) \right\} CA. \tag{20}$$

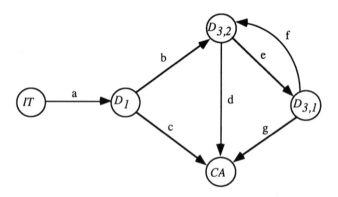

Figure 7-10. Generic graph for the direct-combination type II hybrid-ARQ protocol.

The reliability function is easily determined as

$$P(E) = P_E^{(1)} + \frac{P_E^{(3)} P_R^{(1)}}{1 - P_R^{(3)}},$$

and the throughput is

$$\eta = \frac{k \left(1 - P_R^{(3)^2} \right)}{n_1 + n_2 P_R^{(1)} + n_1 P_R^{(1)} P_R^{(3)} - n_1 P_R^{(3)^2}}.$$

TABLE 3   Graph Labels for the Derivation of Throughput and Reliability Generating Functions for the Direct Combination Extension

Branch Label	Throughput Label	Reliability Label
a	T^{n_1}	1
b	$p_R^{(1)} \cdot T^{n_2}$	$p_R^{(1)}$
c	$1 - p_R^{(1)}$	$p_E^{(1)}$
d	$1 - p_R^{(3)}$	$p_E^{(3)}$
e	$p_R^{(3)} \cdot T^{n_1}$	$p_R^{(3)}$
f	$p_R^{(3)} \cdot T^{n_2}$	$p_R^{(3)}$
g	$1 - p_R^{(3)}$	$p_E^{(3)}$

The *a posteriori* or modified BER for the combined decoding operation must be averaged to account for the additional errors in the unreliable code word and the raw channel BER from the new code word.

For the (8,4) MDS code considered above, the direct-combination approach reduces the decoder processing complexity and results in a slight throughput performance improvement. These results are shown in Figure 7-11. The direct-combination approach is possible because of the excellent incremental redundancy available in MDS codes. The direct-combination approach justifies the assumption in Section 5.2 that the modified BER for the combined decoding operation does not differ significantly from the modified BER after a single decoding operation.

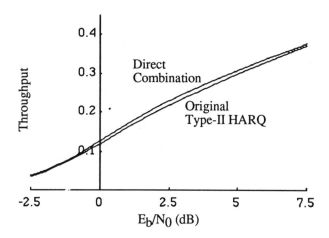

Figure 7-11. Comparison of the type II protocol and the direct-combination extension for the (8,4) code.

7 CONCLUSION AND COMMENTS

MDS codes have been shown to exhibit a series of properties that make them well suited for use in type II hybrid-ARQ protocols. Strong separability and strong invertibility allow for the use of a decomposition process through which an (n, k) MDS code is used to create a pair of punctured $(n/2, k)$ MDS codes. The original code and the two derived codes are used individually in type I hybrid-ARQ protocols. Together the three type I protocols create a type II protocol whose throughput and reliability performance is superior to that of any of the individual protocols.

The MDS decomposition process can be extended to develop more powerful code combining schemes. For example, a (64,4) MDS code can be decomposed into eight (8,4) codes to create a code-combining system with eight different code rates similar to the variable rate systems developed by Pursley and Sandberg [16]. Such a system will offer better performance than a type II HARQ protocol in applications in which the channel varies slowly over a wide range of ambient noise levels.

APPENDIX: PERFORMANCE BOUNDS ON THE TYPE II SYSTEM

Unfortunately, the complexity of equation (7) increases with the fifth power of the effective diameter of the decoding operation. The computation of equation (7) [as used in equation (8)] thus begins to become a problem for the combined decoding operation D_3 for code lengths of 32 or more. If sufficient computing resources are not available, the following analysis can be used to obtain bounds on the performance of the type II system.

Consider an (n, k) MDS code and a corresponding decoder with effective diameter d_e. A decoding error will occur if the received word is within the decoding sphere of diameter d_e surrounding an incorrect code word. The closest such code word is Hamming distance d_{min} away (the code is assumed to be linear). There must thus be a minimum of $(d_{min} - \lfloor d_e/2 \rfloor)$ symbol errors in the received word for a decoder error to occur. If erasure decoding is available, a decoder error can occur only if, in addition to the above, the number of erasures is not greater than the effective decoding diameter d_e (otherwise a retransmission request will be generated). An upper bound is obtained by treating this pair of required events as if they were independent.

$$P_E \leq \begin{cases} 1 - \sum_{v=0}^{d_{\min}-\lfloor \frac{d_e}{2} \rfloor} \binom{n}{v} p_e^v (1 - p_e)^{n-v} \\ \qquad\qquad\qquad\qquad\qquad\qquad \text{nonerasure decoding} \\[2ex] \left\{ 1 - \sum_{v=0}^{d_{\min}-\lfloor \frac{d_e}{2} \rfloor} \binom{n}{v} p_e^v (1 - p_e)^{n-v} \right\} \cdot \left\{ \sum_{w=0}^{d_e} \binom{n}{w} p_s^w (1 - p_s)^{n-w} \right\} \\ \qquad\qquad\qquad\qquad\qquad\qquad\qquad\quad \text{erasure decoding} \end{cases}$$

$$\tag{21}$$

The probability of retransmission is upper-bounded by the probability that $(2e + s) > d_e$.

$$P_R \leq \begin{cases} 1 - \sum_{v=0}^{\lfloor \frac{d_e}{2} \rfloor} \binom{n}{v} p_e^v (1 - p_e)^{n-v} \\ \qquad\qquad\qquad\qquad\qquad \text{nonerasure decoding} \\[2ex] 1 - \sum_{v=0}^{\lfloor \frac{d_e}{2} \rfloor} \sum_{w=0}^{d_e-2v} \binom{n}{v}\binom{n-v}{w}(1 - p_e - p_s)^{n-v-w} p_e^v p_s^w \\ \qquad\qquad\qquad\qquad\qquad\quad \text{erasure decoding} \end{cases} \tag{22}$$

The probabilities of symbol error and erasure in the above expressions (p_e and p_s, respectively) are obtained from either Figure 7-4 (first attempt to decode) or equations (15) and (19) (second and subsequent attempts to decode). If the code length is such that equations (15) and (19) require unreasonable computation times, then the following approximations can be used.

$$P(\text{code symbol error} \mid \text{request}) = p_e' \approx \frac{1}{n P_R}(n p_e - \Omega_0) \tag{23}$$

$$P(\text{code symbol erasure} \mid \text{request}) = p_s') \approx \frac{1}{n P_R}(n p_s - \Psi_0) \tag{24}$$

where Ω_0 and Ψ_0 are as in equations (12) and (16).

REFERENCES

[1] E. Berlekamp, *Algebraic Coding Theory* (rev. ed.), Laguna Hills, Calif.: Aegean Park Press, 1984.

[2] E. Berlekamp, R. Peile, and S. Pope, "The Application of Error Control to Communications," *IEEE Communications Magazine*, Volume 25, pp. 44–57, April 1987.

[3] D. Chase, "Code Combining—A Maximum-Likelihood Decoding Approach for Combining an Arbitrary Number of Noisy Packets," *IEEE Transactions on Communications*, Volume COM-33, Number 5, pp. 385–393, May 1985.

[4] G. C. Clark, Jr., and J. B. Cain, *Error-Correction Coding for Digital Communications*, New York: Plenum Press, 1981.

[5] J. Du, M. Kasahara, and T. Namekawa, "Separable Codes on Type-II Hybrid-ARQ Systems," *IEEE Transactions on Communications*, Volume COM-36, Number 10, pp. 1089–1097, October 1988.

[6] J. Hagenauer and E. Lutz, "Forward Error Correction Coding for Fading Compensation in Mobile Satellite Channels," *IEEE Journal on Selected Areas in Communications*, Volume SAC-5, Number 2, pp. 215–225, February 1987.

[7] T. Kasami and S. Lin, "On the Probability of Undetected Error for the Maximum Distance Separable Codes," *IEEE Transactions on Communications*, Volume COM-32, Number 9, pp. 998–1006, September 1984.

[8] S. Lin and D. J. Costello, Jr., *Error Control Coding: Fundamentals and Applications*, Englewood Cliffs, N.J.: Prentice-Hall, 1983.

[9] S. Lin, D. J. Costello, Jr., and M. J. Miller, "Automatic-Repeat-Request Error Control Schemes," *IEEE Communications Magazine*, Volume 22, pp. 5–17, December 1984.

[10] S. Lin and P. S. Yu, "A Hybrid-ARQ Scheme with Parity Retransmission for Error Control of Satellite Channels," *IEEE Transactions on Communications*, Volume COM-30, Number 7, pp. 1701–1719, July 1982.

[11] D. L. Lu and J. F. Chang, "Analysis of ARQ Protocols via Signal Flow Graphs," *IEEE Transactions on Communications*, Volume COM-37, Number 3, pp. 245–251, March 1989.

[12] F. J. MacWilliams and N. J. A. Sloane, *The Theory of Error-Correcting Codes*, New York: North-Holland, 1977.

[13] D. M. Mandelbaum, "An Adaptive Feedback Coding Scheme Using Incremental Redundancy," *IEEE Transactions on Information Theory*, Volume 20, pp. 388–389, May 1974.

[14] D. M. Mandelbaum, "On Forward Error Correction with Adaptive Decoding," *IEEE Transactions on Information Theory*, Volume 21, pp. 230–233, March 1975.

[15] M. B. Pursley and S. D. Sandberg, "Variable-Rate Coding for Meteor-Burst Communications," *IEEE Transactions on Communications*, Volume 37, Number 11, pp. 1105–1112, November 1989.

[16] M. B. Pursley and S. D. Sandberg, "Incremental-Redundancy Transmission for Meteor-Burst Communications," *IEEE Transactions on Communications*, Volume COM-39, Number 3, pp. 689–702, May 1991.

[17] R. C. Singleton, "Maximum Distance q^n-ary Codes," *IEEE Transactions on Information Theory*, Volume IT-10, pp. 116–118, 1964.

[18] Y. Wang and S. Lin, "A Modified Selective-Repeat Type-II Hybrid-ARQ System and Its Performance Analysis," *IEEE Transactions on Communications*, Volume COM-31, Number 5, pp. 593–607, May 1983.

[19] S. B. Wicker, "High Reliability Data Transfer over the Land Mobile Radio Channel Using Interleaved Hybrid-ARQ Error Control," *IEEE Transactions on Vehicular Technology*, Volume 39, Number 1, pp. 48–55, February 1990.

[20] S. B. Wicker, "Reed-Solomon Error Control Coding for Slowly Fading Channels with Feedback," *IEEE Transactions on Vehicular Technology*, Volume 41, Number 2, pp. 124–133, May 1992.

Reed-Solomon Codes in Frequency-Hop Communications[1]

Michael B. Pursley
Department of Electrical and Computer Engineering
Clemson University
102 Riggs Hall, Box 340915
Clemson, South Carolina 29634-0915

1 INTRODUCTION

There are many applications of Reed-Solomon codes in which it is highly desirable to obtain information concerning the reliability of the received symbols. This information, which we refer to as side information, can be provided by sources outside the communications receiver in some situations, but for most systems it is obtained as part of the demodulation and decoding processes in the receiver. Examples of the latter are the results of demodulating special symbols that have been inserted in the message or the results of decoding an inner code in a concatenated coding system.

The focus in this chapter is on low-complexity methods for the use and generation of side information. The methods described in Section 3 can be employed in existing communication receivers. Because these methods require only the usual hard-decision output from the demodulator, no modifications to the demodulator are necessary. Consideration is given to more complex techniques that use soft-decision demodulation, but because of the desire for low complexity and applicability to existing systems, full soft-decision decoding

[1] Funding for the research described in this chapter was provided by the Army Research Office under grant DAAH04-93-G-0253 to Clemson University and contract DAAL03-92-C-0018 to Techno-Sciences, Inc.

is not considered in this chapter. Rather, the emphasis here is on single-pass errors-and-erasures decoding of Reed-Solomon codes, although some use is made of parallel errors-and-erasures decoding with two decoders.

The motivation for the methods described in this chapter is that side information can be used to erase some of the unreliable symbols and therefore enhance the error control capability of the Reed-Solomon coding system. Even if the side information is imperfect, it can be used in many systems to provide much lower error probabilities than obtainable with errors-only decoding. Most of the chapter is devoted to slow-frequency-hop spread-spectrum transmission, and this is envisioned as the primary application of the methods that are described. The formulation in Section 2 is more general, however, and it applies to many types of systems that use diversity transmission. Diversity transmission is a common method for combating fading or intermittent interference, and it can be used to compensate for lost packets in a packet radio network. The use of Reed-Solomon codes permits greater efficiency in a diversity transmission system than the more customary simple repetition of the message or packet.

For slow-frequency-hop radios that must communicate in the presence of partial-band interference (e.g., multiple-access interference, jamming, or narrowband interference), the situation is complicated by the fact that interference that is not detected by the side information produces statistically dependent errors within the packet, and interference that is detected by the side information produces dependent erasures within the packet. The analysis described in Section 2 accounts for this statistical dependence, and it also accounts for the fact that the side information is not perfect.

2 EVALUATION OF PACKET ERROR PROBABILITIES

The models employed for the packet format and the channel in this section are general enough that the basic results obtained here are valid for a wide range of applications of Reed-Solomon codes. These basic results are specialized to slow-frequency-hop communications in the next section. A key feature of the packet formats that are considered in this paper is the important role played by the *segments*. A segment is a particular subset of the symbols contained in a packet, and each symbol of the packet is in one and only one segment. Segments are constructed in such a way that no segment has more than one symbol from a given code word.

2.1 Models for the Interference and Noise

The input to the demodulator consists of the *desired signal*, which is a delayed, attenuated version of the transmitted signal, plus two forms of channel disturbance, which are referred to as *interference* and *wideband noise*. The wideband noise is additive, and it is present during the transmission of all of the segments. It is assumed to be a stationary random process that is independent from one symbol period to the next. The most common example of wideband noise is thermal noise. The power density for the wideband noise is typically much less than the symbol energy for the desired signal.

The interference, on the other hand, is not necessarily additive, and in general not all segments are subjected to the interference. The interference is modeled as block interference [16] with a burst length that is not larger than the segment duration. Each interference burst is contained completely within a single segment. When present in a segment, this interference is generally much more disruptive than the wideband noise.

Of particular interest in this section is *catastrophic* block interference, by which we mean interference that, when present in a particular segment, produces an unacceptably high error probability at the output of the demodulator for some or all of the symbols in that segment. Catastrophic interference may be due to a strong interfering signal, a deep fade suffered by the desired signal, or a large increase in the noise power. We also use the term "catastrophic interference" for segments that are lost (i.e., not delivered to the receiver), such as when a packet is dropped in a computer communication network. The approach of the receiver is to ignore those demodulated symbols that are known to have been corrupted by catastrophic interference. For systems with Reed-Solomon codes, this means that erasures are inserted in the positions of these symbols.

It is helpful to introduce two examples that illustrate the kinds of applications that are appropriate and the ways in which block interference arises in these applications. The packet formats for these two examples are described in more detail in subsequent sections.

Example 1. Consider frequency-hop packet transmission with one segment per dwell interval of the frequency hopper. Assume the interference is partial-band interference. Over the duration of the packet, the signal occupies various frequency slots, some of which have interference and wideband noise, while others have wideband noise only. The interference may be band-limited noise that occupies a fixed portion of the RF band [25], or its frequency occupancy may change with time, such as with frequency-hop multiple-access interference [18]. In either case, interference is present during portions of some dwell intervals, but it is totally absent in others. A similar situation results from multiple-access interference in a time-hopping system or pulsed interference in most types of communication systems [17]. Of primary interest in this section is the situation in which the power of the interference, when present in a dwell interval, is sufficiently large compared to the signal power that it is characterized as catastrophic interference. Generally, this is the case as long as the instantaneous power of the interference is not much less than that of the desired signal, such as for multiple-access interference in a network with all signals of nearly equal power [11]. However, the model also includes situations in which the instantaneous power of the interference is much greater than the desired signal, which is true for strong partial-band jamming.

Example 2.   Consider a slotted packet radio network with N_m mini-packets per packet. Time is slotted into mini-slots of duration equal to the time required to transmit a mini-packet. The mini-packets that make up a given packet are sent via different routes from the source to the destination, and the packet is reconstructed from the mini-packets at the destination. In this example, the interference may be due to mini-packet collisions, or it may represent lost or excessively delayed mini-packets. Clearly, these all represent catastrophic interference as defined above. The latter is also an example in which the interference is not additive.

Returning to the general model, we introduce some terminology that facilitates the subsequent presentation. If interference is present for any fraction of the time interval in which a given segment is transmitted, that entire interval is referred to as an *interference interval*, and the corresponding segment as a *corrupted segment*. The symbol error probability in a corrupted segment is very large. This is true for additive interference if the amount of interference power in an interference interval ranges from slightly less to much greater than the power in the desired signal.

The results presented in this section are based on the assumption that all of the code symbols in a corrupted segment are received in error or perhaps not received at all. This assumption leads to an upper bound on the packet error probability, and it provides analytical results that are applicable to a wide range of channels with catastrophic block interference and wideband noise. In addition, this gives a good approximation in many situations. For example, in certain multiple-access systems that employ M-ary orthogonal signaling, interference from a signal that is much stronger than the desired signal gives a symbol error probability of approximately $(M - 1)/M$ if the wideband noise is negligible in comparison to the interference signal. For large values of M, the approximation $(M - 1)/M \approx 1$ gives sufficient accuracy in the evaluation of the performance of the error-correcting code.

For specific systems, a precise evaluation of the error probabilities for symbols in a corrupted segment can be incorporated into the analysis. For example, if the symbol errors within a corrupted segment are independent, the analysis is a straightforward extension of the results of this section (see

Section 3). But in many examples these errors are not independent [8,12,13], and to incorporate the methods required in such examples would unduly limit the applicability of the results of the present section. Moreover, a precise, tractable mathematical model for the interference is necessary for an exact evaluation of the error probabilities for symbols in a corrupted segment, but for many practical applications such a model is not available. Even in the simple multiple-access example cited above, the analysis is very tedious if the number of interference signals is larger than two or three, especially if the signals have unequal power.

If there is more than one symbol per segment, the analysis is complicated by the statistical dependence between symbol errors within a segment. Block interference produces errors at the demodulator output that are strongly statistically dependent within the segments, but the effects of the wideband interference on the demodulation of different symbols are statistically independent. It is necessary that the analysis handle any combination of both types of interference. A method for dealing with this problem is given below.

2.2 Packet Format

Each packet is divided into N equal-length segments, and each segment consists of L symbols from a given alphabet of size M. Assume that an (n, k) Reed-Solomon code is used and that N is a multiple of n. If a packet consists of multiple code words, it is desirable to interleave the code symbols to some degree. With full interleaving of code symbols, no two code symbols from a given code word are transmitted in the same segment. One frame of a packet is illustrated in Figure 8-1. There are L code words in each frame and $J = N/n$ frames in each packet. Thus, there are Ln code symbols per frame and JLn code symbols per packet. Each packet contains $JLk \log_2(M)$ bits of information. The symbol labeled i-j in Figure 8-1 is the jth symbol of the ith code word of the frame that is illustrated.

In Example 1 of Section 2, the value of L, the number of symbols per segment, is constrained to be the ratio of the length of the dwell interval to the duration of the symbol. If full interleaving is employed, L is also the number of code words per frame, so in order to have more than L code words per packet, it is necessary to have multiple frames per packet.

For Example 2 of Section 2, it is not necessary to have more than one frame per packet. The length of the mini-packet can be large enough to provide for the required number of bits per packet. Each segment is a mini-packet in Example 2, and the ith mini-packet consists of the ith symbol of each of the L code words.

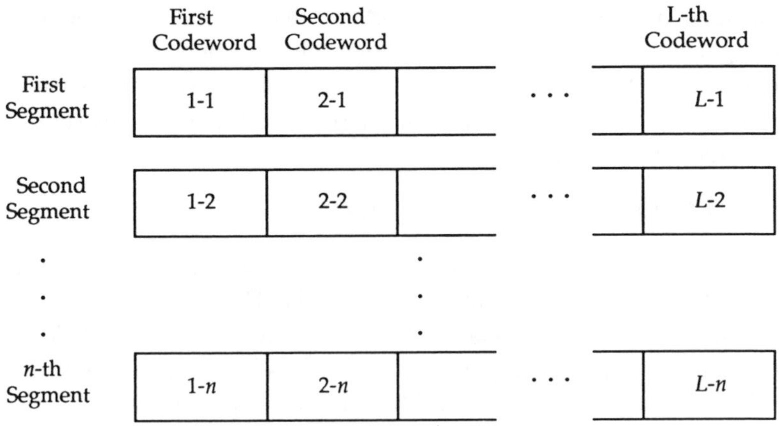

Figure 8-1. One frame of a packet.

2.3 Side Information for Segments

Side information is available in the receiver to indicate which of the segments are corrupted, but this side information may not be completely accurate. For each segment in the packet, the side information takes the form of a single binary decision which indicates that interference is present or absent in that segment. For the method considered in this section, erasures are made for entire segments. If the side information indicates interference is present in a certain segment, all of the symbols from that segment are declared unreliable and they are erased. For each such symbol, the demodulator output is ignored, and an erasure symbol is passed on to the decoder. If the side information indicates the absence of interference in a segment, all symbols in that segment are judged to be reliable, and the corresponding outputs of the hard-decision demodulator are passed on to the decoder.

For each code word in the transmitted packet, a corresponding *received word* is formed at the demodulator output. Each received word consists of a combination of incorrect symbols, correct symbols, and erasures. Correct decoding of a received word occurs if the numbers of errors and erasures in the received word are within the correction capability of the code; otherwise, the decoder produces an incorrect code word (decoding error) or it will fail to produce a code word at all (decoding failure).

Full interleaving ensures that the errors and erasures within a code word are independent. But, because of the statistical dependence between symbol errors and erasures within a segment, the decoding errors and failures in different code words within a frame are not independent. Although this complicates the analysis, it is not something that one should strive to avoid. By using a suitable packet format together with an appropriate error control coding scheme, the dependence can be exploited to give a better packet error probability than is obtained from interference that produces statistically independent errors [19].

2.4 The Frame Error Probability

A transmitted frame consists of L code words, and the received frame consists of the L corresponding received words. The frame is correct if each of the L received words is decoded into the correct code word. The derivation of the frame error probability is given in [19] and [21]. The results are best described as a sequence of probabilities, and these probabilities are given in terms of the false alarm probability α, the detection probability β, and the quiescent probability of error p.

In this section, the goal of the side information is to identify the segments that are corrupted, and all symbols in a segment that is identified as corrupted are erased. A segment that is corrupted and is identified by the side information as such is said to be *detected*. A corrupted segment that is not identified as such by the side information is said to be a *miss*. The detection probability is the probability that a corrupted segment is detected, and its complement is the *miss probability*. A segment that is not corrupted but is identified by the side information as being corrupted is said to be a *false alarm*. The quiescent probability of error is the probability of error for symbols that are not in corrupted segments.

A symbol that is in a corrupted segment is said to be *hit*. Thus, β is the probability that a hit is detected and erased, α is the probability that a symbol that is not hit is erased, and p is the probability of error for a symbol that is neither hit nor erased.

The probability that the frame is correct is given in terms of $P(j)$, the probability that there are j hits in the frame. This probability depends on the particular application, but the only requirement for the results presented here is that the process by which the hits are generated must be stationary. If $P(j)$ denotes the probability of j hits in a sequence of n segments, the probability that the frame is correct is

$$P_C = \sum_{j=0}^{n} P(j) P_3(j) \tag{1}$$

where $P_3(j)$ is the conditional probability that the frame is correct given that there are j hits in the n segments. The frame error probability is $P_E = 1 - P_C$.

An (n, k) Reed-Solomon code can correct at most $r = n - k$ erasures and even fewer errors. Under the assumption that hits that are not erased result in errors, $P_3(j) = 0$ for $j > r$. For $j \le r$,

$$P_3(j) = \sum_{i=i'}^{j} \binom{j}{i} \beta^i (1 - \beta)^{j-i} P_2(i; j) \tag{2}$$

where $i' = \max\{0, 2j - r\}$. The probability $P_2(i; j)$ is the probability that the frame is correct given that there are j hits and i of them are erased. The lower limit $i' = \max\{0, 2j - r\}$ in (2) is a consequence of the fact that among the code symbols, each unerased hit is assumed to result in an error. For an (n, k) Reed-Solomon code, correct decoding requires that $i + 2(j - i)$ not exceed r, which is equivalent to $i \ge 2j - r$. It follows that $P_2(i; j) = 0$ for $i < i'$ if all unerased hits result in errors. The conditional probability that the frame is correct given j hits and given that i of these are detected is

$$P_2(i; j) = \sum_{s=0}^{s^*} \binom{n-i}{s} \alpha^s (1 - \alpha)^{n-j-s} \{P_1(s; i, j)\}^L, \tag{3}$$

where $P_1(s; i, j)$ is the conditional probability that a particular received word is decoded correctly given that there are j hits, i detected hits, and s false alarms. The limit s^* is selected to ensure the errors-and-erasures correcting capability of the code is not exceeded. For an (n, k) Reed-Solomon code with redundancy $r = n - k$, this limit is $s^* = r - 2j + i$. For $s \ge s^*$, $P_1(s; i, j) = 0$.

If the integer L is set equal to 1, the expression in (3) reduces to the conditional probability that a particular received word is correctly decoded given there are j hits, i of which are detected (for $L = 1$ there is only one code word per frame). For convenience, the probability that a particular received word is not decoded correctly is often referred to as the code word error probability. Comparisons of code word error probabilities are useful in situations for which it is difficult to compute the frame error probability.

Finally, the probability $P_1(s; i, j)$ is given by

$$P_1(s; i, j) = \sum_{t=0}^{t^*} \binom{n-j-s}{t} p^t (1 - p)^{n-j-s-t}. \tag{4}$$

The upper limit of the sum in (4) is $t^* = \lfloor (r - i - s)/2 \rfloor - j$, where $\lfloor x \rfloor$ denotes the integer part of the real number x. The integer t^* is the maximum number of errors that the code can correct if there are j hits, i detected hits, and s false alarms among the n symbols.

For an application in which the hits are independent and identically distributed from one segment to the next and the probability of a hit in a particular segment is $\mathcal{P}$, the probability of a particular pattern of j hits in a sequence of n segments is $\mathcal{P}^j (1 - \mathcal{P})^{n-j}$, and (1) becomes

$$P_C = \sum_{j=0}^{r} \binom{n}{j} \mathcal{P}^j (1 - \mathcal{P})^{n-j} P_3 (j). \tag{5}$$

2.5 Packet Error Probability

For systems with more than one frame per packet, the calculation of the packet error probability depends on the specific application. For some applications, the errors from frame to frame can be considered to be independent, and the error probability for a packet with J frames is

$$P_{E,p} = 1 - P_C^J \tag{6}$$

In other applications, the errors in different frames of the same packet are highly dependent because of the nature of the interference.

Wideband noise is independent from frame to frame in the packet, but block interference is not. For certain types of block interference, however, errors in different frames are *conditionally* independent given the level of the interference. For example, in a slotted frequency-hop multiple-access packet radio system with *synchronous* frequency hopping, errors due to the multiple-access interference are conditionally independent given the number of simultaneous transmissions in a given packet interval. This approach permits evaluation of the conditional probability of packet error using (6) with the probabilities interpreted as conditional probabilities, and then we can average out the conditioning as the last step.

2.6 Numerical Results

One of our goals of this section is to determine the ranges of values of the false alarm and miss probabilities that are required to provide satisfactory performance. Although the best performance is obtained if the false alarm and miss probabilities are as small as possible, there is a tradeoff between the performance and the cost. An efficient system may have false alarm and miss probabilities in the range 0.01 to 0.05, or perhaps even larger for some applications.

The numerical results presented in this section are for systems with one frame per packet ($J = 1$). In Figures 8-2 through 8-6 the packet error probability is shown as a function of the false alarm and miss probabilities for different values of the quiescent error probability p and hit probability $\mathcal{P}$. In Figures 8-2 through 8-4, the packet error probability for a system with no side information corresponds to $\alpha = 0$ and $1 - \beta = 1$ ($\beta = 0$). It is clear from these three curves that even imperfect side information provides a substantial reduction in packet error probability as compared to no side information at all. In some cases (e.g., Figure 8-3 of this chapter and Figures 8-2 through 8-3 of [21]), this reduction is several orders of magnitude.

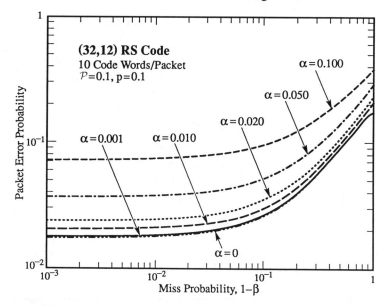

Figure 8-2. Packet error probability as a function of the miss probability for the (32,12) RS code in a system with $\mathcal{P} = 0.1$ and $p = 0.1$.

The results for perfect side information ($\alpha = 1 - \beta = 0$) can also be obtained from the limiting values of the curves in Figures 8-2 through 8-6. Packet error probabilities for systems with perfect side information are the limiting values of the $\alpha = 0$ curves as $1 - \beta \to 0$ in Figures 8-2 through 8-4 and the limiting values of the $\beta = 1$ curves as $\alpha \to 0$ in Figures 8-5 through 8-6. It can be seen from Figures 8-2 through 8-6 that the values $\alpha = 0.001$ and $\beta = 0.999$ give approximately the same packet error probability as perfect side information (i.e., $\alpha = 0$ and $\beta = 1$). Notice also that the packet error probability does not decrease very much as α or $1 - \beta$ is decreased below 0.001. Clearly, the side information does not have to be perfect in order to provide acceptable performance.

If the values for α and $1 - \beta$ are increased to 0.01, there is still not a significant degradation as compared with perfect side information. If the false alarm and miss probabilities are increased to 0.05, the degradation in packet error probability is definitely noticeable, but even these levels may be acceptable for many applications, and they certainly give far better performance than systems with no side information at all.

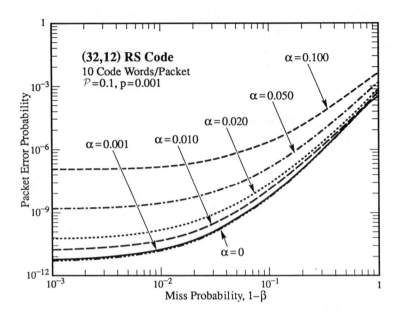

Figure 8-3. Packet error probability as a function of the miss probability for the (32,12) RS code in a system with $\mathcal{P} = 0.1$ and $p = 0.001$.

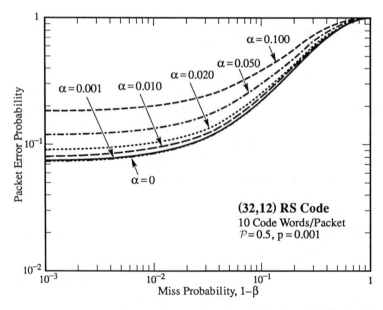

Figure 8-4. Packet error probability as a function of the miss probability for the (32,12) RS code in a system with $\mathcal{P} = 0.5$ and $p = 0.001$.

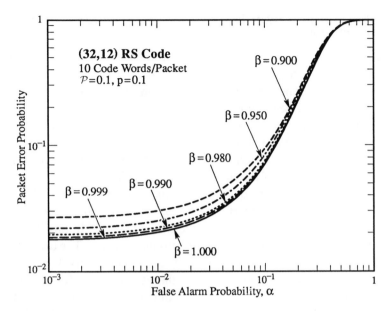

Figure 8-5. Packet error probability as a function of the false alarm probability for the (32,12) RS code in a system with $\mathcal{P} = 0.1$ and $p = 0.1$.

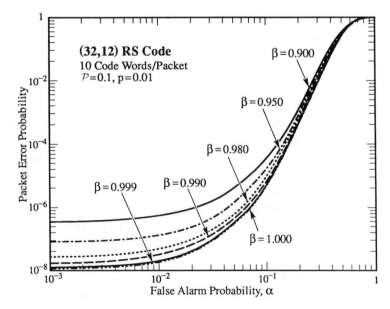

Figure 8-6. Packet error probability as a function of the false alarm probability for the (32,12) RS code in a system with $\mathcal{P} = 0.1$ and $p = 0.01$.

3 SIDE INFORMATION FROM TEST SYMBOLS FOR FREQUENCY-HOP TRANSMISSION

In Example 1, the desired signal is a slow-frequency-hop signal and the interference occupies a part of the frequency band. Two common forms of partial-band interference are frequency-hop multiple-access interference and partial-band noise. One method for obtaining side information for frequency-hop communication systems is to transmit special symbols, called *test symbols*, in each dwell interval along with the data symbols. The demodulation of the test symbols from a particular dwell interval provides information on the presence or absence of interference in that dwell interval.

The use of test symbols to obtain side information is illustrated in Figure 8-7 for a system with two interfering frequency-hop signals, each of which has the same dwell interval length as the desired signal. In this illustration, partial-band noise occupies two separate frequency bands. The desired signal is hit by another frequency-hop signal in one dwell interval, and it is hit by partial-band noise in another. Notice that it is possible for hits by other frequency-hop signals to affect only a part of the dwell interval of the desired signal, whereas the stationary partial-band noise is present during the entire dwell interval.

The transmission of a code word from a Reed-Solomon code of block length n is accomplished by including one symbol from the code word in each of n consecutive dwell intervals. Although the illustration in Figure 8-7 shows the relative locations within the dwell interval to be the same for all symbols from a given code word, some applications dictate variations in these locations from one dwell interval to the next. Regardless of the positions within the dwell intervals, the key feature is that the interleaving of the Reed-Solomon code word should be done in a way that no two symbols from a given code word are in the same dwell interval. As a result, a single hit interferes with at most one symbol from a code word.

The test symbols are denoted by the letter T in Figure 8-7. In practice there are typically several test symbols per dwell interval. Also, the test symbols need not be from the same alphabet as the code symbols. For example, it is convenient in radios that use binary modulation that the test symbols are binary and the code symbols are words formed from sets of binary symbols. This provides the nonbinary symbols necessary for Reed-Solomon codes, yet it permits a simple method for detecting the presence of hits using binary decisions on the test symbols. For example, for a system with binary frequency-shift-key (BFSK) modulation and a Reed-Solomon code with a 32-ary symbol alphabet, each symbol is formed from a sequence of five consecutive binary symbols, and it is transmitted as a sequence of five consecutive BFSK signals.

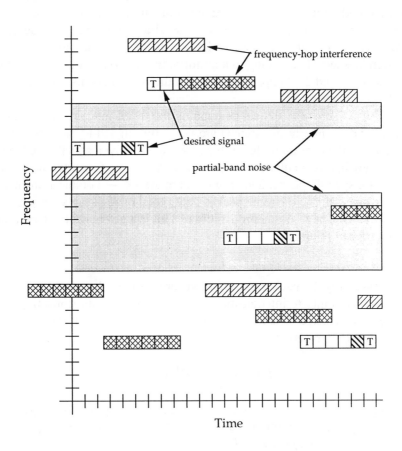

 positions for symbols from a single Reed-Solomon code word

Figure 8-7. Slow-frequency-hop transmission with test symbols.

For multiple-access interference, there is an advantage in locating the test symbols at the ends of the dwell intervals to make sure that any multiple-access interference that hits one or more code symbols within a dwell interval also hits at least one set of the test symbols in that same dwell interval [20]. For partial-band noise, however, there is no such advantage, and for some applications there are other considerations that may dictate a more uniform distribution of test symbols among the code symbols in a dwell interval. The choice depends on the application and the type of interference that is more prevalent or has more serious consequences in the system.

For many applications, the hopping pattern design is not under the control of the communications engineer, and the hopping patterns are generated in some pseudorandom way. In such situations it is common that the hopping pattern for a given transmission is modeled as a sequence of independent, identically distributed random variables. Each frequency in each hopping pattern is selected according to a uniform distribution on the set of available frequencies, and the hopping patterns for different transmissions are statistically independent [11].

For synchronous frequency hopping the dwell intervals for the desired signal and all interfering signals are perfectly aligned at the receiver. If q frequency slots are used, the probability that two given signals use the same frequency in a particular dwell interval is $P_h = 1/q$. Consider the transmission of a specific packet and assume there are $(K - 1)$ other transmissions taking place during the same packet slot (a total of K packets are sent in that packet slot). The resulting probability of a hit in a given dwell interval for the given transmission is

$$\mathcal{P} = 1 - (1 - P_h)^{K-1} \tag{7}$$

Assuming the packet transmissions are also synchronous (i.e., slotted), the number of interfering transmissions is constant over the transmission time of a given packet, and so the probability of j hits in a given frame (n consecutive dwell intervals) is

$$P(j) = \binom{n}{j} \mathcal{P}^j (1 - \mathcal{P})^{n-j}$$

as employed in (5). Therefore, equations (2)–(5) apply to the slow-frequency-hop multiple-access communication system with synchronous frequency hopping if $\mathcal{P}$ is given by (7) with $P_h = 1/q$.

If the frequency hopping is *asynchronous* among the different transmitters in the system or network, the situation is more complicated, but upper bounds on the packet and frame error probabilities can be obtained and the exact error probabilities can be calculated (e.g., see [7], [8], [12], [13], and [18]). In this chapter, we use an upper bound on the error probability that is obtained by replacing the asynchronous frequency-hop network by a synchronous frequency-hop network with the same number of frequency slots, but a larger value of P_h is used. The simplest bound is obtained by letting $P_h = 2/q$ and interpreting $K - 1$ as the *maximum* number of interfering transmissions at any time during the reception of the desired packet [18]. The desired upper bound follows from equations (2)–(5) and (7).

The transmitter and receiver know the sequence of test symbols that is to be included in each dwell interval. The received signals that correspond to the transmission of these test symbols are demodulated, and the demodulator decisions for the test symbols are compared with the symbols from the known sequence. The number of incorrectly demodulated test symbols for a given dwell interval is used as a statistic upon which to base the decision regarding the reliability of the data symbols in that dwell interval. This method can provide an arbitrarily small probability of a miss by increasing the number of test symbols in the sequence. Because an increase in the number of side information symbols produces a decrease in the information rate for the packet, a tradeoff can be carried out to maximize the information throughput subject to the constraints on the error probability [20].

The number of test symbols inserted in each dwell interval is $2N_t$. If there is one set of N_t test symbols at each end of the dwell interval, each hit that overlaps one or more data symbols must also overlap at least one entire set of test symbols. One erasure insertion procedure that has been suggested [20] is to determine the number of errors in each of the two sets of test symbols, and if either of these two numbers exceeds a predetermined threshold γ, the data symbols in that dwell interval are declared unreliable. Subject to some constraints, the unreliable symbols are erased before the sequence of data symbols is passed on to the decoder, as illustrated in Figure 8-8. One such constraint is that the number of erasures in each received word should not exceed the erasure correction capability of the Reed-Solomon code. Variations in this system, such as the use of parallel decoders (e.g., [4], [9], [17], and [23]), effectively handle the situation in which the side information suggests erasure of more symbols in a received word than the Reed-Solomon code can correct.

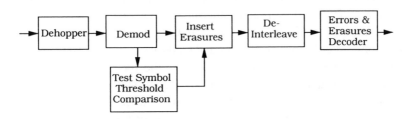

Figure 8-8. Receiver for the development and use of side information from test symbols.

The false alarm probability depends on the probability of error for a test symbol that is not hit. The probability of error for a test symbol that is not hit is denoted by p_t. Its value depends on the type of modulation and demodulation and the ratio of the test symbol energy to the power spectral density for the wideband noise.

Unlike for the code symbols, it is not assumed that all test symbols in a corrupted segment are received in error. The probability of error for a test symbol that is hit is a critical parameter in the performance analysis because it determines the probability of a miss for the side information. The probability of error for a test symbol that is hit is denoted by $P(E|\text{hit})$.

If the only interference is frequency-hop multiple-access interference, $P(E|\text{hit})$ depends on the type of modulation and demodulation, the ratio of the test symbol energy to the power spectral density for the wideband noise, the number of interfering transmissions that cause the hit, and the power in these transmissions. Exact values of $P(E|\text{hit})$ are difficult to obtain for asynchronous frequency-hop multiple-access interference, but approximations and bounds are sufficient for most applications.

The values for the miss and false alarm probabilities are given in [21] for a frequency-hop system with N_t test symbols at each end of each dwell interval. The range $1 \leq N_t \leq 15$ is considered, and it is shown that if $P(E|\text{hit}) \geq 0.3$, then $\alpha \leq 0.03$ and $1 - \beta \leq 0.01$ for some choices of N_t. For $P(E|\text{hit}) = 0.2$ it is possible to achieve $\alpha \leq 0.03$ and $1 - \beta \leq 0.04$ for $N_t = 15$ and $\gamma = 0$, and a larger value of γ gives a smaller probability of packet error. It is concluded that if $P(E|\text{hit}) \geq 0.2$, the reliability of the side information obtained from test symbols is sufficient to provide a considerable reduction in the packet error probability as compared with a receiver that uses errors-only decoding. In addition, the resulting packet error probability is, for most applications, acceptably close to that obtainable with perfect side information.

If BFSK is employed with noncoherent demodulation and there is a single interfering signal with the same power as the desired signal, it can be shown that under certain conditions the probability of error for a test symbol that is hit satisfies $1/4 \leq P(E|\text{hit}) \leq 1/2$. Furthermore, $P(E|\text{hit}) \approx 1/2$ if the power in the interfering signal is much greater than the power in the desired signal.

If the only interference is partial-band Gaussian noise, $P(E|\text{hit})$ is easily calculated from the energy per test symbol and the spectral densities for the partial-band noise that is present in the frequency slot used for that dwell interval and the wideband noise (which is present in all frequency slots). Fewer test symbols are required if the predominant form of interference is stationary partial-band noise because all test symbols are hit if the interference is present in the dwell interval, whereas we can guarantee only that half are hit if the interference is frequency-hop multiple-access interference. If $\mathcal{E}$ is the energy per test symbol and $N_T/2$ is the total two-sided noise density for the noise that is present in the frequency slot occupied by the desired signal, then

$$P(E|\text{hit}) = 0.5 \exp\left(\frac{-0.5\mathcal{E}}{N_T}\right)$$

for noncoherent demodulation of BFSK test symbols. In this case $\mathcal{E}/N_T \leq$ 1.4 dB suffices to ensure $P(E|\text{hit}) \geq 1/4$, $\mathcal{E}/N_T = -3.5$ dB gives $P(E|\text{hit}) \approx$ 0.4, and $\mathcal{E}/N_T \leq -14$ dB guarantees that $P(E|\text{hit}) > 0.49$. These values indicate that acceptable false alarm and miss probabilities are obtained for combating strong partial-band Gaussian noise interference.

4 OTHER METHODS FOR OBTAINING AND EMPLOYING SIDE INFORMATION

There are several methods for obtaining side information in frequency-hop communications that require less redundancy than is introduced by the transmission of test symbols, and there are others that attempt to obtain greater benefit from the redundancy that is added. For frequency-hop systems with binary modulation, the nonbinary symbols used in Reed-Solomon encoding and decoding are sequences of binary symbols. Lam and Sarwate [15] proposed the addition of a binary parity-check symbol to each such sequence of binary symbols at the output of the Reed-Solomon encoder. These parity-check symbols are used in place of test symbols in the determination of which dwell intervals to erase. For many applications, the parity-symbol method gives a higher false alarm probability than the test-symbol method described in Section 3, but for the parity-symbol method the unerased symbols have a higher probability of being correct. This leads to a different tradeoff in the false alarm and miss probabilities, and for some ranges of channel parameters it gives better performance. The coding scheme just described is a simple form of concatenated coding, the subject of Section 5.

One method for obtaining side information that does not require the transmission of extra redundancy is the ratio-threshold test (RTT) introduced by Viterbi [24] for protection against tone and partial-band noise interference. The reliability of a symbol is derived from a comparison of the soft-decision outputs of matched filters, and the erasure decision is based on the ratio of the largest magnitude to the second largest. A threshold is set, and erasures are made if this ratio does not exceed the threshold. Performance analyses (e.g., [1], [3], [5], [24]) show the RTT is very effective in frequency-hop receivers with soft-decision capability. Investigations of the sensitivity of the performance of the RTT to the choice of threshold have been completed, and results are given in [1].

A Bayesian decision-theoretic framework is employed in [1] to find erasure insertion strategies that minimize a linear combination of the symbol error probability and symbol erasure probability. The decision statistics that are required are the outputs of the soft-decision demodulator, which for a noncoherent communication system is a bank of envelope detectors. As with the RTT approach, the only symbols in the dwell interval are code symbols.

No test symbols or additional parity symbols are needed. When applied to frequency-hop communications with partial-band interference, this Bayesian erasure insertion is far superior to errors-only decoding. Under many conditions, it gives better performance than systems which erase all symbols that are hit, *even if the side information is perfect*. This is because all symbols are affected by wideband noise, so it is likely that even some of the the symbols that are not hit should be erased. On the other hand, some symbols that are hit can be demodulated correctly, so they should not be erased. The Bayesian method makes better decisions on both of these classes of symbols.

A typical performance curve for the Bayesian method of erasure insertion is shown in Figure 8-9 for an asynchronous frequency-hop multiple-access system with BFSK modulation, noncoherent demodulation, and a (32,12) Reed-Solomon code. The parameter λ is defined by $\lambda = K/q$, where K is the total number of transmitted signals and q is the number of frequency slots. For the results in Figure 8-9, $K \rightarrow \infty$ and $q \rightarrow \infty$ with λ held constant at a value of 0.2. The two-sided density for the wideband noise is $N_0/2$, and the energy per information bit is denoted by E_b. In general, systems that employ Reed-Solomon codes and use the Bayesian erasure insertion method provide far better performance than systems without side information that employ errors-only decoding. The performance differences can be quite large in some applications. As shown in Figure 8-9, for example, the Bayesian method gives several orders of magnitude of improvement in the probability of not decoding correctly for E_b/N_0 greater than about 14 dB.

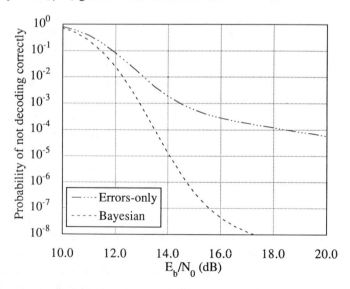

Figure 8-9. Performance of the Bayesian erasure insertion technique for asynchronous frequency-hop multiple-access communications.

5 CONCATENATED CODING FOR FREQUENCY-HOP COMMUNICATIONS

If redundancy is to be added in the transmission, the form of the redundancy can be selected to permit the correction of some error patterns in addition to the detection of errors for subsequent erasure. Concatenated coding gives one method for accomplishing this goal. If concatenated coding is used, the inner code provides much more than a method for obtaining side information, so this section departs slightly from the theme of the derivation and use of side information.

One strategy to improve performance beyond that obtainable with Reed-Solomon codes alone is to try to provide coding protection within the dwell intervals, rather than just across them as is done with the interleaved Reed-Solomon codes described in Section 2. In particular, such additional coding protection can give better performance in systems with a poor signal-to-noise ratio. If the signal-to-noise ratio is too small, the false alarm probability may be too large for the side information derived from the demodulation of test symbols. In addition, the error probability may be unacceptably large, even in the absence of interference, so that it is necessary to reduce the error probability at the input to the Reed-Solomon decoder.

The above considerations have led to the examination of concatenated coding for frequency-hop communication systems. The outer code is a Reed-Solomon code, and several types of block and convolutional codes have been considered for the inner code (e.g., [6], [9], and [10]). The decoding of the inner code can correct errors, and the results of the decoding process can provide side information to the outer Reed-Solomon decoder. It is common to set a threshold on the number of detected errors and erase the entire dwell interval if this threshold is exceeded, even if some or all of these errors are corrected. The observation of a large number of detected errors in a dwell interval is an indication that strong interference may be present during that dwell interval, so that there may be a large number of undetected errors.

Performance bounds are given for the Reed-Solomon outer codes and convolutional inner codes in [6], and simulation results are presented in [9] for both convolutional and block inner codes with hard-decision decoding. Two methods of interleaving are compared in [10]. The results of [6], [9], and [10] are for partial-band interference, but the same concatenated coding techniques can also be applied to frequency-hop multiple-access systems.

The use of parallel decoding of Reed-Solomon codes is introduced in [17] and shown to be effective in the decoding of Reed-Solomon codes for frequency-hop systems with side information. Further investigations of parallel decoding are presented in [4], [9], [23], and several other papers. The simplest parallel decoder consists of an errors-only decoder in parallel with an errors-and-erasures decoder. Each received word is the input to each decoder, and the results of the two separate decoding attempts are compared. Under fairly general conditions, Reed-Solomon decoders are much more likely to fail to decode than to decode into an incorrect code word; thus it is rare for the two decoders to produce different code words at their outputs. The most likely situation is that both decoders succeed in decoding and produce the same code word, and the next most likely situation is that one of the decoders fails to decode and the other produces a code word at its output. The simplest example of an advantage of using parallel decoding is the situation that arises if the side information or the decoding of the inner code indicate that the number of symbols that should be erased is beyond the erasure correction capability of the Reed-Solomon code. In such situations, there is no need to attempt the decoding of the received word with such a large number of erasures, and the system should be designed so that the errors-and-erasures decoder simply defaults to the errors-only decoder. Although soft-decision decoding of the Reed-Solomon codes can be even more effective, it is also considerably more complex than parallel decoding.

6 THE USE OF SIDE INFORMATION IN PROTOCOLS FOR FREQUENCY-HOP PACKET RADIO NETWORKS

In order to deliver packets to their destinations efficiently, the protocols employed in a packet radio network should have available a precise measure of the quality of the links in the network. This permits reliable decision making in the selection of a radio to which to forward a packet and the choice of a route by which to get a packet from its source to its destination. Designs of forwarding and routing protocols that utilize side information to account for link conditions in a frequency-hop packet radio network are given in [22] and related papers.

The general framework for the routing protocols considered in [22] is referred to as least-resistance routing (LRR). The LRR routing protocol can use any of a number of metrics in order to quantify link quality, but the one most closely related to the use of side information in the decoding of Reed-Solomon codes is a metric that is based on the number of errors and erasures made in the receiver. The erasure decisions can employ any of the types of side information discussed in the previous sections. We focus here on the use of test symbols to derive side information.

The errors-and-erasures (EE) metric is defined to be the number of erasures plus twice the number of errors that occur in the demodulation of the code symbols in a packet. For each received word that is decoded, the number of errors is determined by comparing the received word and the decoder output word. For each received word in the packet that fails to decode, the number of errors is taken to be the smallest number of errors that will cause the received word to fail to decode when the number of erasures is also taken into account. The number of erasures depends on the outcome of the demodulation of the test symbols, as discussed in Section 3.

Simulations of a frequency-hop packet radio network with 12 radios have been carried out, and the results are reported in [22]. In addition to the radios that are part of the network, additional frequency-hop radio interference is simulated to represent other radios that are not part of the network but are within range and use the same band of frequencies in their transmissions. Such radios may be used for point-to-point voice or data transmission, or they may belong to another packet radio network that is operating in the vicinity. Also included are two mobile sources of partial-band interference, each of which affects only one radio at a time.

A comparison of LRR and tier routing, a well-known routing method [14] devised for packet radio networks in the early 1980s, is shown in Figure 8-10. The (32,16) extended Reed-Solomon code is employed with errors-and-erasures decoding based on side information that is derived from 10 test symbols per dwell interval. The throughput for the LRR protocol with the EE metric is compared with the throughput for tier routing for $E_b/N_0 = 14$ dB. The fractional bandwidth for the partial-band interference is 0.2. It is clear that much larger throughput is obtained with LRR and the EE metric, especially at the higher traffic levels.

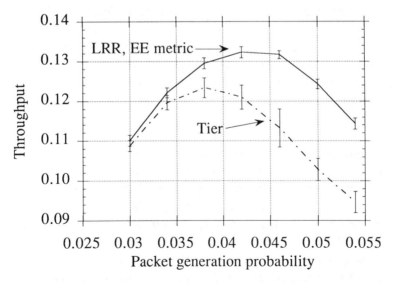

Figure 8-10. Throughput for two routing protocols in a frequency-hop packet radio network.

ACKNOWLEDGMENTS

The author wishes to thank William Sander of the Army Research Office for his support and encouragement in this research. The material presented in this chapter draws heavily on [21], an invited paper published in the IEICE Transactions on Communications, Special Issue on Spread Spectrum Techniques and Applications. The author wishes to thank the editors of the special issue for the opportunity to prepare and publish that paper.

Thanks are also due Dilip Sarwate and Jim McChesney for several discussions on the use of side information in frequency-hop packet radio systems. Carl Baum, Colin Frank, and Harlan Russell made several of the original contributions reviewed in Sections 4–6; in particular, Carl Baum obtained the results shown in Figure 8-9 and Harlan Russell developed the frequency-hop packet radio network simulation and obtained the results presented in Figure 8-10. Finally, I would like to thank Stephen Wicker and Vijay Bhargava, the editors of this volume, for their invitation to prepare this chapter and their editorial suggestions.

REFERENCES

[1] C. W. Baum and M. B. Pursley, "Bayesian Methods for Erasure Insertion in Frequency-Hop Communications with Partial-Band Interference," *IEEE Transactions on Communications*, Volume 40, pp. 1231–1238, July 1992.

[2] E. R. Berlekamp, "The Technology of Error-Correcting Codes," *Proceedings of the IEEE*, Volume 68, pp. 564–593, May 1980.

[3] K. G. Castor and W. E. Stark, "Performance of Diversity/Reed-Solomon Coded SSFH Communications with Errors/Erasures via Ratio Thresholding," *Proceedings of the 21st Annual Allerton Conference on Communication, Control, and Computing*, University of Illinois, pp. 869–877, October 1985.

[4] K. G. Castor and W. E. Stark, "Parallel Decoding of Diversity/Reed-Solomon Coded SSFH Communications with Repetition Thresholding," *Proceedings of the 20th Annual Conference on Information Sciences and Systems*, Princeton University, pp. 75–80, October 1985.

[5] L. F. Chang and R. J. McEliece, "A Study of Viterbi's Ratio-Threshold AJ Technique," *1984 IEEE Military Communications Conference Record*, pp. 11.2.1–5, October 1984.

[6] G. M. Chiasson and M. B. Pursley, "Concatenated Coding for Frequency-Hop Packet Radio," *1991 IEEE Military Communications Conference Record*, Volume 3, pp. 1235–1239, October 1991.

[7] C. D. Frank and M. B. Pursley, "Comments on 'Packet Error Probabilities in Frequency-Hopped Spread-Spectrum Packet Radio Networks—Memoryless Frequency-Hopping Patterns Considered,'" *IEEE Transactions on Communications*, Volume 37, pp. 295–298, March 1989.

[8] C. D. Frank and M. B. Pursley, "On the Statistical Dependence of Hits in Frequency-Hop Multiple Access," *IEEE Transactions on Communications*, Volume 38, pp. 1483–1494, September 1990.

[9] C. D. Frank and M. B. Pursley, "Tradeoffs in Concatenated Coding for Frequency-Hop Packet Radio with Partial-Band Interference," *1992 IEEE Military Communications Conference Record*, Volume 1, pp. 125–129, October 1992.

[10] C. D. Frank and M. B. Pursley, "Concatenated Coding Alternatives for Frequency-Hop Packet Radio," *IEICE Transactions on Communications*, Special Issue on Spread Spectrum Techniques and Applications, Volume E76-B, pp. 863–873, August 1993.

[11] E. A. Geraniotis and M. B. Pursley, "Error Probabilities for Slow-Frequency-Hopped Spread-Spectrum Multiple-Access Communications over Fading Channels, *IEEE Transactions on Communications*, Volume COM-30, pp. 996–1009, May 1982.

[12] M. Georgiopoulos, "Packet Error Probabilities in Frequency-Hopped Spread-Spectrum Packet Radio Networks—Memoryless Frequency-Hopping Patterns Considered," *IEEE Transactions on Communications*, Volume 36, pp. 720–723, June 1988.

[13] M. V. Hegde and W. E. Stark, "On the Error Probability of Coded Frequency-Hopped Spread-Spectrum Multiple-Access Systems," *IEEE Transactions on Communications*, Volume 38, pp. 571–573, May 1990.

[14] J. Jubin and J. D. Tornow, "The DARPA Packet Radio Network Protocols," *Proceedings of the IEEE*, Volume 75, pp. 21–32, January 1987.

[15] A. W. Lam and D. V. Sarwate, "Comparison of Two Methods for Generation of Side Information in Frequency-Hopping Spread-Spectrum Multiple-Access Communications," *Proceedings of the 21st Annual Conference on Information Sciences and Systems*, Johns Hopkins University, pp. 426–431, March 1987.

[16] R. J. McEliece and W. E. Stark, "Channels with Block Interference," *IEEE Transactions on Information Theory*, Volume IT-30, pp. 44–53, January 1984.

[17] M. B. Pursley, "Coding and Diversity for Channels with Fading and Pulsed Interference," *Proceedings of the 1982 Conference on Information Sciences and Systems*, Princeton University, pp. 413–418, March 1982.

[18] M. B. Pursley, "Frequency-Hop Transmission for Satellite Packet Switching and Terrestrial Packet Radio Networks," *IEEE Transactions on Information Theory*, Volume IT-32, pp. 652–667, September 1986.

[19] M. B. Pursley, "Packet Error Probabilities in Frequency-Hop Radio Networks—Coping with Statistical Dependence and Noisy Side Information," *IEEE Global Telecommunications Conference Record*, Volume 1, pp. 165–170, December 1986.

[20] M. B. Pursley, "Tradeoffs Between Side Information and Code Rate in Slow-Frequency-Hop Packet Radio Networks," *1987 IEEE International Conference on Communications Conference Record*, Volume 2, pp. 947–952, June 1987.

[21] M. B. Pursley, "The Derivation and Use of Side Information in Frequency-Hop Spread Spectrum Communications," *IEICE Transactions on Communications*, Special Issue on Spread Spectrum Techniques and Applications, Volume E76-B, pp. 814–824, August 1993.

[22] M. B. Pursley and H. B. Russell, "Routing in Frequency-Hop Packet Radio Networks with Partial-Band Jamming," *IEEE Transactions on Communications*, Volume 41, pp. 1117–1124, July 1993.

[23] M. B. Pursley and W. E. Stark, "Performance of Reed-Solomon Coded Frequency-Hop Spread-Spectrum Communications in Partial-Band Interference," *IEEE Transactions on Communications*, Volume COM-33, pp. 767–774, August 1985.

[24] A. J. Viterbi, "A Robust Ratio-Threshold Technique to Mitigate Tone and Partial Band Jamming in Coded MFSK Systems," *1982 IEEE Military Communications Conference Record*, pp. 22.4.1–5, October 1982.

[25] A. J. Viterbi and I. M. Jacobs, "Advances in Coding and Modulation for Noncoherent Channels Affected by Fading, Partial Band, and Multiple-Access Interference," in *Advances in Communication Systems*, Volume 4, pp. 279–308, Academic Press, New York, 1975.

Chapter 9

Reed-Solomon Codes and the Design of Sequences for Spread-Spectrum Multiple-Access Communications[1]

Dilip V. Sarwate
Coordinated Science Laboratory
and the
Department of Electrical and Computer Engineering
University of Illinois at Urbana-Champaign
Urbana, Illinois 61801

1 INTRODUCTION

A digitally modulated signal is called a *spread-spectrum signal* if its spectrum is very much wider than the spectrum of the modulating signal and if this spectral spreading does not depend on the spectrum of the modulating signal. The two most common methods for creating a spread-spectrum signal are frequency hopping and direct-sequence modulation [3,27,33]. In a frequency-hopped spread-spectrum (FH/SS) communication system, a transmitter changes (hops) its RF carrier frequency at regular intervals as prescribed by a *frequency-hopping pattern*. The time interval during which the carrier frequency is constant is called a *dwell*, and during each dwell, data communication occurs via some conventional (narrowband) digital modulation technique such as M-ary frequency-shift-keying or differential phase-shift-keying. Thus, during each dwell, the transmitted signal is just a conventional digitally modulated signal occupying a small frequency band (called a *frequency slot*) centered at the carrier frequency. However, since the transmitted signal

[1]Preparation of this material was supported by the U. S. Army Research Office under Grant DAAL03-91-G-0154 and the Joint Services Electronics Program under Grant NOOO14-90-J-1270.

occupies different frequency slots during different dwells, the total signal energy is spread over a wide frequency band. Note that the spectral spreading is determined by the spacing of the slots and by the frequency-hopping pattern and not by the data rate or data modulation method. In contrast, a direct-sequence spread-spectrum (DS/SS) transmitter creates a wideband signal by phase-shift-keying its RF carrier with the sum of the data sequence and a *signature sequence* whose pulse rate is very much larger than the pulse rate of the data sequence. Since the bandwidth of the signal depends on the rate at which phase transitions occur in the RF carrier, the spectral spreading is determined by the signature sequence pulse rate and not the data rate. Note that in contrast to a FH/SS signal, the energy in a DS/SS signal is present in all parts of the frequency band at all times.

Most spread-spectrum communication systems are multiple-access communication systems; that is, several transmitters are simultaneously active in the frequency band allotted to the system. Thus, in general, several signals are present at the input to a receiver, and while attempting to demodulate one of these signals, the receiver must contend with the interference caused by the other (undesired) signals. System designers can reduce this *multiple-access interference* by careful choice of the frequency-hopping patterns or signature sequences assigned to the various transmitters. The use of Reed-Solomon codes in the design of these patterns and sequences is the topic of this chapter. Section 2 contains a brief survey of various FH/SS communication systems and describes several methods for the design of frequency-hopping patterns for these systems. Some of these methods explicitly use Reed-Solomon codes, and the resulting frequency-hopping patterns are code words from low-rate Reed-Solomon codes. Other methods were originally described using different terminology, but the resulting frequency-hopping patterns also can be viewed as code words from low-rate Reed-Solomon codes. Section 3 shows that several well-known signature sequence sets for DS/SS communications (such as the Gold sequences and Kasami sequences [23]) also can be viewed in terms of code words from low-rate Reed-Solomon codes. However, there seems to be no apparent connection between the properties of the Reed-Solomon codes and the resulting signature sequences.

2 FREQUENCY-HOPPED SPREAD-SPECTRUM SYSTEMS

2.1 Desirable Properties of Frequency-Hopping Patterns

Let q denote the number of frequency slots in a FH/SS system and let f_i denote the center frequency of the ith slot, $0 \leq i \leq q - 1$. The center frequencies are usually chosen so that the slots are spaced uniformly across the frequency band allotted to the system. A frequency-hopping pattern is a sequence $x = (x_0, x_1, \ldots, x_{N-1})$ of N elements from the set $\{f_0, f_1, \ldots, f_{q-1}\}$ specifying the order in which the slots are to be used by a particular transmitter. Long messages are transmitted by repeating the frequency-hopping pattern as often as necessary. As in [23], let T denote the operator that shifts a sequence x cyclically to the left by one place, that is, $Tx = (x_1, x_2, \ldots, x_{N-1}, x_0)$. If T is applied k times to x, where $0 < k < N$, the result is $T^k x = (x_k, x_{k+1}, \ldots, x_{N-1}, x_0, x_1, \ldots, x_{k-1})$, while $T^N x = x$. The *period* of x is the least positive integer M such that $T^M x = x$. Generally, M can be any divisor of N, but in most cases of interest, $M = N$. The sequences $x, Tx, T^2 x, \ldots, T^{M-1} x$ are distinct but *cyclically equivalent*; they are cyclic shifts of each other.

The *composition vector* $\mathcal{N}(x)$ of the sequence x is defined as

$$\mathcal{N}(x) = [N_0(x), N_1(x), \ldots, N_{q-1}(x)],$$

where, for $0 \leq i \leq q - 1$, $N_i(x)$ denotes the number of times that frequency f_i occurs in x. Note that cyclically equivalent sequences have the same composition vector. Obviously,

$$N_i(x) \geq 0 \text{ for all } i, \text{ and } \sum_{i=0}^{q-1} N_i(x) = N. \tag{1}$$

It can be shown [10] that (1) implies that

$$\sum_{i=0}^{q-1} N_i^2(x) = \| \mathcal{N}(x) \|^2 \geq N \left\lfloor \frac{N}{q} \right\rfloor + \left\lceil \frac{N}{q} \right\rceil (N \bmod q) \tag{2}$$

where $\| \cdot \|$ denotes the norm of a vector and $(N \bmod q)$ denotes the least positive residue of N modulo q. Equality holds in (2) if and only if

$$N_i(x) = \left\lceil \frac{N}{q} \right\rceil \quad \text{for } (N \bmod q) \text{ values of } i, \tag{3}$$

$$N_i(x) = \left\lfloor \frac{N}{q} \right\rfloor \quad \text{for } q - (N \bmod q) \text{ values of } i. \tag{4}$$

Note that

$$N \left\lfloor \frac{N}{q} \right\rfloor + \left\lceil \frac{N}{q} \right\rceil (N \bmod q) = N \quad \text{if } N \leq q, \tag{5}$$

and that

$$N \left\lfloor \frac{N}{q} \right\rfloor + \left\lceil \frac{N}{q} \right\rceil (N \bmod q) \geq \frac{N^2}{q} \tag{6}$$

with equality if and only if N is an integer multiple of q. As will be shown below, it is often possible to find frequency-hopping patterns that satisfy (3) and (4). Such hopping patterns spread the signal energy as uniformly as possible across the entire frequency band allotted to the FH/SS system. Uniform usage of the frequency slots can also be justified by a minimax approach to the design of frequency-hopping patterns for FH/SS systems operating in jamming or fading environments. If a signal visits one slot much more often than others, then it is more vulnerable to jamming or fading in that slot. Of course, such a signal is less vulnerable in those slots that it visits less frequently, but clearly the maximum vulnerability is minimized if the slots are utilized as uniformly as possible. It is shown below that uniform usage of slots also minimizes the average multiple-access interference from other transmitters.

A receiver attempting to receive the signal from a particular transmitter in a FH/SS system must track the frequency-hopping pattern of that transmitter. A local oscillator is frequency-hopped in synchronism with the incoming signal so that when the incoming signal is in the ith slot, the oscillator is producing a tone at frequency $f_i - f_{int}$. Consequently, even though the incoming signal is hopping from slot to slot, heterodyning the local oscillator output with the incoming signal produces a signal at the fixed intermediate frequency f_{int}. Since the signal being transmitted during each dwell is a conventional digitally modulated signal, this process of *dehopping* produces a conventional digitally modulated signal at frequency f_{int}, and this can be detected by conventional means [3,33]. It is assumed that the intermediate frequency is chosen so that there are no problems with image frequencies showing up in the mixer output. Also, it is assumed that the slots are spaced far enough apart in frequency that when the receiver is tuned to a slot, there is no interference from signals being transmitted in adjacent slots. However, when several FH/SS transmitters are simultaneously active, it is possible that two or more transmitters may hop to the *same* frequency slot at the same time. Such an event is called a *collision* or *hit*, and it usually causes such severe signal degradation that it is best to detect collisions whenever possible, to delete the most severely degraded symbols, and then to reconstruct these deleted symbols by use of an erasures-and-errors correcting channel code [1]. In fact, as detailed elsewhere [19] in this book, the powerful erasures-and-errors correcting capabilities of Reed-Solomon codes make them natural candidates for this purpose. This chapter, however, is more concerned with minimizing the number of collisions that occur.

The dwell duration T_h is the length of the time interval during which a transmitter signal occupies one frequency slot. If at least one symbol is transmitted during a dwell, the system is called a *slow* FH/SS system. A *fast* FH/SS system is one in which the duration of each transmitted symbol is larger than the dwell time, so that the demodulator must observe the signal over several dwells in order to decide which symbol was transmitted. Clearly, a collision between hopping patterns affects only part of a transmitted symbol in a fast FH/SS system, but it can affect several transmitted symbols in a slow FH/SS system. Thus, collisions can be more of a problem in slow FH/SS systems than in fast FH/SS systems. There is also another aspect to be considered. Suppose that at a given receiver, the desired signal and the signal from an interfering transmitter are *dwell-synchronous*; that is, each carrier signal changes frequency at exactly the same time. In other words, the relative delay between the two signals is an integer multiple of T_h. In this case, when the two signals hop to the same slot, they collide for the entire dwell. However, most FH/SS systems are not dwell-synchronous; that is, the relative delay between two signals need not be an integer multiple of T_h. Thus, when the desired signal hops into a slot, a receiver tracking the signal may find that an interfering signal is already present in that slot, but that this interfering signal disappears before the end of the dwell interval. On the other hand, an interfering signal may suddenly appear during a dwell and last until the end of the dwell interval. Such *partial hits* can be accounted for quite easily if one knows the number of (full) collisions that occur for each given delay between the two patterns in a dwell-synchronous system. These collisions are counted by the Hamming correlation functions which are considered next.

2.2 The Hamming Correlation Functions

Let x and y denote two frequency-hopping patterns with common period N. The number of hits that occur in one period of x due to interference from y is counted by the *Hamming cross-correlation function* which was defined by Lempel and Greenberger [10] as

$$H_{x,y}(j) = \sum_{i=0}^{N-1} h(x_i, y_{i+j}), \quad 0 \le j \le N - 1 \tag{7}$$

where j is the relative delay between the two frequency-hopping patterns, the sum $i + j$ is taken modulo N, and

$$h(a, b) = \begin{cases} 1 & \text{if } a = b, \\ 0 & \text{if } a \ne b. \end{cases}$$

Equivalently,

$$H_{x,y}(j) = N - d(x, T^j y) \tag{8}$$

where $d(x, y)$ denotes the Hamming distance between the sequences x and y. Naturally, one would like to have x and y such that $H_{x,y}(j)$ is as small as possible for all $j, 0 \le j \le N - 1$. The *Hamming autocorrelation function* $H_x(j)$ for the hopping pattern x is just $H_{x,x}(j)$ and has the obvious property that $H_x(0) = N$. One would like to choose x such that the *out-of-phase autocorrelation* values $H_x(j)$, $0 < j < N$, are as small as possible. Note that the out-of-phase autocorrelation is a measure of the self-interference suffered by a signal from a delayed replica of itself. Such replicas may be received because of specular multipath propagation or because a repeat jammer is rebroadcasting the signal. The out-of-phase autocorrelation can also be used to estimate the likelihood of false lock in the initial acquisition and synchronization process that aligns the hopping pattern of the receiver's local oscillator with the received signal.

How small can the Hamming cross-correlation and out-of-phase Hamming autocorrelation be? First, note that $0 \le H_{x,y}(j) \le N$ for all j. Let $\bar{H}_{x,y}$ denote the *average Hamming cross-correlation value* and $\langle \cdot, \cdot \rangle$ denote the usual inner product of two vectors. Then,

$$N\bar{H}_{x,y} = \sum_{j=0}^{N-1} H_{x,y}(j) = \sum_{i=0}^{q-1} N_i(x)N_i(y) = \langle \mathcal{N}(x), \mathcal{N}(y) \rangle. \quad (9)$$

Similarly, $\bar{H}_x$, the *average out-of-phase Hamming autocorrelation* for the sequence x is given by

$$(N - 1)\bar{H}_x = \sum_{j=1}^{N-1} H_x(j) = \langle \mathcal{N}(x), \mathcal{N}(x) \rangle - N = \| \mathcal{N}(x) \|^2 - N. \quad (10)$$

If $N \le q$, then (2), (5), and (10) lead to the trivially obvious conclusion that $\bar{H}_x \ge 0$. Furthermore, $\bar{H}_x = 0$ if and only if the hopping pattern satisfies (3) and (4), that is, if and only if each $N_i(x)$ is either 0 or 1. Such sequences are called *nonrepeating* hopping patterns because each frequency is used at most once in each period [28], and they are of interest for the purposes of initial acquisition and synchronization. Note that $\bar{H}_x = 0$ implies that $H_x(j) = 0$ for *all* j, $0 < j < N$. More generally, (2) and (6) show that the right side of (10) is at least $N^2/q - N$ and hence, for *any* sequence x,

$$\bar{H}_x > \frac{N}{N - 1} \left(\frac{N}{q} - 1 \right). \quad (11)$$

The right side of (11) is nonpositive for $N \le q$, and in this case, $\bar{H}_x \ge 0$ as discussed above. On the other hand, if $N > q$, the right side of (11) exceeds $N/q - 1$. Since the Hamming correlation functions are integer-valued, it follows that for *any* sequence x,

$$\max_{0 < j < N} H_x(j) \ge \left\lceil \frac{N}{q} \right\rceil - 1. \quad (12)$$

In comparison, for any j, $0 < j < N$, the expected value of $H_x(j)$, averaged over all possible q^N N-tuples in the set $\{f_0, f_1, \ldots, f_{q-1}\}^N$, is N/q. In other words, it is not possible to design hopping patterns whose autocorrelation values are significantly smaller than the average value for a randomly chosen hopping pattern.[2]

Next, suppose that x and y are chosen randomly and independently from the set of q^N N-tuples in the set $\{f_0, f_1, \ldots, f_{q-1}\}^N$. Then, for all j, $0 \leq j < N$, the expected value of $H_{x,y}(j)$ is N/q. Once again, it is not possible to do much better than this with nonrandom designs except in the following special cases. Suppose that the set $\{f_0, f_1, \ldots, f_{q-1}\}$ is partitioned into a collection of K disjoint subsets where $K < q$, and that K patterns are constructed with each pattern being restricted to the slots in a different subset in the collection. Then, the composition vectors of the patterns are orthogonal vectors and it follows from (9) that $\bar{H}_{x,y} = 0$ and therefore $H_{x,y}(j) = 0$ for all j. If these patterns happen to be nonrepeating patterns, then $\bar{H}_x = 0$ for all x as well. However, the common period N of these nonrepeating patterns is at most $\lfloor q/K \rfloor$ since at least one pattern is restricted to no more than $\lfloor q/K \rfloor$ slots. On the other hand, if the patterns are not nonrepeating patterns so that the common period exceeds $\lfloor q/K \rfloor$, then from (11) it follows that $\bar{H}_x > KN/q - 1$ for some of the sequences. Thus, although the Hamming cross-correlations of these K hopping patterns are identically zero, their maximum out-of-phase Hamming autocorrelations are much larger than those of patterns that hop to all q slots. Of course, these special cases essentially correspond to frequency-division multiple-access (FDMA) systems (possibly spiced with a little frequency diversity if $\lfloor q/K \rfloor \geq 2$) and are not of much interest in FH/SS applications.

More generally, let $\mathcal{X}$ denote a set of K hopping patterns of period N. Then, from (9) it follows that

$$\sum_{x \in \mathcal{X}} \sum_{y \in \mathcal{X}} \sum_{j=0}^{N-1} H_{x,y}(j) = \| \sum_{x \in \mathcal{X}} \mathcal{N}(x) \|^2 . \tag{13}$$

Since

$$\sum_{x \in \mathcal{X}} N_i(x) \geq 0 \text{ for all } i, \text{ and } \sum_{i=0}^{q-1} \sum_{x \in \mathcal{X}} N_i(x) = KN,$$

which is analogous to (1), it follows that the right side of (13) is smallest when

---

[2]A more careful analysis [10] leads to a more precise estimate for the right side of (11), but these results generally do not improve on the right side of (12). It is also worth noting that all these results can also be deduced by applying the well-known Plotkin upper bound on the average minimum distance of a block code [11] to a length-N q-ary block code whose N code words are $\{x, Tx, \ldots, T^{N-1}x\}$.

$$\sum_{x \in \mathcal{X}} N_i(x) = \left\lceil \frac{KN}{q} \right\rceil \quad \text{for } (KN \bmod q) \text{ values of } i, \tag{14}$$

$$\sum_{x \in \mathcal{X}} N_i(x) = \left\lfloor \frac{KN}{q} \right\rfloor \quad \text{for } q - (KN \bmod q) \text{ values of } i. \tag{15}$$

Let $\bar{H}_c(\mathcal{X})$ and $H_c(\mathcal{X})$, respectively, denote the average and maximum values of $H_{x,y}(j)$ over all $K(K-1)$ pairs of distinct hopping patterns x and y in $\mathcal{X}$ and all j, $0 \le j < N$. Similarly, let $\bar{H}_a(\mathcal{X})$ and $H_a(\mathcal{X})$, respectively, denote the average and maximum values of $H_x(j)$ over all K patterns $x \in \mathcal{X}$ and all j, $0 < j < N$. Let $\bar{H}_{\max}(\mathcal{X}) = \max\{\bar{H}_c(\mathcal{X}), \bar{H}_a(\mathcal{X})\}$ and $H_{\max}(\mathcal{X}) = \max\{H_c(\mathcal{X}), H_a(\mathcal{X})\}$. Then, it follows from (6) and (13) that

$$K(K-1)N H_c(\mathcal{X}) + K(N-1) H_a(\mathcal{X})$$

$$\ge K(K-1)N \bar{H}_c(\mathcal{X}) + K(N-1) \bar{H}_a(\mathcal{X})$$

$$= \| \sum_{x \in \mathcal{X}} \mathcal{N}(x) \|^2 - KN \ge \frac{(KN)^2}{q} - KN, \tag{16}$$

and hence, if $KN > q$,

$$H_{\max}(\mathcal{X}) \ge \bar{H}_{\max}(\mathcal{X}) > \frac{N}{q} - \frac{1}{K}. \tag{17}$$

Thus, one or both of the maximum (and average) correlation values are bounded from below by a quantity that is almost the same as the expected value when random patterns are used.

The bound (17) on $H_{\max}(\mathcal{X})$ is useful if $N \gg q$. However, if N is no larger than q, the bound is not only small but it hardly increases at all as K increases. In such instances, a larger lower bound on $H_{\max}(\mathcal{X})$ can be obtained as follows. Consider all the KN cyclic shifts of the hopping patterns in $\mathcal{X}$ as a q-ary nonlinear cyclic code of length N. The Singleton bound on the minimum distance of this code [11] together with (8) implies that

$$H_{\max}(\mathcal{X}) \ge \lceil \log_q(KN) \rceil - 1. \tag{18}$$

For example, according to (18), for a set of q^s hopping patterns of length $N \le q$, the maximum Hamming correlation value is at least s. However, bound (18) increases only logarithmically with N, whereas bound (17) increases linearly with N, and thus the latter is tighter when applied to small sets of long hopping patterns.

Returning to (16), note that this can be written as

$$H_c(\mathcal{X}) + \frac{1}{K-1}H_a(\mathcal{X}) \geq \bar{H}_c(\mathcal{X}) + \frac{1}{K-1}\bar{H}_a(\mathcal{X})$$

$$\geq \frac{1}{K-1}\left(\frac{KN}{q} - 1\right) \qquad (19)$$

showing that there is a tradeoff between the maximum (or average) cross-correlation and maximum (or average) autocorrelation values—if careful design of hopping patterns reduces one maximum (or average) correlation value substantially below N/q, then the other maximum (or average) correlation value will be larger than N/q. However, since different weights are attached to the quantities in (19), a set of patterns with very small maximum (or average) cross-correlation will necessarily have large maximum (or average) autocorrelation but a set of patterns with very small maximum (or average) autocorrelation need not necessarily have very large maximum (or average) cross-correlation value. As an example, it was shown above that if $\bar{H}_c(\mathcal{X}) = 0$ (which implies that $H_c(\mathcal{X}) = 0$), then $H_a(\mathcal{X}) \geq \bar{H}_a(\mathcal{X}) > KN/q - 1 \gg N/q - 1$. In contrast, if $\bar{H}_a(\mathcal{X}) = 0$ (which implies that $H_a(\mathcal{X}) = 0$ and all the patterns are nonrepeating), (19) shows that

$$H_c(\mathcal{X}) \geq \bar{H}_c(\mathcal{X}) \geq \frac{K}{K-1}\frac{N}{q} - \frac{1}{K-1}$$

where the right side is only slightly larger than the right side of (17).

The average out-of-phase autocorrelation $\bar{H}_x$ is minimized for each sequence x if x is such that (3) and (4) hold, whereas the right side of (13) is smallest when (14) and (15) hold. Fortunately, it is sometimes possible to satisfy both conditions in the important special case when K is a multiple of q. Let x denote a hopping pattern of period N whose composition vector $\mathcal{N}(x)$ satisfies (3) and (4). Construct $(q-1)$ other hopping patterns with composition vectors $T\mathcal{N}(x), T^2\mathcal{N}(x), \ldots, T^{q-1}\mathcal{N}(x)$. For example, a hopping pattern with composition vector $T^j\mathcal{N}(x)$ can be constructed from x by replacing each occurrence of f_i in x by $f_{((i-j) \bmod q)}$. Then, the composition vectors of the q hopping patterns constructed in this fashion all satisfy (3) and (4), and the set of q sequences satisfies (14) and (15). In fact, since the number of sequences is a multiple of q, the stronger condition $\sum_x \mathcal{N}(x) = (N, N, \ldots, N)$ holds. This construction can be applied to other sequences satisfying (3) and (4) to create a set of K sequences, where K is any integer multiple of q. Note that the construction may have the following undesirable property: if the sequence x contains long runs of the form $(\ldots, f_i, f_{i+1}, f_{i+2}, f_{i+3}, \ldots)$, then the sequence y with composition vector $T\mathcal{N}(x)$ contains runs of the form $(\ldots, f_{i-1}, f_i, f_{i+1}, f_{i+2}, \ldots)$, and thus $H_{x,y}(1)$ may be unacceptably large even though $\bar{H}_{x,y}$ is reasonably small. This matter is discussed in more detail in the next subsection. Note, however, that in some cases, it might be possible to renumber the frequency slots in a way that such problems do not arise.

Finally, suppose that the relative delay between two signals using x and y, respectively, as hopping patterns is $(j + \epsilon)T_h$, where $0 < \epsilon < 1$. Then, the receiver synchronized to x suffers partial hits in $H_{x,y}(j)$ of the N dwells. In these dwells, the interfering signal is already present when the receiver tunes to that slot, and the interfering signal disappears $(1 - \epsilon)T_h$ seconds after the beginning of the dwell. The receiver also suffers partial hits in $H_{x,y}(j + 1)$ of the N dwells, and in these dwells the interfering signal suddenly appears $(1 - \epsilon)T_h$ seconds after the beginning of the dwell and lasts until the end of the dwell. Thus, partial hits occur in a total of $H_{x,y}(j) + H_{x,y}(j + 1)$ dwells, and the total duration of the time interval hit is $[(1 - \epsilon)H_{x,y}(j) + \epsilon H_{x,y}(j+1)]T_h$. Of course, if for some i, $x_i = y_{i+j} = y_{i+j+1}$, the two partial hits in the ith dwell combine to give a full hit in that dwell. This phenomenon cannot occur in some applications in which it is required that any two consecutive symbols from any hopping pattern be distinct [6, 18]. However, in general, a hopping pattern may well contain a succession of identical symbols, and the effects of this are considered in the next subsection.

2.3 Runs and Bursts

A hopping pattern x of length N is said to contain a *run* of length r of the frequency f_i beginning at position j if

$$(x_{j-1}, x_j, x_{j+1}, \ldots, x_{j+r-1}, x_{j+r}) = (f_k, f_i, f_i, \ldots, f_i, f_l)$$

$$\text{where } f_k \neq f_i \text{ and } f_l \neq f_i,$$

and the subscripts on x are taken modulo N. Long runs are undesirable for several reasons. First, the signal stays in the same slot for r successive dwells and is thus more vulnerable if that slot is being jammed or is in a deep fade. Second, long occupancy of a slot also makes the signal more vulnerable to interception by an unauthorized receiver. Finally, if long runs of the same frequency occur in two different patterns, then long *bursts* of full hits will occur whenever the relative delay is such that the runs arrive at the same time at a receiver. Although hits often can be detected and the corresponding symbols erased (and later restored by an errors-and-erasures correcting code), a burst of hits causes a large number of erasures in a short period of time, and this may well lead to a decoding failure in the error control system. This is because the block length of the error control code is usually much smaller than the length of the hopping patterns, and thus a code that can handle H hits scattered over N dwells may well fail if many of these H hits occur in a burst and affect symbols belonging to the same code word.

Bursts of hits are caused not only by runs of the same frequency but also by the occurrence of identical subsequences in two hopping patterns; that is, if $(x_i, x_{i+1}, \ldots, x_{i+r-1}) = (y_j, y_{j+1}, \ldots, y_{j+r-1})$, where, as before, the subscripts are taken modulo N, then a burst of r hits occurs for a relative delay of $(j - i)T_h$. Generally, these hits become partial hits if the relative delay is $(j - i + \epsilon)T_h$ unless the subsequences contain repetitions of the same frequency. Now, let $B(\mathcal{X})$ denote the length of the longest burst of hits between any two hopping patterns in $\mathcal{X}$ and note that $H_{\max}(\mathcal{X}) \geq B(\mathcal{X})$. The KN subsequences of the form $(x_i, x_{i+1}, \ldots, x_{i+r-1})$, $x \in \mathcal{X}$, cannot all be distinct if $q^r < KN$, and therefore bursts of length r must occur for all r satisfying this inequality. It follows that

$$H_{\max}(\mathcal{X}) \geq B(\mathcal{X}) \geq \lceil \log_q(KN) \rceil - 1, \tag{20}$$

which not only provides a direct proof of (18) but also shows that one or more *bursts* of hits of length at least $\lceil \log_q(KN) \rceil - 1$ must occur.

2.4 The Design of Hopping Patterns Using Reed-Solomon Codes

Hopping patterns were defined earlier as sequences of elements from the set $\{f_0, f_1, \ldots, f_{q-1}\}$. However, it is not necessary that the elements of the set be the center frequencies of the slots. All the various properties of hopping patterns discussed above hold provided only that the set contains q distinct elements. In short, one can also regard a hopping pattern as a sequence of elements from some arbitrary set of q distinct elements, and the pattern can always be transformed into a sequence of frequencies by a suitable one-one mapping from this set to $\{f_0, f_1, \ldots, f_{q-1}\}$. This is the viewpoint that will be taken in the remainder of this section. In particular, hopping patterns will be viewed as sequences of elements from the finite field $\mathrm{GF}(q) = \mathrm{GF}(p^k)$, where p denotes a prime. Thus, it should not be too surprising that Reed-Solomon codes over $\mathrm{GF}(q)$ are a source of excellent designs of hopping patterns. The concept is as follows.

Let N be a divisor of $q - 1$ and let α denote a primitive Nth root of unity in $\mathrm{GF}(q)$. Let $\mathcal{C}(N, t+1; i)$ denote the cyclic $(N, t+1)$ Reed-Solomon code over $\mathrm{GF}(q)$ with parity-check polynomial

$$h(x) = \prod_{j=i}^{i+t}(x - \alpha^{-j}),$$

generator matrix

$$G = \begin{bmatrix} 1 & \alpha^i & \alpha^{2i} & \cdots & \alpha^{(N-1)i} \\ 1 & \alpha^{(i+1)} & \alpha^{2(i+1)} & \cdots & \alpha^{(N-1)(i+1)} \\ 1 & \alpha^{(i+2)} & \alpha^{2(i+2)} & \cdots & \alpha^{(N-1)(i+2)} \\ \vdots & \vdots & \vdots & \ddots & \vdots \\ 1 & \alpha^{(i+t)} & \alpha^{2(i+t)} & \cdots & \alpha^{(N-1)(i+t)} \end{bmatrix}, \tag{21}$$

and minimum distance $N - t$. Suppose that two *cyclically inequivalent* code words x and y are chosen to be hopping patterns. Since the code is cyclic, $T^j y$ is a code word for any j. Furthermore, since the sequences are cyclically inequivalent, $T^j y \neq x$ for any j. Hence, $H_{x,y}(j) = N - d(x, T^j y) \leq t$. Similarly, if x is of period M, where M is a divisor of N, then $H_x(j) = N - d(x, T^j x) \leq t$ for $j \not\equiv 0 \bmod M$. Thus, hopping patterns can be constructed by choosing one code word from each cyclic equivalence class. However, for reasons noted earlier, it is usually desirable to use only those patterns that have full period N. Furthermore, since a pattern of period N may leave as many as $(q - N)$ slots unused, this construction is usually applied only to Reed-Solomon codes of length $q - 1$. Interestingly, in the early 1970s, the above idea was discussed by both Reed [20] and Solomon [28] in separate papers. Their solutions to the problem were somewhat different, and these solutions are considered next.

2.5 Reed's Construction

In [20], Reed considered hopping patterns obtained by choosing one code word from each cyclic equivalence class of the code words belonging to the code $C(q - 1, t + 1; 0)$ with generator matrix

$$G = \begin{bmatrix} 1 & 1 & 1 & \cdots & 1 \\ 1 & \alpha & \alpha^2 & \cdots & \alpha^{(q-2)} \\ 1 & \alpha^2 & \alpha^4 & \cdots & \alpha^{2(q-2)} \\ \vdots & \vdots & \vdots & \ddots & \vdots \\ 1 & \alpha^t & \alpha^{2t} & \cdots & \alpha^{t(q-2)} \end{bmatrix}. \tag{22}$$

Note that α is a primitive element of the field GF(q). The number of cyclic equivalence classes (i.e., the number of different hopping patterns) is given by [20]

$$\frac{1}{q-1} \sum_{d|(q-1)} \phi(d) q^{1+\lfloor t/d \rfloor}$$

where $\phi(\cdot)$ is Euler's totient function. Of course, many of these equivalence classes contain code words of period less than $q-1$ (referred to as *nonprimitive* code words henceforth) and thus are usually not of interest. Reed also gave a lower bound on the number of hopping patterns of period $q - 1$ (these are *primitive* code words) that can be obtained from this code. This bound is based on the following simple argument. If α^j is a nonprimitive element of GF(q), then the jth row $(1, \alpha^j, \alpha^{2j}, \ldots, \alpha^{j(q-2)})$ of the generator matrix in (22) is a nonprimitive code word. Suppose that s rows of **G** are nonprimitive code words. The q^s linear combinations of these rows *usually* are nonprimitive code words but can be primitive code words in some cases. On the other hand, nonzero linear combinations of the other $(t + 1 - s)$ rows are always primitive code words. Since the sum of a primitive code word and a nonprimitive code word is a primitive code word, it follows that there are *at least* $q^s(q^{t+1-s} - 1) = q^{t+1} - q^s$ primitive code words in the code. Hence, the set $\mathcal{X}$ of hopping patterns of period $q - 1$ obtained from $C(q - 1, t + 1; 0)$ contains at least $(q^{t+1} - q^s)/(q - 1) = \sum_{j=s}^{t} q^j \geq q^t$ hopping patterns. Furthermore, $H_{\max}(\mathcal{X}) = t$, and since $KN = K(q - 1) < q^{t+1}$ (which implies that $\log_q \lceil KN \rceil - 1 = t$), it follows that both (18) and (20) are satisfied with equality. In other words, these hopping patterns are optimal with respect to these bounds.

The obvious (but generally very time-consuming) explicit construction of the hopping patterns requires finding all the code words, dividing them into cyclic equivalence classes, and then choosing one member from each equivalence class of primitive code words. Fortunately, it is possible to construct the $\sum_{j=s}^{t} q^j$ hopping patterns promised by Reed's lower bound very easily. The method, which is based on a slight modification of the argument that produced the bound itself, can be explained as follows [29]. Let $\hat{\mathbf{G}}$ denote a matrix obtained by reordering the rows of **G** so that the s nonprimitive code words appear above the $(t + 1 - s)$ primitive code words. Let $\mathbf{u}^{(j)}$, $s \leq j \leq t$, denote a vector of length $t + 1$ over GF(q) in which the leading j elements are arbitrary, the $(j + 1)$th element is 1, and remaining $(t - j)$ elements are 0. Clearly, there are q^j such vectors $\mathbf{u}^{(j)}$. It is easily shown that code words of the form $\mathbf{u}^{(j)}\hat{\mathbf{G}}$, $s \leq j \leq t$, are cyclically inequivalent primitive code words. These code words are the $\sum_{j=s}^{t} q^j$ hopping patterns promised by Reed's lower bound. As a specific simple example of this construction process, consider $C(q - 1, 2; 0)$ whose generator matrix has rows $(1, 1, \ldots, 1)$ and $(1, \alpha, \alpha^2, \ldots, \alpha^{q-2})$ of period 1 and $q - 1$, respectively. Thus, $t = s = 1$, $\mathbf{G} = \hat{\mathbf{G}}$, and the q hopping patterns are given by $(\beta, 1)\mathbf{G}$, where $\beta \in$ GF(q). Put another way, let β_j, $0 \leq j \leq q - 1$, denote the elements of GF(q). Then, the q sequences obtained via Reed's construction can be expressed as

$$x^{(j)} = (\beta_j, \beta_j, \ldots, \beta_j) + (1, \alpha, \alpha^2, \ldots, \alpha^{q-2}), \quad 0 \leq j \leq q - 1. \quad (23)$$

Since the ith element of the jth sequence is

$$x_i^{(j)} = \beta_j + \alpha^i, \quad 0 \le i < q - 1, \ 0 \le j \le q - 1, \tag{24}$$

and since $\alpha^i \ne 0$, the element β_j does not occur in $x^{(j)}$, while any other β_l occurs exactly once. Thus, these hopping patterns are nonrepeating and they also satisfy (14) and (15) with each element of GF(q) occurring a total of $(q - 1)$ times in the q hopping patterns. Note also that for $i \ne j$, $\langle \mathcal{N}(x^{(i)}), \mathcal{N}(x^{(j)}) \rangle = q - 2$ and that $H_{x^{(i)}, x^{(j)}}(l)$ has value 0 if $l = 0$ and value 1 otherwise.

Applying Reed's construction to $C(q - 1, t + 1; i)$, where $i \ne 0$, sometimes provides *minor* improvements on the above results. If $q = 2^k$, Reed's construction applied to $C(2^k - 1, 2; 0)$ provides 2^k hopping patterns with $H_{\max} = 1$ as described by (23). In comparison, the construction provides $(2^k + 1)$ hopping patterns with $H_{\max} = 1$ when it is applied to $C(2^k - 1, 2; 1)$. This is because both α and α^2 are primitive elements, and hence the code words of the form $(1, 0)G$ and $(\beta, 1)G$ are cyclically inequivalent primitive code words. Letting x and y denote the two rows of G and noting that $T^i x = \alpha^i x$, this set of $(2^k + 1)$ hopping patterns can be expressed as

$$\{x, y, x + y, Tx + y, T^2 x + y, \ldots, T^{2^k - 2} x + y\}$$

which is very similar to the representation of Gold sequences in (4.4) of [23]. Similarly, applying Reed's construction to $C(2^k - 1, 3; 0)$ provides $(2^{2k} + 2^k)$ hopping patterns with $H_{\max} = 2$, whereas it provides $(2^{2k} + 2^k + 1)$ hopping patterns with $H_{\max} = 2$ when it is applied to $C(2^k - 1, 3; 1)$, where k is odd. More generally, if $(2^k - 1)$ is a Mersenne prime, then all the rows of the generator matrix of $C(2^k - 1, t + 1; 1)$ are primitive code words, and hence Reed's construction provides $(2^{k(t+1)} - 1)/(2^k - 1) = \sum_{j=0}^{t} 2^{jk}$ hopping patterns of period $2^k - 1$ with $H_{\max} = t$.

In contrast to the situation when q is even, α^i and α^{i+1} both cannot be primitive elements when q is odd. Thus, the zeroth, second, fourth, $\ldots$, etc., rows of G in (22) are nonprimitive code words and therefore $s \ge \lceil (t + 1)/2 \rceil$. For other choices of i in $C(q - 1, t + 1; i)$, fewer than $\lceil (t + 1)/2 \rceil$ rows of G in (21) may be nonprimitive. For example, $s = 2$ for the code $C(q - 1, 3; 0)$ but $s = 1$ for the code $C(q - 1, 3; q - 2)$ because both $\alpha^{q-2} = \alpha^{-1}$ and α are primitive elements. The former code provides q^2 hopping patterns with $H_{\max} = 2$, while the latter code provides $(q^2 + q)$ hopping patterns with $H_{\max} = 2$.

Although the hopping patterns obtained via Reed's construction are optimal with respect to the bounds (18) and (20), they can have some undesirable properties when $t > 1$. For example, consider the q^2 hopping patterns with

$H_{max} = 2$ obtained from $C(q - 1, 3; 0)$, where q is assumed to be odd. These hopping patterns are all of the form $(\gamma, \delta, 1)\hat{\mathbf{G}}$, where γ and δ are arbitrary elements of GF(q), and the ith element of a typical sequence is of the form $\gamma + \alpha^i + \delta\alpha^{2i}$. Suppose that $\delta \neq 0$. Now, an element β occurs in this hopping pattern if there is an i such that $\beta = \gamma + \alpha^i + \delta\alpha^{2i}$; i.e., if the quadratic equation $\delta x^2 + x + (\gamma - \beta) = 0$ has a nonzero root in the field. It is easily verified that γ occurs once in the hopping pattern (the other root of the quadratic is 0) as does $\gamma - (4\delta)^{-1}$ (the quadratic has repeated roots), and that any other β occurs either twice (the quadratic has two distinct nonzero roots) or not at all (the quadratic is irreducible over GF(q).) Thus, this hopping pattern uses roughly half of the available frequency slots, and this is usually undesirable.

2.6 Solomon's Construction

In [28], Solomon considered the construction of hopping patterns based on *cosets* of Reed-Solomon codes. The code $C(q - 1, t; 0)$ is a subcode of $C(q - 1, t + 1; 0)$, and hence the latter can be be partitioned into q cosets of $C(q - 1, t; 0)$. The coset representatives can be taken to be multiples of the last row of **G** in (22), i.e., $\beta(1, \alpha^t, \alpha^{2t}, \ldots, \alpha^{t(q-2)})$, where β is an element of GF(q). Now, cyclically shifting all the code words in one such coset results in another such coset (usually distinct from the first). Solomon suggested using the coset with representative $(1, \alpha^t, \alpha^{2t}, \ldots, \alpha^{t(q-2)})$ as a set of hopping patterns. Each coset contains q^t hopping patterns, and since these are all code words in $C(q - 1, t + 1; 0)$, $H_{max} = t$ for this set. In comparison, recall that Reed's set of hopping patterns also has $H_{max} = t$ but contains *at least* q^t hopping patterns.

As an example of Solomon's construction technique, consider the repetition code $C(q - 1, 1; 0)$ which is a subcode of $C(q - 1, 2; 0)$. The code words in the coset are all of the form

$$(1, \alpha, \alpha^2, \ldots, \alpha^{q-2}) + (\beta, \beta, \ldots, \beta), \quad \beta \in GF(q)$$

and these are *identical* to the hopping patterns exhibited in (23). On the other hand, Reed's construction can provide $(2^k + 1)$ hopping patterns with $H_{max} = 1$ when it is applied to $C(2^k - 1, 2; 1)$ over GF(2^k), while Solomon's construction provides only 2^k hopping patterns.

There is a minor problem (that did not show up in the above simple examples) with the general version of Solomon's construction. If α^t is not a primitive element, then the coset representative $(1, \alpha^t, \alpha^{2t}, \ldots, \alpha^{t(q-2)})$ is not a primitive code word, and hence the hopping patterns do not all have period $q - 1$ (even though $H_{max} = t$ for the set.) Fortunately, there is a simple way around this difficulty. The code $C(q - 1, t; 0)$ is also a subcode of $C(q-1, t+1; q-2)$, and Solomon's set can be taken to be the coset with representative $(1, \alpha^{q-2}, \alpha^{2(q-2)}, \ldots, \alpha^{(q-2)^2})$. As noted previously, α^{q-2} is a primitive element. Hence all the hopping patterns in the coset are of period $q-1$, and the problem is thus eliminated. As a final comment, suppose that α^t is a primitive element and suppose that the last row of the permuted matrix $\hat{\mathbf{G}}$ of the previous subsection is the last row of $\mathbf{G}$ in (22). Then, Solomon's coset is just the set of code words of the form $\mathbf{u}^{(t)}\hat{\mathbf{G}}$, where $\mathbf{u}^{(t)} = (u_1, u_2, \ldots, u_t, 1)$, and is thus generally a subset of the hopping patterns obtained by Reed's construction.

2.7 Titlebaum's Construction

Let $k = 1$ so that $\mathrm{GF}(q) = \mathrm{GF}(p)$ and consider the code generated by the matrix

$$\mathbf{G} = \begin{bmatrix} 1 & 1 & 1 & \cdots & 1 \\ 0 & 1 & 2 & \cdots & p-1 \end{bmatrix}.$$

It was shown by Roth and Seroussi [21] that this code is a maximum distance separable (MDS) *cyclic* code and that the code is *equivalent* under column permutations to an *extended* cyclic Reed-Solomon code over $\mathrm{GF}(p)$. The minimum distance of this code is $p-1$, and hence the representatives of the $(p-1)$ equivalence classes of period p form a set of nonrepeating hopping patterns with $H_a(\mathcal{X}) = 0$ and $H_c(\mathcal{X}) = 1$. The hopping patterns thus satisfy (3), (4), (14), and (15) with equality and are optimal with respect to the bounds of Section 2.2. It is easily shown that the representatives of these equivalence classes may be taken to be

$$(0, 1i, 2i, \ldots, (p-1)i), \quad 1 \le i \le p-1.$$

This form of the construction is due to Titlebaum [30] and Shaar and Davies [24]. Extensions to larger sets of hopping patterns can be found in [14] and [31].

A related construction, due to Shaar and Davies [25], is as follows. Suppose that $2^k - 1$ is a Mersenne prime and consider the generator matrix of the Reed-Solomon code $C(2^k - 1, 2^k - 2; 1)$ over $\mathrm{GF}(2^k)$. All the rows of this generator matrix are primitive code words of the form $(1, \alpha^i, \alpha^{2i}, \ldots, \alpha^{i(2^k-2)})$. Shaar and Davies proposed that these rows be considered as hopping patterns of period $2^k - 1$ over the alphabet $\mathrm{GF}(2^k) - \{0\}$ of size $2^k - 1$. Clearly, $\mathcal{N}(x) = (1, 1, \ldots, 1)$ for all these hopping patterns, and hence $H_a(\mathcal{X}) = 0$ and $\bar{H}_c(\mathcal{X}) = 1$. In fact, $H_{x,y}(l) = 1$ for all $x \ne y$ and all l. This is because if the ith and the jth sequence collide in the mth and the nth dwells when the relative time delay is l dwells, then it must be that $\alpha^{im} = \alpha^{j(l+m)}$ and

$\alpha^{in} = \alpha^{j(l+n)}$. However, these two equations cannot be satisfied simultaneously when $i \neq j$. Note that the Shaar-Davies construction cannot be used with fields of characteristic greater than 2 because $p^k - 1$ is always composite when $p > 2$ (except in the trivial case $p = 3$, $k = 1$). Another construction that also requires an alphabet of prime cardinality is given in [4]. However, this is not directly related to Reed-Solomon codes and will not be discussed further here.

2.8 The Lempel-Greenberger Construction

The Reed and Solomon constructions use code words from cyclic Reed-Solomon codes and hence the hopping patterns have period at most $q - 1$. However, the constructions can be used to create large sets of hopping patterns of these relatively short periods. In contrast, in their seminal paper [10], Lempel and Greenberger showed how to create small sets of hopping patterns of a very large period. In hindsight, the Lempel-Greenberger construction can also be viewed as a construction based on Reed-Solomon codes and thus it fits in perfectly with the theme of this chapter.

Let X denote an m-sequence (that is, a maximal-length linear feedback shift register sequence) of period $N = p^n - 1$ over GF(p). Two important properties of X are as follows:

1. For any i, $0 < i < N$, there is a j, $0 < j < N$, such that $X - T^i X = T^j X$.

2. With subscripts on X being taken modulo N, the n-tuples $(X_i, X_{i+1}, \ldots, X_{i+n-1})$, $0 \leq i < N$, are distinct and nonzero; that is, each of the $p^n - 1$ nonzero n-tuples occurs exactly once in a period of X.

Suppose that $k \leq n$. Then, since each nonzero k-tuple can be extended into p^{n-k} different nonzero n-tuples, the nonzero k-tuples all occur p^{n-k} times in a period of X. Similarly, since the zero k-tuple can be extended into $(p^{n-k} - 1)$ different *nonzero* n-tuples, it occurs $(p^{n-k} - 1)$ times in a period of X.

Sequences of k-tuples are the basis of the Lempel-Greenberger construction. Let x denote the sequence whose elements are successive overlapping k-tuples from X. Thus,

$$x_i = (X_i, X_{i+1}, X_{i+2}, \ldots, X_{i+k-1}), \quad 0 \leq i < N. \tag{25}$$

Since GF$(q) = $ GF(p^k) can be regarded as a k-dimensional vector space over GF(p), one can also think of the x_i as elements of GF(q). Property 2 of X above thus implies that each nonzero element of GF(q) occurs p^{n-k} times in a period of x, while 0 occurs $(p^{n-k} - 1)$ times, and thus x satisfies (3) and

(4). The Lempel-Greenberger set of hopping patterns can then be defined as the set of q sequences $\{x^{(j)} : 0 \le j \le q - 1\}$, where

$$x_i^{(j)} = \beta_j + x_i, \ 0 \le i < N, \ \beta_j \in \mathrm{GF}(q). \tag{26}$$

Note that x itself is one of the members of this set of hopping patterns. Note also that each $x^{(j)}$ satisfies (3) and (4) with the element β_j occurring $(p^{n-k} - 1)$ times and all the other elements occurring p^{n-k} times. Thus, the Lempel-Greenberger set also satisfies (14) and (15) with each element of $\mathrm{GF}(q)$ occurring a total of N times in the q hopping patterns.

It was shown in [10] that for $1 < l < N$,

$$H_{x^{(i)}}(l) = p^{n-k} - 1 = \left\lceil \frac{N}{q} \right\rceil - 1 \tag{27}$$

and that if $i \ne j$, then $H_{x^{(i)}, x^{(j)}}(0) = 0$ and

$$H_{x^{(i)}, x^{(j)}}(l) = p^{n-k} = \left\lceil \frac{N}{q} \right\rceil > \frac{N}{q} - \frac{1}{q} \tag{28}$$

for $1 < l < N$. Thus, the hopping patterns are optimal with respect to the bounds (12) and (17). These properties can be proved straightforwardly using the properties of X. These properties can also be deduced from the fact that the Lempel-Greenberger hopping patterns can be obtained by mapping a set of Reed and Solomon sequences over $\mathrm{GF}(p^n)$ of the form exhibited in (23) to $\mathrm{GF}(q)$. This idea is considered next.

Suppose without loss of generality that the m-sequence X is in its *characteristic phase* so that there is a primitive element $\xi \in \mathrm{GF}(p^n)$ such that $X_i = \mathrm{Tr}(\xi^i)$, $0 \le i < N$, where $\mathrm{Tr}(z) = z + z^p + z^{p^2} + \cdots + z^{p^{n-1}}$ is the *trace* function from $\mathrm{GF}(p^n)$ to $\mathrm{GF}(p)$ [16]. Now, a standard polynomial basis for $\mathrm{GF}(p^n)$ over $\mathrm{GF}(p)$ is $\{1, \xi, \xi^2, \ldots, \xi^{n-1}\}$. The n-tuple $(a_0, a_1, \ldots, a_{n-1})$ represents the element $\sum_{i=0}^{n-1} a_i \xi^i \in \mathrm{GF}(p^n)$ with respect to this standard polynomial basis. Let $\{\zeta_0, \zeta_1, \ldots, \zeta_{n-1}\}$ denote the *dual* basis of the standard polynomial basis. With respect to this dual basis, the n-tuple $(b_0, b_1, \ldots, b_{n-1})$ represents the element $Y = \sum_{j=0}^{n-1} b_j \zeta_j \in \mathrm{GF}(p^n)$. But, according to the properties of dual bases, the b_j are given by $b_j = \mathrm{Tr}(Y \cdot \xi^j)$ for $0 \le j \le n - 1$ [16]. Thus the n-tuple

$$(X_i, X_{i+1}, \ldots, X_{i+n-1}) = (\mathrm{Tr}(\xi^i), \mathrm{Tr}(\xi^{i+1}), \ldots, \mathrm{Tr}(\xi^{i+n-1})),$$
$$= (\mathrm{Tr}(\xi^i \cdot \xi^0), \mathrm{Tr}(\xi^i \cdot \xi^1), \ldots, \mathrm{Tr}(\xi^i \cdot \xi^{n-1})),$$

is just the representation of ξ^i with respect to the *dual* of the standard polynomial basis. Hence, the sequence $\hat{X}$ of successive overlapping n-tuples from

X with ith element given by

$$\hat{X}_i = (X_i, X_{i+1}, \ldots, X_{i+n-1}) \tag{29}$$

represents the sequence of elements $(1, \xi, \xi^2, \ldots, \xi^{N-1})$ over $\mathrm{GF}(p^n)$ with respect to the dual of the standard polynomial basis.

Consider the Reed and Solomon set of sequences from the Reed-Solomon code $\mathcal{C}(p^n - 1, 2; 0)$ over $\mathrm{GF}(p^n)$. Denoting the elements of $\mathrm{GF}(p^n)$ as γ_i, $0 \le i \le N$, the ith sequence is just

$$\hat{X}^{(i)} = (1, \xi, \xi^2, \ldots, \xi^{N-1}) + (\gamma_i, \gamma_i, \ldots, \gamma_i) \tag{30}$$

which is exactly of the form given in (23). Note that γ_i does not occur in $\hat{X}^{(i)}$, while all the other elements of $\mathrm{GF}(p^n)$ occur exactly once. Suppose that $\mathrm{GF}(p^n)$ is represented as an n-dimensional vector space over $\mathrm{GF}(p)$ with respect to some *arbitrary* basis and suppose that L denotes an *arbitrary linear* transformation of rank k from this n-dimensional space to a k-dimensional vector space. The range of L is a representation of $\mathrm{GF}(p^k) = \mathrm{GF}(q)$ with respect to some basis, and thus L is a map from $\mathrm{GF}(p^n)$ to $\mathrm{GF}(q)$. However, there is no elegant algebraic description of this map when n is not a multiple of k. Let $L(\hat{X}^{(i)})$ denote the result of applying L to the elements of $\hat{X}^{(i)}$ as exhibited in (30) so that

$$L(\hat{X}^{(i)}) = (L(1), L(\xi), L(\xi^2), \ldots, L(\xi^{N-1})) + (L(\gamma_i), L(\gamma_i), \ldots, L(\gamma_i)).$$

Since $\ker(L)$, the kernel of the linear transformation L, has dimension $n - k$, exactly p^{n-k} elements $\gamma_i \in \mathrm{GF}(p^n)$ are mapped onto each element $\beta_j \in \mathrm{GF}(q)$. Since the first sequence in the above equation does not depend on i, it follows that p^{n-k} Reed-Solomon code words $\hat{X}^{(i)}$ are mapped to the same sequence over $\mathrm{GF}(q)$; that is, only q different sequences over $\mathrm{GF}(q)$ are obtained from this mapping. The Lempel-Greenberger hopping patterns as defined in (26) are obtained when the elements of $\mathrm{GF}(p^n)$ in (30) are represented as n vectors with respect to the dual of the standard polynomial basis, and the transformation L is a projection mapping that maps an n vector onto its first k components. In this case, the Reed-Solomon code word $(1, \xi, \xi^2, \ldots, \xi^{N-1})$ is represented by $\hat{X}$ as defined in (29), and its image under L is just x as defined in (25). As a special case, the Lempel-Greenberger hopping patterns are identical to the Reed and Solomon patterns when $n = k$ and all field elements are represented with respect to the dual of the standard polynomial basis.

As shown above, the Lempel-Greenberger hopping patterns are a special case of a more general sequence design based on the idea of mapping Reed and Solomon hopping patterns over $\mathrm{GF}(p^n)$ onto $\mathrm{GF}(q)$. All the Hamming correlation properties described above for the Lempel-Greenberger hopping patterns also apply to the more general sets. To see this, note that $\hat{X}^{(i)}$ and $\hat{X}^{(j)}$ are both code words in a linear cyclic code and hence $\hat{X}^{(i)} - T^l\hat{X}^{(j)}$ is also a code word in the same code. Furthermore, if $l = 0$, this code word consists of $\gamma_i - \gamma_j$ repeated N times, whereas if $0 < l < N$, then every element of $GF(p^n)$ except $\gamma_i - \gamma_j$ appears exactly once in this code word. Now, for a relative time delay of l dwells, the Hamming correlation between $L(\hat{X}^{(i)})$ and $L(\hat{X}^{(j)})$ is just the number of times that 0 appears in the sequence $L(\hat{X}^{(i)}) - T^l L(\hat{X}^{(j)})$. But this sequence is just the image of $\hat{X}^{(i)} - T^l\hat{X}^{(j)}$ under L. Thus, if $\gamma_i - \gamma_j \in \ker(L)$, then $L(\hat{X}^{(i)}) = L(\hat{X}^{(j)})$, the correlation under consideration is an autocorrelation, and 0 appears $(p^{n-k} - 1)$ times for any l, $0 < l < N$. On the other hand, if $\gamma_i - \gamma_j \notin \ker(L)$, then $L(\hat{X}^{(i)}) \neq L(\hat{X}^{(j)})$, the correlation under consideration is a cross-correlation, and 0 appears p^{n-k} times if $l \neq 0$ and never appears if $l = 0$. Thus, the Hamming correlation properties (27) and (28) of the Lempel-Greenberger hopping patterns also hold in the more general case.

Another interesting property of the Lempel-Greenberger hopping patterns arises from the fact that the underlying sequence X is an m-sequence of period $p^n - 1$. According to Property 2 above, X contains a run of length n of each nonzero element of $GF(p)$. It follows that the sequence x defined in (25) has a run of length $n - k + 1$ corresponding to each nonzero element of $GF(p)$. Thus, at some time during each period, the signal will hop to the frequency slot corresponding to $(i, i, \ldots, i) \in GF(q)$ and stay there for $(n - k + 1)$ successive dwells. Since X also contains runs of lengths $n - 1, n - 2, \ldots$, the signal will return to the same slot many more times in each period though it will stay there for fewer successive dwells. Since $x^{(j)} = x + \beta_j$, the other Lempel-Greenberger patterns hop to slots corresponding to $\beta_j + (i, i, \ldots, i)$ and stay there for $(n - k + 1)$ successive dwells. In fact, given any frequency slot, there are $(p - 1)$ Lempel-Greenberger patterns that will hop to that slot and stay there for $(n - k + 1)$ successive dwells. All this is clearly undesirable for the reasons discussed in Section 2.3. Note that the maximum length of a burst of hits for Lempel-Greenberger hopping patterns is at least $n - k + 1$, which is approximately k times larger than the lower bound of (20). These properties also hold for the more general version of the Lempel-Greenberger sequences discussed above. The proof is a straightforward but not particularly interesting exercise in linear algebra and the theory of equivalent matrices.

2.9 Generalizations of the Lempel-Greenberger Construction

The Lempel-Greenberger construction is optimal with respect to various correlation bounds but has the defect that long runs occur in the sequences and these runs are undesirable for the reasons outlined in Section 2.3. Various generalizations of this construction are possible. For example, one can use an arbitrary basis for $GF(p^n)$ and an arbitrary linear transformation L of rank k from the n-dimensional vector space to the k-dimensional vector space as discussed in the previous subsection. However, there is no particular advantage to such generalizations because the generalized hopping patterns have the same properties as the original Lempel-Greenberger hopping patterns. In fact, the implementation of sequence generators is very easy for the original Lempel-Greenberger hopping patterns but somewhat more complicated for the generalized versions.

Another generalization of the Lempel-Greenberger hopping patterns uses the extension field $GF(p^s)$ instead of the prime field $GF(p)$. Thus, X is an m-sequence of period $(p^s)^n - 1$ over $GF(p^s)$, and these generalized Lempel-Greenberger hopping patterns are formed by considering the sequence x of successive overlapping k-tuples from X and adding a fixed k-tuple over $GF(p^s)$ to each element of x. The hopping patterns are thus elements of $GF((p^s)^k)$, and so on. None of the proofs in [10] really require the base field $GF(p)$ to be a *prime* field—they all hold *mutatis mutandis* if the base field is the extension field $GF(p^s)$ instead. Unfortunately, this also means that all the results asserted in the previous subsection also hold. In particular, these generalized Lempel-Greenberger hopping patterns also have runs of the same frequency and produce bursts of hits for certain relative time delays, etc.

Recently, a different solution to the runs problem, based on a combination of the Lempel-Greenberger and Reed-Solomon approaches, has been proposed by Burger [2]. This method can be viewed as a product code construction in which one code is a Lempel-Greenberger hopping pattern and the other code is a Reed-Solomon hopping pattern. The method begins by constructing a set of q Lempel-Greenberger hopping patterns of period $p^n - 1$ over $GF(q)$ as usual. Each transmitter uses a different $(q - 1, 1)$ Reed-Solomon code (actually a coset of a $(q - 1, 1)$ Reed-Solomon code) over $GF(q)$ to encode each symbol in its Lempel-Greenberger pattern. In other words, each symbol in the Lempel-Greenberger pattern is replaced by a code word of length $q - 1$ from the Reed-Solomon coset. This creates a hopping pattern of length $(p^n - 1)(q - 1) = p^{n+k} - p^n - p^k + 1$ over $GF(q)$. Now, the Reed-Solomon coset is a coset of $C(q - 1, 1; 0)$, and the q different cosets assigned to the q transmitters are all subsets of $C(q - 1, 3, q - 2)$. Hence, any two code words in the coset assigned to a transmitter collide in at most one position, while code words from the cosets assigned to two different transmitters collide in at most two positions. The Hamming correlations of these patterns are not quite optimal but are nonetheless very good. More important, however, is the fact that the runs of the same frequency that occur in the Lempel-Greenberger patterns have been broken up. It is also easy to show that at most four successive collisions can occur between two patterns, which alleviates the burden on the error control system as well. Further details of this construction can be found in [2].

2.10 Vajda's Construction

The use of a product code construction of hopping patterns has also been explored by Vajda [32] who took a cyclic product of two codes. The first code is obtained from $C(N, t + 1; 0)$ over GF(q), where N is a prime. As described in Section 2.5, q^t hopping patterns of period N can be obtained from this code. Let r denote the largest integer such that $N^{r-1} \leq q^t$. This code is a (nonlinear) cyclic code consisting of a set of N^{r-1} hopping patterns of period N and all their cyclic shifts. Note that the minimum distance of this nonlinear cyclic code is $N - t$. The other code is a coset of $C(M, K - 1; 2)$ over GF(N^r) that is a subcode of $C(M, K + 1; 0)$ over GF(N^r). Note that M is a divisor of $N^r - 1$. Thus, this code has $N^{r(K-1)}$ code words over an alphabet of size N^r, and since the code words belong to $C(M, K + 1; 0)$, the minimum distance between cyclic shifts of two code words is at least $M - K$. Vajda has proposed using the cyclic product of these codes instead of the direct product discussed in the previous subsection. Thus, each of the M N^r-valued symbols in a code word of the second code is replaced by a column vector of length N consisting of a code word of the first code. This creates an $N \times M$ matrix $\mathbf{Q} = Q_{i,j}$. Now, M and N are relatively prime, and hence the entries in $\mathbf{Q}$ can be read off in cyclic fashion to form a hopping pattern of length MN whose ith symbol is $Q_{i \bmod N, i \bmod M}$. Since the cyclic product of an (n_1, k_1, d_1) cyclic code with an (n_2, k_2, d_2) cyclic code is an $(n_1 n_2, k_1 k_2, d_1 d_2)$ cyclic code [13], this hopping pattern is actually a code word in an $[MN, (k + 1)(K + 1), (M - K)(N - t)]$ cyclic code over GF(q). There are $N^{r(K-1)}$ such hopping patterns, and it follows from (8) that, as shown in [32],

$$H_{\max} \leq MN - (M - K)(N - t) = Mt + KN - Kt.$$

As an example of this construction, let $q = 32$, $N = 31$, $t = 2$, $r = 3$, and $M = (31^3 - 1)/(31 - 1) = 993$. Let $K = 4$. Then, a set of $31^{3 \cdot 2} = 887,503,681$ hopping patterns of period $31 \cdot 993 = 30,783$ over GF(32) is obtained. The maximum Hamming correlation is 2102, so that there is, on the average, one hit every 14.64 symbols. In contrast, the Reed and Solomon sets of hopping patterns from $C(31, 3; 0)$ over GF(32) provide 1024 hopping patterns of period 31 with a maximum Hamming correlation of 2, that is, one hit every 15.5 symbols, which is very slightly better.

2.11 Einarsson's Construction

Because of technological limitations on the frequency synthesizers used to produce the frequency-hopped signals, the hopping rate in a FH/SS system is limited to a few thousand dwells per second. In a fast FH/SS system, the transmission of a symbol occurs over several hops, and it is necessary to use M-ary signaling in order to achieve a reasonably large data rate. Einarsson [5] proposed a combined design of hopping patterns and M-ary modulation for use in such systems. In systems using this design, each transmitter is assigned a *collection* of M hopping patterns of length N and transmits one M-ary data symbol per N dwells by choosing and transmitting one of the hopping patterns. The data rate is thus $\log_2(M)/NT_h$ bits per second. Note, however, that the receiver is now more complicated since it must track all M possible hopping patterns in order to determine which one is being transmitted. Thus, M different frequency synthesizers might be needed in each receiver.

The Einarsson design uses all the nonzero code words in the Reed-Solomon code $C(q - 1, 2; 0)$. Each transmitter is assigned all the code words in a cyclic equivalence class. Thus, $M = N = q - 1$, and the hopping patterns assigned to jth transmitter are of the form

$$(\beta_j, \beta_j, \ldots, \beta_j) + \alpha^i(1, \alpha, \alpha^2, \ldots, \alpha^{q-2}), \ 0 \leq j \leq q - 1.$$

Since all these sequences are from $C(q - 1, 2; 0)$, the number of hits between two patterns assigned to different transmitters is at most 1 regardless of the relative time delay between the two patterns. However, the number of hits per period can be guaranteed to be 1 only if the two transmitters are *frame-synchronous*. If the transmitters are only dwell-synchronous, then the tail end and the front end of *two possibly different* hopping patterns from an interfering transmitter can cause collisions,[3] and thus the number of hits per period can be two in some cases. There is also the question of the initial acquisition of synchronization in the receivers in such systems since the hopping patterns assigned to a transmitter are not cyclically inequivalent. In fact, the Hamming cross-correlation between two hopping patterns assigned to the same transmitter can have values as large as $N - 1$.

2.12 Other Constructions

There are several other constructions of frequency hopping patterns that are not directly related to Reed-Solomon codes except in certain special cases.

---

[3] A similar phenomenon in DS/SS systems gives rise to the *odd cross-correlation function* of binary sequences (cf. [23]).

Among these are those described by Cooper and Nettleton [4], Jevtić and Alkhatib [8], and Kumar [9]. This last paper is of interest because it considers hopping patterns with large *linear span*, that is, hopping patterns that can be generated by relatively short shift registers with nonlinear feedback but that require very long shift registers if the feedback is restricted to be linear. However, since these constructions do not fit within the topic of this chapter, the interested reader is invited to consult the literature for details.

3 DIRECT-SEQUENCE SPREAD-SPECTRUM SYSTEMS

In contrast to the detailed exposition of the use of Reed-Solomon codes in the design of frequency-hopping patterns, this section on the use of Reed-Solomon codes in the design of signature sequences for DS/SS systems is mercifully brief. There are two reasons for this. First, the desirable properties of signature sequences for DS/SS systems are described in [23], and a detailed tutorial survey of various constructions for these signature sequences is also given there. Thus, all that information need not be repeated here. Second, although many signature sequences can be described in terms of images of Reed-Solomon codes, the properties of Reed-Solomon codes *per se* do not appear to have much bearing on the desirable properties of the sequences themselves. Thus, although many new results on the design of signature sequences for DS/SS systems have appeared since the publication of [23], this section merely points out that many of the elementary constructions described in [23], as well as many of the more advanced constructions published since then, can be viewed as images of code words from Reed-Solomon codes.

3.1 Binary *m*-Sequences and Their Decimations

Let $N = 2^n - 1$ and let $x^{(1)}$ denote a binary *m*-sequence of period N. Suppose that $x^{(1)}$ is in its characteristic phase, that is, $x_{2i}^{(1)} = x_i^{(1)}$. Then there is a primitive element α of $GF(2^n)$ such that $x_i^{(1)} = \mathrm{Tr}(\alpha^i)$, $0 \le i < N$, where, as in Section 2.8, $\mathrm{Tr}(z) = z + z^2 + z^{2^2} + \cdots + z^{2^{n-1}}$ is the trace function which maps $GF(2^n)$ to $GF(2)$. Thus, $x^{(1)}$ is the image of the sequence

$$X^{(1)} = (1, \alpha, \alpha^2, \ldots, \alpha^{N-1})$$

over $GF(2^n)$. But $X^{(1)}$ is a (primitive) code word in the cyclic Reed-Solomon code $C(N, 1; 1)$ with parity-check polynomial $h(x) = (x - \alpha^{-1})$, and thus, the binary *m*-sequence $x^{(1)}$ can be obtained by mapping the Reed-Solomon code word $X^{(1)}$ to $GF(2)$.

More generally, for $0 < s < N$, the *s*th *decimation* of $x^{(1)}$ is the sequence $x^{(s)}$ defined by $x_i^{(s)} = x_{si}^{(1)}$, where the subscripts are taken modulo N. Then,

$x_i^{(s)} = \text{Tr}(\alpha^{si}) = \text{Tr}((\alpha^s)^i)$, so that $x^{(s)}$ is the image of

$$X^{(s)} = (1, \alpha^s, (\alpha^s)^2, \ldots, (\alpha^s)^{N-1})$$

which is a code word in $\mathcal{C}(N, 1; s)$. Thus, the decimations of $x^{(1)}$ are also images of Reed-Solomon code words. If $\gcd(N, s) = 1$, the element α^s is primitive, and hence $X^{(s)}$ is a primitive code word and $x^{(s)}$ is an m-sequence. Otherwise, $X^{(s)}$ is nonprimitive and both $X^{(s)}$ and $x^{(s)}$ have period $N / \gcd(N, s) < N$. Note that since $x^{(1)}$ is in its characteristic phase, so is $x^{(s)}$; that is,

$$x_{2i}^{(s)} = x_{2si}^{(1)} = x_{si}^{(1)} = x_i^{(s)}.$$

It follows that $x^{(s \cdot 2^k)} = x^{(s)}$ for all s, $0 < s < N$, and all k, $0 \le k < n$. Furthermore, $X^{(s)}$ is not the only Reed-Solomon code word that is mapped to $x^{(s)}$ by the trace function—$X^{(s \cdot 2^k)}$ is also mapped to $x^{(s \cdot 2^k)} = x^{(s)}$. Note that $X^{(s \cdot 2^k)}$ is a code word in the cyclic Reed-Solomon code $\mathcal{C}(N, 1; s \cdot 2^k)$ with parity-check polynomial $h(x) = (x - \alpha^{-s \cdot 2^k})$. This idea is used repeatedly in the remainder of this section.

3.2 Dual-BCH Sequences

Consider the Reed-Solomon code $\mathcal{C}(N, 2; 2)$ over $\text{GF}(2^n)$ whose generator matrix $\mathbf{G}$ has two rows: $X^{(2)}$ and $X^{(3)}$. Both rows are primitive code words if n is odd, while if n is even, $X^{(3)}$ has period $N/3$. Thus, this Reed-Solomon code has $(2^n + 1)$ or 2^n cyclically inequivalent code words of period N according as n is odd or even. A typical primitive code word is of the form $X^{(2)} + \beta X^{(3)}$, where $\beta \in \text{GF}(2^n)$. Now, suppose that n is odd and that $\beta \ne 0$. Then $\beta X^{(3)}$ is just a cyclic shift of $X^{(3)}$, and hence the trace function (which is a *linear* map from $\text{GF}(2^n)$ to $\text{GF}(2)$) maps $X^{(2)} + \beta X^{(3)}$ to the binary sequence $x^{(2)} + T^i x^{(3)} = x^{(1)} + T^i x^{(3)}$ for some i, $0 \le i < N$. If $\beta = 0$, the sequence is just $x^{(1)}$. One other sequence that can be added to the list of binary sequences obtained from $\mathcal{C}(N, 2; 2)$ is $x^{(3)}$ itself. Thus, the collection of $2^n + 1$ sequences can be written as

$$\{x^{(1)}, x^{(3)}, x^{(1)} + x^{(3)}, x^{(1)} + T x^{(3)}, x^{(1)} + T^2 x^{(3)}, \ldots, x^{(1)} + T^{N-1} x^{(3)}\}. \quad (31)$$

When n is even, matters are slightly more complicated. Now, the image of $\beta X^{(3)}$ can be a cyclic shift of one of three different binary sequences $y^{(0)} = x^{(3)}$, $y^{(1)}$, and $y^{(2)}$ of period $N/3$. Thus, the 2^n binary sequences obtained can be written as

$$\{x^{(1)}, x^{(1)} + T^i y^{(0)}, x^{(1)} + T^i y^{(1)}, x^{(1)} + T^i y^{(2)} \mid 0 \le i < N/3\}. \quad (32)$$

The sets exhibited in (31) and (32) are exactly those in Eq. (4.4) and (4.12) of [23]. They are called dual-BCH sequences because they can be obtained from the dual codes of double-error-correcting binary BCH codes.

3.3 Gold and Gold-like Sequences

The Gold sequences are a set of $(2^n + 1)$ binary sequences of the form

$$\{x, y, x + y, x + Ty, x + T^2y, \ldots, x + T^{N-1}y\} \tag{33}$$

where x and y are m-sequences of period N and y is a *preferred decimation* of x. Some preferred decimations of the form $2^k + 1$ and $2^{2k} - 2^k + 1$ are given in Theorem 1 of [23]. Clearly, if the decimation $2^k + 1$ is being used, then these sequences can be obtained from the (2^n+1) cyclically inequivalent code words of period N from $\mathcal{C}(N, 2; 2^k)$, where $X^{(2^k)}$ maps to $x^{2^k} = x^{(1)} = x$ and $X^{(2^k+1)}$ maps to y. A similar construction does not always work with the decimation $2^{2k} - 2^k + 1$. Similarly, there are several other preferred decimations that have been discovered experimentally, and the Gold sequences corresponding to these cannot be generated by this method.

The classical Gold decimation $2^{\lfloor (n+2)/2 \rfloor} + 1$ does not produce an m-sequence when $n \equiv 0 \bmod 4$, and thus the set of sequences obtained in this case cannot be expressed in the form (33). In this case, the set of *Gold-like* sequences contains 2^n sequences of period N of the form exhibited in (32) or (4.12) of [23]. The reason for this is that these sequences are the images of code words from $\mathcal{C}(N, 2; 2^{(n+2)/2})$, but $\alpha^{2^{(n+2)/2}+1}$ is an element of order $N/3$, and hence, only 2^n different cyclically inequivalent Reed-Solomon code words can be formed. As in the case of Gold sequences, all sets of Gold-like sequences need not be obtainable from Reed-Solomon code words.

3.4 Kasami Sequences

Let n be even and let $w = x^{(2^{n/2}+1)}$. Then, w is an m-sequence of period $2^{n/2} - 1$, and the *small set of Kasami sequences* [23] is given by

$$\{x, x + w, x + Tw, x + T^2w, \ldots, x + T^{2^{n/2}-2}w\}.$$

The reader who has followed the above discussion will have no difficulty in recognizing that the small set of Kasami sequences is obtained as the images of code words from the Reed-Solomon code $\mathcal{C}(N, 2; 2^{n/2})$. The case of the *large set of Kasami sequences* is slightly complicated because it is necessary to consider the cases $n \equiv 0 \bmod 4$ and $n \equiv 2 \bmod 4$ separately. In either case, the sequences are the images of code words from the Reed-Solomon code $C(N, 2; 2^{(n+2)/2})$, but the numbers of sequences obtained depends on whether $n \equiv 0 \mod 4$ or $n \equiv 2 \mod 4$. The details can be found in [23].

3.5 Remarks

This section has shown how many of the classical sequence designs for signature sequences can be obtained as the images of code words from Reed-Solomon codes. However, this relationship does not seem to be of much use for suggesting new design methods. All the Reed-Solomon codes considered have rate $2/N$, but although there are only minor differences between the various Reed-Solomon codes of a given rate, the binary sequences obtained from them have vastly different correlation properties. Thus, this connection between binary signature sequences and Reed-Solomon codes is in essence just a curiosity.

4 CONCLUSIONS

This chapter has discussed how Reed-Solomon codes can be used in the design of frequency-hopping patterns for FH/SS systems and signature sequences for DS/SS systems. Although signature sequences for DS/SS systems can be viewed as the images of Reed-Solomon code words, there seems to be no obvious connection between the properties of the Reed-Solomon code and the correlation properties of the resulting signature sequences. Thus, the primary application of Reed-Solomon codes in sequence design for spread-spectrum systems remains the design of hopping patterns for FH/SS systems.

ACKNOWLEDGMENTS

Much of the material in Sections 1 and 2 of this chapter is an updated and considerably expanded version of [22], while some of the material in Section 3 is drawn from [23]. The author wishes to thank Professor Michael B. Pursley, his coauthor on those papers, for suggesting the fascinating topic of sequence design for spread-spectrum systems as an area for research collaboration and for many helpful discussions on this topic (and many others in the general area of spread-spectrum systems) over a period of twenty years. The author also wishes to thank Professors Stephen B. Wicker and Vijay K. Bhargava, the editors of this volume, for the invitation to prepare this chapter.

REFERENCES

[1] C. A. Baum and M. B. Pursley, "Bayesian Methods for Erasure Insertion in Frequency-Hop Communication Systems with Partial-Band Interfer-

ence," *IEEE Transactions on Communications,* Volume 40, pp. 1231–1238, July 1992.

[2] N. Burger, "The Design of Frequency Hopping Patterns for Multiple-Access Communications," M. S. Thesis, Department of Electrical and Computer Engineering, University of Illinois at Urbana-Champaign, Urbana, January 1994.

[3] G. R. Cooper and C. D. McGillem, *Modern Communications and Spread Spectrum,* New York: McGraw-Hill, 1984.

[4] G. R. Cooper and R. W. Nettleton, "A Spread Spectrum Technique for High-Capacity Mobile Communications," *IEEE Transactions on Vehicular Techology,* Volume VT-27, pp. 264–275, 1978.

[5] G. Einarsson, "Address Assignment for a Time-Frequency-Coded, Spread Spectrum System," *Bell System Technical Journal,* Volume 59, pp. 1241–1255, 1980.

[6] E. A. Geraniotis and M. B. Pursley, "Error Probabilities for Slow Frequency-Hopped Spread-Spectrum Multiple-Access Communication over Fading Channels," *IEEE Transactions on Communications,* Volume COM-30, pp. 996–1009, 1982.

[7] S. W. Golomb, *Shift Register Sequences,* San Francisco: Holden-Day, 1967.

[8] D. B. Jevtić and H. B. Alkhatib, "Frequency-Hopping Codes for Multiple-Access Channels: A Geometric Approach," *IEEE Transactions on Information Theory,* Volume 35, pp. 477–481, March 1989.

[9] P. V. Kumar, "Frequency-Hopping Code Sequence Designs Having Large Linear Span," *IEEE Transactions on Information Theory,* Volume 34, pp. 146–151, January 1988.

[10] A. Lempel and H. Greenberger, "Families of Sequences with Optimal Hamming Correlation Properties," *IEEE Transactions on Information Theory,* Volume IT-20, pp. 90–94, January 1974.

[11] J. H. van Lint, *A Course in Coding Theory,* Berlin: Springer-Verlag, 1989.

[12] F. J. MacWilliams and N. J. A. Sloane, "Pseudorandom Sequences and Arrays," *Proceedings of the IEEE,* Volume 64, pp. 1715–1729, December 1976.

[13] F. J. MacWilliams and N. J. A. Sloane, *The Theory of Error-Correcting Codes,* Amsterdam: North-Holland, 1977.

[14] S. V. Maric and E. L. Titlebaum, "Frequency Hop Multiple Access Codes Based upon the Theory of Cubic Congruences," *IEEE Transac-*

tions on Aerospace and Electronic Systems, Volume 25, pp. 1035–1039, November 1990.

[15] R. J. McEliece, "Some Combinatorial Aspects of Spread Spectrum Communication Systems," in *New Concepts in Multi-User Communications,* J. K. Skwirzynski (ed.), Dordrecht, The Netherlands: NASI Sirjhoff and Noordhoff, 1981.

[16] R. J. McEliece, *Finite Fields for Computer Scientists and Engineers,* Boston: Kluwer Academic Press, 1989.

[17] R. M. Mersereau and T. S. Seay, "Multiple Access Frequency Hopping Patterns with Low Ambiguity," *IEEE Transactions on Aerospace and Electronic Systems,* Volume AES-17, pp. 571–578, 1981.

[18] M. B. Pursley, "Frequency-Hop Transmission for Satellite Packet Switching and Terrestrial Packet Radio Networks," *IEEE Transactions on Information Theory,* Volume IT-32, pp. 652–667, September 1986.

[19] M. B. Pursley, "Reed-Solomon Codes in Frequency-Hop Communications," in *Reed-Solomon Codes and Their Applications,* S. B. Wicker and V. K. Bhargava (eds.), Piscataway, N.J.: IEEE Press, 1994.

[20] I. S. Reed, "k-th Order Near-Orthogonal Codes," *IEEE Transactions on Information Theory,* Volume IT-15, pp. 116–117, January 1971.

[21] R. M. Roth and G. Seroussi, "On Cyclic MDS Codes of Length q over GF(q)," *IEEE Transactions on Information Theory,* Volume IT-32, pp. 284–285, March 1986.

[22] D. V. Sarwate and M. B. Pursley, "Hopping Patterns for Frequency Hopped Multiple Access Communications," *IEEE International Conference on Communications Conference Record*, Toronto, Ontario, June 4–8, 1978, Volume 1, pp. 7.4.1–7.4.3.

[23] D. V. Sarwate and M. B. Pursley, "Crosscorrelation Properties of Pseudorandom and Related Sequences," *Proceedings of the IEEE,* Volume 68, pp. 593–619, May 1980.

[24] A. A. Shaar and P. A. Davies, "Prime Sequences: Quasi-Optimal Sequences for OR Channel Code Division Multiplexing," *Electronics Letters,* Volume 19, pp. 888–890, 1981.

[25] A. A. Shaar and P. A. Davies, "A Survey of One-Coincidence Sequences for Frequency-Hopped Spread-Spectrum Systems," *IEE Proceedings— Part F: Communications, Radar, and Signal Processing,* Volume 131, pp. 719–724, December 1984.

[26] A. A. Shaar, C. F. Woodcock, and P. A. Davies, "Number of One-Coincidence Sequence Sets for Frequency-Hopping Multiple Access Communication Systems," *IEE Proceedings—Part F: Communications,*

Radar, and Signal Processing, Volume 131, pp. 725–728, December 1984.

[27] M. K. Simon, J. K. Omura, R. A. Scholtz, and B. K. Levitt, *Spread Spectrum Communications*, Rockville, Md.: Computer Science Press, 1985.

[28] G. Solomon, "Optimal Frequency Hopping Sequences for Multiple Access," *Proceedings of a Symposium on Spread Spectrum Communication,* Volume 1, AD-915852, pp. 33–35, 1973.

[29] H. Y. Song, I. S. Reed, and S. W. Golomb, "On the Nonperiodic Cyclic Equivalence Classes of Reed-Solomon Codes," *IEEE Transactions on Information Theory,* Volume 39, pp. 1431–1434, July 1993.

[30] E. L. Titlebaum, "Time Frequency Hop Signals, Part I: Coding Based upon the Theory of Linear Congruences," *IEEE Transactions on Aerospace and Electronic Systems,* Volume AES-17, pp. 490–494, July 1981.

[31] E. L. Titlebaum and L. H. Sibul, "Time Frequency Hop Signals, Part II: Coding Based upon the Theory of Quadratic Congruences," *IEEE Transactions on Aerospace and Electronic Systems,* Volume AES-17, pp. 494–501, July 1981.

[32] I. Vajda, "Code Sequences for Frequency-Hopping Multiple-Access Systems," *IEEE Transactions on Communications* (in press).

[33] R. E. Ziemer and R. L. Peterson, *Digital Communications and Spread Spectrum Systems,* New York: Macmillan, 1985.

A Hypersystolic
Reed-Solomon Decoder[1]

Elwyn Berlekamp
University of California
Berkeley, California 94720

Gadiel Seroussi
Hewlett-Packard Laboratories
1501 Page Mill Road
Palo Alto, California 94304

Po Tong
Amati Communications Corporation
101 University Ave.
Palo Alto, California 94301

1 INTRODUCTION

Reed-Solomon (RS) coding, once considered an esoteric art, has become, in recent years, an ubiquitous technology widely used in many applications. These range from space communications to consumer products such as audio CD players. Today's system designer can find "off the shelf" RS solutions in the form of VLSI integrated circuits and macro cells [19] that satisfy a wide range of encoding/decoding needs. However, when the highest possible performance (in error correction power, throughput, or both) is sought, solutions based on highly customized algorithms and architectures are still an appropriate choice.

This chapter presents an example of such an architecture. We describe a *hypersystolic Reed-Solomon decoder* (HRSD) designed to achieve very high sustained data rates, in the gigabit/second order of magnitude (the term "hypersystolic" will be precisely defined in Section 3). The architecture was developed and implemented at Kodak/Cyclotomics, Inc., in 1986–1988, when a hardware prototype of the HRSD was built and demonstrated. This prototype decoder corrected all patterns of up to five errors/block in the (63,53) code over $GF(2^6)$, running at sustained data rates of 820 Mbits/s. A conceptual

_____
[1]This work was essentially done while the authors were with Kodak/Cyclotomics Inc., Berkeley, CA, USA.

model of hypersystolic architectures was presented in [1], and the HRSD architecture is described in detail in [3] and [6]. However, these references are quite obscure, and this chapter is the first attempt to present a complete description of the HRSD in the open literature. A companion hypersystolic RS *encoder* architecture is described in [14] and [15].

Pipelined and systolic designs for RS decoding are discussed in [17] and [16]. These architectures are significantly different than the one presented here. In particular, some of the systolic cells in [17] and [16] are of significantly higher complexity, and although they have a systolic structure, these designs do not seem to be amenable to the stricter constraints of a hypersystolic architecture. In a related research area, systolic architectures for Galois field arithmetic operations have also received attention in recent years [7,22,23]. These architectures are motivated by cryptographic applications where the size of a field element is large. In practical RS decoders, the symbol size is usually small enough (e.g., $m = 8$) that field operations can be realized using combinational logic. In this chapter, the hypersystolic structure is applied at the decoder "system" level and not to the field operations. In Section 7, however, we do discuss an implementation of Galois field division that is advantageous in the context of the hypersystolic decoder.

The rest of the chapter is organized as follows: Section 2 describes the procedures for Reed-Solomon encoding and decoding. The main purpose of the section is to define the mathematical terminology and notation used here, and to describe, in general terms, the decoding algorithm used in the HRSD, which is based on the extended Euclidean algorithm. Detailed proofs and explanations of how and why the algorithm works can be found, for example, in [12 (Chap. 8)] and [10 (Chap. 12)]. Section 3 defines hypersystolic arrays, the basic constraints they obey, and the advantages, in terms of system design and ultimately in throughput, which are obtained once the constraints are satisfied. Section 4 gives a high-level description of the HRSD architecture, its subsystems, and data flow through them. Sections 5–7 describe the HRSD subsystems in more detail. In particular, in Section 6, we present an implementation of Euclid's algorithm whose salient feature is that it completes its computation after a *predetermined* number of iterations, which depends on the parameters of the code but not on the input data. This is very desirable in a systolic implementation since the computation can be distributed among many systolic cells, each of which can determine the termination of the computation locally (just by counting cycles) without needing to check a global condition. Finally, Section 8 describes some additional properties of the HRSD and enhancements that can be easily incorporated into the basic architecture. The emphasis throughout will be on the algorithmic aspects of the HRSD and how the algebraic algorithms are matched to the hypersystolic constraints. In order to keep the chapter to a reasonable length, many implementation details will be omitted.

2 REED-SOLOMON ENCODING AND DECODING

2.1 Encoding

We consider Reed-Solomon (RS) codes defined over the Galois field $F = GF(2^m)$, where m is a positive integer. Let n and r be integers satisfying $1 \leq n \leq 2^m - 1$ and $0 < r < n$ and let L be an arbitrary integer. Also, let $k = n - r$ and let α be a primitive element of F. We define an $(n, k, r+1)$ RS code by its set of *roots* $\alpha^L, \alpha^{L+1}, \ldots, \alpha^{L+r-1}$, and its *generator polynomial*

$$g(x) = (x - \alpha^L)(x - \alpha^{L+1}) \cdots (x - \alpha^{L+r-1}). \tag{1}$$

It follows readily from (1) that $g(x)$ has degree r. The parameters r and k are called the *redundancy* and the *dimension* of the code, respectively. For the sake of simplicity, we assume that r is even.[2]

To encode a *message word* $\mathbf{u} = (u_{k-1} u_{k-2} \ldots u_0), u_i \in F$, we consider the associated polynomial

$$u(x) = u_{k-1}x^{k-1} + u_{k-2}x^{k-2} + \cdots + u_1x + u_0. \tag{2}$$

The *code word* $\mathbf{c}$ corresponding to $\mathbf{u}$ is defined by

$$\mathbf{c} = (c_{n-1} c_{n-2} \cdots c_r c_{r-1} \cdots c_1 c_0), \tag{3}$$

where $c_{r+i} = u_i, 0 \leq i \leq n - r - 1 = k - 1$, and $c_0, c_1, \ldots, c_{r-1}$ (the *check symbols*) are the coefficients of

$$\bar{c}(x) \overset{\text{def}}{=} c_{r-1}x^{r-1} + c_{r-2}x^{r-2} + \cdots + c_0 = x^r u(x) \bmod g(x). \tag{4}$$

If $n = 2^m - 1$, the RS code is *primitive* and *cyclic*. Otherwise, we are dealing with a *shortened* code, which, in general, is not cyclic. Notice that this is just one of several equivalent ways of defining RS codes (see, for instance, [2], [10], and [12]). For fixed n and r, all choices of the parameter L yield codes with the same error correction capability. In Section 7, we specify a preferred choice of L.

We adopt the convention that code words are sent over the channel with the highest-order coefficient c_{n-1} first, and the lowest-order coefficient c_0 last. Hence, message symbols are sent before check symbols.

---

[2]However, the HRSD works also for odd values of r, and can take advantage of the error detection capability provided by the "odd" check symbol.

2.2 Decoding

This section follows, loosely, the treatment of RS decoding in [12 (Chap. 8)]. Upon transmission over the channel, the code word **c** may be corrupted by noise, and a *received word*

$$\mathbf{y} = (y_{n-1}\, y_{n-2}\, \cdots\, y_0) \tag{5}$$

arrives at the decoder end. The code word **c** and the received word **y** are related by the equation $\mathbf{y} = \mathbf{c} + \mathbf{e}$, where

$$\mathbf{e} = (e_{n-1}\, e_{n-2}\, \cdots\, e_0) \tag{6}$$

is a *noise vector*, with $e_i \in F, 0 \le i \le n - 1$, and addition is taken over F. The goal of the decoder is to recover **c** (or, equivalently, **e**) from **y**. As is well known, this goal is attainable if the Hamming weight (number of nonzero entries) τ of **e** satisfies

$$\tau \le t \stackrel{\text{def}}{=} \frac{r}{2}. \tag{7}$$

Let $0 \le i_1 < i_2 < \cdots < i_\tau \le n - 1$ be the indices of the locations where $e_{i_j} \ne 0$. As is customary, we recast the error vector **e** as a set of *error locations*

$$X_j = \alpha^{-i_j}, \quad 1 \le j \le \tau, \tag{8}$$

and a set of *error values*

$$Y_j = e_{i_j}, \quad 1 \le j \le \tau. \tag{9}$$

We define the *error locator polynomial*

$$\sigma(x) = \prod_{j=1}^{\tau}(x - X_j), \tag{10}$$

and the *error evaluator polynomial*

$$\omega(x) = \sum_{j=1}^{\tau} Y_j X_j^{1-L} \prod_{l \ne j}(x - X_l). \tag{11}$$

Finding the error vector **e** is equivalent to finding the X_j and Y_j, which, in turn, is equivalent to finding $\sigma(x)$ and $\omega(x)$.

The decoding process for RS codes is divided into three main stages:

i. **Syndrome computation:** In this stage, the polynomial $y(x) = \sum_{i=0}^{n-1} y_i x^i$ associated with the received word **y** is evaluated at the roots of the code, producing the *power sums* (or *syndrome digits*)

$$S_j = y(\alpha^{L+j}) = \sum_{i=0}^{n-1} y_i \alpha^{(L+j)i}, \quad 0 \le j \le r - 1. \tag{12}$$

ii. **Finding the error locator and error evaluator polynomials:** This is
the heart of the decoding process. The error locator and error evaluator
polynomials satisfy the *key equation* [2,12]

$$\sigma(x)S(x) \equiv \omega(x) \bmod x^r, \tag{13}$$

where $S(x) = \sum_{j=0}^{r-1} S_j x^j$. In this stage, we start from $S(x)$ as
computed in Stage (i) and solve the key equation (13) for $\sigma(x)$ and
$\omega(x)$. Several efficient methods are known for solving this equation
[2,4,11,13,20]. Which one is used generally depends on the specific
requirements of the application and on the computational means at
hand. A very elegant method, which appears to be the best suited for
systolic implementation, makes use of the *extended Euclidean algorithm* for polynomials. The Euclidean algorithm was first applied to
decoding of RS codes (as a special case of Goppa codes) by Sugiyama
et al. in [18]. The first systolic implementation of the algorithm was
proposed in [5], which is the basis for the designs in [17] and [16].

Without reference to any specific architecture, the Euclidean
computation can be described as follows:

Procedure E1: Extended Euclidean algorithm
1. Initialize

$$\sigma_{(-1)}(x) = 0, \qquad \sigma_{(0)}(x) = 1,$$
$$\omega_{(-1)}(x) = x^r, \qquad \omega_{(0)}(x) = S(x). \tag{14}$$

2. For $i = 0, 1, 2, \ldots$, compute $Q_{(i)}(x)$ and $\omega_{(i+1)}(x)$ satisfying

$$\omega_{(i+1)}(x) = \omega_{(i-1)}(x) - Q_{(i)}(x)\omega_{(i)}(x), \qquad \deg \omega_{(i+1)} < \deg \omega_{(i)},$$

where $\deg f$ denotes the degree of a polynomial $f(x)$, and compute

$$\sigma_{(i+1)}(x) = \sigma_{(i-1)}(x) - Q_{(i)}(x)\sigma_{(i)}(x).$$

Stop at $i + 1 = j$, where j is the smallest integer such that
$\deg \omega_{(j)} < t$.
3. Set

$$\sigma(x) = \sigma_{(j)}(x),$$
$$\omega(x) = \omega_{(j)}(x).$$

iii. **Search for error locations and computation of error values:** In this
stage, we evaluate $\sigma(x)$ at $x = \alpha^{-i}$ for $n-1 \geq i \geq 0$ (this is known as a
Chien search). Values of x for which $\sigma(x) = 0$ correspond to the error
locations X_j. Once an error location X_j is found, the corresponding
error value is given by

$$Y_j = \frac{\omega(X_j)}{\sigma'(X_j)} X_j^{L-1}. \tag{15}$$

Here, $\sigma'(x)$ denotes the formal derivative [12] of the polynomial $\sigma(x)$ with respect to x. The error location X_j can now be corrected by subtracting the value Y_j from the corresponding entry y_{i_j} in $\mathbf{y}$.

3 HYPERSYSTOLIC ARRAYS

A *systolic array* [8] is an array of computing *cells* with a regular interconnection pattern in which every cell communicates only with physically adjacent cells. Data flows through the cells of the array in regular beats (hence the term *systolic*), controlled by a clocking mechanism. In principle, there could be one global clock signal distributed to all the cells, and data transfer between adjacent cells could occur simultaneously throughout the array at each clock cycle. However, if the array contains a large number of cells, the need to distribute a global clock signal, and the resulting clock skews, might become the limiting factor on the switching speed achievable in a practical implementation, hence restricting data throughput.

In a *hypersystolic* array [1,3], clocking signals are passed from cell to adjacent cell along with the data rather than being globally distributed. Each cell receives a clock signal from a unique cell called its *predecessor* and passes a (possibly regenerated) clock signal forward to one or more *successor* cells. Under this clocking scheme, a cell is *synchronous* with its predecessor and with its successors (since they share a clock signal) but is assumed to be *asynchronous* with all other cells and thus cannot communicate with them directly. An immediate consequence of this is that no global signals are allowed in a hypersystolic array. Also, we make no assumptions on the amount of clock skew through a cell and, in particular, we do not assume that the skew is the same through two different cells (even if they are copies of the same cell design). Thus, two-dimensional cell structures like the one shown in Figure 10-1 are not allowed since there is no assignment of clock successors and predecessors that guarantees communication only between synchronous cells. For example, assuming that clocks are distributed from top to bottom in Figure 10-1, cells D and E are asynchronous, even though they are at the same "distance" from cell A. In fact, cells B and C are also asynchronous, even though each is synchronous with A; synchronicity is not transitive. Structures like the one shown in Figure 10-1 are typical in traditional systolic arrays. The additional limitations on the array topology imposed by the hypersystolic constraints make it more challenging for the array designer to map algorithms to the architecture. However, once the right mapping is found, the architecture can be run at much higher clock rates and is very robust since all timing problems are local and no global clock "tweaking" is necessary. Also, each signal line in the array (including clocks) has a fan-in and fan-out of 1; i.e., each cell output is connected to exactly one input in one adjacent cell. Wire connection lengths are minimized, and the regularity of the interconnection pattern allows for simple and efficient layouts of the systolic cells. These properties, again, translate into higher achievable clock rates.

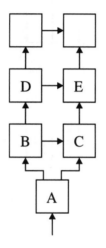

Figure 10-1. Two-dimensional systolic structure.

It follows from the above discussion that a hypersystolic array is physically asynchronous, in the sense that, say, clock cycle i occurs at different physical times in different parts of the array, possibly with large clock skews relative to the clock period. However, since a cell communicates only with cells it shares a clock with, the system can be logically thought of and simulated as a synchronous one; i.e., the concept of "global clock cycle i" is logically meaningful although unrelated to any specific instant of physical time.

Most cells in the HRSD have just one successor. We call these *regular* cells. A regular cell with its predecessor and successor are shown in Figure 10-2. Data going in the same direction as the clock are referred to as *forward data*, while data going in the opposite direction are referred to as *backward* data. Cells with two successors are called *joiners*. One such cell, together with its predecessor and successors, is shown in Figure 10-3. Cells in the HRSD have at most two successors. Some cells have no successors, and one has no predecessor. The function of these cells will be explained when we describe the HRSD in more detail.

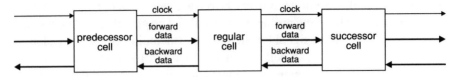

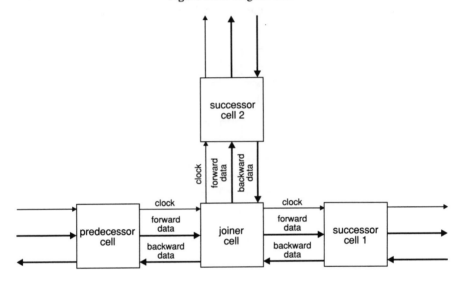

Figure 10-2. Regular cell.

Figure 10-3. Joiner cell.

In addition to the basic hypersystolic constraints, other properties of the architecture are desirable from an implementation point of view. These include very low per-cell complexity, a small number of distinct cell types (which are replicated to form the systolic array), and "narrow" data paths between cells. In the HRSD, the complexity of each cell is restricted to one Galois field multiplier/accumulator, a few registers, and control logic. Also, while the cells perform a variety of different functions, they are all variations of four basic designs. Data paths between adjacent cells are limited to one pair of m-bit signals (one signal in each direction) plus a few 1-bit control signals.

4 HRSD: HIGH-LEVEL DESCRIPTION

4.1 Architecture

The basic structure of the HRSD is shown in Figure 10-4, where each box represents one hypersystolic cell. The HRSD consists of four major subsystems: a horizontal *Main Street* and three vertical *towers*. For the sake of simplicity, Figure 10-4 does not show clock signals. These are assumed to flow from left to right on Main Street, and upwards on the towers (this defines the *forward* direction). Notice that, due to the hypersystolic constraints, there is no "horizontal" communication between towers. The four subsystems are briefly described in the following paragraph. The towers are described in more detail in Sections 5–7.

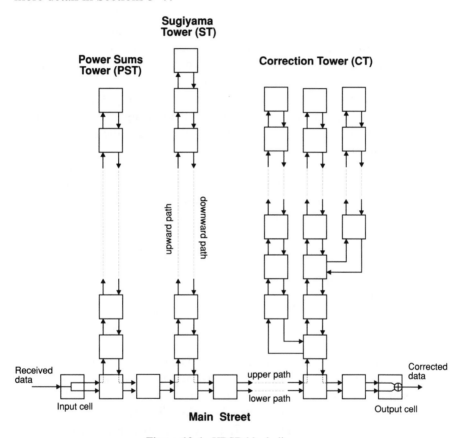

Figure 10-4. HRSD block diagram.

Main Street is a digital delay line with two parallel data paths. Data (received words) enter the HRSD at the leftmost cell of Main Street (the *input* cell). This cell has no predecessor, and it receives its clock and data from an external source. At the input cell, two copies of the input data stream are made, which are fed to the two data paths. The *upper path* is used to communicate with the towers, sending data and control signals in the forward (upward) direction and receiving results from the towers in the backward (downward) direction. The towers process the input data, eventually producing a stream of error values that flows back to the upper path of Main Street. The *lower path* is used to "slow down" the original data so that it matches the delay caused by the computation in the towers. At the end of Main Street, we have a copy of the received data on the lower path and the stream of error values on the upper path. These two streams become synchronized at the *output* cell, where the error values are subtracted (XOR-ed) from the received values, producing a stream of corrected data.

The *power sums tower* (PST) computes the syndrome digits S_0, $S_1, \ldots, S_{r-1}$ from received symbols $y_{n-1}, y_{n-2}, \ldots, y_1, y_0$. The latter arrive from Main Street and flow on the upward path. Syndrome digits S_j are output on the downward path, back to Main Street.

The *Sugiyama tower* (ST) receives the syndrome digits S_j from Main Street on the upward path, runs the extended Euclidean algorithm, and outputs the coefficients of the error locator polynomial $\sigma(x)$ and the error evaluator polynomial $\omega(x)$ on the downward path.

The *correction tower* (CT) is a treelike structure that evaluates the polynomials $\sigma(x)$ and $\omega(x)$ at all the code locations, determines locations that are roots of $\sigma(x)$, and computes the corresponding error values. The output of the CT is a stream of error values that is fed back to Main Street.

Notice that cells at the tops of towers have no successors. All output from these cells flows back to the downward path.

4.2 Data Formats

The various signal paths in the HRSD (upper and lower paths on Main Street, upward and downward paths on the towers) consist of two types of lines.

Data lines carry m-bit symbols from F. Data are divided into n-symbol *blocks*. Blocks are separated by an extra *end-of-packet marker* (EOPM) cycle. The meaning of the data in a block depends on what section of the HRSD the block is flowing in. At the input to the PST, a block is just a received word to be decoded; between the PST and the ST, a block contains the syndrome digits; between the ST and the CT, a block contains the coefficients of the polynomials σ and ω; at the output from the CT, a block is an error vector. The EOPM cycle is used by the systolic cells to finalize computations corresponding to a block and to initialize computations corresponding to the next. This extra cycle, whose effect on the data rate is equivalent to increasing the code redundancy by one symbol, could be eliminated at the expense of increased cell complexity.

Control lines carry 1-bit signals used for control and synchronization of the systolic computation. Most signal paths in the HRSD contain one data line and two control lines associated with the data line. These control lines, denoted, respectively, EOPM and VALID, are described as follows:

- EOPM marks the EOPM cycle.[3] This 1-bit signal is delivered, together with the received data, to the input cell of Main Street. The signal value is 0 while the symbols of a block are being received (n cycles), and it is 1 during the $(n + 1)$st cycle (the EOPM cycle). We assume that the next block starts at the $(n + 2)$nd cycle. The actual value on the data line during the EOPM cycle is ignored (in a practical application, this value could be used for acquisition of block synchronization).

- VALID. This signal marks the cycles in which the corresponding data line carries meaningful information. For example, the output from the PST consists of r syndrome symbols. These symbols are output over a period of n cycles, resulting in $(n - r)$ "idle" cycles. The VALID signal is 0 during those cycles. A similar situation occurs at the output of the ST.

A typical set of signals is shown in Figure 10-5. Each arrow in the HRSD block diagram (Figure 10-4) represents such a set, with the exception of the downward path in the ST which carries one additional control signal. This additional signal will be defined in Section 6. It follows that the number of "wires" running between two adjacent cells (each wire carrying a binary signal), counting clocks, is $2m + 5 + s$. Here, $s = 1$ for cells in the ST, and $s = 0$ otherwise. From an individual cell perspective, the number of input/output wires for each cell is summarized in Table 1.

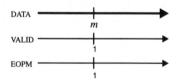

Figure 10-5. Typical signal set.

At times, when describing the towers, it will be necessary to distinguish between signals in the upward and downward paths. We will do so by adding the suffixes _UP and _DN, respectively, e.g., DATA_UP, DATA_DN, EOPM_UP, EOPM_DN, VALID_UP, VALID_DN.

As an example of the foregoing discussion, the following table shows the status of the data and control signals at the input to the PST before, during,

---

[3]The ambiguity here is intentional: we refer to the signal, and to the cycle when the signal is 1, by the same name of EOPM.

TABLE 1   Number of Binary Inputs/
Outputs per Cell.

Cell Type	Inputs	Outputs
Regular	$2m + 5 + s$	$2m + 5 + s$
Joiner	$3m + 7 + s$	$3m + 8 + s$

and after reception of a code block **y**. We denote the code block received before **y** by $\hat{\mathbf{y}}$, and the one received after **y** by $\bar{\mathbf{y}}$. Clock cycle numbers are relative to the beginning of **y**, and □ denotes the EOPM cycle.

Cycle:	$\cdots$	-3	-2	-1	0	1	$\cdots$	$n-1$	n	$n+1$	$n+2$	$\cdots$
Data:	$\cdots$	$\hat{y}_1$	$\hat{y}_0$	□	y_{n-1}	y_{n-2}	$\cdots$	y_0	□	$\bar{y}_{n-1}$	$\bar{y}_{n-2}$	$\cdots$
VALID:	$\cdots$	1	1	0	1	1	$\cdots$	1	0	1	1	$\cdots$
EOPM:	$\cdots$	0	0	1	0	0	$\cdots$	0	1	0	0	$\cdots$

A similar example, for data at the output of the PST, is given in Section 5.

The flow of data through the HRSD is continuous. The input cell receives one symbol per clock cycle, and once the pipeline is full, the output cell emits one corrected symbol per clock cycle (except at the EOPM cycle). Thus, at any given clock cycle, the HRSD may be processing several code blocks simultaneously along its pipeline. The number of such blocks is a function of the total latency of the system, which is estimated in Section 8. Also, in order to keep the data flow uninterrupted, cells in the ST and in the CT may be processing data for one block while fetching coefficients for the next block.

The following sections describe the HRSD towers in more detail. The descriptions include logic diagrams for the core computations of the systolic cells. The schematic symbols used in the diagrams are shown in Figure 10-6.

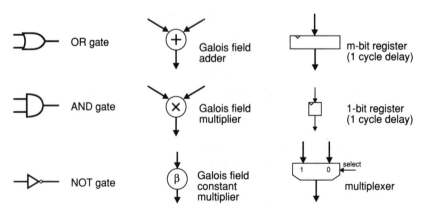

Figure 10-6. Schematic symbols.

5 THE POWER SUMS TOWER

The PST, shown in Figure 10-7, consists of r systolic cells, each computing one syndrome digit. Cell j (starting with $j = 0$ at the top of the tower) evaluates S_j using Horner's rule:

$$S_j = y(\alpha^{L+j}) = (\cdots ((y_{n-1}\alpha^{L+j} + y_{n-2})\alpha^{L+j} + y_{n-3})\alpha^{L+j} + \cdots)\alpha^{L+j} + y_0.$$
$$(16)$$

The core of the circuitry for this computation is shown in Figure 10-8. The code root α^{L+j} is stored in a static register X. Register Y stores successive coefficients y_i as they are received on the upward path. Register S is initialized to 0 at the EOPM cycle *preceding* the block, and it accumulates the result. The basic computation performed is

$$S := S \cdot X + Y, \qquad (17)$$

where := denotes assignment. The computation is completed when the cell is hit by the EOPM_UP signal. At that cycle, the result of the computation is inserted in the downward stream (by an appropriate selection at the multiplexer M1), and the VALID_DN signal is set to 1 (by a similar selection at multiplexer M2). During other cycles, the downward path just propagates results from previous cells. The use of Horner's rule for systolic implementation of polynomial evaluations in RS decoding was suggested in [5] and is also found in the designs of [17] and [16].

Since the cell computing S_{r-1} is at the bottom of the tower, it is the first one hit by the EOPM_UP signal. Therefore, its result S_{r-1} will be output first. The EOPM_UP signal is "bounced" to the downward path upon reaching the top of the tower, becoming EOPM_DN. Notice also that, in Figure 10-8, signals are delayed by one cycle on the upward path, and by two cycles on the downward path. This delay configuration is typical of all the tower cells in the HRSD. Thus, EOPM_UP reaches cell $j - 1$ one cycle later than cell j, and the result from cell $j - 1$ takes two more cycles to reach the downward output of cell j. Therefore, S_{j-1} is output three cycles later than S_j, and, in general, syndrome digits are spaced three cycles apart in the output sequence. Since all the syndrome digits for a block must be output over a period of n cycles, the maximum redundancy of the code is restricted by $3r - 2 \leq n$. The three-cycle structure and the resulting restriction on the code redundancy are actually dictated by the computation on the Sugiyama tower, which actually imposes a slightly stricter bound on r. This is discussed in Section 6. A possible relaxation of the restriction on r is discussed in Section 8.1.

The output from the PST flows back to Main Street. For a typical code block, the PST output sequence is as follows (ϕ denotes undefined data):

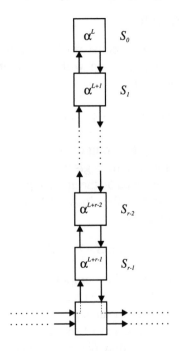

Figure 10-7. The power sums tower.

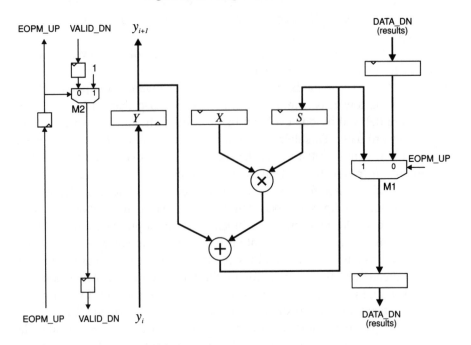

Figure 10-8. Power sums tower cell.

Data:	□	ϕ	$\cdots$	ϕ	S_{r-1}	ϕ	ϕ	S_{r-2}	$\cdots$	ϕ	S_1	ϕ	ϕ	S_0	□
VALID:	0	0	$\cdots$	0	1	0	0	1	$\cdots$	0	1	0	0	1	0
EOPM:	1	0	$\cdots$	0	0	0	0	0	$\cdots$	0	0	0	0	0	1

6 THE SUGIYAMA TOWER

6.1 Data Structure and Algorithm

From the description of the Euclidean algorithm in Procedure E1, it is apparent that one needs to keep track of two sequences of polynomials, namely, the $\omega_{(i)}$ and the $\sigma_{(i)}$, "remembering," at each step, two consecutive elements from each sequence. The implementation of the Euclidean algorithm in the ST is based on the following properties of these sequences of polynomials, which are discussed in more detail in [12]:

P1. The degree of $\omega_{(i)}(x)$, $i \geq -1$, is monotonically decreasing with i. The degree of $\sigma_{(i)}(x)$, $i \geq -1$, is monotonically increasing with i.
P2. The degrees satisfy

$$\deg \omega_{(i-1)} + \deg \sigma_{(i)} = r, \quad i \geq 0, \tag{18}$$

and

$$\deg \omega_{(i)} + \deg \sigma_{(i-1)} < r, \quad i \geq 0. \tag{19}$$

Clearly, (19) follows from (18) and P1. From property P2, it follows that the four polynomials we want to keep track of, namely, $\omega_{(i-1)}$, $\omega_{(i)}$, $\sigma_{(i-1)}$, and $\sigma_{(i)}$, can be nicely "packed" into two rows of $(r+2)$ registers each (a *register* is a memory element capable of storing one element of F). We will refer to these rows as RTOP and RBOT, respectively. RTOP stores the coefficients of $\omega_{(i)}(x)$ and $\sigma_{(i-1)}(x)$, and RBOT stores the coefficients of $\omega_{(i-1)}(x)$ and $\sigma_{(i)}(x)$. This arrangement is shown in Figure 10-9. In each row, the right hand side of the row contains the σ polynomial, with its leading coefficient at the rightmost register, and the left hand side of the row contains the ω polynomial, with its leading coefficient at the leftmost register. The two are separated by a conceptual "comma," which marks the boundary between the polynomials. As the ω shrink and the σ grow (property P1), the positions of the commas in RTOP and RBOT (which are independent) shift to the left. By property P2, $\omega_{(i-1)}(x)$ and $\sigma_{(i)}(x)$ fit tightly in RBOT, while $\omega_{(i)}(x)$ and $\sigma_{(i-1)}(x)$ have some "slack" in RTOP. For the purposes of the algorithm, we assume that this slack is filled with zeros on the side of $\sigma_{(i-1)}$. An arrangement similar to that of Figure 10-9 for the Euclidean algorithm is described in [2 (Chap. 2)], for binary polynomials. Here, we follow the same basic scheme extended to polynomials over F.

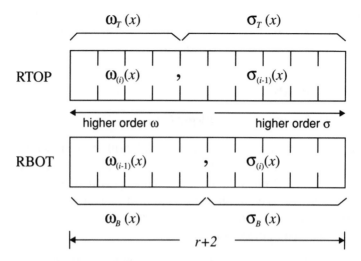

Figure 10-9. Data structure for Euclidean computation.

The scheme combines the steps of the Euclidean algorithm with the internal steps of the polynomial division operations required in the algorithm. Let $\omega_T(x)$ and $\omega_B(x)$ denote the polynomials represented, respectively, by the portions of RTOP and RBOT to the left of the commas. Similarly, let $\sigma_T(x)$ and $\sigma_B(x)$ denote the polynomials represented, respectively, by the portions of RTOP and RBOT to the right of the commas.[4] Let $d_T = \deg^* \omega_T$ and $d_B = \deg^* \omega_B$, where $\deg^*$ denotes a relaxed notion of degree, defined as 1 less than the number of registers to the left of the appropriate comma. This is equal to the true degree when the most significant (leftmost) register in the appropriate row (RTOP or RBOT) is nonzero. As we shall see, at key points in the computation, d_T and d_B do represent the true degrees of ω_T and ω_B, respectively. Define also $\delta = d_B - d_T$. The computation is summarized in the following procedure.

Procedure E2: Extended Euclidean algorithm (modified version)

1. **initialize**

$$
\begin{array}{llll}
\omega_T(x) & := & x^r, & \sigma_T(x) & := & 1, \\
\omega_B(x) & := & S(x), & \sigma_B(x) & := & 0.
\end{array}
\tag{20}
$$

2. **repeat** r **times:**

---

[4]The apparent redundant notation in Figure 10-9 is explained as follows: ω_T, σ_T, ω_B, and σ_B denote the polynomials represented by the appropriate portions of RTOP and RBOT, respectively, *at all stages of the computation*. These polynomials will coincide, at well defined points in the computation, with polynomials from the sequences $\omega_{(i)}$ and $\sigma_{(i)}$ of Procedure E1.

a. **set**

$$\mu_T := \text{leftmost (leading) coefficient of } \omega_T(x),$$
$$\mu_B := \text{leftmost (leading) coefficient of } \omega_B(x). \tag{21}$$

b. **if** $\mu_B \neq 0$ **and** $\delta < 0$ (i.e., the bottom comma is to the left of the top comma), **then**

swap   RTOP and RBOT,

swap μ_T and μ_B.

c. **if** $\mu_B \neq 0$, **then set**

$$\omega_B(x) := \mu_T \omega_B(x) - x^\delta \mu_B \omega_T(x). \tag{22}$$

$$\sigma_T(x) := \mu_T \sigma_T(x) - x^\delta \mu_B \sigma_B(x). \tag{23}$$

d. **shift** RBOT (and its comma) one position to the left.

3. **output** $\omega_B(x)$ as $\omega(x)$, and $\sigma_T(x)$ as $\sigma(x)$.

When initializing ω_B in Step 1, we assume that $S(x)$ is of full degree $r - 1$; i.e., we start with $d_B = r - 1$, regardless of the value of S_{r-1}. Also, initially, we have $d_T = r$, and, thus, $\delta = -1$. Notice that the initialization step in Procedure E2 actually reverses the initial values of $\omega_{(-1)}$ and $\omega_{(0)}$ (and, similarly, $\sigma_{(-1)}$ and $\sigma_{(0)}$) called for in Procedure E1. Since we start with $\delta = -1$, Step 2b will swap the contents of RTOP and RBOT as soon as the leftmost coefficient μ_B of $\omega_B(x)$ is nonzero. This will happen due to the shifting in Step 2d if $S(x) \neq 0$. If $S(x) = 0$, Procedure E2 just "idles," shifting RBOT left r times and then outputting $\sigma(x) = 1$ (this is the initial value of σ_T) and $\omega(x) = 0$. This corresponds to the case where the received block is a code word, and no corrections are made. After the first swap, the values in RTOP and RBOT are consistent with the initialization in Procedure E1, and we always have $\mu_T \neq 0$. Thus, d_T does represent the true degree of ω_T. Also, d_B is guaranteed to represent the true degree of ω_B immediately before and immediately after a **swap** operation in Step 2b, since at those points we have both $\mu_T \neq 0$ and $\mu_B \neq 0$.

Steps 2c and 2d perform one basic step in the polynomial division of $\omega_{(i-1)}$ by $\omega_{(i)}$, except that in a conventional division the computation would be

$$\omega_B(x) := \omega_B(x) - x^\delta \frac{\mu_B}{\mu_T} \omega_T(x). \tag{24}$$

Hence, in Procedure E2, the computed partial remainder at each basic step is multiplied by the scalar factor μ_T. The same factor multiplies the corresponding polynomials in the sequence $\sigma_{(i)}$. Since our final goal is to determine the roots of σ and to compute quotients of the form ω/σ', multiplying σ and ω by the same scalar factor has no effect on the results of interest. The use of "cross-multiplication" instead of division is suggested for the systolic implementation of Euclid's algorithm in [5]. Step 2c zeroes out the leading coefficient of ω_B, which is then "popped out" by the shift in Step 2d. The factors x^δ on the right hand sides of equations (22) and (23) do not require any actual operation, they just indicate that the polynomials in RTOP and RBOT are properly aligned; i.e., the operations in (22) and (23) involve linear combinations of coefficients that are stored opposite each other in RTOP and RBOT. Notice that the quotient polynomials $Q_{(i)}$ are never explicitly stored. Also, in Step 2d, we shift $\omega_{(i-1)}$ to the left, i.e., towards higher-order positions. At that point, we would also need to shift $\sigma_{(i-1)}$ towards higher-order positions, i.e., to the *right*. Instead, we shift $\sigma_{(i)}$, which is in RBOT together with $\omega_{(i-1)}$, to the left, obtaining the same relative effect.

The condition $\delta < 0$ (i.e., the bottom comma overtaking the top comma to the left) in Step 2b marks the end of a division operation. This corresponds to the end of one iteration in the "standard" Euclidean procedure E1. At that point (before the **swap** operations), the polynomials stored in RBOT and RTOP correspond to polynomials in the sequence generated by Procedure E1, and we have $\omega_B(x) = \gamma_j \omega_{(j)}(x)$, $\sigma_T(x) = \gamma_j \sigma_{(j)}(x)$, $\omega_T(x) = \gamma_{j-1} \omega_{(j-1)}(x)$, and $\sigma_B(x) = \gamma_{j-1} \sigma_{(j-1)}(x)$, for some $j \geq 0$, and constants $\gamma_j, \gamma_{j-1} \in F$. Notice that there might be some idle steps between the time the bottom comma overtakes the top comma and the time the swap occurs. During these steps, RBOT is shifted left until its leftmost coefficient is nonzero. However, these shifts do not affect the values of the polynomials in RTOP and RBOT. After the swap in Step 2b, the configuration of polynomials is as shown in Figure 10-9, and a new division operation begins.

A complete numerical example of Procedure E2 is presented in Appendix A.

In the following propositions, we refer to one iteration of Step 2 in Procedure E2 as a *basic iteration*. Also, we use the notation $d_T(i)$, $d_B(i)$, and $\delta(i)$ to denote the values of d_T, d_B, and δ, respectively, at the end of the ith basic iteration.

LEMMA 1   Let $d(i) = d_T(i) + d_B(i)$. Then, after i basic iterations, we have $d(i) = 2r - 1 - i$.

PROOF At the start of the procedure, we have $d_T(0) = r$, $d_B(0) = r - 1$, and, thus, $d(0) = 2r - 1$. The lemma now follows from the observation that, in each basic iteration, Steps 2b and 2c do not affect d, while Step 2d always decreases d by one.

THEOREM 1   At the end of r basic iterations of Procedure E2,

    i. If $\delta(r) < 0$, then the polynomials $\sigma_T(x)$ and $\omega_B(x)$ produced by Procedure E2 are equal, up to a scalar multiple, to the polynomials $\sigma(x)$ and $\omega(x)$ produced by Procedure E1.

    ii. If $\delta(r) \geq 0$, then the syndrome polynomial $S(x)$ corresponds to an uncorrectable error pattern.

PROOF It follows from the discussion following Procedure E2 that the procedure computes the sequences $\omega_{(j)}$ and $\sigma_{(j)}$ produced by the standard Euclidean computation E1, up to scalar multiples that affect both sequences equally. The "synchronization" points between the procedures occur right before **swap** operations in Step 2b. At those points, we have $\omega_B(x) = \gamma_j \omega_{(j)}(x)$, $\sigma_T(x) = \gamma_j \sigma_{(j)}(x)$, $\omega_T(x) = \gamma_{j-1}\omega_{(j-1)}(x)$, and $\sigma_B(x) = \gamma_{j-1}\sigma_{(j-1)}(x)$, for some $j \geq 0$, and constants $\gamma_j, \gamma_{j-1} \in F$.

By Lemma 1, at the end of r basic iterations, we have $d(r) = r - 1$. Since r is even, this implies that

$$\min[d_T(r), d_B(r)] \leq \frac{r}{2} - 1 < t. \tag{25}$$

    i. Assume $\delta(r) < 0$. Then, $d_B(r) < d_T(r)$, and by (25) we have $d_B(r) < t$, while by Lemma 1 we have $d_T(r) = r - 1 - d_B(r) \geq t$. Since $\delta < 0$, the procedure is at a point which is after the end of one division operation and *before* the beginning of the next; i.e., a **swap** is due. Hence, the polynomials ω_B and σ_T correspond to some $\omega_{(j)}$ and $\sigma_{(j)}$ of the sequence generated by Procedure E1. But, since $\deg \omega_{(j)} = d_B(r) < t$, and $\deg \omega_{(j-1)} = d_T(r) \geq t$, this must be the stopping point of Procedure E1. Hence, we have $\omega_B(x) = \gamma_j \omega_{(j)}(x) = \gamma_j \omega(x)$, $\sigma_T(x) = \gamma_j \sigma_{(j)}(x) = \gamma_j \sigma(x)$, as claimed.

    ii. Assume $\delta(r) \geq 0$. Then we are "in the middle" of a division step of Procedure E1, which started with a **swap** at, say, basic iteration number $r - l + 1$, $l \geq 1$. Consider the state of the computation at the end of basic iteration number $r - l$ (i.e., just before the swap). At this point, again, ω_B and σ_T correspond to a pair $\omega_{(j)}$, $\sigma_{(j)}$ from Procedure E1. The polynomial ω_T gets its value from ω_B at the swap operation in basic iteration number $r - l + 1$ and remains unchanged until the end of basic iteration number r. Hence, we have $d_B(r - l) = d_T(r)$ and, using also (25) and the fact that $\delta(r) \geq 0$, we obtain

$$\deg \omega_{(j)} = d_B(r - l) = d_T(r) = \min[d_T(r), d_B(r)] < t. \tag{26}$$

On the other hand, by Lemma 1, (26) and the fact that $r = 2t$, we have

$$\deg \omega_{(j-1)} = d_T(r-l) = r+l-1-d_B(r-l) > t+l-1 \geq t. \qquad (27)$$

Hence, procedure E1 would have stopped at this point, producing $\omega_{(j)}$ and $\sigma_{(j)}$ as its results. The degree of $\sigma_{(j)}$ is the same as that of σ_T, which shares RTOP with ω_T. Hence, using again the result of Lemma 1, we have

$$\begin{aligned}
\deg \sigma_{(j)} &\leq r - \deg \omega_T = r - d_T(r-l) = r - [d(r-l) - d_B(r-l)] \\
&= r - [r+l-1-d_B(r-l)] = d_B(r-l) - l + 1 \qquad (28) \\
&\leq d_B(r-l) = \deg \omega_{(j)}.
\end{aligned}$$

Now, by the properties of the Euclidean algorithm [12 (Chap. 8)], $\sigma_{(j)}$ and $\omega_{(j)}$ are a solution to the key equation (13), satisfying $\deg \sigma_{(j)} \leq t$ and $\deg \omega_{(j)} < t$, and such a solution is essentially unique. However, for a *correctable* error pattern, by equations (10) and (11), we must have $\deg \omega < \deg \sigma$, contradicting (28). Hence, in this case, the syndrome $S(x)$ must correspond to an uncorrectable error pattern.

6.2 Hypersystolic Implementation

To map the data structure of Figure 10-9 onto the Sugiyama tower in the HRSD, we rotate RTOP and RBOT 90 degrees counterclockwise, and assign one pair of registers (one from RTOP, one from RBOT) to each cell, except for the leftmost registers in RTOP and RBOT. The latter, which correspond to the variables μ_T and μ_B in Procedure E2, are replicated in each cell. Thus, the ST consists of $(r+1)$ systolic cells, each containing four basic registers: *rtop*, *rbot*, μ_T, and μ_B (the cells also contain other auxiliary registers that will be discussed below). The bottom of the tower corresponds to the left end of the arrays in Figure 10-9, and the top corresponds to the right end. Thus, for example, the "shift left" operation of Step 2d is realized by transferring coefficients on the downward path of the ST.

In the initialization step, we need to load the *rbot* registers with the syndrome digits $S_{r-1}, S_{r-2}, \ldots, S_0$, which are received on the upward path. This is accomplished by a "coefficient-grabbing" mechanism in which a cell "grabs" the *first* upward data value that is accompanied by an active VALID signal (VALID = 1), resets the VALID signal for that data value to 0, and lets the following data and VALID values go through unchanged. Thus, the cell at the bottom of the tower grabs the first coefficient in the sequence (S_{r-1}), the second cell from the bottom grabs the next coefficient (S_{r-2}), and so on until the cell next to the top grabs coefficient S_0. Notice that, since there are $(r+1)$ cells but only r coefficients, the cell at the top of the tower does not grab any coefficient. The *rbot* register in that cell belongs to $\sigma_{(i-1)}$, which is initialized to 0. The coefficient-grabbing circuitry is shown in Figure 10-10.

The *coeff* register is loaded with a value from the DATA_UP stream the first time the VALID_UP signal is active. The same signal sets flip-flop G to 1. This forces *coeff* to hold its value. G is reset to 0 at the next EOPM_UP cycle. Similar circuitry is used by cells in the CT to grab the coefficients of $\omega(x)$ and $\sigma(x)$ produced by the ST.

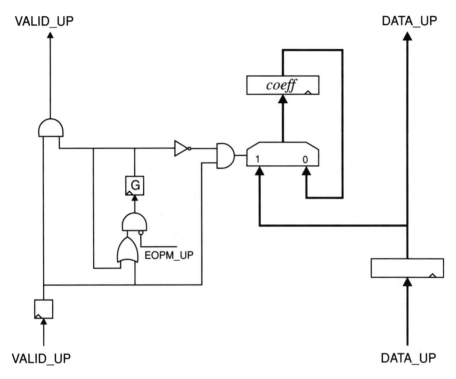

Figure 10-10. Coefficient-grabbing circuitry.

One of the conceptual difficulties in implementing Procedure E2 in a hypersystolic array is the fact that the procedure seems to require cells to share global information. For example, in order to carry out Step 2c, all the cells need to know the values μ_T and μ_B. We satisfy this need without violating the hypersystolic constraints by letting the procedure be *staggered* in time; i.e., at any given instant in "logical" time (ignoring the analog clock skews mentioned in Section 3), different cells are executing different stages of the algorithm. The coefficients μ_T and μ_B are generated at the bottom cell of the tower and flow up the tower through the upward path. Thus, the cell at the bottom generates one pair (μ_T, μ_B) and uses it for computing its contribution to the computation in Step 2c (this will usually involve the second most significant coefficients of ω_B and ω_T). The bottom cell propagates the pair (μ_T, μ_B) to its successor cell,[5] and the latter computes its contribution to the same instance of Step 2c a few cycles later (more precisely, three cycles later, as will be explained below). The process continues in the same way with cells higher up in the tower. Thus, Procedure E2 is distributed both in space (i.e., the different cells) and in time (i.e., different cycles), and no snapshot of the ST at any given clock cycle will actually show the structure depicted in Figure 10-9 or in the example in the Appendix.

The core of the computation in Procedure E2 is Step 2c. The exact behavior of a cell when executing this step depends on the cell's relative position with respect to the commas, as detailed below.

1. If the cell is to the *left* of the commas in both RTOP and RBOT, then both *rtop* and *rbot* hold coefficients from the ω sequence, and the cell executes the computation corresponding to equation (22), namely,

$$rbot := \mu_T \; rbot - \mu_B \; rtop. \tag{29}$$

2. If the cell is to the *right* of the commas in both RTOP and RBOT, then both *rtop* and *rbot* hold coefficients from the σ sequence, and the cell executes the computation corresponding to equation (23), namely,

$$rtop := \mu_T \; rtop - \mu_B \; rbot. \tag{30}$$

3. If the cell is to the right of the comma in RTOP, but to the left of the comma in RBOT, then *rtop* and *rbot* contain mixed coefficients, and the cell executes degenerate versions of the computations corresponding to both (22) and (23), namely,

$$\begin{aligned} rtop &:= \mu_T \; rtop, \\ rbot &:= \mu_T \; rbot. \end{aligned} \tag{31}$$

4. The fourth configuration, in which the cell is to the left of the comma in RTOP and to the right in RBOT, never occurs when computing the linear combinations of Step 2c. This configuration implies that $\delta < 0$, which can hold only in Step 2c if $\mu_B = 0$, in which case the computation of the linear combinations is skipped.

To keep track of its position relative to the commas, each ST cell contains two 1-bit variables, *ctop* and *cbot*. Cells to the right of the comma in RTOP have $ctop = 1$, and cells to the left of the comma have $ctop = 0$. A similar convention for variable *cbot* is used in RBOT. An additional control signal

---

[5] Actually, it is only necessary to propagate the value of μ_B, since the value of μ_T can be derived from the value of μ_B when the registers are swapped.

CBOT, present only in the ST, is used on the downward path to update the contents of *cbot* when RBOT is shifted left. The value of *ctop* is derived from *cbot* when RTOP and RBOT are swapped.

Each cell in the ST also contains a register holding the value of δ. This value is needed in order to determine the "swap" condition in Step 2b. Although the information contained in δ is global in nature, it can be derived locally in each cell by noting the initial positions of the commas (which is fixed, with $\delta = -1$) and keeping track of subsequent swaps ($\delta := -\delta$) and shifts ($\delta := \delta - 1$).

For an individual cell, a basic iteration of Procedure E2 comprises (at most) two multiplication operations and appropriate routing of the results. In order to keep the cell complexity down to one Galois field multiplier, a basic iteration is allotted three clock cycles, and the same multiplier circuitry is used for both multiplication operations. The main operations in the three cycles are broadly described as follows:

Cycle 0: Receive μ_B from the predecessor cell (upward path) and shift RBOT left (downward path).

Cycle 1: Compute the first product in (29), (30), or (31).

Cycle 2: Compute the second product in (29), (30), or (31). Add, if required, to the result of Cycle 1.

A *cycle counter* keeps track of the three cycles in a basic iteration, while an *iteration counter* keeps track of the number of basic iterations. The computation for a block ends after r basic iterations are counted. At that point, the cell outputs its result on the downward path. The core components of the ST cell are shown in Figure 10-11. Notice that all the inputs to the multiplexers at the top of Figure 10-11, except for DATA_UP and DATA_DN, either are constants or originate from internal registers inside the cell.

The three-cycle structure also allows for multiplexing of the ST data paths. Thus, the upward path is used to receive and propagate syndrome symbols from the PST and also to propagate coefficients μ_B. The downward path is used to shift RBOT left and to propagate the coefficients of the computed ω and σ polynomials. Due to this multiplexing, data paths in the ST carry the same number of signals as data paths in the other towers, with the addition of the one-bit signal CBOT on the downward path.

6.3 ST to CT Interface

As in the case of the PST, the coefficients coming out of the ST are spaced three cycles apart. Assuming the polynomials $\sigma(x)$ and $\omega(x)$ attain their full degrees (t and $t - 1$, respectively), a typical output sequence at the data line

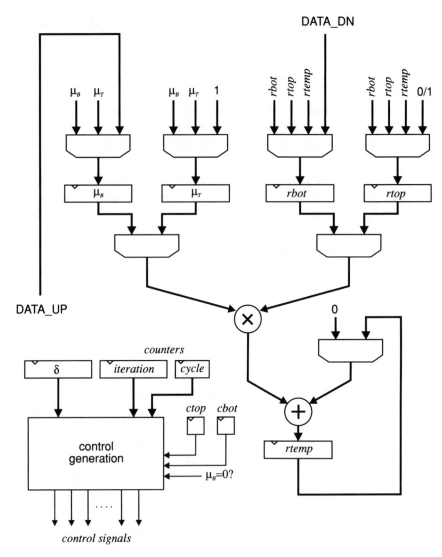

Figure 10-11. Core components of the ST cell.

flowing back to Main Street is as follows:

$$\cdots \square \phi \cdots \phi \, \omega_{t-1} \, \phi \, \phi \, \omega_{t-2} \cdots \phi \, \phi \, \omega_0 \, \phi \, \phi \, \sigma_0 \, \phi \, \phi \, \sigma_1 \cdots \phi \, \phi \, \sigma_{t-1} \, \phi \, \phi \, \sigma_t \square \cdots$$

The total number of coefficients output by the ST is $r + 1$ over a period of n cycles. Hence, the code redundancy is restricted by

$$3r + 1 \leq n, \tag{32}$$

or, equivalently, $r < n/3$.

The data structure in Figure 10-9 keeps polynomials justified towards the ends of RTOP and RBOT, i.e., towards their higher-order positions. Hence, in cases where σ and ω do not attain their full degree, they are padded with zeros at the lower-order positions. When reading the sequence of coefficients from the ST, the CT distributes these padding zeros equally between σ and ω. This results, effectively, in the CT receiving polynomials

$$\overline{\sigma}(x) = x^i \sigma(x),$$
$$\overline{\omega}(x) = x^i \omega(x),$$

for some $i \leq t$, rather than the intended $\sigma(x)$ and $\omega(x)$. However, it can be readily shown that using $\overline{\sigma}$ and $\overline{\omega}$ does not affect the computation of error locations and error values. It is clear that the set of nonzero roots of $\overline{\sigma}$ is the same as that of σ. On the other hand, for a root X of σ, we have

$$\overline{\sigma}'(X) = X^i \sigma'(X) + i X^{i-1} \sigma(X) = X^i \sigma'(X). \tag{33}$$

Hence, the corresponding error value Y can be written as

$$Y = \frac{\omega(X)}{\sigma'(X)} X^{L-1} = \frac{X^i \omega(X)}{X^i \sigma'(X)} X^{L-1} = \frac{\overline{\omega}(X)}{\overline{\sigma}'(X)} X^{L-1}. \tag{34}$$

7 THE CORRECTION TOWER

7.1 Tower Structure

The correction tower determines the roots of the error locator polynomial $\sigma(x)$ and evaluates the error values at the corresponding locations. The CT, shown in Figure 10-12, is composed of three subtowers arranged in a treelike structure, namely, the Ω subtower, the Σ_{odd} subtower, and the Σ_{even} subtower. The three subtowers perform a similar function: evaluate a polynomial at a sequence of n elements of F. The Ω subtower handles the error evaluator polynomial $\omega(x)$. To describe the function of the Σ subtowers, write

$$\sigma(x) = \sigma_{\text{even}}(x^2) + x \sigma_{\text{odd}}(x^2), \tag{35}$$

where

$$\sigma_{\text{even}}(x^2) = \sigma_0 + \sigma_2 x^2 + \cdots + \sigma_{t-\epsilon} x^{t-\epsilon} \tag{36}$$

and

$$\sigma_{\text{odd}}(x^2) = \sigma_1 + \sigma_3 x^2 + \cdots + \sigma_{t+\epsilon-1} x^{t+\epsilon-2}. \tag{37}$$

Here, $\epsilon = t \bmod 2$. The Σ_{even} subtower evaluates the polynomial $\sigma_{\text{even}}(x^2)$, and the Σ_{odd} subtower evaluates the polynomial $\sigma_{\text{odd}}(x^2)$. Partitioning $\sigma(x)$ in this way has the advantage of obtaining the evaluation of $\sigma'(x)$ as a by-product of the evaluation of $\sigma(x)$ since we have

$$\sigma'(x) = \sigma_{\text{odd}}(x^2). \tag{38}$$

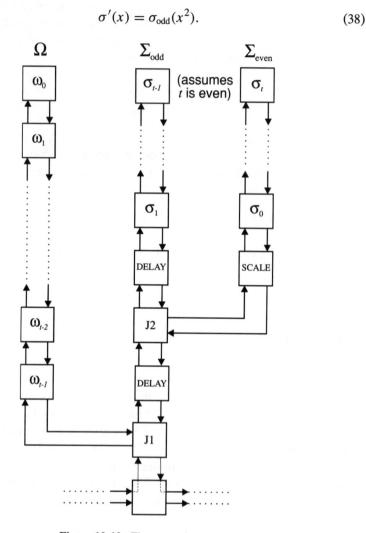

Figure 10-12. The correction tower.

Evaluation of polynomials is done in a similar manner in the three subtowers. The basic computation follows Horner's rule, as in the PST. However, there is a major difference between the PST and the CT: in the PST, each cell evaluates a polynomial at a fixed argument that resides in a static data register in the cell. The polynomial "flows" through the cells, and no coefficient is stored in any particular location for more than one clock cycle. In the CT, each cell grabs a polynomial coefficient and stores it in an internal register for a period of n clock cycles. Coefficients are received on the upward path and are routed to the appropriate subtowers by the joiner cells J1 and J2 (see Figure 10-12). In the subtowers, the cells grab the coefficients using a mechanism similar to the one used in the ST (Figure 10-10). Each cell generates the complete sequence of arguments for the polynomial evaluation and computes a partial result. The partial results flow on the downward path, and the final evaluation result is output from the cell closest to the bottom of the tower. Since one evaluation result is required at every clock cycle (except EOPM), evaluation for one block proceeds in parallel with coefficient-grabbing for the next.

The core of the CT computation is shown in Figure 10-13, which shows the evaluation circuitry for a cell holding a coefficient f_j in a generic subtower computing a polynomial $f(x) = \sum_{j=0}^{s} f_j x^j$. We assume that the polynomial is to be evaluated at the sequence of arguments $x_0, x_1, x_2, \ldots, x_{n-1}$, with $x_i = x_0 \beta^i$ for some $x_0, \beta \in F, 0 \le i \le n - 1$. The values of x_0 and β for each subtower in the CT will be specified in the sequel. Also, we assume that cell s at the top of the tower holds the highest-order coefficient f_s and that cell 0 at the bottom of the tower holds f_0. Register X is initialized to x_0 at the beginning of the computation and is multiplied by β at each cycle, thus running through the sequence $x_0, x_1, x_2, \ldots, x_{n-1}$. The beginning of the computation is triggered by the EOPM_DN signal, which is "bounced back" from EOPM_UP at the top cell. Hence, cell s starts its computation first, followed by cell $s - 1$ two cycles later, and so on. Let

$$f_{(j)}(x) = \sum_{l=j}^{s} f_l x^{l-j}, \qquad 0 \le j \le s. \tag{39}$$

Assuming that register Y at the top cell is permanently set to 0, it can be readily verified that cell j computes the sequence $f_{(j)}(x_0), f_{(j)}(x_1), f_{(j)}(x_2),$ $\ldots, f_{(j)}(x_{n-1})$. In particular, since $f_{(0)}(x) = f(x)$, cell 0 computes $f(x_0)$, $f(x_1), \ldots, f(x_{n-1})$, which is the desired sequence of evaluations.

We now determine the parameters x_0 and β for each subtower. In principle, we want to evaluate $\sigma(x)$ for $x = \alpha^{-(n-1)}, \alpha^{-(n-2)}, \ldots, \alpha^{-1}, \alpha^0$ and then compute Y_j as given in (15) for locations X_j such that $\sigma(X_j) = 0$. However, a few complications stand in our way. First, as discussed above, the odd and even parts of σ are computed separately, and with argument x^2 rather than x. This is accomplished by setting $x_0 = \alpha^{-2(n-1)}$ and $\beta = \alpha^2$ for the σ cells. Since F has characteristic 2, a location X is a root of $\sigma(x)$ if and only if

$$\sigma_{\text{even}}(X^2) = X\sigma_{\text{odd}}(X^2), \tag{40}$$

or, equivalently,

$$X^{-1}\sigma_{\text{even}}(X^2) = \sigma_{\text{odd}}(X^2) \tag{41}$$

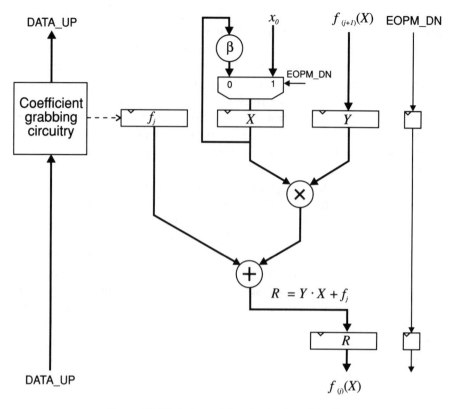

Figure 10-13. Polynomial evaluation in a CT cell.

(recall that locations X are nonzero). The SCALE cell at the bottom of the Σ_{even} subtower (Figure 10-12) multiplies $\sigma_{\text{even}}(x)$ by x^{-1}. This cell is similar to the evaluation cells depicted in Figure 10-13, but with the grabbing circuitry disabled and the coefficient register f_j set to 0. In order for the cell to perform the desired scaling by x^{-1}, its parameters are set to $x_0 = \alpha^{n-1}$, $\beta = \alpha^{-1}$. Notice that we choose to use equation (41) rather than (40) since we want to leave the value $\sigma_{\text{odd}}(x^2) = \sigma'(x)$ intact. The DELAY cell at the bottom of the Σ_{odd} subtower is used to equalize the logical delay of the two Σ subtowers, so that the even and odd results arrive at the joiner cell J2 at the same time.[6] At J2, $\sigma_{\text{odd}}(x^2)$ (arriving from Σ_{odd}) is compared to $x^{-1}\sigma_{\text{even}}(x^2)$ (arriving from Σ_{even}). If they are equal, a root is detected, and the computation of the error value is enabled. This computation is actually distributed between J1 and J2, as will be explained in Section 7.2.

---

[6]Although we show only one cell, a chain of delay cells may be needed, depending on the amount of delay required and on the delay cell implementation.

The second complication in the CT computation stems from the fact that, due to the order in which the ST outputs the coefficients of ω and σ, the ω_j are loaded onto the Ω subtower in reverse order; i.e., ω_0 goes to the top of the tower, and ω_{t-1} goes to the bottom. Hence, the Ω subtower actually evaluates

$$\overleftarrow{\omega}(x) = \omega_0 x^{t-1} + \omega_1 x^{t-2} + \cdots + \omega_{t-2} x + \omega_{t-1} = x^{t-1} \omega(x^{-1}). \qquad (42)$$

Rewriting equation (15) in terms of $\overleftarrow{\omega}$, we obtain

$$Y_j = \frac{\overleftarrow{\omega}(X_j^{-1})}{\sigma'(X_j)} X_j^{L+t-2}. \qquad (43)$$

Setting $x_0 = \alpha^{n-1}$ and $\beta = \alpha^{-1}$ in all the cells of the Ω subtower, we obtain the desired evaluation of $\overleftarrow{\omega}$ at x^{-1} rather than x. Also, by choosing $L = 2 - t$, we eliminate the extra factor on the right hand side of (43), thus reducing the error value computation to one division over F.

The DELAY cell between the joiners J1 and J2 is used to equalize the logical delays of the Ω and Σ structures. The values of x_0 and β for the different cells in the CT are summarized in Table 2.

TABLE 2   Values of x_0 and β.

Cell Type	x_0	β
ω	α^{n-1}	α^{-1}
σ	$\alpha^{-2(n-1)}$	α^2
SCALE	α^{n-1}	α^{-1}

7.2 Computation of Division in the Correction Tower

The last stage in the computation of the error values in the CT calls for the calculation of a quotient u/v, where $u = \overleftarrow{\omega}(X^{-1})$ and $v = \sigma'(X)$, for some root X of σ. The quantity v is available at the joiner cell J2, and u is available at the joiner cell J1. A straightforward approach would be to have a field inverter in J2 and a multiplier in J1. J2 would compute v^{-1} and pass it to J1, which would complete the calculation by computing $u \cdot v^{-1}$. This approach calls for fairly different circuitry in J1 and J2. When m is even, it is possible to structure the computation in a way that results in very similar designs for J1 and J2. Minimizing the variety of cell designs is an important consideration in practical implementations of systolic arrays.

Assume $m = 2p$, for some integer $p \geq 1$. Then, $F = GF(2^m)$ can be represented as a quadratic extension of $G = GF(2^p)$. An element $v \in F$ is represented as $v = V_0 + V_1 \gamma$, where $\gamma \in F$ is the root of an irreducible quadratic polynomial $h(x)$ over G. We can assume, without loss of generality, that $h(x) = x^2 + x + \lambda$, for some $\lambda \in G$. It is easy to verify that the second root of $h(x)$ is $\gamma + 1$. Hence, the *conjugate* of v is $v^* = (V_0 + V_1) + \gamma V_1$, and its *norm* [9] is given by

$$\Delta(v) = v \cdot v^* = V_0^2 + V_1^2 \lambda + V_0 V_1 \in G. \tag{44}$$

We define a *quasi-division* operation • as follows:

$$u \bullet v \stackrel{\text{def}}{=} u \cdot v^*. \tag{45}$$

Assume $v \neq 0$ and consider the following computation:

$$z = v \bullet \frac{1}{\Delta(v)}, \tag{46}$$
$$y = u \bullet z.$$

We claim that $y = u/v$. To prove the claim, we first observe that

$$z = v \bullet \frac{1}{\Delta(v)} = v \cdot \frac{1}{\Delta(v)^*} = \frac{v}{\Delta(v)} = \frac{1}{v^*}. \tag{47}$$

Now,

$$y = u \bullet z = u \cdot z^* = u \cdot \left(\frac{1}{v^*}\right)^* = \frac{u}{v}. \tag{48}$$

Thus, following (46), we can compute the quotient u/v using two quasi-division operations plus the computation of $1/\Delta(v)$. The complexity of a quasi division is similar to the complexity of a multiplication in F, which can be done with three multiplications over G [21]. The computation of $\Delta(v)$ requires one more multiplication over G, and for practical values of m (e.g., $m = 8$) the inverse $1/\Delta(v)$ is simpler than a multiplication over G. Notice that, in the computation of $\Delta(v)$ given in (44), V_0^2 and λV_1^2 are linear operations over $GF(2)$ in the arguments V_0 and V_1, respectively. Thus, they do not require additional G multipliers. In the case of $m = 8$, further complexity savings can be obtained by representing $G = GF(16)$ as a quadratic extension of $GF(4)$. This "recursive" representation is also advantageous when implementing multiplication in the PST, ST, and CT cells. The computation of division in J1 and J2 is shown in Figure 10-14 (the delay cell between J1 and J2 is omitted).

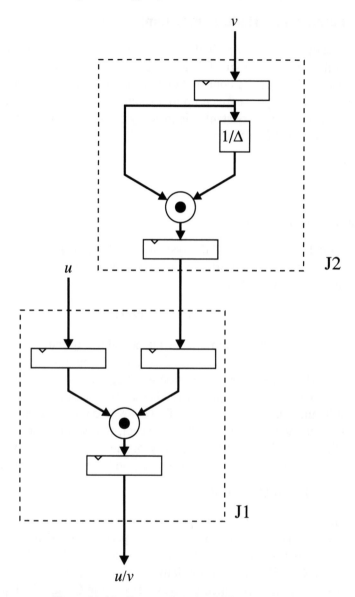

Figure 10-14. Computation of a division in J1 and J2.

8 OTHER PROPERTIES AND ENHANCEMENTS

In this section, we discuss some additional properties and possible enhancements of the HRSD.

8.1 Latency and Redundancy Limitation

The latency of the upper path of the HRSD is an important parameter that determines the amount of logical delay necessary on the lower path of Main Street. Listed below are the contributions of the different subsystems to the total latency. All delays are given up to a small, implementation-dependent additive constant. These constants, denoted by ϵ_i, include pipelining delays on the upper path of Main Street.

PST: $n + 3r + \epsilon_1$
ST: $6r + \epsilon_2$
CT: $3t + \epsilon_3$
Total: $n + 9r + 3t + \epsilon_4$.

Hence, the total digital latency of the system, from the time a received symbol enters the input cell of Main Street to the time the corresponding corrected symbol leaves the output cell, is

$$D = n + 10.5r + O(1).$$

One of the factors that determine the latency of the system, as well as the limitation $r < n/3$ on the redundancy of the code, is the three-cycle computation on the ST. Since the basic iteration requires only two multiplications, it could be possible, in principle, to reduce a basic iteration to two cycles while maintaining one multiplier per cell. This would reduce latency and the limitation in redundancy to $r < n/2$. However, this would also result in a very significant increase in the complexity of the ST cell circuitry and the "lengthening" of critical paths, with the corresponding penalty in throughput.

8.2 Number of Cell Types

As can be seen from the description in the previous sections, many different cell functions are required in the various parts of the HRSD. However, some of these functions are very similar. For example, cells in the Σ and Ω sections of the CT differ only in the initial values x_0 and in the constant β used for advancing their arguments. Also, cells in the CT and PST perform similar basic operations (one iteration in a polynomial evaluation based on Horner's rule) and could share significant parts of their designs. On the other hand, some degree of cell differentiation might be needed even for cells on a single tower. For example, cells at tops of towers perform a slightly different function than cells in the middle (since, for instance, they need to "bounce down" some signals). In another example, the cell at the bottom of the ST is slightly different than other cells in the tower since it generates the coefficients μ_B that then flow up the tower. By allotting a few *mode bits* for cell differentiation, similar cells can be based on one common design and the actual "identity" of the cell can be dynamically determined at system startup time by loading appropriate values into the mode bits. These mode bits reside in static registers whose contents remain unchanged until the decoder is reinitialized, or reconfigured, as discussed in Section 8.3.

In the HRSD prototype implementation, four basic cell designs were used:

Design 1: All Main Street cells
Design 2: All PST and CT cells
Design 3: All ST cells
Design 4: The J1 and J2 joiner cells

Various mechanisms could be used to initialize the cells. In the HRSD prototype, a so-called *vision string* mechanism was used. Under this mechanism, the system could switch to an *initialization mode* in which all the registers and flip-flops in all the cells of the array were "strung" into one very long shift register (the *vision string*). A desired initial state could then be loaded serially into the shift register, with appropriate values reaching mode bits and static variables (e.g., the evaluation argument in a PST cell) in all the cells. Once the initialization was accomplished, the system would switch back to its regular RS decoding mode. The initialization procedure could be run at clock rates orders of magnitude slower than regular operation. Thus, signals related to the vision string mechanism were not required to satisfy the hypersystolic constraints. The vision string mechanism adds three binary I/O signals to each cell: a serial input, a serial output, and an input signal used to switch the cell to initialization mode.

8.3 Variable Code Parameters

One of the benefits of using mode bits for cell differentiation is the possibility of dynamically changing the code parameters. Assume we start with a HRSD designed for given maximum parameters n and r. To obtain a decoder with redundancy $r' < r$, we can program cells in the middle of the PST, ST, and CT to behave like "tops of towers," effectively shortening the lengths of the towers. At the same time, we must program the delay on the lower path of Main Street to adjust for that shortening. To change the length of the code to $n' < n$, we change the initial value of x_0 in the CT cells, and, again, we adjust the delay on Main Street.

8.4 Error Detection

As proven in Theorem 1, the condition $\delta \geq 0$ at the end of the Euclidean computation in the ST indicates the presence of an uncorrectable error pattern. This condition can be detected by the ST cells, and the information can be propagated from the ST to the CT (for example, by setting VALID = 1 at the EOPM cycle, which would otherwise be meaningless) and from there to the output cell on Main Street. This provides some error detection capability in addition to error correction. When r is odd, it can be shown that this condition will detect all error patterns of weight $t + 1$.

ACKNOWLEDGMENTS

We thank Dave Aspinwall, Earl Cohen, Sol Golomb, Robert MacKenzie, Tze-Hwa Liu, Steve Pope, Lloyd Welch, and the other members of Kodak/Cyclotomics' research and engineering team for many fruitful discussions and for their contributions to the implementation of the HRSD prototype.

APPENDIX: EXAMPLE OF PROCEDURE E2

Let $m = 3$, and $\alpha \in \text{GF}(8)$ satisfying $\alpha^3 + \alpha + 1 = 0$. We consider an RS code with parameters $n = 7$, $r = 4$, $t = 2$, $L = 0$, and roots $1, \alpha, \alpha^2, \alpha^3$. Assume the error vector is $(0\,0\,\alpha^2\,0\,0\,0\,1)$, i.e., $e(x) = \alpha^2 x^4 + 1$, and the error locations are $X_1 = \alpha^{-4}$ and $X_2 = 1$, with error values $Y_1 = \alpha^2$, $Y_2 = 1$. The syndrome symbols are $S_0 = e(1) = \alpha^6$, $S_1 = e(\alpha) = \alpha^2$, $S_2 = e(\alpha^2) = \alpha$, and $S_3 = e(\alpha^3) = 0$. The error locator and error evaluator polynomial are given, respectively, by

$$\sigma(x) = (x + \alpha^{-4})(x + 1) = x^2 + \alpha x + \alpha^3$$

and

$$\omega(x) = 1 \cdot 1 \cdot (x + \alpha^{-4}) + \alpha^2 \cdot \alpha^3 \cdot (x + 1) = \alpha^4 x + \alpha^2.$$

The listing below shows the values in RTOP and RBOT obtained by running Procedure E2 for this example. Brackets delineate basic iterations of Procedure E2. As claimed in Theorem 1, results are obtained after $r = 4$ basic iterations.

(0) $\begin{bmatrix}\end{bmatrix}$ Step 1. Initial state:

1	0	0	0	0 ,	1	RTOP
0	α	α^2	α^6 ,	0	0	RBOT

(1) Step 2d. Shift RBOT left:

1	0	0	0	0 ,	1
α	α^2	α^6 ,	0	0	0

(2) Step 2b. Swap RTOP and RBOT

α	α^2	α^6 ,	0	0	0
1	0	0	0	0 ,	1

Step 2c. Multiply and add : $\mu_T = \alpha, \mu_B = 1$

α	α^2	α^6 ,	0	0	1
0	α^2	α^6	0	0 ,	1

Step 2d. Shift RBOT left:

α	α^2	α^6 ,	0	0	1
α^2	α^6	0	0 ,	1	0

(3) Step 2c. Multiply and add : $\mu_T = \alpha, \mu_B = \alpha^2$

α	α^2	α^6 ,	0	α^2	α
0	α^5	α	0 ,	1	0

2d. Shift RBOT left:

α	α^2	α^6 ,	0	α^2	α
α^5	α	0 ,	1	0	0

(4) 2c. Multiply and add: $\mu_T = \alpha, \mu_B = \alpha^5$

α	α^2	α^6 ,	α^5	α^3	α^2
0	α^6	α^4 ,	1	0	0

2d. Shift RBOT left:

α	α^2	α^6 ,	α^5	α^3	α^2
α^6	α^4 ,	1	0	0	0

As expected for a correctable error pattern, we have $\delta = -1$ at the end of the computation. The final results are given by the coefficients to the left of the comma in RBOT and the coefficients to the right of the comma in RTOP, i.e., $\omega_B(x) = \alpha^6 x + \alpha^4$ and $\sigma_T(x) = \alpha^2 x^2 + \alpha^3 x + \alpha^5$. We verify that these are scalar multiples of the desired $\omega(x)$ and $\sigma(x)$, namely,

$$\omega_B(x) = \alpha^2 \omega(x),$$

and

$$\sigma_T(x) = \alpha^2 \sigma(x).$$

REFERENCES

[1] E. R. Berlekamp, Hypersystolic Computers, JASON Workshop on Advanced Computer Architectures, La Jolla, Calif., 1986.

[2] E. R. Berlekamp, *Algebraic Coding Theory*, Laguna Hill, Calif.: Aegean Park Press, 1984.

[3] E. R. Berlekamp, G. Seroussi, and P. Tong, "Hypersystolic Reed-Solomon Decoder," U.S. Patent No. 4,958,348, issued September 18, 1990.

[4] E. R. Blahut, *Theory and Practice of Error Control Codes*, Reading, Mass: Addison-Wesley, 1983.

[5] R. P. Brent and H. T. Kung, "Systolic VLSI Arrays for Polynomial GCD Computations," *IEEE Transactions on Computers*, Volume C-33, pp. 731–736, 1984.

[6] "Hypersystolic Reed-Solomon Decoder," Internal Technical Report, Cyclotomics, Inc., Berkeley, Calif., March 1988.

[7] M. A. Hasan and V. K. Bhargava, "Bit-Serial Systolic Divider and Multiplier for Finite Fields $GF(2^m)$," *IEEE Transactions on Computers*, Volume C-41, pp. 972–980, 1992.

[8] H. T. Kung, "Why Systolic Architectures?" *IEEE Computer Magazine*, Volume 15, pp. 37–45, 1982.

[9] R. Lidl and H. Niederreiter, "Finite Fields," in *Encyclopedia of Mathematics and Its Applications*, Gian-Carlo Rota (Ed.), Reading, Mass.: Addison-Wesley, 1983.

[10] F. J. MacWilliams and N. J. A. Sloane, *The Theory of Error Correcting Codes*, Amsterdam: North-Holland, 1983.

[11] J. L. Massey, "Shift Register Synthesis and BCH Decoding," *IEEE Transactions on Information Theory*, Volume IT-15, pp. 122–127, 1969.

[12] R. J. McEliece, "The Theory of Information and Coding," *Encyclopedia of Mathematics and Its Applications*, Gian-Carlo Rota (Ed.), Cambridge University Press, Cambridge, 1985.

[13] M. Morii and M. Kasahara, "Generalized Key-Equation of Remainder Decoding Algorithm for Reed-Solomon Codes," *IEEE Transactions on Information Theory*, Volume IT-38, pp. 1801–1807, 1992.

[14] G. Seroussi, "Hypersystolic Reed-Solomon Encoder," U.S. Patent No. 4,958,348, issued May 30, 1989.

[15] G. Seroussi, "A Systolic Reed-Solomon Encoder," *IEEE Transactions on Information Theory*, Volume IT-37(4), pp. 1217–1220, July 1991.

[16] H. M. Shao and I. S. Reed, "On the VLSI Design of a Pipeline Reed-Solomon Decoder Using Systolic Arrays," *IEEE Transactions on Computers*, Volume C-37, pp. 1273–1280, 1988.

[17] H. M. Shao, T. K. Truong, L. J. Deutsch, J. H. Yuen, and I. S. Reed, "A VLSI Design of a Pipeline Reed-Solomon Decoder," *IEEE Transactions on Computers*, Volume C-34, pp. 393–403, 1985.

[18] Y. Sugiyama, M. Kasahara, S. Hirasawa, and T. Namekawa, "A Method for Solving Key Equation for Decoding Goppa Codes," *Information and Control*, Volume 27, pp. 87–99, 1975.

[19] P. Tong, "A 40-mHz Encoder-Decoder Chip Generated by a Reed-Solomon Compiler," *Proceedings, Custom Integrated Circuits Conference, Boston, Mass.*, pp. 13.5.1–13.5.4, May 1990.

[20] L. R. Welch and E. R. Berlekamp, "Error Correction for Algebraic Block Codes," U.S. Patent No. 4,633,470, issued December 30, 1986.

[21] S. Winograd, *Arithmetic Complexity of Computations*, Regional Conference Series in Applied Mathematics, Philadelphia: SIAM, 1980.

[22] C. -S. Yeh, I. S. Reed, and T. K. Truong, "Systolic Multipliers for Finite Fields $GF(2^m)$," *IEEE Transactions on Computers*, Volume C-33, pp. 357–360, 1984.

[23] B. B. Zhou, "A New Bit-Serial Systolic Multiplier over $GF(2^m)$," *IEEE Transactions on Computers*, Volume C-37, pp. 749–751, 1988.

Chapter 11

Matching Viterbi Decoders and Reed-Solomon Decoders in a Concatenated System

Joachim Hagenauer

Elke Offer

Lutz Papke
Institute for Communications Technology
German Aerospace Research Establishment (DLR)
D-82230 Wessling, P.O. Box 1116, Germany

1 INTRODUCTION

Reed-Solomon codes have a number of characteristics that have made them quite popular. For example, they have, in the Berlekamp-Massey algorithm, an efficient bounded distance decoding algorithm. Being nonbinary, Reed-Solomon codes also provide significant burst-error-correcting capability. Perhaps the only disadvantage to using Reed-Solomon codes lies in the lack of an efficient maximum likelihood soft-decision decoding algorithm.[1] The difficulty in finding such an algorithm is in part due to the mismatch between the algebraic structure of a Galois field and the real numbers at the output of the receiver demodulator. A well-known information theoretic result holds that on a Gaussian channel with binary input the minimum E_b/N_0 that will support transmission with arbitrarily high reliability is -1.6 dB for soft-decision decoders, increasing to 0.4 dB for hard-decision decoders. E_b/N_0 is the ratio of the received energy per information bit to the one-sided noise power spectral density. These results assume that the code rate approaches zero asymptotically. For a rate-1/2 code the minimum E_b/N_0 necessary for reliable transmission is 0.2 dB for soft-decision decoders and 1.8 dB for hard-decision decoders. These basic results suggest the significant loss of performance entailed when soft-decision decoding is not available for a given code.

---

[1]Chapter 6 describes the state of the art in the search for such an algorithm.

The situation is quite different for convolutional codes with sequential or Viterbi decoding. Soft decisions can be easily incorporated into either decoding algorithm in a very natural way, providing an increase in coding gain of over 2.0 dB with respect to the comparable hard-decision decoder over an additive white Gaussian noise channel. Unfortunately convolutional codes present their own set of problems. For example, they cannot be easily implemented at high coding rates. They also have an unfortunate tendency to generate burst errors at the decoder output as the noise level at the input is increased.

A "best of both worlds" situation can be obtained by combining Reed-Solomon codes with convolutional codes in a concatenated system. The convolutional code (with soft-decision Viterbi decoding) is used to "clean up" the channel for the Reed-Solomon code, which in turn corrects the burst errors emerging from the Viterbi decoder. This chapter shows that such a system can achieve a bit error rate of 10^{-5} at an E_b/N_0 of 1.7 dB and a code rate of approximately 0.5.

The next section of this chapter provides a review of previous work and a discussion of the state of the art in concatenated systems. We then proceed to the soft-output Viterbi decoder. This decoder can provide reliability information *to* the outer Reed-Solomon decoder, while accepting reliability information *from* a previous Reed-Solomon decoding step in an interleaved scheme. This system is thoroughly characterized, and its substantial improvement in performance with respect to the standard concatenated system is demonstrated. One proposed application for this new system is the NASA/ESA standard coding scheme for deep space missions. A particular example for this application is the partial compensation for the failure of the *Galileo* main antenna, an event that caused a desperate need for additional power gains in the image transmission system.

2 CONCATENATED CODING SYSTEM WITH CONVOLUTIONAL CODES AND REED-SOLOMON CODES

2.1 The Problem

In his paper "The How and Why of Channel Coding" [14] J. Massey stated that convolutional codes should be used in the first stage of decoding because they can easily accept soft decisions and channel state information from the channel. Reed-Solomon codes are then used to clean up the errors left over by the Viterbi decoder. Indeed Viterbi decoding and the decoding of Reed-Solomon codes complement each other very nicely: the Viterbi decoder has no problems accepting soft decisions from the channel, and it delivers short bursts of errors. Short error bursts do not affect the Reed-Solomon decoder as long as they are within an α-bit symbol of the Reed-Solomon code. This complementary feature was one of the reasons that this concatenated system has been selected by the Consultative Committee for Space Data Systems (CCSDS) of NASA and ESA for deep space missions, where power savings is the main concern [4]. It is also under consideration for the transmission layer of the digital television system defined by the Moving Pictures Expert Group (MPEG).

We go one step further in this chapter and link the two decoders even further: we use the soft output of a modified Viterbi decoder to generate erasures at the input of the Reed-Solomon decoder, thus improving performance. The result of the Reed-Solomon decoding process is then used for another round of Viterbi decoding. We want to obtain the probability of correct decoding for each individual bit at the output of the Reed-Solomon decoder because this constitutes *a priori* information for the next step of Viterbi decoding. Up to now we have used only very crude information about the reliability of the Reed-Solomon decoding operation. For certain code parameters the probability that a code word and therefore a bit is wrong is very small when the Berlekamp-Massey algorithm terminates within its designed correction capability.

One problem that immediately arises is the fact that Viterbi decoding of convolutional codes works on bits and that Reed-Solomon codes are symbol-oriented. We must thus transform bit error probabilities into symbol error probabilities and vice versa.

2.2 Previous and Related Work

Improvement of the decoding system for the conventional concatenated codes (an outer Reed-Solomon code and an inner convolutional code) has been considered several times in the literature. One of the first authors who worked on this problem was Lin-Nan Lee, in his Ph.D. thesis prepared under the direction of J. Massey in 1976 [12]. Parts of this work were published in *IEEE Transactions on Communications* in 1977 [13]. Lee modified the conventional system by making the inner code a unit-memory convolutional code. He further allowed for the movement of reliability information between the inner and outer decoders. Lee has thus already introduced most of the ideas we propose to discuss in this chapter; the only thing missing from his results is an evaluation of his coding scheme under realistic constraints, something we intend to provide here.

The unit-memory convolutional code encodes k_0-bit information into n_0-bit encoded segments so that they are naturally symbol-oriented, with symbol size equal to k_0 information bits. In his study Lee took the $(18, 6)$ unit-memory code with free distance 16 as the inner code. The outer codes considered are

$t = 4$, 6, and 8 error-correcting Reed-Solomon codes defined over GF(2^6). Lee assumes that the interleaving between the inner and outer encoders is perfect; it is thus only necessary to simulate the inner coding system to get the byte error probability at the inner decoder output. By computing the probability of there being $(t + 1)$ or more erroneous symbols in a Reed-Solomon code word, Lee obtains an upper bound on decoder error for the outer decoder. The overall performance of the concatenated coding system is then estimated under the assumption that all incorrectly decoded Reed-Solomon code words are $d_{\min} = 2t + 1$ symbols away from the correct code word. The quantification of the performance improvements discussed in Lee's article are obtained by comparing the symbol error rates of the $t = 4$, 6, and 8 error-correcting Reed-Solomon codes as outer codes on a simulated AWGN channel with an E_S/N_0 of -3.5 dB. Here E_S denotes the average signal energy, and N_0 the one-sided noise spectral density.

The unit-memory code has a free distance that is greater by 1 than that of the conventional $(3, 1)$ convolutional code with $M = 6$ (and thus a 64-state trellis diagram). This improved free distance and the symbol-oriented nature of the unit-memory code provide an improvement of approximately 0.3 dB when this code replaces the bit-oriented convolutional inner code. But even if the number of states in the trellis diagram is equal for both convolutional codes, the $2^6 = 64$ branches per state for the $(18, 6)$ unit-memory code require a significant increase in decoder complexity when compared to the two branches per state for the conventional convolutional code.

Another improvement discussed by Lee is the use of a minimal-symbol-error probability decoding algorithm; in other words, he considers a symbol-by-symbol maximum *a posteriori* (MAP) decoder instead of the Viterbi decoder. The outer decoder may then use reliability information about the estimated code symbol to perform "errors-and-erasures" decoding. This scheme improves the performance by only 0.05 to 0.1 dB, clearly not enough to justify substitution of the symbol-by-symbol MAP decoder for the less complex Viterbi decoder.

Lee also presents performance results for a concatenated decoding system in which there is information feedback from the outer decoder to the inner decoder. When the outer decoder detects and corrects errors made by the inner decoder, the corrected estimates of the outer decoder are fed back to the inner decoder to eliminate error bursts. Other authors have called this technique *forced-state decoding* or *state pinning* [16]. The further improvement obtained by feedback is about 0.3 to 0.4 dB, assuming that the outer decoder always makes correct decisions. In Lee's work the symbol-by-symbol MAP decoder receives a greater benefit from the feedback than does the Viterbi decoder.

Finally, Lee compares his approach to the tail annexation scheme proposed by Zeoli [20] and Jelinek [10]. This approach requires the feedback of symbols previously decoded by the Viterbi decoder and uses the output of the outer decoder to restart the inner Viterbi decoder whenever an error is corrected by the outer decoder.

Zeoli's scheme is less successful than the symbol-by-symbol MAP decoder followed by an errors-and-erasures Reed-Solomon decoder with feedback when both are applied to the $(18, 6)$ unit-memory convolutional code with a three-branch-long "random tail" (the resulting code is actually an $M = 4$ $(18, 6)$ convolutional code). Combining all his ideas into a single system, Lee achieves a symbol error rate of about 10^{-5} at an E_b/N_0 of 1.9 dB and a total code rate of 0.29.

E. Paaske has also been working on improvements for the conventional concatenated coding system [16–18]. In particular he focuses on the coding system recommended as a standard for telemetry channel coding by the Consultative Committee for Space Data Systems. This coding system has an outer $(255, 223)$ Reed-Solomon code with symbols out of $GF(2^8)$ followed by an inner, rate-1/2 convolutional code with memory $M = 6$. The interleaver size proved to be an important parameter in the decoding process, so Paaske investigated interleaving blocks with $I = 12$ and $I = 16$ Reed-Solomon code words as well as the usual interleaving size of $I = 8$ used in the system implemented by ESA. In the conventional coding system both decoders work independently of each other, without any exchange of side information. The two decoding steps in the standard coding system can therefore be viewed separately. Paaske reintroduced the idea of exchanging information between the two decoders and the deinterleaver to increase the error correction capability of the overall system [16]. His proposals are mainly based on the fact that the output of the Viterbi decoder is not statistically independent but is bursty, and that the error correction capability of Reed-Solomon codes (or any block code) can be increased if errors are transformed into erasures. The output of the standard Viterbi decoder does not indicate where to place the erasures in the received Reed-Solomon code words. Paaske's idea was to use repeated Reed-Solomon decoding trials on the output of the Viterbi decoder, thereby making it possible to place erasures by examining the block deinterleaver. Assuming that at least one Reed-Solomon code word in the block deinterleaver can be correctly decoded in the first Reed-Solomon decoding run, Paaske developed several strategies for erasing symbols in the neighboring but not yet decodable Reed-Solomon code words. This is feasible because a successful decoding operation shows the positions of the former erroneous symbols in the corrected code word. Since there is a significant probability that the symbols at the same position in the neighboring Reed-Solomon code word are also erroneous, they are erased. If none of these strategies leads to a decoding success, Paaske erases arbitrarily chosen symbols in the received word. This procedure is repeated until either the received word can be decoded or a maximal number of runs has been reached. This last strategy seldom terminates successfully.

For example, with interleaver size $I = 8$ and $E_b/N_0 = 2.0$ dB, these improvements reduce the percentage of outer decoder failures from 33.8% to 2.2%. This is equivalent to a gain of 0.1 to 0.2 dB in E_b/N_0. The improvement in frame error rate is slightly higher, about 0.3 dB in E_b/N_0. Of course the price to be paid is a significant increase in decoding effort. For every decoded Reed-Solomon code word, the decoder needs an average of 21.6 trials in this particular example.

Paaske also examines the use of repeated decoding trials for both the Viterbi and Reed-Solomon decoders, with an exchange of decoding information between the two. The Viterbi decoder is constrained in such a way that the symbols that are already decoded by the Reed-Solomon decoder must be part of the decoded path in the next decoding run of the Viterbi decoder (forced-state decoding). As noted earlier, a similar feedback scheme was already used by Lee in [13]. The coding gain is 0.25 dB at a bit error rate (BER) of 10^{-5} and 0.3 dB for a frame error rate (FER) of 10^{-5}. The interleaver size was chosen in this example to be $I = 8$ [18]. The bit error rate of 10^{-5} is thus achieved with a signal-to-noise ratio of 2.05 dB. Paaske proposes the use of another technique when no Reed-Solomon code word in the interleaver block is successfully decoded. The objective is to determine which symbols in the yet-to-be decoded Reed-Solomon code words should be erased or substituted. Paaske found alternative symbols by tracing back through the Viterbi algorithm and looking for a zero difference in the partial path metric comparisons performed at each node. This procedure, called *list-of-2 Viterbi decoding*, is restricted to finding only one alternative for a Reed-Solomon symbol. The improvement in coding gain is about 0.4 dB for the FER (interleaver size $I = 8$) when a maximum number of 2000 feedback circles for the decoding of one interleaver block is allowed.

Paaske's most recent work [18] deals with the implementation of nonuniform Reed-Solomon code profiles as opposed to the list-of-2 Viterbi decoding. This means that some Reed-Solomon code words in the interleaver block have a greater error correction capability than others. The overall code rate remains nearly the same. However, the probability that one Reed-Solomon code word in an interleaver frame is successfully decoded increases, and consequently the probability that the whole interleaver frame is totally decoded increases as well. In contrast to the high complexity of the list-of-2 Viterbi decoding algorithm, the use of nonuniform Reed-Solomon code profiles results in no overall complexity increase. In this case the gain is about 0.4 dB for the BER and about 0.45 dB for the FER as compared to the standard concatenated coding system when a $t = 10$ error-correcting Reed-Solomon code alternates with a $t = 22$ error-correcting Reed-Solomon code [18].

The use of nonuniform Reed-Solomon code profiles was further investigated by D. Linne von Berg and S. Wilson [3]. Through a simulation study they found profiles that are quite nonuniform but have the same overall code rate as the standard concatenated coding system. Unfortunately, the optimal code profile varied with the E_b/N_0, but the main characteristic was one very strong code ($t = 45$) in the middle flanked by weaker codes, where on the left side the codes had to be stronger than on the right side. The coding gain was found to be about 0.6 dB for the BER as compared to the standard coding system.

3 SOFT-OUTPUT VITERBI DECODING AND REED-SOLOMON CODES

3.1 The Soft-Output Viterbi Algorithm with *A Priori* Information

In this section we briefly describe a Viterbi algorithm that delivers soft decisions [8] to the outer decoder. We restrict ourselves to binary transmitted data and use log-likelihood ratios that are clearly related to bit error probabilities. The concept of the log-likelihood or algebraic value $L(u)$ [1,2] of a binary random variable u is first formulated. Let u be in GF(2) = $\{+1, -1\}$ with $+1$ as the "null" element under the addition $\oplus$ and define its log-likelihood ratio $L(u)$ as the real number

$$L(u) = \log \frac{P(u = +1)}{P(u = -1)}. \tag{1}$$

Unless otherwise stated the logarithm is the natural logarithm. We subsequently call $L(u)$ the "soft" value or L-value of a binary random variable. The sign of $L(u)$ corresponds to the hard decision, and the magnitude $|L(u)|$ is the reliability of this decision. It is easy to show that for statistically independent u,

$$L(u_1 \oplus u_2) = \log \frac{1 + e^{L(u_1)}e^{L(u_2)}}{e^{L(u_1)} + e^{L(u_2)}} \tag{2}$$

$$\approx \text{sign}[L(u_1)] \cdot \text{sign}[L(u_2)] \cdot \min[|L(u_1)|, |L(u_2)|] \tag{3}$$

For the log-likelihood or algebraic values $L(u)$, the soft values, we define a special algebra where $\boxplus$ denotes the addition for this set:

$$L(u_1) \boxplus L(u_2) = L(u_1 \oplus u_2), \tag{4}$$

with the rules

$$L(u) \boxplus \infty = L(u) \tag{5}$$

$$L(u) \boxplus 0 = 0. \tag{6}$$

By complete induction one can further prove that

$$L\left(\sum_{j=1}^{J} \oplus u_j\right) = \sum_{j=1}^{J} \boxplus L(u_j) = \log \frac{\prod_{j=1}^{J}(e^{L(u_j)} + 1) + \prod_{j=1}^{J}(e^{L(u_j)} - 1)}{\prod_{j=1}^{J}(e^{L(u_j)} + 1) - \prod_{j=1}^{J}(e^{L(u_j)} - 1)} \tag{7}$$

and finally approximate it as in equation (3) by

$$L\left(\sum_{j=1}^{J} \oplus u_j\right) = \sum_{j=1}^{J} \boxplus L(u_j) \approx \prod_{j=1}^{J} \text{sign}[L(u_j)] \cdot \min_{j=1...J} |L(u_j)|. \tag{8}$$

The reliability of the sum is therefore determined by the smallest reliability of the terms. After transmission over a binary symmetric channel (BSC) or a Gaussian channel we calculate the log-likelihood ratio (soft value) of a coded bit x conditioned on the matched filter output y. For a binary channel or a Gaussian channel the quantity

$$\log \frac{p(y|x = +1)}{p(y|x = -1)} = L_c \cdot y \tag{9}$$

is what has been transmitted over the channel, namely, the difference between the *a posteriori* and the *a priori* soft values of x. We call it the soft value of the channel and use it as soft input for the inner decoder stage. The channel reliability factor L_c equals

$$L_c = \log \frac{1 - P_0}{P_0} \tag{10}$$

for the BSC with crossover probability P_0, and

$$L_c = 4 \frac{E_s}{N_0} \tag{11}$$

for the Gaussian channel.

We further want to obtain a soft-output form for the inner Viterbi decoder stage that can serve as the soft input for the erasure setting in the next stage of Reed-Solomon decoding.

The Viterbi algorithm (VA) is usually derived as a maximum likelihood sequence estimator. Similar to Forney [7], we start a step before the *a posteriori* estimation of the state sequence of a binary trellis and rederive a more general VA. The branches of the trellis are labeled with the information bits u_k and with the coded bits $\mathbf{x}_k = (x_{k1}, \ldots, x_{kn}, \ldots, x_{kN})$ of a convolutional code of rate $1/N$. The decoder searches for the state sequence $\mathbf{s}^{(m)}$ and thus the desired information sequence $\mathbf{u}^{(m)}$ by maximizing the *a posteriori* probability

$$\max_m P(\mathbf{s}^{(m)}|\mathbf{y}) = \max_m p(\mathbf{y}|\mathbf{s}^{(m)}) \frac{P(\mathbf{s}^{(m)})}{p(\mathbf{y})}. \tag{12}$$

Since $\mathbf{y}$ is fixed, we can equivalently maximize

$$\max_m p(\mathbf{y}|\mathbf{s}^{(m)})P(\mathbf{s}^{(m)}). \tag{13}$$

We assume statistical independence of the relevant u_k within the observation window of the VA and further assume that we know $L(u)$. After some manipulations with the L values [9], we finally obtain the path metric in the form

$$M_k^{(m)} = M_{k-1}^{(m)} + \sum_{n=1}^{N} x_{k,n}^{(m)} L_{c_{k,n}} y_{k,n} + u_k^{(m)} L(u_k). \tag{14}$$

With the normalization used, the probability of the path m at time k and the metric are related by

$$P(\text{path } m) = P(\mathbf{s}_k^{(m)}) = e^{M_k^{(m)}/2}. \tag{15}$$

This slight modification of the metric of the VA in equation (14) incorporates the *a priori* or *a posteriori* information about the probability of the source bits.

This modified VA will therefore be called the APRI-VA. Forney [7] mentioned the possibility of using *a priori* values in his paper but did not give any use or application for it. In Figure 11-1 it is shown how the VA uses the soft values $L(u_k)$. If the channel is very good, $L_{c_{k,n}}$ is larger than $|L(u_k)|$ and decoding relies on the received channel values. If the channel is bad, as during a deep fade, decoding relies on the APRI information $L(u_k)$. If $L(u_k)$ is very large, the VA is forced through certain states and thus improves the decoding of the neighboring bits.

The Soft-Output Viterbi Algorithm (SOVA).

We need the probability of decoder errors for bits and symbols in order to declare erasures for the following Reed-Solomon decoder. We thus need an estimate from the VA about the reliability of each of its decisions, i.e., we need a soft output. The soft-output Viterbi algorithm (SOVA) can be implemented in the register exchange mode [8] or in the trace-back mode. It is described here for the latter mode using the $L(u)$ algebra.

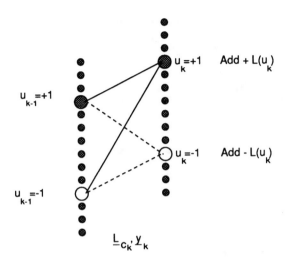

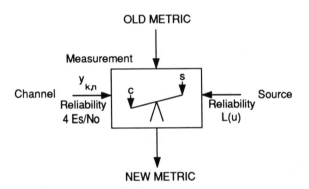

Figure 11-1. Trellis and weighting property of the Viterbi algorithm with *a priori* information (APRI-VA).

The VA proceeds in the usual way by calculating the metrics for the m path using equation (14) with or without $L(u)$. For each state it selects the path with the larger metric $M_j^{(m)}$. Figure 11-2 shows an example trellis where the VA has selected at time j the ML path with index m_0 and has discarded the path with index m_0'. Define the metric difference

$$\Delta_j^l = \frac{1}{2}\left(M_j^{(m_l)} - M_j^{(m_l')} \right). \tag{16}$$

The probability that the path decision was correct at this point is then from equation (15),

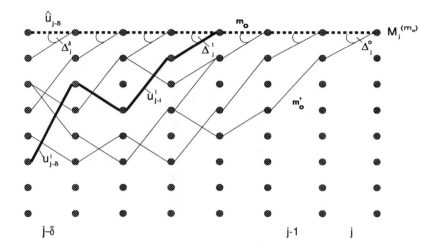

Figure 11-2. Example with metric differences for the derivation of the trace-back SOVA.

$$P(\text{correct}) = \frac{P(\text{path } m_0)}{P(\text{path } m_0) + P(\text{path } m_0')} = \frac{e^{M_j^{(m_0)}/2}}{e^{M_j^{(m_0)}/2} + e^{M_j^{(m_0')}/2}} = \frac{e^{\Delta_j^0}}{1 + e^{\Delta_j^0}}.$$

$$(17)$$

The likelihood ratio or soft value of this binary path decision is thus

$$\log \frac{P(\text{correct})}{1 - P(\text{correct})} = \Delta_j^0. \tag{18}$$

Along the ML path m_0, which decides the bit $\hat{u}_{j-\delta}$, $(\delta + 1)$ nonsurviving paths with indices $l = 0, \ldots, \delta$ have been discarded. The difference between their metrics is $\Delta_j^l \geq 0$.

If the bit $u_{j-\delta}^l$ on the discarded path equals the decided bit $\hat{u}_{j-\delta}$, we certainly would have made no bit error if we had selected the discarded path. Thus the reliability of this bit decision is ∞. Otherwise, if the bits differ, i.e., $e_{j-\delta}^l = u_{j-\delta}^l \oplus \hat{u}_{j-\delta} = -1$, the log-likelihood value of a bit error $e_{j-\delta}^l$ equals Δ_j^l. Consequently we have

$$L(e_{j-\delta}^l) = \log \frac{P(e_{j-\delta}^l = +1)}{P(e_{j-\delta}^l = -1)} = \begin{cases} \infty & u_{j-\delta}^l = \hat{u}_{j-\delta} \\ \Delta_j^l & u_{j-\delta}^l \neq \hat{u}_{j-\delta} \end{cases} \tag{19}$$

and the total error resulting from all possibly discarded paths for bit $\hat{u}_{j-\delta}$ is

$$e_{j-\delta} = \sum_{l=0}^{\delta} \boxplus\; e^l_{j-\delta}. \tag{20}$$

If the Δ^l_j and the e^l_j are statistically independent with respect to the indices l—which is a good assumption for reasonable codes—then the log-likelihood ratio of the decisions, the soft output of the VA (SOVA), is the decision $\hat{u}_{j-\delta}$ times the L-value of the errors:

$$L(\hat{u}_{j-\delta}) = \hat{u}_{j-\delta} \cdot \sum_{l=0}^{\delta} \boxplus\; L(e^l_{j-\delta})$$

$$= \hat{u}_{j-\delta} \cdot \sum_{l=0}^{\delta} \boxplus\; \Delta^l_j \tag{21}$$

$$\approx \hat{u}_{j-\delta} \cdot \min_{l=0,\dots,\delta} \Delta^l_j.$$

It is clear from the relation (5) that the sum and the minimum in the last lines of equation (21) have to be taken only over those indices l where the bits differ. We therefore have the same hard decisions $\hat{u}_{j-\delta}$ as with the classical VA. The reliability of these decisions is obtained by taking the minimum of the metric differences along the ML path whenever the update sequences $e^l_{j-\delta}$ indicate this. Typically only two to three updates are necessary.

In the trace-back implementation, SOVA proceeds as in the classical VA. For each state it stores the metric difference as well as the metric and renews the update sequences e^l_{j-i} by modulo-2 addition of two words. For the decision and its reliability a trace-back is performed as described above.

We now have a modified Viterbi algorithm that accepts log-likelihood (soft) L-values from *a priori* information and from the channel and delivers such values for the output bits. The L-values of the bits are directly related to their probabilities through the inverse of equation (1) and are thus well-defined quantities.

3.2 Reliability Information and Reed-Solomon Codes

The soft output of the SOVA enables us to implement an errors-and-erasures decoding algorithm for the Reed-Solomon code words. However, the SOVA outputs the reliability of every outgoing bit, whereas the Reed-Solomon code is symbol-oriented. Hence we have to develop a strategy to convert bit reliabilities into symbol reliabilities. One has to keep in mind that the SOVA output is correlated, so that an optimal transformation is not possible. We considered several strategies that were easy to implement but suboptimal. Using the minimum of the bit reliabilities corresponding to a symbol as the symbol reliability turned out to be a good (and simple) compromise.

The errors-and-erasures Reed-Solomon decoder can correct a code word as long as the number of errors t and the number of erasures e satisfy the inequality $2t + e \leq d_{\min} - 1$. For every error transformed into an erasure, the decoding capability is clearly extended. The particular errors-and-erasures Reed-Solomon decoder that we use here is a modified version of the general minimum distance (GMD) decoder introduced by Forney [6]. In contrast to Forney's GMD decoder, we skip the checking of the Euclidean distance between the code words before and after decoding.

The Reed-Solomon control unit uses the symbol reliabilities to set up a list of the most unreliable symbols in the Reed-Solomon code word to be decoded. The Reed-Solomon decoder then performs the first trial without erasures. A block diagram of this scheme, called S1, is shown in the middle part of Figure 11-10. If the Reed-Solomon decoder succeeds in decoding the Reed-Solomon code word, then the decoding is finished and the corresponding information sequence is delivered. For each subsequent decoding failure the Reed-Solomon decoder control unit sets two additional erasures until the Reed-Solomon decoder succeeds or a maximum number of erasures is reached. The objective of this strategy is to reduce the impact of possible errors by converting unreliable symbols to erasures.

Since the Reed-Solomon decoder error probability is $P_{e\,\text{word}} \approx 1/t!$, and t declines with the number of erasures, the balance between erasures and errors must be carefully chosen [15].

We would like to determine bit reliabilities at the output of the Reed-Solomon decoder; unfortunately, the calculation of these $|L(u)|$ values is rather difficult. However, we show a simulation of the bit reliabilities of a Reed-Solomon decoder that follows the SOVA ($r = 1/2$, $M = 6$) in Figure 11-3. The outer code is a (63, 55) Reed-Solomon code defined over $GF(2^6)$, where e varies between 0 and the maximum of 8.

In principle we can use the reliability values in equation (14) for iterative decoding. We have instead chosen to use them in quantized form only. For $GF(2^6)$ we have approximated them by $|L(u)| = \infty$ for $e = 0$ and $|L(u)| = 0$ for $e > 0$. For the (255, 223) Reed-Solomon code defined over $GF(2^8)$ with minimum distance $d_{\min} = 33$, a maximum number of 16 erasures was found to be justifiable. The probability of a decoding error is then $1/t! = 1/8! \approx 2.5 \cdot 10^{-5}$. Beyond 16 erasures, the symbol reliabilities out of the SOVA became so poor that, on average, two erasures hit less than one error. For

$$L=\log[(1-P_{bit\ error})/P_{bit\ error}]$$

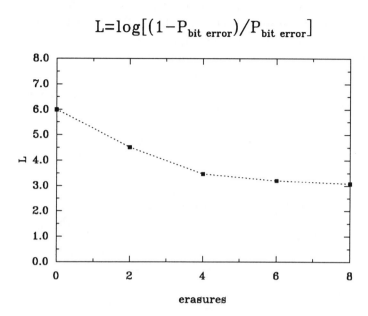

Figure 11-3. Bit reliabilities $|L(u)|$ for the Reed-Solomon decoder after the SOVA. Simulation results for the $(63, 55)$ Reed-Solomon code in $GF(2^6)$ as outer code and the convolutional code with $r = 1/2$, $M = 6$ as inner code. $E_b/N_0 = 1.7$ dB, $L_c = 2.52$.

this code we have thus quantized the reliabilities $|L(u)| = \infty$ for successful decoding and $e <= 16$ and $|L(u)| = 0$ otherwise.

4 ITERATIVE DECODING

4.1 General Principle of Iterative Decoding

In a concatenated system it is possible and desirable to go back to the inner decoding step after the outer decoding step is finished, for we may now have more reliable information about some of the information bits. Of course, if the decoding of certain information bits is correct, a second round of decoding is of no use. However, we might be able to help in the decoding of neighboring bits.

In the conventional concatenated system, Reed-Solomon code words form the columns, and convolutional code words form the rows in an interleaver frame. If we correctly decode a Reed-Solomon code word, all the bits of this code word have $|L(u)| = \infty$, and the SOVA in its second round is forced through known states. The known bits in the area between two known states are now better protected as compared to previous decoding processes because of the forced margin states. Figure 11-4 shows some simulation results for the BER in a bit stream where the 8 bits in the middle were known by the SOVA decoder. This technique has already been used by other authors [13,16–18], as mentioned in Section 2.2.

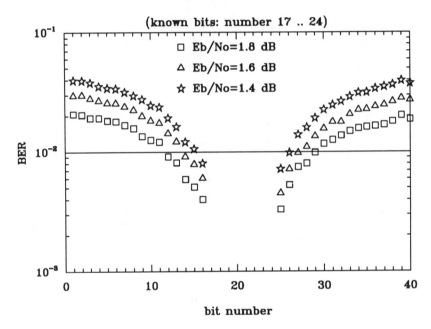

Figure 11-4. Simulation results for rate $r = 1/2$, memory $M = 6$ convolutional code, where bits 17 to 24 were known to the Viterbi decoder.

The bit error rate at the SOVA output is thus reduced and, as a consequence, more Reed-Solomon code words can be decoded. Figure 11-5 shows an example of the progress of the reiterated decoding (=redecoding) procedure.

4.2 Interleaver Design

The effect of the redecoding increases with the size of the interleaver. We observe that with only one successfully decoded Reed-Solomon code word in an interleaver frame in the first decoding process and by using several redecoding runs, a whole interleaver frame can be completely decoded

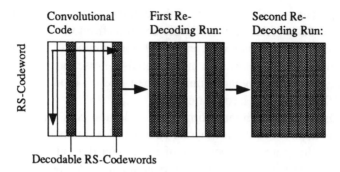

Figure 11-5. Redecoding example with an interleaver of size $I = 8$.

step by step. Simulations with the codes from the standard concatenated coding system in Section 5 have shown that with a signal-to-noise ratio of $E_b/N_0 > 1.9$ dB and an interleaver size of $I = 2$, the number of error-free interleaver frames is improved by a factor of 2 due to the use of redecoding. For an enlarged interleaver of size 8, however, the factor is 100 (see Figure 11-11).

Expanding the interleaver size has two effects on the bit error rate. On the one hand, the number of erroneous Reed-Solomon symbols resulting from one error burst in one Reed-Solomon code word reduces with increasing interleaver size I; on the other hand, the probability that one Reed-Solomon code word in an interleaver frame is decodable grows and, therefore, the redecoding becomes more effective.

Using a rate $r = 1/2$, memory $M = 6$ convolutional code followed by a $(255, 223)$ Reed-Solomon code defined over $GF(2^8)$, an interleaver size of $I = 8$ provides sufficient interleaving of the error bursts in the SOVA output because error paths longer than 64 bits are very unlikely. However, the gain obtained by the redecoding further increases when the interleaver size is extended beyond $I = 8$. For example, a BER of 10^{-5} is reached at $E_b/N_0 = 2.25$ dB when $I = 2$, at $E_b/N_0 = 1.95$ dB when $I = 8$, at $E_b/N_0 = 1.85$ dB when $I = 16$, and finally, at $E_b/N_0 = 1.75$ dB when $I = 32$.

One can expand the coding system in such a way that one Reed-Solomon code word in the interleaver frame gets a higher error correction capability. This increases the probability that one Reed-Solomon code word in an interleaver frame is successfully decoded, as well as increasing the probability that the whole interleaver frame is successfully decoded. The code parameters for this code word can be changed, for example, from $(255, 223)$ to

(255, 175). The overall code rate of the coding system with an interleaver size of $I = 32$ is reduced a negligible amount, from 0.437 to 0.434. The use of additional redundancy in one Reed-Solomon code word results in a further—albeit small—reduction in the signal-to-noise ratio. Simulations of this coding system at a signal-to-noise ratio of 1.62 dB produced no bit errors in 1.4×10^7 transmitted information bits!

We also examined nonuniform Reed-Solomon code profiles in which code words adjacent to the lower-rate code word were also given additional redundancy. In contrast to the work of Linne von Berg and Wilson [3], the overall code rate was not kept the same as the uniform code profile. In any event, the simulations using the code profile described above (only one strong Reed-Solomon code word) delivered the best results.

Having recognized that forcing the SOVA through a few known states improves the estimation of nearby states in the sequence (see Section 4.1), two special versions of interleaving were developed and examined. The first scheme uses a form of bit interleaving, as opposed to symbol interleaving, in which neighboring Reed-Solomon symbols are scrambled with one another. Both schemes are shown in Figure 11-6. Simulation results have shown that bit interleaving provides no significant gain over symbol interleaving. Similar results had been found by Linne von Berg and Wilson, although their interleaving scheme is slightly different [3].

The second idea was to work in another Galois field and to reduce the length of the Reed-Solomon symbols from $\alpha = 8$ bits per symbol to $\alpha = 6$ bits. We thereby hoped to reduce the bit error rate in the neighboring Reed-Solomon code words and hence the number of nondecodable Reed-Solomon code words. In order to keep the code rate approximately the same, a (63, 55) Reed-Solomon code defined over $GF(2^6)$ is used. The interleaver is designed in such a way that for both Reed-Solomon codes about the same number of bits are interleaved. This allows for a fair comparison between $GF(2^6)$ and $GF(2^8)$.

Simulations have shown that the number of erroneous symbols in the neighboring code words of a decodable code word is always smaller for $\alpha = 6$ than for $\alpha = 8$, but this is only true for the number of nondecodable Reed-Solomon code words for an $E_b/N_0 < 1.6$ dB. Figure 11-7 shows the simulation results. Due to the reduced error correction capability of the (63, 55) Reed-Solomon code, only $t = 4$ symbol errors can be corrected compared to the $t = 16$ for the (255, 223) Reed-Solomon code. This results in an increase in the probability of decoding error. This has obvious negative consequences for the redecoding procedure. Even when errors-only Reed-

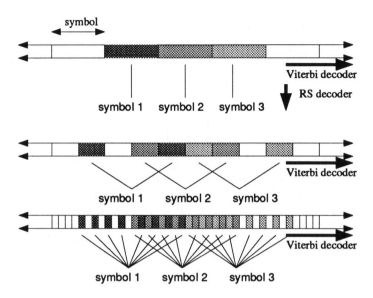

Figure 11-6. Bit-interleaving schemes.

Solomon decoding is used, the probability for an erroneously decoded code word is between 1% and 4% for 1.4 dB $< E_b/N_0 <$ 1.8 dB.

A concatenated coding system with a $(63, 55)$ Reed-Solomon code followed by a rate $r = 1/2$, memory $M = 6$ convolutional code was simulated. The interleaver size was chosen as $I = 43$, which corresponds to an interleaver size of $I = 8$ for the $(255, 223)$ Reed-Solomon code. Every tenth Reed-Solomon code word was given 14 more redundant symbols. These "improved" code words can correct up to $t = 11$ symbol errors, and the overall code rate is reduced from 0.44 to 0.43. As already discussed in Section 3.2, erroneously decoded symbols should not be fed back. Only symbols from successfully decoded $(63, 41)$ Reed-Solomon code words or their direct neighbors were fed back after the first redecoding trial. Furthermore, successfully decoded code words were treated as highly reliable ($|L(u)| = \infty$) if, in the following decoding attempt, two neighboring code words which were previously not decodable could be decoded.

Simulation results are shown in Figure 11-8. The curve is a lower bound because successfully decoded Reed-Solomon code words are assumed to be error-free. For comparison the results for the $(255, 223)$ Reed-Solomon code with interleaver $I = 8$ and without additional redundancy are also presented. We can conclude from Figure 11-8 that the Reed-Solomon codes defined over

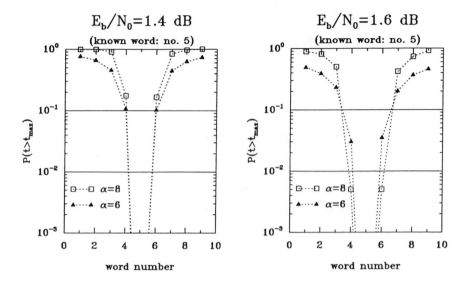

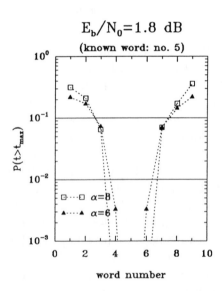

Figure 11-7. Probability for a nondecodable Reed-Solomon code word when code word 5 is known by the SOVA ($\alpha = 8, t_{max} = 16; \alpha = 6, t_{max} = 4$).

GF(2^6) promise no significant gain in E_b/N_0 at a BER of 10^{-5} compared to a Reed-Solomon code defined over GF(2^8).

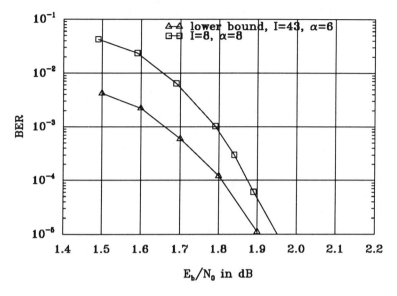

Figure 11-8. Simulation results for the Reed-Solomon codes in GF(2^6).

5 IMPROVEMENTS OF THE NASA/ESA STANDARD CODING SYSTEM FOR DEEP SPACE MISSIONS

5.1 Overview

The exploration of the universe is currently heavily dependent on images from spacecraft. The large distance between the transmitting spacecraft and the receiving earth station and the limited transmitting power result in a very poor signal-to-noise ratio at the receiver side. The consequence is a large number of transmission errors. Furthermore, the data bits are highly compressed before transmission to allow as large a number of images as possible to be transmitted at the limited data rate. Unfortunately compressed data bits are especially sensitive to transmission errors. The channel coding system must thus be selected very carefully.

Today, the National Aeronautics and Space Administration and the European Space Agency are using the coding system recommended by the CCSDS in 1987 as a standard for deep space missions. The coding system consists of the concatenation of an outer $(255, 223)$ Reed-Solomon code defined over the GF(2^8) and an inner rate $r = 1/2$ convolutional code with memory $M = 6$. Between inner and outer coder or decoder there is an interleaver and deinterleaver, respectively. The decoding of the convolutional code is performed by a Viterbi decoder.

In this section, we apply the ideas presented in the previous sections to improve the standard coding system. The modifications are separated into two groups [19]. The first group is composed of modifications concerning only the receiver, which can, therefore, be used in current missions such as the *Galileo* mission where every tenth of a decibel is needed because of an antenna failure. The second group consists of modifications on the transmitter side and, therefore, should be viewed as recommendations for future or still modifiable deep space missions.

The theoretical limit for channel coding for a code with overall rate $R_{over} = 0.44$ and a desired bit error rate of 10^{-5} given by the channel capacity C is $E_b/N_0|_C = -0.1$ dB. If the cut-off rate R_0 of a channel is used instead, a "limit" of $E_b/N_0|_{R_0} = 2.2$ dB is found. The proximity of the performance of the standard coding system to the cut-off rate limit suggests that an improvement of the standard coding system is possible only in small steps.

In the first group additional coding gains of about 0.3 to 0.4 dB, and in the second group of about 0.6 to 0.9 dB, can be achieved with respect to the standard coding system. The increase in complexity is only in the receiver, not in the spacecraft. With these improvements we are only 1.8 dB away from the absolute Shannon limit and already 0.5 dB below the R_0 "bound."

Before we speak about our improvements, we will briefly explain the standard coding system and show its performance.

5.2 Standard Coding System

Figure 11-9 shows the block diagram of the standard coding systems as it is recommended by the CCSDS. The Reed-Solomon coder encodes the data stream to be transmitted in blocks. Out of the 223 information symbols—each symbol consists of 8 bits—the 32 redundant symbols are built, which together with the information symbols form the Reed-Solomon code word. The minimum distance of this code is $d_{min} = 33$, and thus the code can correct up to 16 symbol errors. After encoding, the Reed-Solomon code words are written column-wise into the interleaver and collected together into a frame of I Reed-Solomon code words. The symbols are then read out row-wise and passed to the convolutional encoder. Present missions use an interleaver size from $I = 2$ (e.g., NASA's *Galileo* mission to Jupiter) to $I = 8$ (e.g., ESA's *Giotto* mission to Halley's comet). The second encoding step consists of a rate 1/2 convolutional code with 64 states. The coded data bits are then passed to the PSK modulator.

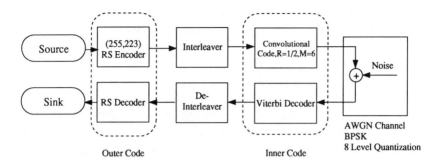

Figure 11-9. Block diagram of the standard coding system.

For the channel model we assume additive white Gaussian noise (AWGN) with mean value 0 and variance $\sigma^2 = N_0/2E_S$.

At the receiver side the signal is demodulated, quantized to 8 levels, and decoded in the Viterbi decoder. The bits are then grouped into symbols, written row-wise into the deinterleaver and passed column-wise to the Reed-Solomon decoder.

The Reed-Solomon decoder can correct up to $t = 16$ symbol errors in one Reed-Solomon code word. If there are more than 16 symbol errors in one code word, the Reed-Solomon decoder has two possible outputs. Either a decoder failure occurs, i.e., the Reed-Solomon decoder recognizes that the number of errors exceeds the code's capabilities and fails to find any code word at all, or a decoder error occurs, i.e., the Reed-Solomon decoder outputs a code word different from the transmitted code word without recognizing its mistake. The probability of a decoder error is less than $1/t! \approx 10^{-14}$ [15] and can, therefore, be excluded for a design bit error rate of 10^{-5}.

We simulated the standard coding system for interleaver sizes $I = 2, 4, 8$ and verified the results using available measurements [11]. For a bit error rate (BER) of 10^{-5}, we need a signal-to-noise ratio of $E_b/N_0 = 2.6, 2.45$, or 2.35 dB, respectively. The results for $I = 2$ and $I = 8$ are plotted in Figure 11-11. Figure 11-12 shows the corresponding curves for the frame error rate (FER), where one frame of $I \cdot 223 \cdot 8$ information bits is declared to be erroneous if it contains one or more errors.

5.3 Modifications on the Receiver Side

In this section we present modifications that concern only the receiver side and, therefore, can be used in ongoing missions. An acute application example is the *Galileo* mission, where parts of the transmitter system broke down at the end of 1990 due to a defect. The resulting severe deterioration of the communication channel now endangers the mission of the spacecraft, and every tenth of a decibel in power savings is welcome.

In principle the effects of the improving strategies depend strongly on the size of the interleaver; unfortunately the *Galileo* mission is working with a very small interleaver of size $I = 2$, so improving strategies will work only in a reduced manner.

For our simulations we use no quantization of the demodulator output. A corresponding sufficiently fine quantization can be realized by a 6-bit A/D converter. Furthermore, the decision length in the Viterbi algorithm is extended from the currently used 70 trellis periods to 100 trellis periods.

Those modifications, as compared with the standard coding system, result in gains less than 0.1 dB.

We first implemented the strategy explained in Section 3. This calls for use of the SOVA followed by the errors-and-erasures Reed-Solomon decoder. Figure 11-10 shows the block diagram of this improving strategy (S1) for the standard coding system.

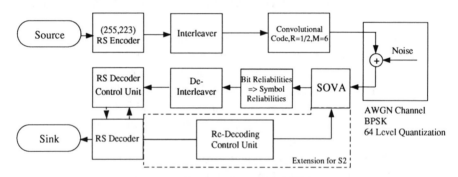

Figure 11-10. Block diagram for the improving strategies S1 and S2.

Another improving strategy, S2, results from applying reiterated decoding, described in Section 4.1. The block diagram is the extension of the block diagram of S1 and is also shown in Figure 11-10.

Simulation results for improving strategies S1 and S2 are plotted in Figure 11-11 and Figure 11-12. Since these curves are very steep, a small gain in E_b/N_0 corresponds to a high gain in bit or frame error rate. For example, a gain of 0.2 dB in E_b/N_0 with the interleaver size $I = 8$ results in a reduction in the bit error rate by a factor of 200! Using the improving strategy S2 for the ESA coding system we achieve a gain of about 0.4 dB at a BER of 10^{-5}, as compared to the standard ESA coding system. Lee obtained a similar gain but used his complex minimal-symbol-error probability decoder (see Section 2.2).

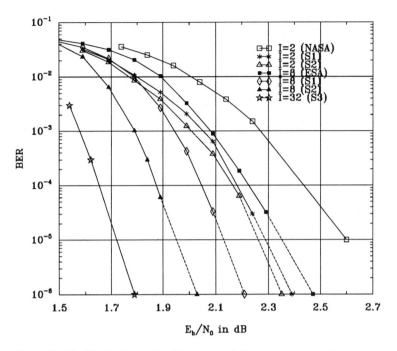

Figure 11-11. Simulation results (bit error rate) for the standard coding system ($I = 2$ and $I = 8$) and the coding systems S1, S2, and S3.

The maximum number of redecoding trials is also very low. For the interleaver size $I = 8$ and the operating points $E_b/N_0 \geq 1.7$ dB, we observed a maximum of four redecoding trials in the whole transmitted information sequence.

For the *Galileo* mission with its small interleaver size of 2, the required SNR could be reduced from 2.6 to 2.25 dB by these receiver-only modifications. Although a gain of 0.35 dB may not seem like much, note that an enlargement of the 70-m ground station antenna by 2.9 meters is necessary to achieve the same effect.

5.4 Modifications on the Receiver and on the Transmitter Sides

In this section we introduce improving strategies that require changes in the interleaver parameters of the standard coding system on both the transmitter side and the receiver side. These strategies result in a bit error rate of 10^{-5} at a signal-to-noise ratio of less than 1.7 dB.

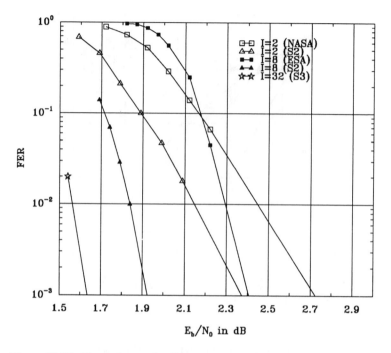

Figure 11-12. Simulation results (frame error rate) for the standard coding system ($I = 2$ and $I = 8$) and the coding systems S2 and S3.

In the last section it was shown that the interleaver size I has a substantial effect on the success of the strategies S1 and S2. Tests have shown that an expansion of the interleaver size of $I = 8$ in coding system S2 to an interleaver size of $I = 32$ results in an additional gain of 0.25 dB in E_b/N_0 at a bit error rate of 10^{-5}. The results for this coding system, named S3, are also plotted in Figures 11-11 and 11-12. The bit error rate of 10^{-5} is now achieved with a signal-to-noise ratio of 1.7 dB. The limit of $E_b/N_0|_C = -0.1$ dB suggested by the channel capacity is now only 1.8 dB away!

A change in the interleaver design is thus a promising strategy. We simulated the strategy (call it S4) described in Section 4.2. One Reed-Solomon code word in the interleaver frame is from the $(255, 175)$ Reed-Solomon code, whereas the others are still from the standard $(255, 223)$ Reed-Solomon code. As already mentioned, we found no bit error with 1.4×10^7 transmitted information bits at a signal-to-noise ratio of 1.62 dB. A bit error rate of 10^{-5} at a signal-to-noise ratio of less than 1.7 dB can thus be achieved. We have shown that by minor parameter changes on the transmitter side and more complex decoding strategies on the earth station decoder we can gain 0.9 dB over the currently used NASA system. In order to achieve the same gain by enlarging the ground station antenna, the diameter would have to be increased by 11%.

5.5 Improving Strategies Used for Image Transmission

An impressive example of the effect of these strategies can be found in the transmission of compressed images. The compression is now done by a discrete cosine transformation combined with a product pyramid vector quantization [5]. The compression factor is 8. The transmission was simulated at a signal-to-noise ratio of $E_b/N_0 = 1.95$ dB. Figures 11-13 through 11-15 show the results for the standard coding system with interleaver size $I = 8$, the coding system S1 and the coding system S2. One can clearly see the increasing error correction capability for the different decoding strategies.

Figure 11-13. Standard coding system $I = 8$, $E_b/N_0 = 1.95$ dB.

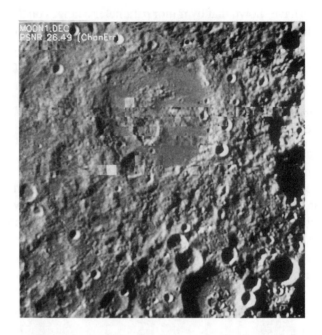

Figure 11-14. Coding system S1, $I = 8$, $E_b/N_0 = 1.95$ dB.

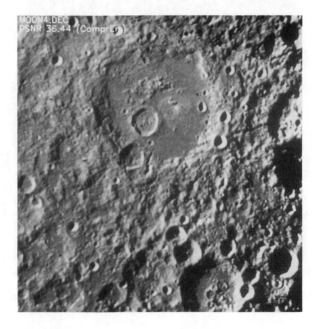

Figure 11-15. Coding system S2, third redecoding run, $I = 8$, $E_b/N_0 = 1.95$ dB.

6 CONCLUSIONS

Reed-Solomon codes and convolutional codes match very well in a concatenated system. Viterbi decoders of convolutional codes can easily accept soft decisions from the channel and produce short error bursts which can readily be handled by Reed-Solomon codes in the outer stage. We have shown that output reliability information can be generated by a modified Viterbi algorithm (SOVA) and passed on to the Berlekamp-Massey algorithm for errors-and-erasures decoding.

For certain code and decoder parameters, Reed-Solomon code words are known to be decoded almost error-free. In an interleaved scheme, we use these decoded words to iterate the outer Viterbi decoding process by "state pinning." We wish we could go a step further and obtain a decoding algorithm for Reed-Solomon codes that accepts bit or symbol soft decisions [$L(u)$ values] and also delivers bit or at least symbol reliabilities.

This would enable us to go beyond "erasure setting" and state pinning to true "soft-in/soft-out" iterative decoding. It is surprising that by improving the decoding process we can additionally gain almost 1 dB while operating well below the R_0 limit. In such a way, we approach the Shannon limit, coming within 1.8 dB. Through the proposed modifications we have shown that at an operating point of $E_b/N_0 = 1.9$ dB, the frame error rate can be reduced by a factor of 500 for the standard coding system of ESA with interleaver size of 8. Further improvements are possible by transmitter and receiver modifications.

REFERENCES

[1] L. R. Bahl, J. Cocke, F. Jelinek, and J. Raviv, "Optimal Decoding of Linear Codes for Minimizing Symbol Error Rate," *IEEE Transactions on Information Theory*, Volume IT-20, pp. 284–287, March 1974.

[2] G. Battail, M. C. Decouvelaere, and P. Godlewski, "Replication Decoding," *IEEE Transactions on Information Theory*, Volume IT-20, pp. 284–287, March 1974.

[3] D. C. L. von Berg and S. G. Wilson, "Improved Concatenated Coding/Decoding for Deep Space Probes," *Proceedings of the IEEE Globecom Conference, Orlando, Fla.*, pp. 707–711, December 1992.

[4] Consultative Committee for Space Data Systems, "Recommendations for Space Data Systems Standard: Telemetry Channel Coding," Blue Book Issue 2, CCSDS 101.0-B2, January 1987.

[5] P. Filip and M. Ruf, "A Fixed-Rate Product Pyramid Vector Quantization Using a Bayesian Model," *Proceedings of the IEEE Globecom Conference, Orlando, Fla.*, pp. 240–244, December 1992.

[6] G. D. Forney, Jr., "Generalized Minimum Distance Decoding," *IEEE Transactions on Information Theory*, Volume IT-12, pp. 125–131, April 1966.

[7] G. D. Forney, Jr., "The Viterbi Algorithm," *Proceedings of the IEEE*, Volume 61, pp. 268–278, March 1973.

[8] J. Hagenauer and P. Hoeher, "A Viterbi Algorithm with Soft-Decision Outputs and Its Applications," *Proceedings of the IEEE Globecom Conference, Dallas, Tex.*, pp. 47.1.1–47.1.7, November 1989.

[9] J. Hagenauer, "Soft-in/Soft-out: The Benefits of Using Soft Decisions in All Stages of Digital Receivers," *Proceedings of the 3rd International Workshop on DSP Techniques Applied to Space Communications, ESTEC Noordwijk, The Netherlands*, September 1992.

[10] F. Jelinek, "Bootstrap Trellis Decoding," *IEEE Transactions on Information Theory*, Volume IT-12, pp. 318–325, May 1975.

[11] R. Johansen, R. J. Reichert, R. C. Barry, and N. Yarnell, "Functional Requirement *Galileo* Orbiter Telemetry Measurements and Data Formats," Technical Report GLL-3-280, Revision D, Jet Propulsion Laboratory, March 1989.

[12] L. N. Lee, *Concatenated Coding Systems Empolying Unit-Memory Convolutional Codes and Byte-Oriented Decoding Algorithms*, Ph.D. Thesis, University of Notre Dame, June 1976.

[13] L. N. Lee, "Concatenated Coding Systems Employing a Unit-Memory Convolutional Code and a Byte-Oriented Decoding Algorithm," *IEEE Transactions on Communications*, Volume COM-25, pp. 1064–1074, October 1977.

[14] J. L. Massey, "The How and Why of Channel Coding," *Proceedings of the 1984 Zurich Seminar on Digital Communications*, IEEE No. 84 CH 1998-4, pp. 67–73, 1984.

[15] R. J. McEliece and L. Swanson, "On the Decoder Error Probability for Reed-Solomon Codes," *IEEE Transactions on Information Theory*, Volume IT-32, pp. 701–703, September 1986.

[16] E. Paaske, "Improved Decoding for a Concatenated Coding System Recommended by CCSDS," *IEEE Transactions on Communications*, Volume COM-38, pp. 1138–1144, August 1990.

[17] E. Paaske, "Efficient Methods for Improving Coding Gains in Concatenated Coding Systems," *Abstracts, International Symposium on Information Theory, Budapest*, p. 297, June 1991.

[18] A. Klindt and E. Paaske, "Generalized Concatenated Coding System in Relation to CCSDS Standard," Technical Report ISSN 0105-8541 Re-

port IT-132, Institute of Circuit Theory and Telecommunication, August 1992.

[19] L. Papke, "Verbesserung des zwei-stufigen Codierverfahrens fuer Raum-flugmissionen," Masters Thesis, DLR, Institute for Communications Technology and Technical University Muenchen, February 1992.

[20] G. W. Zeoli, "Coupled Decoding of Block-Convolutional Concatenated Codes," *IEEE Transactions on Communications*, Volume COM-21, pp. 219–226, March 1977.

Chapter 12

RS-Based Unidirectional Byte Error Control Codes Perform Better than RS Codes

Yuichi Saitoh

Hideki Imai
Institute of Industrial Science
University of Tokyo
Roppongi, Minatoku, Tokyo 106, Japan

1 INTRODUCTION

When two types of errors, 1 to 0 and 0 to 1, occur but do not occur simultaneously in a single word, the errors are called *unidirectional errors* [5–8,14,15 (pp. 325–326),20,21 (pp. 4–5),30]. When two types of errors arise but do not occur simultaneously in a single byte of a byte-organized word, the errors are called a *unidirectional byte error* [11,12,22,23–28] which is a kind of byte error. We refer to a byte error that is not a unidirectional byte error as a *bidirectional byte error*. Examples of unidirectional errors and unidirectional and bidirectional byte errors are shown in Figure 12-1. (When a byte consists of b bits, a byte error is also called a b-bit byte error.)

A number of faults in integrated circuits, which affect address decoders, word lines, power supply, read/write circuits, etc., are known to be regarded as unidirectional errors [14,20]. For example, although short-circuit and open-circuit defects in bus lines turn the levels of signal lines into high, low, or medium levels, the levels of the faulty lines can always be made either high or low [18]. Unidirectional error control codes have been applied to masking bus line faults in 4-Mbit VLSI ROMs by NTT [18]. Such codes are also applicable to parallel asynchronous communications without acknowledgment [7].

The well-known applications of unidirectional error control codes have been found in computer memory systems [5,6,8,21,30]. Faults in some semiconductor LSI nonvolatile memories are apt to cause unidirectional errors

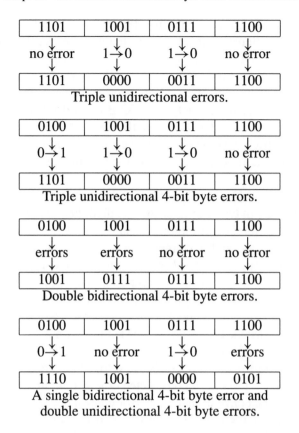

Figure 12-1. Examples of unidirectional errors and unidirectional and bidirectional byte errors.

[21]. The most likely faults in cells of these memories are caused by leakage of the charge, since a charge cannot be created except by a rewrite process. Therefore, the errors in these memories are apt to be unidirectional. When data are stored in a byte-organized fashion, unidirectional byte errors are predominant in these memories [9–12,22], but bidirectional byte errors may also occur. Therefore, codes that correct and detect unidirectional and bidirectional byte errors are important for error control of these byte-organized storage devices.

Hereafter, the following abbreviations are used.

- t-UbEC (or t-UbED): t-fold unidirectional b-bit-byte error-correcting (or -detecting).
- AUbED: All unidirectional b-bit-byte error-detecting.
- AUED: All unidirectional error-detecting.

t-fold error-correcting and d-fold error-detecting Reed-Solomon (RS) codes, which include shortened, extended, and doubly extended RS codes [4 (pp. 220–224),31], over $GF(2^b)$ are capable of t-UbEC/d-UbED, but RS codes are not fit for control of the predominant errors in byte-organized storage devices, i.e., unidirectional byte errors, and more efficient t-UbEC/d-UbED codes ought to be constructed. In fact, 1-UbEC Bose codes [9], t-UbED/AUED Dunning-Dial-Varanasi codes [11,12], and t-UbED/AUED Rao-Feng-Kolluru codes [22] have been developed, and these codes are more efficient than RS codes of the same unidirectional byte error-correcting or -detecting capabilities.

Saitoh and Imai [23,26] have derived the theory of unidirectional byte error control codes in terms of a distance, called the *unidirectional byte distance*, which is different from known distances such as the Hamming, Lee, arithmetic, Euclidean, and asymmetric distances [2 (pp. 204–205),21 (pp. 6–7, 121, 351),15 (pp. 28–29, 32, 327)]. They have derived necessary and sufficient conditions for various unidirectional byte error control codes.

Saitoh and Imai [23,25,26] have also presented code construction techniques for t-UbEC/d-UbED codes. These are based on the combination of two codes. One is a code for encoding the Hamming weights of data bytes and for locating errors. The other is a byte error-correcting code for error evaluation. Saitoh and Imai [27] have also developed generalized concatenated code constructions. They have constructed efficient unidirectional byte error control codes using conventional byte error control codes such as RS codes; i.e., we can construct RS-based t-UbEC/d-UbED codes more efficient than RS codes. They have also derived bounds for a t-UbEC code and analyzed its asymptotic property when the code length goes to infinity [28].

In this chapter, a construction of t-UbEC/d-UbED codes, called Construction I_{RS}, which is an RS-based version of the generalized concatenated code construction in [27], is described, and a new coding scheme for inner codes is proposed. The codes from Construction I_{RS} are RS-based codes, which means codes employing RS codes. Construction I_{RS} calls for two RS codes as outer codes. One is the RS code for selecting one of the inner codes, and it locates unidirectional byte errors. The other is the RS code for selecting one of the code words in the selected inner code, and it evaluates unidirectional byte errors and corrects bidirectional byte errors. These RS-based t-UbEC/d-UbED codes are more efficient than RS codes. This chapter also analyzes the decoding error performance of a t-UbEC code.

The structure of this chapter is as follows. In the next section, we describe the relations between distances and various error control capabilities.

Section 3 gives a construction of t-UbEC/d-UbED codes based on RS codes. Examples of encoding and decoding are found in Section 4. In Section 5, an efficient coding scheme is presented, which is used for the construction in Section 3. In Section 6, we compare the RS-based t-UbEC/d-UbED codes with RS codes in terms of error-correcting capabilities. In Section 7, the decoding error probability of a t-UbEC code is derived, and finally we summarize the chapter in Section 8.

In this chapter, the following notations are used.

- $\mathcal{Z}_q$: alphabet with q elements defined as $\{0, 1, \cdots, q - 1\}$
- $\mathcal{Z}_q^b$: set of all b-tuples over $\mathcal{Z}_q$
- $|A|$: number of elements in the set A
- 0^l (or 1^l): concatenation of l 0's (or 1's)
- $(a, b, c, \ldots)$: concatenation of the words or symbols $a, b, c, \ldots$
- $[n, k, d; q]$ code: code of length n over $\mathcal{Z}_q$ of dimension k and minimum Hamming distance d

2 DISTANCES AND ERROR CONTROL CAPABILITIES

Let b be the number of bits in a single byte and let

$$x = (x_1, x_2, \cdots, x_n),$$
$$y = (y_1, y_2, \cdots, y_n),$$
$$z = (z_1, z_2, \cdots, z_n),$$

where $x_i, y_i, z_i \in \mathcal{Z}_2^b$ for all i.

Suppose that x is transmitted and y is received. Assume that a bidirectional byte error has occurred in x_i. Then y_i is in error. It is possible to consider that x_i is turned into z_i by a unidirectional byte error and z_i is turned into y_i by a unidirectional byte error. Thus a bidirectional byte error is resolved into two unidirectional byte errors. Accordingly it may be convenient to define a distance that increases by 1 for the occurrence of a unidirectional byte error and increases by 2 for the occurrence of a bidirectional byte error. Hence we define the unidirectional byte distance as follows: When N is defined as

$$N((u_1, u_2, \ldots, u_b), (v_1, v_2, \ldots, v_b)) = |\{i \mid u_i = 1 \wedge v_i = 0\}|,$$

where $u_i, v_i \in \mathcal{Z}_2$, the byte crossover $\mathcal{N}$, the unidirectional byte distance $\mathcal{D}$, the minimum unidirectional byte distance $\mathcal{D}_{\min}$, the byte semidistance δ, and the minimum byte semidistance δ_{min} are defined as

$$\mathcal{N}(x, y) = |\{i \mid N(x_i, y_i) \neq 0\}|,$$
$$\mathcal{D}(x, y) = \mathcal{N}(x, y) + \mathcal{N}(y, x),$$
$$\mathcal{D}_{min}(C) = \min_{\substack{x,y \in C \\ x \neq y}} \mathcal{D}(x, y),$$
$$\delta(x, y) = |\{i \mid \mathcal{D}(x_i, y_i) = 2\}|,$$
$$\delta_{min}(C) = \min_{\substack{x,y \in C \\ x \neq y}} \delta(x, y).$$

$\mathcal{D}, \delta,$ and $\mathcal{N}$ satisfy

$$\begin{aligned}
D(x, y) &= \mathcal{N}(x, y) + \mathcal{N}(y, x) \\
&\geq \max[\mathcal{N}(x, y), \mathcal{N}(y, x)] \\
&\geq \min[\mathcal{N}(x, y), \mathcal{N}(y, x)] \\
&\geq \delta(x, y)
\end{aligned}$$

for all x and y. Also we have

$$\mathcal{D}(x, y) \geq d_H(x, y) \geq \delta(x, y),$$

where d_H is the Hamming distance over the alphabet Z_2^b.

Example 1. If $b = 4$ and

$$x = (0100, 1001, 1110, 0110),$$
$$y = (0111, 0000, 0010, 1011),$$

then $\mathcal{N}(x, y) = 3, \mathcal{N}(y, x) = 2, \mathcal{D}(x, y) = 5, \delta(x, y) = 1,$ and $d_H(x, y) = 4$.

It is easily shown that the unidirectional byte distance $\mathcal{D}$ is a "metric" function that is a real-valued function having the following three properties:

$$\begin{aligned}
\mathcal{D}(x, y) &> 0 \text{ for } x \neq y \\
&= 0 \text{ for } x = y \qquad \text{(positive definiteness)} \\
\mathcal{D}(x, y) &= \mathcal{D}(y, x) \qquad \text{(symmetry)} \\
\mathcal{D}(x, y) &+ \mathcal{D}(y, z) \geq \mathcal{D}(x, z). \quad \text{(triangle inequality)}
\end{aligned}$$

When $\delta(x, y) \geq 1$, no unidirectional byte error can turn x into y even if $\mathcal{D}(x, y) = 2$, which is different from the case of the relation between the Hamming distance and ordinary errors. However, in a similar way to the ordinary case, a necessary and sufficient condition for a t-UbEC code is derived in terms of the unidirectional byte distance as follows.

THEOREM 1 (SAITOH-IMAI [23]) C is a t-UbEC code if and only if

$$\mathcal{D}_{\min}(C) \geq 2t + 1.$$

PROOF If $\mathcal{D}_{\min}(C) \geq 2t + 1$, it is straightforward that C is a t-UbEC code. If $\mathcal{D}_{\min}(C) \leq 2t$, there are two distinct code words x and y satisfying $\mathcal{D}(x, y) \leq 2t$; then there is a word z satisfying $\mathcal{D}(x, z) \leq t$ and $\mathcal{D}(z, y) \leq t$. Thus, if C is capable of t-UbEC, we must have $\mathcal{D}_{\min}(C) \geq 2t + 1$.

Theorem 1 says that there might be codes with t-UbEC capability stronger than ordinary codes based on the Hamming distance since the unidirectional byte distance is greater than or equal to the Hamming distance.

With respect to the correction of combinations of bidirectional and unidirectional byte errors, we have the following important theorem.

THEOREM 2 (SAITOH-IMAI [23]) A t-UbEC code corrects all combinations of μ bidirectional byte errors and ν unidirectional byte errors for $0 \leq 2\mu + \nu \leq t$.

PROOF Let C be a t-UbEC code. Also assume that x in C is transmitted and μ bidirectional byte errors and ν unidirectional byte errors arise. Then the distance between x and the received word y is $\mathcal{D}(x, y) = 2\mu + \nu$. Consider any z in C. Then $\mathcal{D}(y, z) \geq \mathcal{D}(x, z) - \mathcal{D}(x, y) \geq 2t + 1 - t = t + 1$ if $0 \leq 2\mu + \nu \leq t$. Hence the t-UbEC code C, for which $\mathcal{D}_{\min}(C) \geq 2t + 1$, can correct those errors if $0 \leq 2\mu + \nu \leq t$.

That is, a unidirectional byte error-correcting code corrects not only unidirectional byte errors but also bidirectional byte errors. Therefore, a t-UbEC code is effective not only for channels where only unidirectional byte errors arise but also for channels where both bidirectional and unidirectional byte errors arise and unidirectional byte errors are predominant.

A necessary and sufficient condition for a t-UbEC/AUbED code is given as follows:

THEOREM 3 (SAITOH-IMAI [26]) A code C has the capability of t-UbEC/AUbED if and only if

$$\delta_{\min}(C) \geq t + 1.$$

PROOF If δ between a code word x and another code word z is t or less, then there is y satisfying $\mathcal{D}(x, y) \leq t, \delta(x, y) = 0$, and $\delta(y, z) = 0$. Assume that x is transmitted and y is received. Then we cannot distinguish the case where t or fewer unidirectional byte errors have occurred in x from the case where arbitrary unidirectional byte errors have occurred in z. Therefore we must have at least $\delta_{\min}(C) \geq t + 1$ for a t-UbEC/AUbED code.

Hereafter suppose that a code satisfies this inequality. When t or fewer unidirectional byte errors have occurred, $\mathcal{D}(x, y) \leq t$ and $\mathcal{D}(y, z) > t$ for any other code word z. Thus the correct decoding can be performed in this case. When more than

t unidirectional byte errors have occurred, $\mathcal{D}(x, y) > t$ and $\mathcal{D}(y, z) > t$. Hence we distinguish this case from the case where t or fewer unidirectional byte errors have occurred and can detect the errors.

We can construct a t-UbEC/AUbED code by the well-known concatenated code construction [17 (p. 307),29], employing an AUED code as the inner code and a t-fold error-detecting code as the outer code.

The condition for a t-UbEC/d-UbED code is given as follows.

THEOREM 4 (SAITOH-IMAI [26]) A code C has the capability of t-UbEC/d ($> t$)-UbED if and only if

$$\mathcal{D}(x, y) \geq t + d + 1 \text{ or } \delta(x, y) \geq t + 1$$

for all distinct $x, y \in C$.

PROOF Suppose that $x, y \in C$ satisfy $\mathcal{D}(x, y) \leq t + d$ and $\delta(x, y) \leq t$. Then we may receive z that satisfies $\mathcal{D}(x, z) \leq t$, $\mathcal{D}(y, z) \leq d$, and $\delta(x, z) = \delta(y, z) = 0$ when x is transmitted. Then we cannot decide whether x is turned into z by t or fewer unidirectional byte errors or y is turned into z by d or fewer unidirectional byte errors. Thus, if C has the capability of t-UbEC/d-UbED, then we must have at least $\mathcal{D}(x, y) \geq t + d + 1$ or $\delta(x, y) \geq t + 1$ for all distinct $x, y \in C$.

Since $\mathcal{D}$ is a mathematical distance function as defined in this section, C has the capability of t-UbEC/d-UbED if $\mathcal{D}_{\min}(C) \geq t + d + 1$. Also if $\delta_{\min}(C) \geq t + 1$, then C has the capability of t-UbEC/d-UbED from Theorem 3. Thus, if $\mathcal{D}(x, y) \geq t + d + 1$ or $\delta(x, y) \geq t + 1$ for all distinct $x, y \in C$, then C has the capability of t-UbEC/d-UbED.

Several code constructions and bounds based on the theorems in this section are known [23,25–28]. In the next section, we describe a construction of t-UbEC/d-UbED codes employing RS codes, which is an RS-based version of Construction I in [27].

3 CONSTRUCTION I$_{RS}$

Construction I$_{RS}$ calls for the following codes:

- A collection of two outer codes A_1, A_2: A_1 is an $[n, n - t - d, t + d + 1; q_1]$ RS code, and A_2 is an $[n, n - t, t + 1; q_2]$ RS code, where $t \leq d$ and $q_1 q_2 \leq 2^b - 2$.
- A collection of q_1 disjoint inner codes $B_0, \ldots, B_{q_1-1}$: B_i is a binary AUED code of length b, where $|B_i| = q_2$ and $B_i \subset \mathcal{Z}_2^b \backslash \{0^b, 1^b\}$.

A code word of $\mathcal{B}_i$ will be denoted by $E_i(j)$, with parameters chosen so that $E_i(j)$ belongs to $\mathcal{B}_i$, and is the jth code word of $\mathcal{B}_i$.

Construction I_{RS} is described as follows: Form an $n \times 2$ array

$$
\begin{bmatrix}
a_1^{(1)} & a_1^{(2)} \\
a_2^{(1)} & a_2^{(2)} \\
\cdots & \cdots \\
a_n^{(1)} & a_n^{(2)}
\end{bmatrix},
$$

where the first column is in $\mathcal{A}_1$ and the second is in $\mathcal{A}_2$. Replace each row $a_i^{(1)}, a_i^{(2)}$ by the binary vector $E_{a_i^{(1)}}(a_i^{(2)})$. The resulting $n \times b$ binary arrays, which can be regarded as the binary vectors of length nb, form the new t-UbEC/d-UbED code.

THEOREM 5   The code from Construction I_{RS} is a t-UbEC/d-UbED code.

PROOF   Let x and y be arbitrary distinct code words in the code from Construction I_{RS}, i.e.,

$$
x = (E_{x_1^{(1)}}(x_1^{(2)}), \ldots, E_{x_n^{(1)}}(x_n^{(2)})),
$$
$$
y = (E_{y_1^{(1)}}(y_1^{(2)}), \ldots, E_{y_n^{(1)}}(y_n^{(2)})),
$$

where

$$
x^{(1)} = (x_1^{(1)}, \ldots, x_n^{(1)}) \in \mathcal{A}_1,
$$
$$
y^{(1)} = (y_1^{(1)}, \ldots, y_n^{(1)}) \in \mathcal{A}_1,
$$
$$
x^{(2)} = (x_1^{(2)}, \ldots, x_n^{(2)}) \in \mathcal{A}_2,
$$
$$
y^{(2)} = (y_1^{(2)}, \ldots, y_n^{(2)}) \in \mathcal{A}_2.
$$

Since $\mathcal{A}_1$ is of minimum distance $t + d + 1$,

$$
\mathcal{D}(x, y) \geq t + d + 1
$$

for $x^{(1)} \neq y^{(1)}$. Furthermore, since $\mathcal{B}_i$ is an AUED code, $\delta_{min}(\mathcal{B}_i) = 1$. Also $\mathcal{A}_2$ is of minimum distance $t + 1$. Therefore, we have

$$
\delta(x, y) \geq t + 1
$$

for $x^{(1)} = y^{(1)}$ and $x^{(2)} \neq y^{(2)}$. Hence the code is a t-UbEC/d-UbED code from Theorem 4.

We note that Construction I_{RS} gives t-UbEC or d-UbED codes when $t = d$ or $t = 0$.

The code can be decoded as follows:

- Decode each byte of the received word by the inner code decoder and determine the code symbols of A_1 and A_2. If the inner code decoder detects errors in a byte, then set the code symbols of A_1 and A_2 corresponding to the byte as erasures. The code symbol sequences of A_1 and A_2 from the received word are called the received words for A_1 and A_2.

- Decode the received word for A_1 by the t-fold error correction and d-fold error detection decoder.

- Set the symbols of A_2 corresponding to the ones of A_1 corrected in the preceding step as erasures, and decode the received word for A_2 by the t-fold erasure correction decoder.

Figure 12-2 illustrates the encoding and decoding process. Examples of encoding and decoding will be found in Section 4.

The rate of the t-UbEC/d-UbED code from Construction I_{RS} is

$$R = \frac{1}{nb} \log_2 q_1^{n-t-d} q_2^{n-t}$$

$$= \frac{n - t - d}{n} \frac{\log_2 q_1 q_2}{b} + \frac{d \log_2 q_2}{nb},$$

where $n \leq q_1 + 1$ and $n \leq q_2 + 1$. Therefore, the larger q_2 is, the more efficient the code is.

4 EXAMPLE OF CONSTRUCTION I_{RS}

Let us construct a 1-U6EC/3-U6ED code. Let $q_1 = 7$ and $q_2 = 8$ and use the codes in Table 1, which have been constructed by trial and error [27], as B_i. In Table 1, the code words are shown by the octal representation.

Let A_1 be the $[8, 4, 5; 7]$ RS code over GF(7) given by the generator matrix

$$G_1 = \begin{bmatrix} 1 & 0 & 0 & 0 & 3 & 1 & 4 & 6 \\ 0 & 1 & 0 & 0 & 6 & 0 & 0 & 5 \\ 0 & 0 & 1 & 0 & 6 & 4 & 3 & 6 \\ 0 & 0 & 0 & 1 & 4 & 1 & 1 & 3 \end{bmatrix}$$

and the parity-check matrix

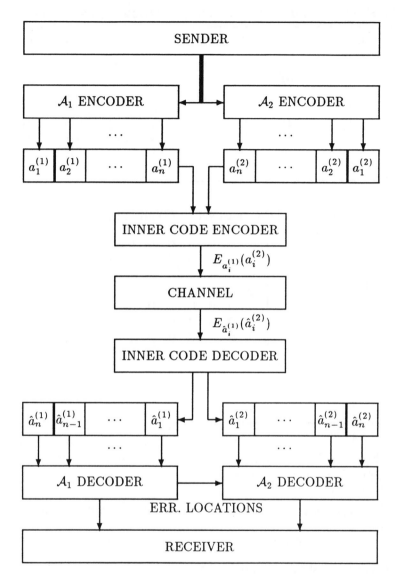

Figure 12-2. Encoding and decoding of the code from Construction I_{RS}.

$$H_1 = \begin{bmatrix} 4 & 1 & 1 & 3 & 1 & 0 & 0 & 0 \\ 6 & 0 & 3 & 6 & 0 & 1 & 0 & 0 \\ 3 & 0 & 4 & 6 & 0 & 0 & 1 & 0 \\ 1 & 2 & 1 & 4 & 0 & 0 & 0 & 1 \end{bmatrix}.$$

TABLE 1 B_i of $b = 6$, $q_1 = 7$, and $q_2 = 8$ (Octal Representation)

Code Word	B_0	B_1	B_2	B_3	B_4	B_5	B_6
0	01	04	05	07	76	73	72
1	02	03	06	13	75	74	71
2	14	11	31	15	63	66	46
3	24	12	32	16	53	65	45
4	44	21	34	70	33	56	43
5	30	22	51	64	47	55	26
6	50	41	52	62	27	36	25
7	60	42	54	61	17	35	23

Let A_2 be the [8, 7, 2; 8] RS code over GF(8) given by the generator matrix

$$
G_2 = \begin{bmatrix}
1 & 0 & 0 & 0 & 0 & 0 & 0 & 1 \\
0 & 1 & 0 & 0 & 0 & 0 & 0 & 1 \\
0 & 0 & 1 & 0 & 0 & 0 & 0 & 1 \\
0 & 0 & 0 & 1 & 0 & 0 & 0 & 1 \\
0 & 0 & 0 & 0 & 1 & 0 & 0 & 1 \\
0 & 0 & 0 & 0 & 0 & 1 & 0 & 1 \\
0 & 0 & 0 & 0 & 0 & 0 & 1 & 1
\end{bmatrix}
$$

and the parity-check matrix

$$H_2 = [\, 1 \quad 1 \quad 1 \quad 1 \quad 1 \quad 1 \quad 1 \quad 1 \,].$$

As a result, we have a 1-U6EC/3-U6ED code with length of 48 bits. This code has $7^4 \cdot 8^7$ code words. Thus we obtain an encoder of this code having $32\ (= \log_2 7^4 + 21)$ input bits, whereas the number of information bits of the RS code with length of 48 bits and the same unidirectional byte error control capability is 24.

We can perform the encoding and the decoding as follows: Let the input bits be

$$010100010101110100101001011110001.$$

We encode the first 11 bits into the 7-ary vector

$$a = (1, 6, 1, 6)$$

and encode the last 21 bits into the 8-ary vector

$$b = (7, 2, 2, 4, 5, 6, 1).$$

We calculate

$$aG_1 = (1, 6, 1, 6, 6, 4, 1, 4),$$
$$bG_2 = (7, 2, 2, 4, 5, 6, 1, 1),$$

so that we have the code word

$(E_1(7), E_6(2), E_1(2), E_6(4), E_6(5), E_4(6), E_1(1), E_4(1))$
$= (100010, 100110, 001001, 100011, 010110, 010111, 000011, 111010).$

Assume that we transmit this code word and receive

$(100010, 100110, 110010, 100011, 010110, 010111, 000011, 111010)$
$\qquad = (E_1(7), E_6(2), E_3(6), E_6(4), E_6(5), E_4(6), E_1(1), E_4(1)).$

We decode $(1, 6, 3, 6, 6, 4, 1, 1)$ by the single error correction and triple error detection decoder of A_1, obtaining $a' = (1, 6, 1, 6)$ as the decoded result, and find that the third byte of the received word is in error. Therefore we decode $(7, 2, *, 4, 5, 6, 1, 1)$, where $*$ is an erasure, by the erasure correction decoder of A_2 and obtain $b' = (7, 2, 2, 4, 5, 6, 1)$ as the decoded result. Hence we have the final decoded result of the 1-U6EC/3-U6ED code

$$0101000101011101001010100101110001$$

from a' and b'.

5 EFFICIENT INNER CODES FOR LARGE q_1 AND q_2

Saitoh and Imai [27] have constructed inner codes by a greedy algorithm or by trial and error. Those codes have no very simple encoding and decoding schemes and require look-up tables in encoding and decoding processes. The codes presented here are based on Berger codes [1,13,21 (pp. 359–360)]. Their encoding and decoding schemes are as simple as those of Berger codes.

Let $\beta_l(x)$ be the l-bit binary representation of the nonnegative integer x, where $x \leq 2^l - 1$, and let $V(x)$ be the number of 0's in the word x. When $j \leq 2^{b-j} - 1$, the encoder of the inner codes is defined as

$$E_i(x) = (\beta_j(x), \beta_{b-j}\{V(\beta_j(x)) + i\})$$

for $i = 0, 1, \ldots, 2^{b-j} - j - 1$ and $x = 0, 1, \ldots, 2^j - 1$. Thus we have

$$q_1 \leq 2^{b-j} - j,$$
$$q_2 = 2^j.$$

The inner codes can be decoded as follows: Assuming that i' and x' are the decoded results corresponding to $E_i(x)$, we have

$$x' = \beta_j^{-1}(x_1),$$
$$i' = \beta_{b-j}^{-1}(x_2) - V(x_1),$$

where $x = (x_1, x_2)$, $x_1 \in \mathcal{Z}_2^j$, $x_2 \in \mathcal{Z}_2^{b-j}$ is the received word.

In order to prove that the encoder proposed here can be applied to one of the inner codes of construction I_{RS}, we must show that the encoder satisfies the following two conditions:

- $\{E_i(x)|x = 0, 1, \ldots, 2^j - 1\}$ for each i is an AUED code.
- $\{E_i(x)|x = 0, 1, \ldots, 2^j - 1\}$ for all i are disjoint.

It is derived immediately that the encoder satisfies the first condition since a Berger code is an AUED code. Also, since we have $E_h(x) \neq E_i(y)$ for $x \neq y$ and $E_h(x) \neq E_i(x)$ for $h \neq i$, the encoder satisfies the second condition.

The number of encoder input bits of the code from Construction I_{RS} is then represented by

$$K = (n - t - d)(b - \Delta) + dj,$$

where $\Delta = b - \log_2 q_1 q_2 = b - j - \log_2 q_1$. That is, the less Δ is and the greater j is, the greater K is.

Parameters of the inner codes described here are listed in Tables 2 and 3.

6 COMPARISONS OF ERROR-CORRECTING CAPABILITIES

We shall compare the RS-based codes from Construction I_{RS} with the RS codes. We consider binary input encoders for which only 2^K code words are used for a positive integer K; i.e., K is the number of encoder input bits. When $b \geq 9$, the inner codes presented in Section 5 provide a number of efficient RS-based codes as listed in Table 4. This table also shows comparisons between the new codes and the RS codes with length of N bits. For example, we have the 10-U12EC code with length of 648 bits and with 458 encoder input bits, whereas an RS code with the same length has the capability of 8-U12EC and 456 encoder input bits.

Note that although the codes from Construction I_{RS} have length of less than $2^{b/2}$ bytes, the complexity of the encoder/decoder is small as compared with that of the encoder/decoder for RS codes over $GF(2^b)$. The complexity for the codes from Construction I_{RS} is the sum of the complexity of the outer encoder/decoder and that of the inner encoder/decoder. The complexity of the outer encoder/decoder approximates that of the encoder/decoder for a code obtained by interleaving RS codes over $GF(2^{b/2})$ twice. The complexity of the inner encoder/decoder approximates that of the encoder/decoder for a Berger code of length b.

TABLE 2   Parameters of the Inner Codes for $9 \leq b \leq 16$

b	Maximum Selectable q_1	Maximum Selectable q_1 That Is a Power of a Prime Number	q_2	Δ
9	126	125	2^2	3.422e−2
	61	61	2^3	6.926e−2
	28	27	2^4	2.451e−1
10	254	251	2^2	2.846e−2
	125	125	2^3	3.422e−2
	60	59	2^4	1.174e−1
	27	27	2^5	2.451e−1
11	510	509	2^2	8.478e−3
	253	251	2^3	2.846e−2
	124	121	2^4	8.114e−2
	59	59	2^5	1.174e−1
12	1022	1021	2^2	4.233e−3
	509	509	2^3	8.478e−3
	252	251	2^4	2.846e−2
	123	121	2^5	8.114e−2
	58	53	2^6	2.721e−1
13	2046	2039	2^2	6.354e−3
	1021	1021	2^3	4.233e−3
	508	503	2^4	2.559e−2
	251	251	2^5	2.846e−2
	122	121	2^6	8.114e−2
14	4094	4093	2^2	1.057e−3
	2045	2039	2^3	6.354e−3
	1020	1019	2^4	7.062e−3
	507	503	2^5	2.559e−2
	250	241	2^6	8.711e−2
	121	121	2^7	8.114e−2
15	8190	8179	2^2	2.291e−3
	4093	4093	2^3	1.057e−3
	2044	2039	2^4	6.354e−3
	1019	1019	2^5	7.062e−3
	506	503	2^6	2.559e−2
	249	241	2^7	8.711e−2
16	16382	16381	2^2	2.642e−4
	8189	8179	2^3	2.291e−3
	4092	4091	2^4	1.762e−3
	2043	2039	2^5	6.354e−3
	1018	1013	2^6	1.558e−2
	505	503	2^7	2.559e−2
	248	241	2^8	8.711e−2

TABLE 3   Parameters of the Inner Codes for $b = 24, 32$

b	Maximum Selectable q_1	Maximum Selectable q_1 That Is a Prime Number	q_2	Δ
24	65528	65521	2^8	3.3024e$-$4
	32759	32749	2^9	8.3676e$-$4
	16374	16369	2^{10}	1.3214e$-$3
	8181	8179	2^{11}	2.2912e$-$3
	4084	4079	2^{12}	6.0002e$-$3
	2035	2029	2^{13}	1.3446e$-$2
	1010	1009	2^{14}	2.1289e$-$2
32	2097141	2097133	2^{11}	1.3070e$-$5
	1048564	1048559	2^{12}	2.3389e$-$5
	524275	524269	2^{13}	5.2283e$-$5
	262130	262127	2^{14}	9.3561e$-$5
	131057	131041	2^{15}	3.4125e$-$4
	65520	65519	2^{16}	3.7428e$-$4
	32751	32749	2^{17}	8.3676e$-$4
	16366	16363	2^{18}	1.8503e$-$3
	8173	8171	2^{19}	3.7030e$-$3
	4076	4073	2^{20}	8.1239e$-$3

TABLE 4   Comparisons Between Newly Constructed and RS t-UbEC Codes

b	n	j	q_1	N	K, t New	K, t RS
9	17	4	27	153	67, 6	63, 5
10	28	5	27	280	128, 10	120, 8
11	33	5	59	363	191, 10	187, 8
12	54	6	53	648	458, 10	456, 8
16	129	7	503	2064	1811, 10	1808, 8
16	242	8	241	3872	3588, 11	3584, 9
					3493, 15	3488, 12
					3398, 19	3392, 15
					3302, 23	3296, 18
					2659, 50	2656, 38
24	2030	13	2029	48720	48342, 10	48336, 8
					48203, 14	48192, 11
					46944, 50	46944, 37
					31206, 500	31200, 365
24	4080	12	4079	97920	96096, 50	96096, 38
					79901, 500	79872, 376
32	8172	19	8171	261504	261068, 9	261056, 7
					260933, 12	260928, 9
					259224, 50	259200, 36
					238977, 500	238976, 352

7 DECODING ERROR PERFORMANCE

We consider the bounded distance decoder. Let t be the error-correcting capability. The case where no more than t errors occur and the decoder corrects the errors is called *correct decoding*. The decoder cannot deal with errors correctly when more than t errors occur. This case is called *incorrect decoding*. In this section, we discuss the probability of incorrect decoding for a t-UbEC code.

Let P_b and P_u be the probabilities of bidirectional and unidirectional byte errors occurring, respectively, when a 1-byte word has been transmitted. Assume that P_b and P_u are constant. Let $P = P_b + P_u$. Then P is the probability of a byte error occurring in a single-byte word, and we have

$$P_b = \frac{r}{1+r} P,$$

$$P_u = \frac{1}{1+r} P,$$

where $r = P_b / P_u$. Then we have the probability of incorrect decoding

$$P_E = 1 - \sum_{i=0}^{\lfloor t/2 \rfloor} \sum_{j=0}^{t-2i} \binom{n}{i} \binom{n-i}{j} \frac{r^i}{(1+r)^{i+j}} P^{i+j} (1-P)^{n-i-j}$$

for a t-UbEC code since a t-UbEC code can correct all combinations of μ bidirectional byte errors and ν unidirectional byte errors for $2\mu + \nu \leq t$. We also have the probability of incorrect decoding

$$P_E^{(RS)} = 1 - \sum_{i=0}^{t^{(RS)}} \binom{n}{i} P^i (1-P)^{n-i}$$

for an $[n, n - 2t^{(RS)}, 2t^{(RS)} + 1; 2^b]$ RS code, since the RS code can correct $t^{(RS)}$ or fewer byte errors.

Tables 5 and 6 show values of P and r for several values of P_E in the cases where $P_E = P_E^{(RS)}$. We set (54, 10, 8) and (242, 50, 38) as $(n, t, t^{(RS)})$ for Tables 5 and 6, respectively, since we have found a combination of the 10-U12EC code and the 8-U12EC RS code with length of 54 bytes, and that of the 50-U16EC code and the 38-U16EC RS code with length of 242 bytes from Table 4. Tables 5 and 6 indicate the ranges of r in the case where the t-UbEC code is superior to the RS code in terms of decoding error performance. For example, when $P_E = P_E^{(RS)} = 10^{-6}$, we have $P = 0.070$ and $r = 0.321$ from Table 6. This implies that the 50-U16EC code is better than the RS code of the same rate when r is less than 0.321.

TABLE 5   Parameters for Several Values
of P_E for $(n, t, t^{(RS)}) = (54, 10, 8)$

P_E	P	r
10^{-6}	0.0195468	0.119489
10^{-9}	0.00863523	0.0804280
10^{-12}	0.00392378	0.0541614
10^{-15}	0.00180394	0.0233201

TABLE 6   Parameters for Several Values
of P_E for $(n, t, t^{(RS)}) = (242, 50, 38)$

P_E	P	r
10^{-6}	0.0698804	0.320887
10^{-9}	0.0536952	0.287605
10^{-12}	0.0423683	0.260240
10^{-15}	0.0339620	0.256810

8 CONCLUSIONS

We have introduced the theory of unidirectional byte error control codes and
have described a construction of RS-based codes. The comparisons between
RS-based unidirectional byte error-correcting codes and RS codes have been
shown in terms of the error-correcting capabilities and decoding error performance. As a result, we have unidirectional byte error-correcting codes that
employ RS codes and are superior to RS codes.

The codes in this chapter are nonsystematic codes, whereas several systematic code constructions are known [11,12,22,23,26]. Note that the systematic unidirectional byte error-correcting codes in [23] and [26] are less
efficient than the nonsystematic codes in this chapter and [27].

The unidirectional byte error control codes described in this chapter provide better efficiency to error control coding in devices where unidirectional
byte errors are predominant. It implies that we have more efficient coding if
we make unidirectional byte errors predominant in devices by devising mod-
ulation/demodulation in transmitted/received or written/readback processes
[24]. This way is one of combined coded modulation techniques [3,15 (pp.
313–322)]. Unidirectional byte error control codes will find not only applications to memory systems but also wide applications if we develop the
modulation that makes unidirectional byte errors predominant.

REFERENCES

[1] J. M. Berger, "A Note on Error Detecting Codes for Asymmetric Channels," *Information Control*, Volume 4, pp. 68–73, March 1961.

[2] E. R. Berlekamp, *Algebraic Coding Theory* (rev. ed.), Laguna Hills, Calif.: Aegean Park Press, 1984.

[3] E. Biglieri and M. Luise (eds.), *Coded Modulation and Bandwidth-Efficient Transmission*, Amsterdam: Elsevier, 1992.

[4] R. E. Blahut, *Theory and Practice of Error Control Codes*, Reading, Mass: Addison-Wesley, 1984.

[5] M. Blaum and H. C. A. van Tilborg, "On t-Error Correcting/All Unidirectional Error Detecting Codes," *IEEE Transactions on Computers*, Volume 38, pp. 1493–1501, November 1989.

[6] M. Blaum, *Codes for Detecting and Correcting Unidirectional Errors*. Los Alamitos, Calif.: IEEE Computer Society Press, 1993.

[7] M. Blaum and J. Bruck, "Coding for Skew-Tolerant Parallel Asynchronous Communications," *IEEE Transactions on Information Theory*, Volume 39, pp. 379–388, March 1993.

[8] F. J. H. Böinck and H. C. A. van Tilborg, "Constructions and Bounds for Systematic tEC/AUED Codes," *IEEE Transactions on Information Theory*, Volume 36, pp. 1381–1390, November 1990.

[9] B. Bose, "Byte Unidirectional Error Correcting Codes," in *Digest of Papers 19th International Symposium on Fault-Tolerant Computers, Chicago, June 1989*, pp. 222–228.

[10] B. Bose and S. Al-Bassam, "Byte Unidirectional Error Correcting and Detecting Codes," *IEEE Transactions on Computers*, Volume 41, pp. 1601–1606, December 1992.

[11] L. A. Dunning, G. Dial, and M. R. Varanasi, "Unidirectional 9-Bit Byte Error Detecting Codes for Computer Memory Systems," in *Digest of Papers 19th International Symposium on Fault-Tolerant Computers, Chicago, June 1989*, pp. 216–221.

[12] L. A. Dunning, G. Dial, and M. R. Varanasi, "Unidirectional Byte Error Detecting Codes for Computer Memory Systems," *IEEE Transactions on Computers*, Volume 39, pp. 592–595, April 1990.

[13] C. V. Freiman, "Optimal Error Detecting Codes for Completely Asymmetric Channels," *Information Control*, Volume 5, pp. 64–71, March 1962.

[14] E. Fujiwara and D. K. Pradhan, "Error-Control Coding in Computers," *IEEE Computers*, Volume 23, Number 7, pp. 63–72, July 1990.

[15] H. Imai, *Coding Theory*, Tokyo: IEICE, 1990 (in Japanese).

[16] H. Imai (ed.), *Essentials of Error-Control Coding Techniques*, San Diego: Academic Press, 1990.

[17] F. J. MacWilliams and N. J. A. Sloane, *The Theory of Error-Correcting Codes*, Amsterdam: North-Holland, 1977.

[18] K. Matsuzawa and E. Fujiwara, "Masking Asymmetric Line Faults Using Semi-distance Codes," *Digest of Papers 18th International Symposium on Fault-Tolerant Computers, Tokyo, June 1988*, pp. 354–359; also *Transactions of the IEICE*, Volume E73, pp. 1278–1286, August 1990.

[19] W. W. Peterson and E. J. Weldon, Jr., *Error-Correcting Codes* (2nd ed.), Cambridge, Mass.: MIT Press, 1972.

[20] D. K. Pradhan, "A New Class of Error-Correcting/Detecting Codes for Fault-Tolerant Computer Applications," *IEEE Transactions on Computers*, Volume C-29, pp. 471–481, June 1980.

[21] T. R. N. Rao and E. Fujiwara, *Error-Control Coding for Computer Systems*, London: Prentice-Hall, 1989.

[22] T. R. N. Rao, G. L. Feng, and M. S. Kolluru, "Efficient Multiple Unidirectional Byte Error-Detecting Codes for Computer Memory Systems," *Digest of Papers 22nd International Symposium on Fault-Tolerant Computers, Boston, July 8–10, 1992*, pp. 502–509.

[23] Y. Saitoh and H. Imai, "Multiple Unidirectional Byte Error-Correcting Codes," *IEEE Transactions on Information Theory*, Volume 37, Number 3, pp. 903–908, May 1991.

[24] Y. Saitoh and H. Imai, "Runlength-Limited Codes which Turn Peak-Shift Errors into Unidirectional Byte Errors," *IEICE Transactions, Fundamentals*, Volume E75-A, Number 7, pp. 898–900, July 1992.

[25] Y. Saitoh and H. Imai, "Runlength-Limited Short-Length Codes for Unidirectional-Byte-Error-Control," *IEICE Transactions Fundamentals*, Volume E75-A, Number 9, pp. 1057–1062, September 1992.

[26] Y. Saitoh and H. Imai, "Some Codes for Correcting and Detecting Unidirectional Byte Errors," *IEEE Transactions on Computers*, Volume 42, Number 5, pp. 547–552, May 1993.

[27] Y. Saitoh and H. Imai, "Generalized Concatenated Codes for Channels Where Unidirectional Byte Errors Are Predominant," *IEEE Transactions on Information Theory*, Volume 39, Number 3, pp. 1014–1022, May 1993.

[28] Y. Saitoh and H. Imai, "Asymptotic Bounds for Unidirectional Byte Error-Correcting Codes," *IEICE Transactions, Fundamentals*, Volume E76-A, Number 9, pp. 1437–1441, September 1993.

[29] H. van Tilborg and M. Blaum, "On Error-Correcting Balanced Codes," *IEEE Transactions on Information Theory*, Volume 35, pp. 1091–1095, September 1989.

[30] J. H. Weber, C. de Vroedt, and D. E. Boekee, "Bounds and Constructions for Codes Correcting Unidirectional Errors," *IEEE Transactions on Information Theory*, Volume 35, pp. 797–810, July 1989.

[31] J. K. Wolf, "Adding Two Information Symbols to Certain Nonbinary BCH Codes and Some Applications," *Bell System Technical Journal*, Volume 48, pp. 2405–2424, September 1969.

Chapter 13

Reed-Solomon and Algebraic Geometry Codes

Tomik Yaghoobian

Ian F. Blake
Department of Electrical and Computer Engineering
University of Waterloo, Waterloo, Ontario, Canada

1 INTRODUCTION

As discussed in Chapter 1, Reed-Solomon codes were originally described by Reed and Solomon as polynomials evaluated over the points in a finite field. Some 20 years later Tsfasman, Vladut, and Zink extended this approach through the use of algebraic geometry to create, for the first time, specific codes that exceed the Varshamov-Gilbert lower bound for alphabet sizes larger than 49. This spectacular result produced a surge of research by mathematicians and engineers into the application of algebraic geometry to error-correcting codes and sequence theory. In one of the seminal papers to emerge from this research, Van Lint and Springer [18] gave an elegant introduction to codes from curves in algebraic geometries by first interpreting Reed-Solomon codes in this light and then extending the resulting concepts to more general codes. This chapter is very much in that spirit, attempting to first interpret Reed-Solomon codes as codes obtained from the evaluation of a class of polynomials on a line in projective space, as in van Lint and Springer [18], and then considering the slightly more general case of codes obtained from elliptic curves. It concludes with a brief discussion of more general constructions of codes using algebraic geometries.

In this chapter we attempt to illustrate that the transition from RS codes to algebraic geometry codes is natural by introducing the concepts from algebraic geometry and how they are used in the coding theoretic setting, in a progressive way. The treatment of the algebraic geometric notions is intuitive; for a more formal treatment the reader is referred to Fulton [5].

The chapter begins with a brief introduction to Reed-Solomon (RS) codes and maximum distance separable codes and their important properties. In Section 3 concepts that generalize the construction of RS codes using notions of algebraic geometries are given. This situation is generalized in Section 4 by considering codes derived from elliptic curves. At this point the situation is already considerably more involved than that for RS codes and the methods required more intricate. A review of the structure of elliptic codes and most of the known facts concerning them are given. Elliptic codes over extension fields of GF(2) are of particular interest here, and some deeper questions considering them are raised. In a sense, codes from elliptic curves can be considered as the closest "cousins" of RS codes. Section 5 considers the further difficulties encountered by going beyond these and looks at codes from more general curves. Here the work is even more involved, and only a few special cases are considered.

The intuition gained from the construction of RS codes and algebraic geometry codes prompted the construction of a new class of codes, hyperelliptic codes. The purpose was to mimic the ideas of algebraic geometry codes while, by construction, establishing their fundamental properties without the use of the deep theorems of algebraic geometry. While this effort was successful, it is nonetheless clear that the powerful theorems of algebraic geometry cannot, in general, be avoided for the construction of good codes. Finally it is noted that decoding algorithms for codes derived from algebraic geometry are not considered here.

2 REED-SOLOMON AND MAXIMUM DISTANCE SEPARABLE CODES

Let $K = \text{GF}(q)$ be the finite field with q elements. A code C that is a linear subspace of K^n of dimension k and minimum distance d is said to be a *linear code* with parameters $[n, k, d]_q$. Only linear codes will be considered in this chapter, unless otherwise noted. The *information rate* of C is k/n. If $wt(x)$ denotes the number of nonzero coordinate positions in the vector x, then the minimum distance of C is

$$d = \min\{wt(x) \mid x \in C, \ x \neq 0\}.$$

Any matrix that has as its rows k independent vectors of C is called a *generator matrix* of C.

For a linear code C the *dual code* C^* is defined as

$$C^* = \{y \in K^n \mid y \cdot x = 0 \ \text{for all} \ x \in C\},$$

where the $\cdot$ operation denotes the usual inner product. The dual code C^* has parameters $[n, n-k, d']_q$. A generator matrix for C^* is called a *parity-check matrix* for the code C.

The *Singleton bound* for a linear code states that for an $[n, k, d]_q$ code the minimum distance d is bounded above by $n - k + 1$. A code that achieves the Singleton bound is called a *maximum distance separable* (MDS) code. When they exist, MDS codes are the best possible linear codes in the sense that they have the largest possible minimum distance for a given length, dimension, and alphabet size, and thus the search for MDS codes is an important problem in coding theory. We introduce the terminology of referring to a code as quasi-MDS (QMDS) if it has parameters $[n, k, d]_q$, where $d = n - k$, 1 less than the distance for MDS codes.

Some basic properties of MDS codes, which includes the class of RS codes, are first reviewed. References [1] and [8] should be consulted for many of the details and proofs of the statements made here.

DEFINITION 1   An RS code is the set of vectors of the form,

$$\{(f(\alpha^0), \ldots, f(\alpha^{q-2}))|\ f(x) \in GF(q)[x] \ and \ \deg f \le k - 1\},$$

where the RS code has parameters $[n = q - 1, k, n - k + 1]_q$.

RS codes can be extended to form a code of increased length and minimum distance.

DEFINITION 2   An extended RS code is the set of vectors of the form

$$\{(f(\alpha^0), \ldots, f(\alpha^{q-2}), f(0)) \mid f(x) \in K[x], \ \deg[f(x)] < k\}.$$

where the RS code has parameters $[n = q, k, n - k + 1]_q$.

Assume C is the above extended RS code. It is easy to see that C is a code with parameters $[n = q, k, d = n - k + 1]_q$, where the minimum distance is $n - k + 1$, as a polynomial of degree $k - 1$ can have at most $(k - 1)$ zeros.

For a more thorough treatment of MDS codes the reader is referred to [2 (pp. 54-56)] and [8 (Chap. 11)]. The definition of an MDS code is simple, and yet they possess remarkable properties which will be briefly noted. Recall that these properties apply to RS codes since they are MDS.

The dual code C^* of an MDS code C is also MDS. If C has parameters $[n, k, n - k + 1]_q$, then C^* has parameters $[n, n - k, k + 1]_q$. Let the $k \times n$ matrix G be the generator matrix for C, and let the $n - k \times n$ matrix H be the generator matrix for C^*; that is, H is the parity-check matrix for the code C. Then every k columns of G and also every $(n - k)$ columns of H are independent.

Assume C is an $[n, k, d]_q$ code and that A_i, $i = 0, \ldots, n$, is the number of code words of weight i. Then the polynomial

$$W(x) = \sum_{i=0}^{n} A_i x^i$$

is the *weight enumerator* of the code C. Let B_i, $i = 0, \ldots, n$, be the number of code words of weight i in the dual code C^*; the weight enumerator of C^* is

$$W^*(x) = \sum_{i=0}^{n} B_i x^i.$$

It can be shown that the weight enumerator of C and C^* are related. A particular version of the MacWilliams [1] identities states that

$$\sum_{i=0}^{n-j} \binom{n-i}{j} A_i = q^{k-j} \sum_{i=0}^{j} \binom{n-i}{j-i} B_i, \quad j = 0, \ldots, n. \qquad (1)$$

The weight enumerator of a code reveals information regarding the structure of the code and assists in computing bounds on the error probability of using the code on a communication channel.

If C is MDS $[n, k, d = n - k + 1]_q$, then $A_0 = 1$ and $A_i = 0$ for $i = 1, \ldots, n - k$, and for C^* we have $B_0 = 1$ and $B_i = 0$ for $i = 1, \ldots, k$. Then the MacWilliams identities reduce to

$$\sum_{i=n-k+1}^{n-j} \binom{n-i}{j} A_i = \binom{n}{j}(q^{k-j} - 1), \quad j = 0, \ldots, k - 1.$$

The above equations can be solved to obtain the solutions

$$A_{n-i} = \sum_{j=i}^{k-1} (-1)^{j-i} \binom{j}{i}\binom{n}{j}(q^{k-j} - 1), \quad i = 0, 1, \ldots, k - 1. \qquad (2)$$

Thus the weight enumerator of MDS codes, and in particular RS codes, is completely determined. It is well known that RS codes can be extended by one or two symbols while retaining the MDS property. In [8] it is shown that there exist triply extended RS codes that are MDS and have parameters $[2^m + 2, 3, 2^m]_{2^m}$. Aside from the triply extended RS codes, no other MDS codes are known for $n > q + 1$; and in fact there is good evidence to suggest that for MDS codes $n \le q + 1$, assuming $k \ge 2$ and $n - k \ge 2$.

There exist codes from algebraic geometry curves, such as elliptic curves, for which it is known that most are not MDS [9] but that they are QMDS of length at most $q + 1 + \lfloor 2\sqrt{q} \rfloor$.

3 CODES FROM ALGEBRAIC GEOMETRIES

Extended RS codes were constructed by using the q points of GF(q) and evaluating polynomials in one variable, where the degree was upper-bounded, on these points. To extend the idea of this construction it will be shown that the points given by a curve and special polynomials in two variables can be used.

The affine 2-space over GF(q) is the set of 2-tuples (x, y) with $x, y \in$ GF(q). An affine plane curve $\mathcal{X}$ is the set of zeros of a polynomial $F(x, y)$

$$\mathcal{X} = \{(x, y) \mid x, y \in GF(q), \ F(x, y) = 0\}.$$

The degree of the curve $\mathcal{X}$ is the degree of the polynomial $F(x, y)$. For example, a curve of degree 1 is a *line*; the line obtained by $F(x, y) = y$ is the set of points $\mathcal{X} = \{(x, 0) \mid x \in \mathrm{GF}(q)\}$ and is equivalent to GF(q). Thus the extended RS code is obtained by evaluating polynomials in one variable of certain degree on the points of the curve $\mathcal{X}$.

An elliptic curve in affine coordinates is the set of solutions over GF(q) to the cubic (called the *dehomogenized Weierstrass* equation)

$$y^2 + a_1 xy + a_3 y = x^3 + a_2 x^2 + a_4 x + a_6, \tag{3}$$

where $a_i \in GF(q)$.

With each curve $\mathcal{X}$ we can associate a nonnegative integer g which is called the *genus* of $\mathcal{X}$. For our purposes it suffices to say that the quantity g can be computed from the given curve. The genus of a curve $\mathcal{X}$ is a measure of its complexity. A curve $\mathcal{X}$ has genus 0 if and only if it is equivalent (birationally) to a line. A curve $\mathcal{X}$ has genus 1 if and only if it is equivalent (birationally) to an elliptic curve.

In order to make all the points on a plane curve $\mathcal{X}$ visible, including what are called points at infinity, projective coordinates must be used. The *projective* 2-space P^2 over GF(q) is defined to be the set of all lines passing through the origin in the affine 3-space A^3, which consists of all 3-tuples (x, y, z) and $x, y, z \in$ GF(q). If we consider two nonzero points $x, y \in A^3$ to be equivalent whenever $x = \lambda y$ for some $\lambda \in$ GF(q), then P^2 is the set of equivalence classes of nonzero points in A^3. A plane curve $\mathcal{X}$ can be represented in affine or projective coordinates. A projective plane curve is the set of zeros of a homogeneous polynomial $F(x, y, z)$ (a polynomial that is a sum of terms $x^i y^j z^k$, where i, j, and k are nonnegative integers and $i + j + k$ is fixed),

$$\mathcal{X} = \{(x, y, z) \mid x, y, z \in \mathrm{GF}(q), \ F(x, y, z) = 0\}.$$

By abuse of notation we will refer to $F(x, y, z)$ as the projective plane curve. For example, (3) represents an elliptic curve in affine coordinates, and

$$y^2z + a_1xyz + a_3yz^2 = x^3 + a_2x^2z + a_4xz^2 + a_6z^3 \qquad (4)$$

represents the same curve in projective coordinates. In (4) there is a point $O = (0, 1, 0)$ which is called the *point at infinity* and which is not visible in (3). A projective plane curve $F(x, y, z)$ is *irreducible* (absolutely) if the polynomial $F(x, y, z)$ is irreducible over any extension field of GF(q).

RS codes were defined by evaluating a set of suitable functions, polynomials, on the projective line. To define codes on curves in a similar fashion, curves must be found for which a description of the points on the curve, and a set of suitable functions to be evaluated on the points of the curve, are given. In order to achieve this goal some more definitions from algebraic geometry are given. For a more thorough and complete introduction to concepts from algebraic geometry the reader is referred to the references mentioned previously.

A projective plane curve $F(x, y, z)$ is said to be *nonsingular* if there exists no point P such that $F(P) = F_x(P) = F_y(P) = F_z(P) = 0$, where F_x, F_y, and F_z are partial derivates of F with respect to x, y, and z, respectively. Henceforth let $\mathcal{X}$ denote a nonsingular projective plane curve.

A *divisor* on $\mathcal{X}$ is a formal sum $D = \sum_{P \in \mathcal{X}} n_P P$, where the coefficients n_P are integers of which all but a finite number are zero. Divisors can be added term by term in the obvious manner. This operation makes the set of all divisors on $\mathcal{X}$, denoted Div($\mathcal{X}$), into an Abelian group (the free Abelian group generated by $\mathcal{X}$). The *degree* of a divisor D is $\deg(D) = \sum_{P \in \mathcal{X}} n_P$. The *support* of D is the set $\{P \in \mathcal{X} | n_P \neq O\}$. A divisor $D = \sum_{P \in \mathcal{X}} n_P P$ is called *effective*, denoted $D \succ 0$, if $n_P \geq 0$ for all $P \in \mathcal{X}$. If $D_1, D_2 \in \text{Div}(\mathcal{X})$, then we write $D_1 \succ D_2$ if $D_1 - D_2 \succ 0$. Assume $k(\mathcal{X})$ is the function field of $\mathcal{X}$, the set of rational functions on $\mathcal{X}$ [5]. Let $f \in k(\mathcal{X})$. Since the number of poles and zeros of a rational function is finite, we can define the *divisor of f* to be $\text{Div}(f) = (f) = \sum_{P \in \mathcal{X}} \text{ord}_P(f)P$, where ord_P is a function which gives the order of the pole or zero of f at the point $P \in \mathcal{X}$. If $\text{ord}_P(f) = n_P > 0$, we say that f has a zero of order n_P, and if $\text{ord}_P(f) = n_P < 0$, we say that f has a pole of order $-n_P$. Essentially the divisor Div(f) is an "accounting" device to keep track of the zeros and poles and their orders.

We define the following vector space [over GF(q)] of rational functions,

$$L(D) = \{f \in k(\mathcal{X}) \mid (f) + D \succ 0\} \cup \{0\},$$

where $D \in \text{Div}(\mathcal{X})$. This vector space consists of functions that have zeros of at least a certain order and poles of at most a certain order, depending on the divisor D.

The dimension of the vector space $L(D)$ is related to the genus g of the curve $\mathcal{X}$ in a well-known theorem referred to as the Riemann-Roch theorem. The Riemann-Roch theorem is used to prove Theorem 1. Given a projective curve $\mathcal{X}$ over GF(q) we say the point P is GF(q)-*rational* if all the components of P are in GF(q).

Assume $P_1, \ldots, P_n$ are GF(q)-rational points on the curve $\mathcal{X}$ and let $D = P_1 + \cdots + P_n$. Assume G is a divisor on X with support consisting of only GF(q)-rational points and disjoint from D (i.e., G contains P_i for $i = 1, \ldots, n$ with coefficient zero). We also restrict the degree of G to the range $2g - 2 < \deg(G) < n$.

DEFINITION 3   The linear code $C(D, G)$ over GF(q) is the image of the linear map

$$\alpha : L(G) \longrightarrow \mathrm{GF(q)}^n, \tag{5}$$

defined by

$$\alpha(f) = [f(P_1), \ldots, f(P_n)].$$

The following theorem gives the parameters of the code $C(D, G)$. The proof is quite simple and uses the Riemann-Roch theorem.

THEOREM 1   The code $C(D, G)$ has parameters $[n, k, d]_q$ with

$$n = \deg(D),$$

$$k = \deg(G) - g + 1,$$

$$d \geq d^* = n - \deg(G).$$

The parameter d^* is called the *designed minimum distance*. For a given field size q and genus g, the number of rational points on a projective curve is upper-bounded by the Hasse-Weil bound (see Theorem 2). Note that $k + d^* = n - g + 1$, and thus we obtain good codes from algebraic geometry, from curves that for a given field size q have the largest possible number of points for a given genus g; in such a case $k + d^*$ is the largest possible value it can be for a given genus. Thus in designing algebraic geometry codes we are interested in curves that have the maximum possible number of rational points.

A general construction using algebraic geometry techniques that produces a code dual to the code $C(D, G)$ also exists but will not be presented here.

The number of GF(q)-rational points of $\mathcal{X}$ is clearly finite. Let $N_q(g)$ be the *maximum number* of GF(q)-rational points on a curve of genus g over GF(q).

THEOREM 2 (HASSE-WEIL)   The number N of GF(q)-rational points on a nonsingular projective curve $\mathcal{X}$ of genus g satisfies

$$|N - (q + 1)| \leq 2g\sqrt{q}.$$

By the Hasse-Weil bound, one has $N_q(g) \leq q + 1 + \lfloor 2g\sqrt{q} \rfloor$, where $\lfloor n \rfloor$ denotes the largest integer $\leq n$. Serre [10,11] showed that this can be improved to $N_q(g) \leq q + 1 + g\lfloor 2\sqrt{q} \rfloor$. For elliptic curves, Serre proved the following.

THEOREM 3 (SERRE) Assume $q = p^e$ with $e \geq 1$ and $m = \lfloor 2\sqrt{q} \rfloor$. Then we have

i. $N_q(1) = q + m$ if e is odd, $e \geq 3$, and p divides m,
ii. $N_q(1) = q + m + 1$ otherwise.

In [15] the values of the maximum number of points for genus-2 curves, $N_q(2)$, are given. However for genus-3 curves the value of $N_q(3)$ is known only for some values of q.

We will now briefly mention a method of obtaining the number of points of the curve over an extension field, knowing the number of points over the base field. Let $\mathcal{X}$ be a projective curve and denote by N_r the number of $GF(q^r)$-rational points on the curve $\mathcal{X}$. Thus the number of $GF(q)$-rational points on $\mathcal{X}$ is N_1 (or simply N). We can associate an important function to the curve $\mathcal{X}$; let the zeta function $Z(t)$ of $\mathcal{X}$ over $GF(q)$ be given by the formal power series with rational coefficients

$$Z(t) = \exp\left(\sum_{r=1}^{\infty} \frac{N_r t^r}{r}\right).$$

The following important result [15] gives the intimate relationship of the zeta function to the curve.

THEOREM 4   The zeta function $Z(t)$ of a curve $\mathcal{X}$ of genus g is given by the rational function of the form

$$Z(t) = \frac{P(t)}{(1-t)(1-qt)}, \tag{6}$$

where $P(t) = q^g t^{2g} + p_1 t^{2g-1} + \cdots + p_{2g-1}t + 1$ is a polynomial with integer coefficients. Furthermore,

$$P(t) = \prod_{i=1}^{2g}(1 - \omega_i t),$$

where ω_i are complex numbers having the properties that the complex conjugate of ω_i is equal to $\bar{\omega}_i = \omega_{g+i}$, and that $|\omega_i| = \sqrt{q}$.

It is easy to show that

$$N_r = \frac{1}{(r-1)!} \frac{d^r}{dt^r}(\log Z(t))|_{t=0}, \tag{7}$$

and using the last expression in the above theorem for $P(t)$, we have that

$$N_r = q^r + 1 - \sum_{i=1}^{2g} \omega_i^r. \tag{8}$$

To illustrate the above ideas consider the elliptic curve X $(g = 1)$ given by affine coordinates as $y^2 + y = x^3$. Then the number of GF(2) points on X is 3; in terms of projective coordinates they are $(0, 1, 1)$, $(0, 0, 1)$, and $(0, 1, 0)$. Then the polynomial $P(t) = 2t^2 + pt + 1$, and all that is undetermined in the expression for $Z(t)$ is the integer p. We know that $N = N_1 = 3$, and also from equation (7) that $N_1 = q + 1 - p = 3 - p$, and thus $p = 0$. In this case $P(t) = (1 - \sqrt{2}it)(1 + \sqrt{2}it)$, where $i = \sqrt{-1}$. Then we have from equation (8) that $N_r = 2^r + 1 - (\sqrt{2}i)^r - (-\sqrt{2}i)^r$.

The polynomial $P(t)$ has $(2g - 1)$ unknown coefficients, and thus it can be shown that if the values of $N_1, \ldots, N_{2g-1}$ are known, then $P(t)$ can be determined, and as a result the number of points on the curve X, for any extension N_r, obtained.

A central problem of coding theory is the construction of asymptotically long codes that meet the Varshamov-Gilbert lower bound. The existence of such codes is established by the random coding theorem of Shannon [12]. Thus codes (in general, nonlinear) of length n and M code words and minimum distance d are sought for which, as n approaches infinity, k/n is maximized for a fixed d/n or vice versa. Define the ratio $\delta = d/n$ and $A_q(n, d)$ to be the maximum M for which an (n, M, d) code exists over F_q. The asymptotic rate is defined as

$$\alpha(\delta) = \limsup_{n \to \infty} \log_q A_q(n, \lfloor \delta n \rfloor).$$

The codes of interest would have the property that as $n \to \infty$, δ is maximized for a fixed $\alpha(\delta)$ or vice versa.

A relatively simple lower bound on the performance of good long codes known as the Varshamov-Gilbert bound [17] is given as follows. Let $H_q(x)$ be the entropy function on $[0, (q-1)/q]$ defined by

$$H_q(x) = x \log_q(q - 1) - x \log_q x - (1 - x) \log_q(1 - x).$$

Then the Varshamov-Gilbert bound states that a sequence of codes exists such that

$$\alpha(\delta) \geq 1 - H_q(\delta). \tag{9}$$

The search for codes that achieve this lower bound has been intensive over the past 30 years. Some interesting constructions were found, but none surpassed it. In 1982 Tsfasman, Vladut, and Zink [16] showed that a sequence of algebraic geometry codes can be constructed that exceed this lower bound for certain alphabet sizes. An outline of their argument is as follows. In [18] the following theorem is given.

THEOREM 5   Let $q = p^{2r}$. There exists a sequence of curves over GF(q) such that

$$\lim_{n \to \infty} \frac{g}{n} = (\sqrt{q} - 1)^{-1}.$$

From Theorem 1 the parameters of a sequence of algebraic geometry codes satisfy

$$\frac{k}{n} = \frac{\deg G - g + 1}{n},$$

$$\frac{d}{n} \geq \frac{n - \deg G}{n}.$$

Using the result of Theorem 5 and taking limits above, we obtain

$$\alpha(\delta) \geq 1 - (\sqrt{q} - 1)^{-1} - \delta. \tag{10}$$

It is easy to show that the line represented by (10) intersects the curve of (9) when $q \geq 49$. For $q \geq 49$ the Varshamov-Gilbert lower bound is exceeded by a new lower bound.

It is an open question as to the existence of binary codes from algebraic curves that exceed the Varshamov-Gilbert bound.

4 CODES FROM ELLIPTIC CURVES

With the background of the material of the previous section, we consider QMDS codes in order to illustrate the techniques of constructing codes from curves in algebraic geometries as a natural evolution from RS codes and as an intermediate step to consider the more general situation in the next section. The QMDS codes will be obtained from elliptic curves, curves of genus 1. The references [3], [4], and [6] are particularly useful on this topic.

Assume $\mathcal{X}$ is an elliptic curve over the field GF(q) given by the homogeneous *Weierstrass* equation

$$y^2 z + a_1 xyz + a_3 yz^2 = x^3 + a_2 x^2 z + a_4 xz^2 + a_6 z^3,$$

where $a_i \in GF(q)$.

Assume $P_1, \ldots, P_n$ are GF(q)-rational points on $\mathcal{X}$ and let $D = P_1 + \cdots + P_n$. To pick a specific code we choose a divisor G such that G has support disjoint from D. One possible choice for the divisor G is $G = mO$, where $O = (0, 1, 0)$ is the point at infinity on $\mathcal{X}$ and $0 < m < n$.

Since $\mathcal{X}$ has genus $g = 1$, according to Theorem 1 the code $C(D, G)$ above has parameters $[n, m, d \geq n - m]_q$. There are several important problems to be considered. In order to find the specific code we need a method of determining a generating matrix of the code or, equivalently, determining a basis of $L(mO)$. This problem for $\text{char}(\text{GF}(q)) = 2$ will be addressed below. Another important problem is to determine the conditions, if any, for which the minimum distance $d = n - m + 1$; that is, under what conditions will the code $C(D, G)$ obtained from an elliptic curve yield an MDS code. The following results of [6] address this problem:

LEMMA 6   For $q < 13$ there are no elliptic MDS codes with length greater than the length of previously known codes.

LEMMA 7   For $q \geq 13$ there exist no nontrivial elliptic MDS codes of length $n > q + 1$.

Thus "most" elliptic codes are QMDS, $[n, k, n - k]_q$ (rather than MDS). The general algebraic geometry construction that produces the dual code to the elliptic code shows that the dual of an elliptic code is either QMDS or MDS. If an elliptic code C is MDS, then its dual is MDS, and the weight enumerator is given by (2). Thus if the elliptic code C is QMDS, then its dual must also be QMDS. Assume the weight enumerator of C with parameters $[n, k, n - k]_q$ is given by

$$W(x) = \sum_{i=0}^{n} A_i x^i,$$

and the weight enumerator of the dual C^* with parameters $[n, n - k, k]_q$ is given by

$$W^*(x) = \sum_{i=0}^{n} B_i x^i.$$

Since C and C^* are QMDS, $A_0 = 1$ and $A_i = 0$ for $i = 1, \ldots, n - k - 1$, and for C^* we have $B_0 = 1$ and $B_i = 0$ for $i = 1, \ldots, k - 1$. Then the MacWilliams identities (1) reduce to

$$\sum_{i=n-k}^{n-j} \binom{n - i}{j} A_i = \binom{n}{j}(q^{k-j} - 1), \quad j = 0, \ldots, k - 1. \qquad (11)$$

The system of equations (11) is a set of k equations in $(k + 1)$ unknowns and can be solved in the one unknown A_{n-k} to obtain [15 (p. 302)],

$$W(x) = x^n + \sum_{i=0}^{k-1} \binom{n}{i}(q^{k-i} - 1)(x - 1)^{n-i} + A_{n-k}(x - 1)^{n-k}. \qquad (12)$$

It is well known that the points on the elliptic curve form an Abelian group. The number of minimum weight code words in C, A_{n-k}, is related to the structure of the Abelian group on the elliptic curve. It can be shown that

$$A_{n-k} = (q-1)M,$$

where M is the number of ways an element of the group on the elliptic curve can be represented as a sum of k different elements from the elliptic curve [15]. If the number of elements on the elliptic curve $\mathcal{X}$, n, and the dimension of the code k, are relatively prime, then the elliptic code C with parameters $[n, k, n-k]_q$ has

$$A_{n-k} = (q-1)\binom{n}{k}/n$$

minimum weight vectors. In other cases the formula for A_{n-k} is not interesting. The important point is that, in cases of interest, A_{n-k} and hence $W(x)$ can be computed explicitly.

There are some general bounds that can be given for the weight enumerator of codes from a curve of genus g [6], however the weight enumerator can be computed explicitly, in this general way, only for MDS and elliptic codes.

The MDS conjecture states that the length of MDS codes with parameters $[n, k, n-k+1]_q$ is upper-bounded by $n \leq q+1$, assuming $k \geq 2$ and $n-k \geq 2$. It is possible to make a similar conjecture for QMDS codes based on results from elliptic codes. Thus we make the following conjecture that the length of QMDS codes with parameters $[n, k, n-k]_q$ is, in general, upper-bounded by $n \leq q+1+\lfloor 2\sqrt{q}\rfloor$. There is limited evidence for the conjecture that says, in essence, that the "best" QMDS codes are those obtained from elliptic curves.

Assume that $\mathcal{X}$ is an elliptic curve and $C(D, G)$ a code with D and G defined as above. Assume that $\text{char}(\text{GF}(q)) = 2$, a case of particular interest from an implementation point of view. In this case a basis of $L(mO)$ can be found that has a simple structure.

THEOREM 8   (DRIENCOURT AND MICHON) Let $\mathcal{X}$ be an elliptic curve over $\text{GF}(2^m)$. Then $L(mO)$ has as basis the following m polynomials

$$1, x, x^2, \ldots, x^\delta, y, yx, yx^2, \ldots, yx^{\widehat{\delta}},$$

where $\delta = \lfloor m/2 \rfloor$ and $\widehat{\delta} = \lfloor (m-3)/2 \rfloor$.

Example 1.   Consider the elliptic curve

$$y^2 + y = x^3$$

over GF(4) $= \{0, 1, \alpha, \alpha^2\}$, where $\alpha^2 + \alpha + 1 = 0$. There are $N_4(1) = 9$, GF(4)-rational points on the curve. They are

$$
\begin{aligned}
P_1 &= (0, 0) & P_5 &= (0, 1) \\
P_2 &= (1, \alpha) & P_6 &= (1, \alpha^2) \\
P_3 &= (\alpha, \alpha) & P_7 &= (\alpha, \alpha^2) \\
P_4 &= (\alpha^2, \alpha) & P_8 &= (\alpha^2, \alpha^2)
\end{aligned}
$$

and the point at infinity O. If we take $D = P_1 + \cdots + P_8$ and $G = mO$, where $0 < m < 8$, then we know that the code $C(D, G)$ has parameters $[8, m, d \geq 8 - m]_4$. By Theorem 8, the vector space $L(4O)$ has basis $\{1, x, x^2, y\}$, and thus the code $C(D, 4O)$ has the following generator matrix:

$$
\begin{pmatrix}
1 & 1 & 1 & 1 & 1 & 1 & 1 & 1 \\
0 & 1 & \alpha & \alpha^2 & 0 & 1 & \alpha & \alpha^2 \\
0 & 1 & \alpha^2 & \alpha & 0 & 1 & \alpha^2 & \alpha \\
0 & \alpha & \alpha & \alpha & 1 & \alpha^2 & \alpha^2 & \alpha^2
\end{pmatrix}.
$$

In the above matrix the first row is obtained by evaluating the function 1 on the eight points $P_1, \ldots, P_8$, the second row by evaluating x, the third by evaluating x^2, and the fourth by evaluating y.

There still remain some important problems associated with elliptic codes. To construct an elliptic code of length N, an elliptic curve that has $(N + 1)$ rational points on it should be found; a general solution for this problem is not known.

Consider elliptic curves over GF(2). It will later be shown that these curves achieve the bounds of Serre (Theorem 3) for many extensions of GF(2), and thus these elliptic curves can be used to construct good codes.

There are 32 Weierstrass polynomials over GF(2), of which 16 are singular. The remaining 16 are all equivalent to one of the five curves below:

i. $y^2 + y = x^3 + x^2 + 1$,
ii. $y^2 + xy = x^3 + x^2 + x$,
iii. $y^2 + y = x^3$,
iv. $y^2 + xy = x^3 + x$,
v. $y^2 + y = x^3 + x^2$.

Since it is easy to find the number of GF(2)-rational points on any of the five types of elliptic curves, we can find the number of points of these elliptic curves over any finite extension of GF(2) by using the zeta function of the curve. We see that there are two parameters, ω_1 and ω_2, associated with each of the five types of curves such that the number of $GF(2^r)$-rational points on a curve of the corresponding type is given by

$$N_r = 2^r - \omega_1^r - \omega_2^r + 1.$$

The parameters for the five types of curves above are:

   i. $\omega_1 = 1 + i$, $\omega_2 = 1 - i$,
  ii. $\omega_1 = (1 + i\sqrt{7})/2$, $\omega_2 = (1 - i\sqrt{7})/2$,
 iii. $\omega_1 = i\sqrt{2}$, $\omega_2 = -i\sqrt{2}$,
  iv. $\omega_1 = (-1 + i\sqrt{7})/2$, $\omega_2 = (-1 - i\sqrt{7})/2$,
   v. $\omega_1 = -1 + i$, $\omega_2 = -1 - i$.

Thus, for example, the curve of type (iii) above, $y^2 + y = x^3$, has nine points over the field GF(8) since $N_3 = 2^3 - (i\sqrt{2})^3 - (-i\sqrt{2})^3 + 1 = 9$.

In obtaining codes from elliptic curves we are most interested in curves that have the maximum number of points, that is, curves that achieve the bounds of Theorem 3. Table 1 shows for different finite extensions of GF(2) which one of the five types of curves above achieves the bound set forth in Theorem 3. A dash indicates that none of the five types of curves above achieve the bounds of Serre (Theorem 3), and thus in order to find such a curve, elliptic curves with coefficients in some extension of GF(2) should be considered.

TABLE 1   Maximal Elliptic Curves for char(K) = 2.

r	Type of Curve	r	Type of Curve
1	(v)	11	(–)
2	(iii)	12	(i)
3	(ii)	13	(ii)
4	(i)	14	(iii)
5	(iv)	15	(–)
6	(iii)	16	(–)
7	(–)	17	(–)
8	(iv)	18	(iii)
9	(–)	19	(–)
10	(iii)	20	(i)

5 BEYOND ELLIPTIC CURVES

The codes obtained from elliptic curves are perhaps the simplest step from RS codes into the domain of codes obtained from curves in algebraic geometries.

This section considers a few classes of more general types of codes obtained in this manner, specifically codes from the Hermitian curves and the Klein quartic, as examples of the more general situation. Other classes, such as codes from modular curves or Shimura curves, would require more background yet and would take us beyond the purpose of this chapter.

The Hermitian curve over $GF(q^2)$ in affine (u, v)-coordinates is

$$C: u^{q+1} + v^{q+1} + 1 = 0. \tag{13}$$

Tiersma [14] has studied codes obtained from Hermitian curves. Stichtenoth [13] generalized and simplified Tiersma's results. Stichtenoth shows that by the change of coordinates $x = b/(v - bu)$ and $y = ux - a$, where $a^q + a = b^{q+1} = -1$, the Hermitian curve C is equivalent to the curve

$$\mathcal{X}: y^q + y = x^{q+1}, \tag{14}$$

which from now on will be referred to as the *Hermitian curve*. It is easy to check that $\mathcal{X}$ is nonsingular, and the genus of $\mathcal{X}$ is $g = (q^2 - q)/2$. There are $(q^3 + 1)$ rational points on $\mathcal{X}$ (as we shall see below), q^3 points satisfying (14) and a point at infinity which will be denoted by O. Notice that the curve $\mathcal{X}$ has the maximum number of rational points allowed by the Hasse-Weil bound (2).

The following theorem from [13] gives a convenient bivariate polynomial basis for $L(mO)$.

THEOREM 9   For each $m \geq 0$, the set

$$\{x^i y^j \mid 0 \leq i; \ 0 \leq j \leq q - 1; \ iq + j(q + 1) \leq m\}$$

is a basis of $L(mO)$.

The *Hermitian code* is $\mathcal{H}_m = C(D, mO)$, where $D = P_1 + \cdots + P_n$, with $n = q^3$, and the P_i are the rational points on $\mathcal{X}$ excluding O. If $2g - 2 < m < n$, then the dimension of $\mathcal{H}_m$ can be determined from Theorem 1 of the previous section and is equal to $m - g + 1$. However, by Theorem 9, the dimension of the code $\mathcal{H}_m$ can be determined for any non-negative integer m (see [13]). Stichtenoth [13] shows that not only is it possible to obtain a lower bound on the minimum distance of $\mathcal{H}_m$ (see Theorem 1), but that for a large number of nonnegative integers m it is possible to find the exact minimum distance.

THEOREM 10   Let $m = iq + j(q + 1) \leq q^3 - 1$, with $0 \leq i, 0 \leq j \leq q - 1$, and either

   i. $m \equiv 0 \pmod{q}$, or

   ii. $m \leq q^3 - q^2$.

Then the minimum distance of $\mathcal{H}_m$ is $q^3 - m$.

   In [20] the minimum distance of $\mathcal{H}_m$ is given for the case $m > q^3 - q^2$. Thus the minimum distance of Hermitian codes is known for all values of the parameter m.

   In summary, the parameters of $\mathcal{H}_m$ are $[n, k, d]_{q^2}$, with $n = q^3$, $k = m - g + 1$ (if $2g - 2 < m < n$), and $d \geq n - m$, for $g = (q^2 - q)/2$. If m is not in the range $2g - 2 < m < n$, then the dimension of $\mathcal{H}_m$ can be found by finding the number of basis elements of $L(mO)$.

   A complete description of the GF(q^2)-rational points on the Hermitian curve

$$\mathcal{X}: \quad y^q + y = x^{q+1} \tag{15}$$

is considered. Assume GF$(q) = \{0, 1, \alpha, \ldots, \alpha^{q^2-2}\}$ for a primitive element $\alpha \in K$.

LEMMA 11 $y^q + y = 0$ has q solutions in $GF(q^2)$.

PROOF If char$(\mathrm{GF}(q)) = 2$, the solutions are the elements of the subfield F_q. If char$(\mathrm{GF}(q)) \neq 2$ then $2(q - 1)$ divides $q^2 - 1$ since q is odd. Thus there exists a primitive $2(q-1)$th root of unity γ in GF(q). It follows that γ^{2i+1}, $i = 0, 1, \ldots, (q-2)$, along with the zero element, are the solutions to the equation.

   Denote the set of solutions to the equation as $\mathcal{B}$, $|\mathcal{B}| = q$. Notice that if (x, y) is a particular solution to (15), with $x \neq 0$, then

$$(\eta x, \eta^{q+1} y + \beta), \quad \beta \in \mathcal{B}, \quad \eta \in GF(q)$$

are the q^3 solutions to (15). For the sequel, let y_0 be the solution to (15) with $x = 1$. Then the q^3 solutions can be written as a $(q^2 \times q)$ array

$$S = [s_{\eta, \beta}]$$

with rows labeled by elements of $\eta \in GF(q)$, columns by elements $\beta \in \mathcal{B}$, and $s_{\eta, \beta} = (\eta, \eta^{q+1} y_0 + \beta)$.

   Example 2.   Let $q = 4$ and $m = 37$, then the parameters of $\mathcal{H}_{37}$ are $[64, 32, 27]_{16}$. The base field is $F_{16} = \{0, 1, \omega, \ldots, \omega^{14}\}$, where $\omega^4 + \omega^3 + 1 = 0$. The $64 = q^3$ rational points of the curve $y^4 + y = x^5$ are

$$
\begin{array}{llll}
P_1 = (0,0) & P_{17} = (0,1) & P_{33} = (0,\omega^5) & P_{49} = (0,\omega^{10}) \\
P_2 = (1,\omega^7) & P_{18} = (1,\omega^{13}) & P_{34} = (1,\omega^{14}) & P_{50} = (1,\omega^{11}) \\
P_3 = (\omega^1,\omega^1) & P_{19} = (\omega^1,\omega^{12}) & P_{35} = (\omega^1,\omega^4) & P_{51} = (\omega^1,\omega^3) \\
P_4 = (\omega^2,\omega^2) & P_{20} = (\omega^2,\omega^9) & P_{36} = (\omega^2,\omega^6) & P_{52} = (\omega^2,\omega^8) \\
P_5 = (\omega^3,\omega^7) & P_{21} = (\omega^3,\omega^{13}) & P_{37} = (\omega^3,\omega^{14}) & P_{53} = (\omega^3,\omega^{11}) \\
P_6 = (\omega^4,\omega^1) & P_{22} = (\omega^4,\omega^{12}) & P_{38} = (\omega^4,\omega^4) & P_{54} = (\omega^4,\omega^3) \\
P_7 = (\omega^5,\omega^2) & P_{23} = (\omega^5,\omega^9) & P_{39} = (\omega^5,\omega^6) & P_{55} = (\omega^5,\omega^8) \\
P_8 = (\omega^6,\omega^7) & P_{24} = (\omega^6,\omega^{13}) & P_{40} = (\omega^6,\omega^{14}) & P_{56} = (\omega^6,\omega^{11}) \\
P_9 = (\omega^7,\omega^1) & P_{25} = (\omega^7,\omega^{12}) & P_{41} = (\omega^7,\omega^4) & P_{57} = (\omega^7,\omega^3) \\
P_{10} = (\omega^8,\omega^2) & P_{26} = (\omega^8,\omega^9) & P_{42} = (\omega^8,\omega^6) & P_{58} = (\omega^8,\omega^8) \\
P_{11} = (\omega^9,\omega^7) & P_{27} = (\omega^9,\omega^{13}) & P_{43} = (\omega^9,\omega^{14}) & P_{59} = (\omega^9,\omega^{11}) \\
P_{12} = (\omega^{10},\omega^1) & P_{28} = (\omega^{10},\omega^{12}) & P_{44} = (\omega^{10},\omega^4) & P_{60} = (\omega^{10},\omega^3) \\
P_{13} = (\omega^{11},\omega^2) & P_{29} = (\omega^{11},\omega^9) & P_{45} = (\omega^{11},\omega^6) & P_{61} = (\omega^{11},\omega^8) \\
P_{14} = (\omega^{12},\omega^7) & P_{30} = (\omega^{12},\omega^{13}) & P_{46} = (\omega^{12},\omega^{14}) & P_{62} = (\omega^{12},\omega^{11}) \\
P_{15} = (\omega^{13},\omega^1) & P_{31} = (\omega^{13},\omega^{12}) & P_{47} = (\omega^{13},\omega^4) & P_{63} = (\omega^{13},\omega^3) \\
P_{16} = (\omega^{14},\omega^2) & P_{32} = (\omega^{14},\omega^9) & P_{48} = (\omega^{14},\omega^6) & P_{64} = (\omega^{14},\omega^8)
\end{array}
$$

We find from Theorem 9 that a basis of $L(37O)$ has the following form

$$
L(37O) =
$$
$$
\{f_0(x) + yf_1(x) + y^2 f_2(x) + y^3 f_3(x) \mid \deg f_j(x) < k(j),\ 0 \le j \le 3\},
$$

where $k(0) = 10, k(1) = 9, k(2) = 7, k(3) = 6$. Having determined a basis of $L(37O)$, the generator matrix of $\mathcal{H}_{37}$ can be constructed.

Hermitian codes are one of a few classes of codes derived from curves in algebraic geometries that have been well studied. In [19] the structure of Hermitian codes is studied further, and it is shown that Hermitian codes are combinations of generalized Reed-Solomon codes.

The Klein quartic $\mathcal{X}$ is given by the homogeneous polynomial

$$
F(x, y, z) = x^3 y + y^3 z + z^3 x. \tag{16}
$$

It can be shown that $\mathcal{X}$ is nonsingular and has genus 3, and if we consider the Klein quartic over GF(8), then it is maximal; the number GF(8)-rational points satisfying $F(x, y, z) = 0$ is equal to the bound given in Theorem 2. For $q = 8$ and $g = 3$ the Hasse-Weil bound states that for N the maximum number of GF(8)-rational points on a curve of genus g, $N \le 8 + 1 + 3\lfloor 2\sqrt{8} \rfloor = 24$. Let α be a primitive element in GF(8) satisfying $\alpha^3 + \alpha + 1 = 0$. The three points $O_1 = (1, 0, 0)$, $O_2 = (0, 1, 0)$, and $O_3 = (0, 0, 1)$ are solutions to

(16). Take $z = 1$, $y = \alpha^i$ for some i in the range $0 \leq i \leq 6$ and write $x = \alpha^{3i}v$. Then we find that $v^3 + v + 1 = 0$ and there are three solutions to this equation $v = \alpha, \alpha^2, \alpha^4$. Thus there are $3 + 7 * 3 = 24$ points on the Klein quartic over GF(8), and it has the maximum number of points for given $q = 8$ and $g = 3$. In order to construct a code on the Klein quartic we choose two divisors, D and G, as in Definition 3. Let $D = P_1 + \cdots + P_{21} + O_3$, where the P_j, $j = 1, \cdots, 21$, are the points with coordinates $(\alpha^{3i}v, \alpha^i, 1)$ for $i = 0, 1, \ldots, 6$ and $v = \alpha, \alpha^2, \alpha^3$, and $G_m = m(O_1 + 3O_2)$ [15]. The vector space $L(G_m)$ has generating functions

$$\{x^i y^j \mid 2i + 3j \leq 3m, \text{ and } i - 2j \leq m\},$$

from which a basis can be formed [15]. The the Klein quartic code thus constructed has parameters $[22, 2(2m - 1), d \geq 2(11 - 2m)]_8$. The basis of $L(G_m)$ over GF(8) for $m = 2, 3, 4, 5$ are

$$m = 2: \quad \{1, x, x^2, y, yx, y^2\},$$

$$m = 3: \quad \{1, x, x^2, x^3, y, yx, yx^2, yx^3, y^2, y^2x\},$$

$$m = 4: \quad \{1, x, \ldots, x^4, y, yx, \ldots, yx^4, y^2, \ldots, y^2x^3\},$$

$$m = 5: \quad \{1, x, \ldots, x^5, y, yx, \ldots, yx^6, y^2, \ldots, y^2x^4\}.$$

It is recognized that algebraic geometry is a powerful tool in understanding and constructing codes. A question arises as to whether there may be techniques that can use the insight obtained from this approach, i.e., evaluating bivariate polynomials on curves, for which the proofs of the fundamental properties of distance and dimension do not rely on the Riemann-Roch theorem. One example of this approach is considered here with hyperelliptic curves to obtain good codes. We will define a class of codes for which we will obtain the parameters using basic principles.

The class of hyperelliptic curves over a finite field GF(q) [7] is defined by

$$\mathcal{X}: \quad y^2 + h(x)y = k(x),$$

where $h(x)$ is a polynomial of degree at most g and $k(x)$ is a polynomial of degree $2g + 1$. The curve $\mathcal{X}$ is called the hyperelliptic curve of genus g. It is assumed that $\mathcal{X}$ is non-singular in the affine part, and furthermore that $h(x_0) + 2y_0 \neq 0$ for any point $P = (x_0, y_0) \in \mathcal{X}$. Note that the point at infinity represented in projective coordinates as $O = (0, 1, 0)$ is a nonordinary multiple point of multiplicity $2g - 1$.

The class of hyperelliptic curves contains the class of elliptic curves; for example, the elliptic curve $y^2 + y = x^3$ has $h(x) = 1$ and $k(x) = x^3$. The size $| \mathcal{X} | = n$ can be bounded by the Hasse-Weil theorem:

$$| n - (q + 1) | \leq 2g\sqrt{q}.$$

As illustrated in the previous chapter (for an algebraic geometry code), one would define a set of rational functions on the curve and proceed to use the Riemann-Roch theorem to establish bounds on the minimum distance of the code. Our approach here is to attempt to use the hyperelliptic curves and define a set of bivariate polynomials to define the code and construct an argument that establishes a lower bound on its minimum distance using only elementary algebra.

Consider the vector space of polynomials

$$\mathcal{L} = \{f(x) + yg(x) \mid \deg f(x) \leq i, \ \deg g(x) \leq j, \ f, g \in GF(q)[x]\}$$

a vector space of dimension $i + j + 2$ over $GF(q)$. Notice that if $P = (x, y) \in \mathcal{X}$, then there exists a point $\hat{P} = [x, -y - h(x)] \in \mathcal{X}$. The point $\hat{P}$ in $\mathcal{X}$ is called the opposite point of P. The point $P = (x_0, y_0)$ is called an s-zero (single) if there exists a polynomial in $\mathcal{L}$ such that

$$f(x_0) + y_0 g(x_0) = 0,$$

and the opposite point of P does not satisfy the same polynomial. A point P is a d-zero (double) if

$$f(x_0) + y_0 g(x_0) = 0,$$

and

$$f(x_0) + [-y_0 - h(x_0)]g(x_0) = 0.$$

It is noted that if $P = (x_0, y_0)$ is a d-zero of $f(x) + yg(x)$, then by subtracting the above two equations and invoking the condition that $h(x_0) + 2y_0 \neq 0$, we obtain $g(x_0) = f(x_0) = 0$, and thus $x - x_0$ divides $f(x)$ and $g(x)$,

$$f(x) + yg(x) = (x - x_0)[\hat{f}(x) + y\hat{g}(x)],$$

where $\hat{f} = f/(x - x_0)$ and $\hat{g} = g/(x - x_0)$. Thus the problem of determining the number of zeros of $f(x) + yg(x)$ reduces to determining the number of s-zeros.

We *define* a code

$$\mathcal{C} = \{(l(P_1), \ldots, l(P_n)), \ l \in \mathcal{L}, \ P_i \in \mathcal{X}\}.$$

The code clearly has length n, which is the number of points on the curve $\mathcal{X}$ and does not have a general description, and dimension $k = i + j + 2$. The only question is its minimum distance. This will be governed by the maximum number of zeros the bivariate polynomials of $\mathcal{L}$ have on the n points of the curve, which generally requires the use of the Riemann-Roch theorem.

Consider the polynomial

$$a(x) = f^2(x) + f(x)g(x)h(x) - k(x)g^2(x),$$

and note that if $(x_0, y_0) \in \mathcal{X}$, then $f(x_0) + y_0 g(x_0) = 0$, and $a(x_0) = 0$. The converse is also true; again assuming x_0 is an x component of a point on $\mathcal{X}$, then if $a(x_0) = 0$, then either $P = (x_0, y_0) \in \mathcal{X}$ is a zero of $f(x) + yg(x)$, or $\hat{P}$ is a zero. Assume $a(x_0) = 0$, then

$$a(x_0) = f^2(x_0) + f(x_0)g(x_0)h(x_0) - k(x_0)g^2(x_0).$$

Since $y^2 + h(x_0)y = k(x_0)$ for some y, that is, $y = y_0$ or $y = -y_0 - h(x_0)$ for $(x_0, y_0) \in X$, we have

$$f^2(x_0) + f(x_0)g(x_0)h(x_0) - y^2g^2(x_0) - h(x_0)yg^2(x_0) = 0.$$

Factoring, we obtain

$$[f(x_0) + yg(x_0)]\{f(x_0) + [-y - h(x_0)]g(x_0\} = 0.$$

Thus either $P = (x_0, y_0) \in \mathcal{X}$ is a zero of $f(x) + yg(x)$ or $\hat{P}$ is a zero.

As a polynomial in one variable, the number of zeros of $a(x)$ may be bounded by its degree. The degree of $a(x)$ is

$$\eta = \max\{2i, i + j + g, 2j + 2g + 1\},$$

or in terms of a fixed k,

$$\eta = \max\{2i, k + g - 2, 2k + 2g - 2i - 3\}.$$

For a given g the best code is obtained by minimizing η. The following theorems can be established by this minimization process.

THEOREM 12   For $g = 1$ the optimum choices of i and j are: (i) if $k = 2m$ then $i = m$, $j = m - 2$, and $\eta = 2m$; (ii) if $k = 2m + 1$ then $i = m$, $j = m - 1$, and $\eta = 2m + 1$. In both cases the resulting code is an $[n, k, d \geq n - k]$ code.

PROOF   Assume $k = 2m$. Then $j = 2m - i - 2$ and

$$\eta = \max\{2i, 2m - 1, 2(2m - i) - 1\}.$$

If $i < m$ then $2m - i > m + 1$, and thus $\eta > 2(m + 1) - 1 = 2m + 1$. If $i > m$ then $2(2m - i) - 1 < 2m - 1$, and therefore $\eta = 2i > 2m$. If $i = m$ then $\eta = 2m$. Thus the minimum value of η is $2m$, occurring when $i = m$.

Assume $k = 2m + 1$. Then $j = 2m - i - 1$ and

$$\eta = \max\{2i, 2m, 2(2m - i) + 1\}.$$

If $i < m$ then $2m - i > m$, and thus $\eta > 2m + 1$. If $i > m$ then $2(2m - i) + 1 < 2m + 1$, and thus $\eta = 2i > 2m$. If $i = m$ then $\eta = 2m + 1$. Thus the minimum value of η is $2m + 1$, and this occurs when $i = m$.

Since elliptic curves are a special subclass of hyperelliptic codes, the results of the above theorem are known in another setting. Note, however, that to derive these codes only elementary concepts have been used. We continue with this procedure to derive codes from $g = 2$ and 3 hyperelliptic curves.

THEOREM 13 For $g = 2$ the optimum choices of i and j are: (i) if $k = 2m$ then $i = m$, $j = m - 2$, and $\eta = 2m + 1$; (ii) if $k = 2m + 1$, then $i = m + 1$, $j = m - 2$, and $\eta = 2m + 2$. In both cases the resulting code is an $[n, k, d \geq n - k - 1]$ code.

PROOF The proof is similar to Theorem 12.

THEOREM 14 For $g = 3$ the optimum choices of i and j are: (i) if $k = 2m$ then $i = m + 1$, $j = m - 3$, and $\eta = 2m + 2$; (ii) if $k = 2m + 1$ then $i = m + 1$, $j = m - 2$, and $\eta = 2m + 3$. In both cases the resulting code is an $[n, k, d \geq n - k - 2]$ code.

PROOF Assume $k = 2m$. Then $j = 2m - i - 2$ and

$$\eta = \max\{2i, 2m + 1, 2(2m - i) + 3\}.$$

If $i < m$ then $2m - i > m$, and thus $\eta > 2m + 3$. If $i = m$ then $\eta = 2m + 3$. If $i = m + 1$ then $\eta = 2m + 2$. If $i > m + 1$ then $2(2m - i) + 3 < 2(m - 1) + 3 = 2m + 1$, and thus $\eta = 2i > 2m + 3$. Therefore the minimum value of η is $2m + 2$, occurring when $i = m + 1$. Assume $k = 2m + 1$. Then $j = 2m - i - 1$ and

$$\eta = \max\{2i, 2m + 2, 2(2m - i) + 5\}.$$

If $i < m$ then $2m - i > m$, and thus $\eta > 2m + 5$. If $i = m$ then $\eta = 2m + 5$. If $i = m + 1$ then $\eta = 2m + 3$. If $i > m + 1$ then $2(2m - i) + 5 < 2(m - 1) + 5 = 2m + 3$, and thus $\eta = 2i > 2m + 3$. Thus the minimum value of η is $2m + 3$, and it occurs when $i = m + 1$.

As far as is known these families of codes are new. They were established by mimicking a technique drawn from algebraic geometry, but without the use of the deep results from that theory. The maximum length n that such codes can have is bounded by the Hasse-Weil theorem mentioned previously. For a given g it will depend on the particular polynomials $h(x)$, $k(x)$ chosen. Similar results can be established for higher values of g. Notice that we have been able to give a construction of codes with parameters $[n, k, d \geq n - k + 1 - g]$ which does not require any algebraic geometry.

6 COMMENTS

This chapter has attempted to introduce the subject of codes derived from curves in algebraic geometries by first interpreting the familiar subject of RS and MDS codes in the language of algebraic geometries. By the generalization from MDS codes to QMDS codes an appreciation of the complexities of the subject is obtained. The QMDS codes obtained from elliptic curves exhibit this complexity while retaining the essential flavor of both RS codes and of deriving codes from curves in algebraic geometries. The more general situation was introduced by considering only two classes of curves, Hermitian and the Klein quartic, and again the complexity was noted. The class of codes from hyperelliptic curves was also discussed as an attempt to derive good codes using the experience of algebraic geometries but proving their properties without the machinery of algebraic geometry. While that effort was largely successful, it has not led to date to other classes of codes constructed in a like manner.

REFERENCES

[1] R. Blahut, *Theory and Practice of Error Control Codes*, Reading, Mass.: Addison-Wesley, 1983.

[2] I. F. Blake and R. C. Mullin, *The Mathematical Theory of Coding*, New York: Academic Press, 1975.

[3] Y. Driencourt, "Some Properties of Elliptic Codes over a Field of Characteristic 2," *Proceedings of AAECC-3*, pp. 185–193, Lecture Notes in Computer Science, Volume 229, 1985.

[4] Y. Driencourt and J. F. Michon, "Elliptic Codes over a Field of Characteristic 2," *Journal of Pure and Applied Algebra*, Volume 45, pp. 15–39, 1987.

[5] W. Fulton, *Algebraic Curves*, New York: Benjamin, 1969.

[6] G. L. Katsman and M. A. Tsfasman, "Spectra of Algebraic-Geometric Codes," *Problems of Information Transmission*, Volume 23, pp. 262–275, 1988.

[7] N. Koblitz, "Hyperelliptic Cryptosystems," *Journal of Cryptology*, Volume 1, pp. 139–150, 1989.

[8] F. MacWilliams and N. Sloane, *The Theory of Error-Correcting Codes*, Amsterdam: North-Holland, 1977.

[9] A. J. Menezes, I. F. Blake, R. C. Mullin, X. Gao, S. A. Vanstone, and T. Yaghoobian, *Applications of Finite Fields*, Dordrecht, The Netherlands: Kluwer Academic, 1993.

[10] J. -P. Serre, "Nombres de points des courbes algébriques sur F_q," *Séminaire de Théorie des Nombres*, Volume 22, pp. 1–8, 1983.

[11] J. -P. Serre, "Sur le nombre de points rationnels d'une corbe algébrique sur un corps fini," *Comptes Rendus de l'Academie des Sciences Paris, Series 1*, Volume 296, pp. 397–402, 1983.

[12] C. E. Shannon, "A Mathematical Theory of Communications," *Bell System Technical Journal*, Volume 27, pp. 379–423, 623–656, 1949.

[13] H. Stichtenoth, "A Note on Hermitian Codes over $GF(q^2)$," *IEEE Transactions on Information Theory*, Volume 34, Number 5, pp. 1345–1348, September 1988.

[14] H. J. Tiersma, "Remarks on Codes from Hermitian Curves," *IEEE Transactions on Information Theory*, Volume 33, Number 4, pp. 605–609, July 1987.

[15] M. A. Tsfasman and S. G. Vladut, *Algebraic-Geometric Codes*, Dordrecht, The Netherlands: Kluwer Academic, 1991.

[16] M. A. Tsfasman, S. G. Vladut, and T. Zink, "Modular Curves, Shimura Curves and Goppa Codes Which Are Better Than the Varshamov-Gilbert Bound," *Mathatische Nachrichten*, Volume 109, pp. 21–28, 1982.

[17] J. H. van Lint, *Introduction to Coding Theory*, New York: Springer-Verlag, 1982.

[18] J.H. van Lint and T.A. Springer, "Generalized Reed-Solomon Codes from Algebraic Geometry, *IEEE Transactions on Information Theory*, Volume 33, pp. 305–309, 1987.

[19] T. Yaghoobian and I. F. Blake, "Hermitian Codes as Generalized Reed-Solomon Codes, *Designs, Codes, and Cryptography*, Volume 2, pp. 5–17, 1992.

[20] K. Yang and P. V. Kumar, "On the True Minimum Distance of Hermitian Codes," in *Coding Theory and Algebraic Geometry*, pp. 99–107, Lecture Notes in Mathematics, Volume 1518, 1991.

Index

Editors' Biographies

Stephen B. Wicker (S'83-M'83-SM'93) was born in Hazelhurst, Mississippi, USA on September 25, 1960. He received the B.S.E.E. with High Honors from the University of Virginia in 1982. He received the M.S.E.E. from Purdue University in 1983 and the Ph.D. degree in Electrical Engineering from the University of Southern California in 1987.

From 1983 through 1987 Professor Wicker was a subsystem and system engineer with the Space and Communications Group of the Hughes Aircraft Company in El Segundo, California. In September 1987 he joined the faculty of the School of Electrical Engineering at the Georgia Institute of Technology, where he currently holds the title of Associate Professor. From June 1991 until March 1992 Professor Wicker served as the Academic Coordinator for Georgia Tech–Lorraine in Metz, France. Professor Wicker was named a Visiting Fellow of the British Columbia Advanced Systems Institute in 1992. He has also served as a consultant in telecommunications systems, error control coding, and cryptography for various companies in North America, Europe, and West Asia.

Professor Wicker's current research interests center on the development of algorithms for error control, data compression, and data security for digital communication systems. He is the author of *Error Control Systems for Digital Communication and Storage* (Prentice Hall, 1994).

Professor Wicker is a member of the IEEE Communications, Information Theory, and Vehicular Technology Societies. He is also a member of Eta Kappa Nu, Tau Beta Pi, Sigma Xi, and Omicron Delta Kappa.

Vijay K. Bhargava (F'92) received the B.Sc. degree with honors from the University of Rajasthan in 1966, the B.Sc. degree in mathematics and engineering, and the M.Sc. and Ph.D. degrees, both in electrical engineering, from Queen's University in Kingston, ON, Canada, in 1970, 1972, and 1974, respectively.

After brief stays at the Indian Institute of Science and the University of Waterloo, he joined Concordia University in Montreal and was promoted to Professor in 1984. From 1982 to 1983, he was on sabbatical leave at l'Ecole Polytechnique de Montreal. In 1984 he joined the newly formed Faculty of Engineering at the University of Victoria as a Professor of Electrical Engineering. In 1988 he was appointed a Fellow of the BC Advanced Systems Institute. He is co-author of the book *Digital Communications by Satellite* (New York: Wiley, 1981). A Japanese translation of the book was published in 1984, and a Chinese translation was published in 1987. During 1988 to 1990, he served at the Editor of the Canadian Journal of Electrical and Computer Engineering. In 1992 he became the Director of IEEE Region 7 for a two-year term.

Dr. Bhargava is a recipient of the IEEE Centennial Medal, the EIC Centennial Medal, and the 1987 A. F. Bulgin Premium awarded by the Institute of Radio and Electronic Engineers (UK). In 1988 he was elected a Fellow of the Engineering Institute of Canada. In 1990 he received the John B. Stirling Medal of the EIC.